NOURISHED

A Cookbook for Health, Weight Loss, and Metabolic Balance

JUDY BARNES BAKER

Author of *Carb Wars: Sugar is the New Fat*

Preface by Mary C. Vernon, M.D. ▪ Foreword by Jackie Eberstein, R.N.
SCIENTIFIC PERSPECTIVE BY RICHARD D. FEINMAN, PH.D., R.D.

Duck In A Boat LLC
Snohomish, Washington

CLASSIC DAY
PUBLISHING
Seattle, Washington
Portland, Oregon
Vancouver, B.C.

NMS
PRESS
Nutrition & Metabolism Society
New York, New York

Copyright © 2012 Judy Barnes Baker

ISBN: 978-09792018-1-3
Library of Congress Control Number: 2011939709

Printed in the United States of America

Design: Soundview Design Studio
Photographs on pages 42 and 46 were taken by Ian Eloff.
Author's photograph on back cover was taken by Christopher Conrad.
Index: Carol Roberts

Disclaimer and Limit of Liability: *Nourished* is a cookbook. Its intent
is to serve as a guide to great tasting, low-carbohydrate cooking. The
author is neither a physician nor a nutritionist. The nutritional and
supplementary information in this book, while believed to be accurate,
is solely informational and educational. It is not intended to be, and
must never be used as, a replacement for the advice from your physician
or nutritionist. None of the information in this book is intended to
treat any disease, medical condition, or health concern. If you believe
that you have a medical problem, please consult your physician. The
author and publisher make no representations or warranties with
respect to the accuracy or completeness of the contents of this book and
specifically disclaim any implied warranties of merchantability or fitness
for a particular purpose. Neither the author nor the publisher shall be
liable for any loss of profit or any other commercial damages including
but not limited to special, incidental, consequential, or other damages.

Requests for such permissions should be addressed to:

Classic Day Publishing
2925 Fairview Avenue East
Seattle, Washington 98102
877-728-8837
www.classicdaypub.com

Table of Contents

"It ain't what we don't know that gives us trouble. It's what we know for sure that ain't so."

— *Variously attributed to Mark Twain, Josh Billings, and Artemus Ward.*

Acknowledgments

I would like to express my gratitude to all those who so generously offered their help and advice to make this project a success:

To the low-carb experts, researchers, and diabetes specialists who served as advisors:

Dr. Richard Feinman	Dr. Mary C. Vernon
Jackie Eberstein	Dr. Richard Bernstein
Dr. Eric Westman	

To the Nutrition and Metabolism Society for their sponsorship and support, especially founder, Dr. Richard Feinman, who made sure I got the science right; president, Jeffrey P. Feinman, for his wise council; and director, Laurie Cagnassola, for her friendship and encouragement.

To Dr. Mary C. Vernon, Dr. Eric Westman, and Gary Taubes of *Innovative Metabolic Solutions* for endorsing *Nourished* and allowing me to use the IMS logo on the cover.

To Elliott Wolf of Classic Day Publishing for his guidance and expertise in the publication of *Nourished*.

To Amy Vaughn and David Marty of Soundview Design Studio and Stephanie Martindale for creating a beautiful book.

To editor, Cherie Tucker, for her contribution to the project, and indexer, Carol Roberts, for a job well done.

To photographer, Christopher Conrad, of Conrad & Company, for sharing his artistic vision and practical advice, and to Penny Haviland for reviewing and adding the finishing touches to my images.

To the cookbook authors, food writers, and low-carb experts who enthusiastically shared the best of the best from their own repertoires to be included in this book:

Dr. Richard Bernstein	Dr. Mary Dan Eades
Jennifer Eloff	George Stella
Greg Atkinson	Jamie Van Eaton

To Jimmy Moore, whose Website serves as Grand Central Station for the low-carb community. Whenever I needed to consult with an educator, researcher, or doctor for advice about nutrition and metabolism, Jimmy could always put me in touch. He also helped me recruit a crack team of recipe testers through his blog at www.livinlavidalowcarb.com.

To all my wonderful recipe testers who volunteered their time, work, and talent with no compensation and even paid for the ingredients out of their own pockets to help me decide which recipes were keepers and to suggest improvements or point out mistakes.

Jonathon Campbell	Regina DiLavore
Amy Dungan	Grace Gulick
Kim Eidson	Debbi Randolf
C. M. (Nell) McVeigh	Gisela Rodriguez
Regina Parsons	Christina Robertson
Genevieve Futrelle	Sarah Florek
Michelle Randolph	Gary K. Noreen
Mylan Hawkins	Juli Brandshaw
Sue O'Donnell	Julie Pascoe
Mary Anne Ward	Kay Witt

Thank you also to the following individuals and companies who responded promptly to my questions, cheerfully searched for answers about products and ingredients, and offered suggestions and advice to make this collection of recipes the best it could be:

Allison Furbish and the Hotline experts at The King Arthur Flour Company

Elizabeth Arndt at Con Agra Foods, Inc.

Erin Quann of the National Dairy Council

Mary-Clare Holst, who put in many hours researching the Sources and Recommended Reading sections of *Nourished*, merits a special mention. She offered to help with the project in any way she could because she believes in the importance of the message. Her special talent for technical writing was a great help and very much appreciated.

I am indebted also to Rob Anthony, the director of book publishing for the American Diabetes Association; this book owes its existence to him. A chance meeting with Rob at an IACP conference in Chicago led to a contract to write a low-carb cookbook for those with diabetes. Although the organization ultimately choose to continue with their current guidelines, I'm confident they will soon revise their policies to better serve the people who look to them for guidance.

Writing a book is like a very long pregnancy, and while it is ultimately worthwhile, it requires a lot of patience from those who suffer through it along with the writer. Thank you to my family for their love and support, especially my husband, Dean. He makes me laugh and eats whatever I put on his plate without grumbling (much). He keeps my computer working, my car running, my clocks set, my pencils sharpened, and my feet warm. I couldn't have done it without you.

– JBB

Preface

BY MARY C. VERNON, M.D.

I spend most of my professional time helping patients to regain their metabolic health. As 75% of adult Americans today (and sadly, more and more children) have obesity and obesity-related disorders such as metabolic syndrome, prediabetes, and Type 2 diabetes mellitus, I have plenty to do. The foods that make America gain weight are exactly what our skilled Kansas farmers use to fatten food animals. We are, after all, the breadbasket of the nation. As sugars and starches are the backbone of the weight-gain industry, my farmers immediately grasp the changes they need to make in their diet to manage their diabetes or metabolic syndrome once I review the link between fattening a steer for market and their carbohydrate intake. ("Oh, you mean no biscuits?") One of the biggest hurdles I face is the translation of science and scientific conversation into the day-to-day life of my patients. I might know the carbohydrate count of a potato or banana, but many of my patients do not. I might know how to fry a cutlet without breading, but my patients may not share this experience. And what to eat instead of the biscuit?

Judy Barnes Baker in *Nourished* provides a superb resource for those of us who work with patients. She accurately translates carbohydrate restriction into food choices and recipes that my patients can follow and enjoy. The recipes taste good. They are easy to follow and easy to prepare. The food choices are accessible. So when I recommend this book to my patients, I do it with confidence. Using this excellent tool, they are well on their way to changing their life and health with all the benefits I see every day for this lifestyle: fewer drugs, fewer health problems, more energy, less pain. If they have questions about the science, well, the answer is often here. Judy addresses some of the most common issues and discusses the science. So if I can't be there to explain, this book can help.

I will be using this in my clinic, but I'll enjoy cooking from it as well. When I bring in these delicious recipes, the hospital staff will gather around pronto. I'm already considering what to prepare for the next holiday when I work.

Thanks, Judy. My patients needed this book, and so did I.

– Mary C. Vernon, M.D.

Foreword

BY JACQUELINE EBERSTEIN, R.N.

The phrase "diets don't work" is mindlessly repeated these days. Our response to this is that they can and they do work. To be successful, it is imperative that your weight loss plan become a lifestyle. One that is maintained over the long term, allowing you to stay within a healthy weight but more importantly to function at your top capacity, enhance your health, and prevent diseases like diabetes, heart disease, and even some cancers, common in those who are overweight.

When choosing a weight-loss plan, it is important to understand that one size does not fit all. Choose the plan that you can follow for a lifetime while maintaining or normalizing your metabolism, one that contains foods that are easily obtained while controlling hunger and cravings. No one can maintain a weight loss plan for long if you are required to live with hunger and cravings or spend hours a day exercising. Diets that severely restrict calories usually fail, as do those that are very low in fat. Keep in mind that no matter what experts tell you, carbohydrate (the basis of many diets) is not an essential nutrient; fat and protein are. Humans evolved eating natural fats and protein with very few carbs. We are still genetically programmed to eat this way.

Since the U.S. government initiated dietary guidelines in the 1980's as a one-size-fits-all approach, obesity and diabetes among all age groups continues to rapidly rise. More than ⅔ of adults are over fat, and our children are following suit. Do we really think that more of the same advice will lead to a different outcome? We must return to eating whole, minimally processed foods the way we did generations ago.

Judy Barnes Baker highlights in easy-to-understand terms the importance of keeping blood sugar and insulin levels normal while choosing the foods humans were meant to eat. She references some of the important research published in the last decade that supports the safety and effectiveness of controlling carbs.

Controlling both the quality and quantity of carbs is especially important for those of us who are carbohydrate intolerant. Carb intolerance is common in people with a family history of diabetes, obesity, too much belly fat, metabolic syndrome, and type 2 diabetes. This applies to many millions in the U.S.

To change a diet into a lifestyle, you need to be fully educated about your plan of choice. *Nourished* will provide information about books, websites, and even support forums to help you along the way. Be sure to spend time to develop all of the tools you need to succeed, even if you have failed in the past. Remember that your quality of life depends on it and perhaps even your life itself.

The "meat" of this book is the extensive culinary information, recipes, and meal plans that will make losing weight and establishing your lifestyle not only nourishing but fun and tasty. Recipes for a variety of very low levels of carbohydrate intake are included.

Fats and oils have been the most maligned and misunderstood nutrients, given their essential need in the body. This book provides an easy-to-understand lesson on the uses and benefits of natural fats, along with some interesting history.

Sweeteners and fiber are also given a good review. Recipes and meals cover everything from breakfast protein shakes to desserts to full meal plans for entertaining and holidays.

Hints on how to adapt recipes with substitutions, find ingredients, including Internet sources, and snacks and travel food ideas are also provided.

Having lost weight, people will need to find their level of carbohydrate intake that maintains their weight, controls hunger and craving, and keeps their individual metabolism in a healthy range. Many of the recipes in this book will be appropriate for all; some of us who are more carbohydrate intolerant will be more limited. Yet we can all benefit from the extensive hands-on information provided here.

Many of the common ills we suffer in our modern but unhealthy environment that diminish our quality of life and significantly stress our healthcare system are simply lifestyle-related. It is up to each of us to care for the only body we will ever have. Luckily our bodies have a tremendous capacity to heal. Take advantage of that and start now to take back control of your health and your life.

– Jacqueline Eberstein, R.N.

Scientific Perspective

BY RICHARD D. FEINMAN, PH.D, R.D.

"This process is alchemy; its founder is the smith Vulcan. What is accomplished by fire is alchemy-whether in the furnace [chemistry] or in the kitchen stove. And he who governs fire is Vulcan, even if he be a cook or a man who tends the stove [chemist]." – Paracelsus

Paracelsus was a sixteenth century doctor and an alchemist. He had one foot in the medieval world and one foot in modern science, and he was probably a bit of a madman. He recognized that cooking and chemistry were the same thing and he saw that it was all about food and transformation. Chemists like to cook. *Nourished* gives you good recipes to try. (If you are new to carbohydrate restriction, the cauliflower recipes are an important place to start.) Chemists even like to read about food. *Nourished* is a good read from a scientist's perspective. I've always made fricos in the frying pan. I liked reading about how it could have been less messy if I followed the recipe on page 159.

It's the connections that scientists like. Chemistry, in particular, is called "the central science" by educators, because it connects very basic stuff, like atomic structure, to practical problems, like making a better detergent, or what to cook for dinner. *Nourished* flows from the science, science that it explains well. Like Judy Barnes Baker's first book, *Carb Wars; Sugar is the New Fat*, it provides a good introduction to the metabolic theory that makes dietary carbohydrate restriction the best diet for weight loss, diabetes, metabolic syndrome, and, for most people, general health. Carbohydrate-restricted diets are really insulin-control diets, and the science is clear on the need to control insulin fluctuations.

Insulin is a kind of master hormone, and although it is under the control of glucose and therefore, dietary carbohydrate, its effects are global: it regulates protein synthesis, and, most of all, it regulates lipid metabolism. In this sense, diabetes is as much a disease of lipid metabolism as of carbohydrate intolerance. Insulin determines whether fat will be stored or broken down—the enzyme, hormone sensitive lipase (HSL), is the primary target of insulin. If insulin is high, the effect is to inhibit the breakdown of fat (lipolysis). Reducing carbohydrate will relieve this inhibition, providing fatty acids (components of fat) as fuel for tissues of the body. Persistent high insulin and high carbohydrate, however, give rise to accommodation, and cells become insulin resistant. Now, fat cells may continue to put out fatty acids, even when insulin is high. These fatty acids may not be oxidized, and it is observed that they may stimulate further insulin resistance, especially if there is high glucose or fructose. So, fatty acids in the blood, a current concern of researchers, is a double-edged sword. In the context of high glucose and high insulin, they will exacerbate the metabolic condition reflected in insulin resistance. On a carbohydrate-restricted diet however, high fatty acids are a sign that fat is being broken down and oxidized for energy.

Insulin-control diets are primarily therapeutic. Many metabolic diseases are hormonal and are either controlled by or interact with insulin. The science is clear but, even if you do not have a medical reason to adopt an insulin-control diet, you may like the food better. So, as

Paracelsus said, it's about cooking and chemistry. But there is one big scientific question, the question everybody really wants to know.

The science is now compelling. There is little doubt that carbohydrate restriction is the best place to start for weight loss and diabetes and, while we don't really understand the causes of cardiovascular disease, we are pretty sure that reducing fat, even saturated fat, will not make much difference. The big question is why so many experts and so many health organizations continue to repeat the same old advice: low fat, high carb. In the way of an answer, I would go back to Paracelsus, to alchemy. Now when I was a kid, I couldn't understand how alchemists could get away with pretending to make gold. You learn pretty early on that transmutation of elements is not possible outside of nuclear reactions, which are a recent thing. So clearly they couldn't be making gold. How did they get away with it? When I was much older, I understood that there were people who wanted to believe they had gold (analogous to believing that their health would be improved by cutting out fat). There were people who were willing to certify that they had gold. There were people who wanted to believe that the certifiers were telling the truth, and, of course, the alchemists themselves wanted everybody to believe that what they were doing (which might be copper-plating an iron object to look like gold) was making gold. As long as nobody broke into the circle, it moved right along. So, it requires an understanding of human nature to understand the big question, but the cycle of pro-low-fat researchers, their friends in large organizations, physicians, the press, and others, perpetuate the outdated science. It is my hope that *Nourished* will help many to finally break the circle. Alchemy is strong, but you have *Nourished* telling you both the science and the cooking. Go with real gold.

– Richard D. Feinman, Ph.D, R.D.

Introduction

One of the national dishes of Poland is fried lard. Almost every meal features a crock of creamy lard, flecked with browned bits, to slather on thick slices of bread. In France the food fairly floats in butter, duck fat, goose fat, and heavy cream. Their ultimate luxury—rich, silky lobes of *foie gras*—must be cooked very tenderly lest it dissolve into a pool of very expensive grease. But in the airports and cities of Europe you will see very few overweight people, and if you get within earshot of those who are, they are usually speaking English. (I asked a tour guide in Poland what the natives thought of all the fat Americans. She replied that they thought it meant that we are all rich.)

Back home in the U.S., the stores are full of fat-free and low-fat products, substitutes for butter and eggs, and boneless, skinless, tasteless cuts of meat, yet we are the fattest and most medicated people in the world. For the past 40 years we have been told that fat is bad and carbohydrates are good because of the supposed link between heart disease and fat intake. But heart disease is still a leading killer, and diabetes and obesity have reached epidemic proportions. We are starting to realize that we have targeted the wrong enemy.

It is counter-intuitive, but undeniable: eating fat doesn't make you fat any more than eating peaches makes you fuzzy. *Storing* fat is what makes you fat, and insulin is required to store fat. It is carbohydrates that raise blood sugar levels and trigger the release of insulin. Insulin signals the body to store energy and shuts off fat burning. As long as insulin is present, the fat remains locked in the cells, even if the body must break down muscle tissue in order to function. In the absence of sugar, insulin levels drop, and the body turns to fat as its primary fuel.

Fats and proteins are essential for life. Dietary carbohydrates are not.[1] Some sugar is required by the body, but it can be produced through a process called gluconeogenesis.[2] This provides only the amount needed and does so in a way that wastes energy, resulting in what has been dubbed the *metabolic advantage,* because it promotes weight loss beyond what would be expected from the calorie equation. The authors of the latest Atkins book call it the *Atkins Edge.* For most people, it happens when the daily intake of carbohydrates falls below 50 digestible grams, the point at which the body switches from burning sugar to burning fat.

It is time for us to return to the good, natural fats that have taken the blame for the mess created by the heavily promoted, "heart-healthy," low-fat and fat-free foods that replaced them in the American diet. Such products are invariably higher in sugar and starch, which is quickly converted into sugar when ingested.

High blood pressure, high insulin levels, belly fat, and abnormal cholesterol levels are all symptoms of carbohydrate intolerance. They occur together and increase the risk for obesity, heart disease, stroke, and diabetes. Evidence-based science shows that it is carbohydrates that promote fat storage and that weight gain is the first of a cascade of reactions called collectively, *the metabolic syndrome.*

---

1   "The brain can run on glucose produced in the body and ketones produced by burning fat for energy." (DRI, Ch. 6, 277) The Dietary Reference Intakes (DRI) of the National Institute of Medicine, part of the National Academies. (This is the document on which the government supposedly bases its guidelines.)

2   "The lower limit of dietary carbohydrate compatible with life is apparently zero." (DRI, Ch. 6, 275)

Emerging research continues to validate that low-carb diets are safe and effective. Those who try the lifestyle will discover that it stabilizes blood glucose levels, lowers blood pressure, eliminates hunger, reduces triglycerides, and improves blood lipid profiles. It decreases or eliminates the need for medications and increases satiety on fewer calories. It is a get-out-of-jail-free card for those with diabetes. When blood glucose is stabilized with food rather than medications, there are no side effects from drugs, there is no danger of hypoglycemia, no damage caused by excessive insulin or high glucose levels, and there is a reduction in medical expenses.

Logic dictates that since diabetes is a disease of defective carbohydrate metabolism, minimizing carbs should be the first line of defense, the prime directive. If blood glucose is kept within the normal range, a person with diabetes can be as healthy and symptom-free as a person who does not have diabetes. That is what normal means. As long as glucose is well-controlled, diabetes will not progress to cause blindness, kidney failure, amputation, heart failure, stroke, or any of its other complications. Eating a diet that minimizes the need for insulin can turn diabetes from a deadly disease into an inconvenience.

If you have diabetes, you can choose to keep your sight, your limbs, and your health, or you can choose bread and sugar. The decision reminds me of an old comedy routine: A man with a gun accosts skinflint Jack Benny and demands, "Your money or your life!" After a long pause, the robber repeats, "I SAID, YOUR MONEY OR YOUR LIFE!" Finally, Benny responds: "I'm thinking; I'm thinking."

I saw a news report recently that said that more Americans are living to be 100 years old (with the caveat that it will probably change as the Baby Boomer generation ages). The very next day there was a story about the skyrocketing rate of Alzheimer's and dementia. We've gotten better at prolonging life, worse at preserving the *quality* of life. Obesity, diabetes, auto-immune and degenerative diseases, disability, and the staggering costs of medical care suck the joy out of living longer.

A long, *healthy* life should be our aim, not simply racking up a few more years of misery. I hope to be like the Japanese man I read about in *National Geographic*. More than 100 years old, he was out digging in his garden every day. Every morning, he pulled back his curtains to let his neighbors know he was still alive. That's the goal, to be healthy and active to the end, then to go quickly and quietly after a long, productive, and purposeful life.

An unattributed essay called, *The Ride of Your Life*, made the rounds on the Internet a few years ago. It ended with this line:

"Life's journey is not to arrive at the grave safely in a well preserved body, but rather to skid in sideways, totally worn out, shouting, "…what a ride!"

About Low-Carb Diets

Metabolism 101

Foods consist of three *macronutrients*, carbohydrate, protein, and fat, and two *micronutrients* (because they are needed in small amounts), vitamins and minerals. Dietary fats and proteins are necessary for life; carbohydrates are not. Some foods that contain important micronutrients also contain carbohydrates, but it is the micronutrients we need, and they can be obtained from low-carb sources, such as green vegetables and low-sugar fruits. The human body requires some sugar in the form of glucose, but the liver can convert proteins and some other small particles to provide it through a process called *gluconeogenesis*.

Carbohydrates comprise various compounds including sugars (such as glucose, sucrose, fructose, and lactose) and starches, which are made up of long chains of glucose molecules. Starches are quickly broken down into simple glucose (blood sugar) after ingestion. Some are actually absorbed into the blood stream more quickly than simple sugars and can cause a greater rise in blood sugar levels than pure glucose. Carbohydrates are used for energy or to make fat to be stored as an energy reserve. The only part of your body that can tell much difference between sugar and starch is your tongue; sugar tastes sweet, starch does not. (To see this for yourself, try the old student experiment of chewing a piece of bread long enough to allow the enzymes in your saliva to break down the starch. It will taste sweet.) Starches and sugars provoke the release of insulin, the hormone that drives fat storage.

Proteins are used for building body tissues and for making enzymes and hormones. Proteins are the machines that make a living cell function. They are polymers (long chains, like beads on a string) of amino acids. Some amino acids can stimulate a certain amount of insulin secretion.

Fat is a source of energy, and stored fat is an energy reservoir. Some fat is incorporated into the body as part of cell membranes and other tissues. Fat does not provoke the release of insulin. The whole process is orchestrated by hormones. This is the way the system should work: when we eat sugar or starch, the beta cells in the pancreas produce insulin. Insulin is the master hormone. It regulates the amount of glucose in the blood to keep the level within the narrow range necessary to prevent organ damage. It also allows glucose to enter the cells. A small amount of glucose is stored as glycogen, and some is used to produce heat or power muscles. Any that remains is turned into fat and stored for future energy needs. Excess sugar is far more damaging to the body than fat, so the process of converting it into fat for storage protects the body from greater harm.

Fat is constantly broken down and burned or re-synthesized and stored. The process is controlled by hormones, the most important of which is insulin. When insulin is high, the cycle favors synthesis and storage of fat; when insulin is low, the cycle is biased toward breaking it down into fatty acids that can be used as the major source of fuel for cells, with a few exceptions, most notably the brain. Gluconeogenesis can supply glucose, derived primarily from protein, to the brain and the other tissues that need it.

When carbohydrates are low, insulin levels drop, and the hormone glucagon initiates fat burning, and at very low carbohydrate levels, a state called ketosis. Ketosis is a natural part of metabolism, and it was and is the normal state for people in non-agricultural societies; it occurs every night while you are sleeping and ends when you consume more sugar or starch to start the cycle over again. For most people, ketosis happens when the daily intake of carbohydrates falls below 50 grams per day on a 2,000-calorie diet.

There is a common misconception that ketosis is harmful because in untreated type 1 diabetes, ketone bodies are produced without the regulation of insulin. Ketone bodies are acids, and at very high levels they can cause *ketoacidoses*. Ketone bodies are only a danger at very high levels in untreated type 1 diabetes where glucose is also dangerously high.

A low-carb diet can supply all the nutrients you need without the excess sugar and starch that cause high blood sugar and the high insulin level needed to bring it under control. Excessive insulin is also toxic and comes with its own set of health problems; in addition to weight gain and obesity and all its consequences, insulin can damage the lining of the blood vessels, increase blood pressure, and heighten the risk for heart attacks and strokes.

"All I'm saying to obesity researchers is, pay attention to the hormonal and enzymatic regulation of the fat tissue. And if you do, you'll get a different answer for what causes obesity and what cures it."
– *Gary Taubes,* Why We Get Fat and What To Do About It

Dr. Cynthia Kenyon, a geneticist at the University of California at San Francisco, believes she has discovered how a simple change in diet can control aging. Scientists already knew they could make laboratory animals live longer by cutting down their food intake. Dr. Kenyon discovered why this works when she tweaked the genes that control insulin production in round worms. She found that carbohydrates affect two genes, also found in rodents and humans, that regulate longevity.

When one gene is turned down, it activates a second gene, which acts as a restorative "elixir of life." The scientists dubbed the first gene, "the Grim Reaper." The second one, whose proper name is DAF 16, they called, "The Sweet Sixteen" gene, because it kept the worms young and active long past their normal life expectancy.

The report in the *Daily Mail*[3] said the discovery has, "…prompted the professor to dramatically alter her own diet, cutting right back on carbohydrates. That's because carbs make your body produce more insulin… so the vital second gene, the 'elixir' one, won't get turned on."

This new study shows that the benefits of low-calorie diets are due to the reduction in insulin. But you don't have to reduce calories to cut down on insulin; you only have to reduce the carbohydrates that provoke the release of insulin.

3   www.dailymail.co.uk/health/article-1323758/Can-cutting-Carbohydrates-diet-make-live-longer.html#ixzz18LgvrA3Q

What is a Low Carb Diet?

An international panel of experts suggested these definitions, describing three different levels of reduction:

- A low-carbohydrate ketogenic diet (LCKD): 50 grams or fewer per day or 10% of calories.
- Low carbohydrate diet (LCD): 50 to 130 grams per day or 10% to 26% of calories.
- Moderate-carbohydrate Diet (MCD): 130 to 225 grams per day or 26% to 45% of calories.[4]

I have added one more definition, one for the typical high-carb diet (the current USDA dietary recommendation is for 300 grams per day):

- Standard American diet (SAD): 300 to 500 grams of carbohydrate per day.

Note: The common perception of low carb is that it requires the consumption of huge amounts of meat and fat. First, let me point out that most of us who follow a reduced carbohydrate way of life do not eat more protein and fat than we did before. It becomes a larger *percentage* of our diet because we eat less overall. I still eat the same small steak, two chops, or one hamburger that I always did. It was my consumption of vegetables that increased when I replaced breads and starchy side dishes with non-starchy vegetables.

Carbohydrates make you hungry. Fat and protein actually reduce the total number of calories needed to keep you feeling satisfied. Gary Taubes, author of *Good Calories, Bad Calories*, said that studies showed that those who cut down on carbs ate less, but that it was important to remember that "no one was *telling* them to eat less!"

Here are some studies that show that reducing sugar and starch in the diet leads to a spontaneous reduction in appetite and total calories:

Boden, G.; Sargrad, K.; Homko, C.; Mozzoli, M; Stein, T.P.: "Effect of a low carbohydrate diet on appetite, blood glucose levels, and insulin resistance in obese patients with type 2 diabetes." *Ann Intern Med* 2005, 142(6):403-411.

Yancy, W.S. Jr; Foy, M.; Chalecki, A.M.; Vernon, M.C.; Westman, E.C.: "A low carbohydrate, ketogenic diet to treat type 2 diabetes." *Nutr Metab (Lond)* 2005, 2:34.

Volek, J.S.; Sharman, M.J.; Gomez, A.L.; Judelson, D.A.; Rubin, M.R.; Watson, G.; Sokmen, B.; Silvestre, R.; French, D.N.; Kraemer, W.J.: "Comparison of energy-restricted very low-carbohydrate and low-fat diets on weight loss and body composition in overweight men and women." *Nutr Metab (Lond)* 2004, 1(1):13.

---

4   Dietary carbohydrate restriction in type 2 diabetes mellitus and metabolic syndrome: Time for a critical appraisal, *Nutrition & Metabolism*, 8 April 2008, 5:9doi:10.1186/1743-7075-5-9, Anthony Accurso, Richard K. Bernstein, Annika Dahlqvist, Boris Draznin, Richard D. Feinman, Eugene J. Fine, Amy Gleed, David B. Jacobs, Gabriel Larson, Robert H. Lustig, Anssi H. Manninen, Samy I. McFarlane, Katharine Morrison, Jørgen Vesti Nielsen, Uffe Ravnskov, Karl S. Roth, Ricardo Silvestre, James R. Sowers, Ralf Sundberg, Jeff S. Volek, Eric C Westman, Richard J. Woo, Jay Wortman, and Mary C. Vernon. Article is here: http://www.nutritionandmetabolism.com/content/5/1/9/abstract/

Who Can Benefit from a Low Carb Diet?

- The overweight and obese. This is by far the largest group who could benefit from carb restriction; they now make up over two-thirds of the population of the United States.
- Bariatric surgery patients. Hundreds of thousands of people a year in the United States are having gastric bypass procedures for the treatment of obesity. Patients are routinely put on a low-carb diet before the surgery to reduce fatty liver disease to help them survive the operation; afterwards, most of them are advised to avoid eating sugar and starch to prevent a painful condition called "dumping" and to avoid regaining weight.
- Those who suffer from epilepsy. Carb restriction has been shown to be effective in reducing the number and severity of epileptic seizures in both adults and children. Some children have been completely cured of the condition after two years on a strict ketogenic diet (lower in carbs than the ketogenic diet defined above). Ongoing research indicates that an Atkins-type diet may be as effective as the more restrictive ketogenic diet and much less stressful.
- Women who have fertility problems caused by polycystic ovary syndrome.
- Bodybuilders and fitness enthusiasts. Many trainers and coaches have embraced this lifestyle including: Dr. Jeff Volek, a professor at the University of Connecticut, and Adam Campbell, the fitness editor for *Men's Health Magazine*, who co-authored the *TNT Diet;*[5] Fred Hahn, author of *The Slow Burn Fitness Revolution*.[6] Dr. Jonny Bowden, author of *The 150 Healthiest Foods on Earth*[7] also recommends limiting carbs.
- Others. Low carb diets are being used to treat acne, eczema, acid reflux, ulcerative colitis, irritable bowel syndrome, gout, attention deficit disorder, Alzheimer's, cancer, and many other diseases and conditions.

---

5 Rodale Books, 2007

6 Broadway, 2002

7 Fair Winds Press, 2007

A 2008 study from Duke University compared a low-glycemic index diet to a low-carbohydrate diet to see which led to greater improvement in blood sugar control. Eighty-four obese volunteers with type 2 diabetes were randomized into either a ketogenic (fat-burning) diet with 20 grams of carbs or fewer per day or a low-glycemic index, reduced-calorie diet with a reduction of 500 calories per day from the amount needed for weight maintenance. Of the participants who completed the study, those eating fewer carbohydrates lost more weight and had greater improvements in HDL (good) cholesterol, triglyceride levels, and glycemic control, and 95.2% were able to significantly reduce or eliminate their diabetes medications.

The conclusion of the abstract from the study states, "Lifestyle modification using low carbohydrate interventions is effective for improving and reversing type 2 diabetes."[8]

---

8   Westman, E.C.; Yancy, W.S. Jr; Mavropoulos, J.C.; Marquart, M.; McDuffie, J.R.; "The effect of a low-carbohydrate, ketogenic diet versus a low-glycemic index diet on glycemic control in type 2 diabetes mellitus," *Nutr Metab* (Lond), 2008 Dec 19;36.

How Long Can You Safely Stay on a Low-Carb Diet?

Many people are not comfortable trying a new and untested diet. This is not one. This is the diet that matches our bodies, the one that sustained humans the world over for millennia before the agricultural revolution.

The low-fat/high-carbohydrate diet that we have been eating for the last 30 years or so is the untested, experimental one, and it is obviously a disastrous failure.

As a former sugar addict myself, I can testify that after reducing my carbohydrate consumption in 2000, I have seen nothing but positive changes in my health. My only regret is that I didn't start sooner. And I am just a beginner compared to some, such as diabetes specialist, Dr. Richard Bernstein, who was diagnosed with type 1 diabetes in 1947 when he was 12 years old. Based on his life expectancy at that time, he should have been dead by 1976. He was well on his way to meeting that fate, with advanced kidney disease, peripheral neuropathy, and a damaged heart when he managed to obtain his own blood glucose meter. He became the first diabetic patient to monitor his own blood- sugar levels and through trial and error, he learned how to normalize his blood sugar with diet. He reversed his diabetic complications and is still healthy and still practicing medicine and writing books at the age of 76, having spent almost 40 years eating a very low-carb diet.

> "…If you overfeed somebody with fat you don't increase their risk of cancer at all….Overfeed with carbohydrates and you drastically increase their cancer risk. Protein is halfway between. That's why we are going to have a huge debate about these carbohydrate-based diets."
>
> –*Dr. Craig B. Thompson, President and CEO of Sloan Kettering Cancer Center*

In *The Diabetes Diet*,[9] he tells about attending his 50th college reunion. He was the only one from his original class who had type 1 diabetes. He was one of only two who were still recognizable from fifty years earlier. "…I am healthier today not *in spite* of having a potentially fatal illness, but *because* of it…It's an odd twist of fate that I am likely much healthier now than I would have been had I not been a diabetic. The diet is why."

Note: A reduced carbohydrate diet may not be appropriate for everyone. Some people with a rare genetic condition called familial dyslipidemia, may need to restrict certain types of dietary fats.

---

9   Richard Bernstein, M.D, *The Diabetes Diet*, Little, Brown and Company, 2005.

The Birth of Fat Phobia:

In an all-too-typical scenario, a young man in my family went to the hospital complaining of chest pains. He learned that he had suffered a heart attack, but at the same time he was told that he had type 2 diabetes. The doctors sent him to a nutritionist for advice, who explained her dilemma—he had two separate conditions that required two opposing dietary interventions: a low-carbohydrate diet for diabetes, but a low-fat diet for the heart condition.

For the past 30 years, much of medical practice has been based on the lipid hypothesis, the belief that dietary fat causes heart disease. Since heart attacks are the leading cause of death for those with diabetes, carbohydrates would seem to be the lesser of two evils. Emerging science is showing that heart disease and diabetes are really manifestations of one syndrome, two sides of the same coin. They tend to happen together, which indicates that they share a common cause.

Ancel Keys, a University of Minnesota physiologist and government consultant, introduced the theory that dietary fats, especially saturated fats, raise cholesterol and cause heart disease. The conclusions he reached in his study of seven countries, which ran from 1958 to 1970, became the cornerstone for medical practice for the next 40 years.

It should be noted that Keys was measuring *total* cholesterol in his subjects, as the tests he used could not differentiate between HDL ("good") and LDL ("bad") cholesterol, so his results were totally meaningless. There are many kinds of cholesterol, and some are associated with a reduced risk of heart disease. A study by CHORI scientists found that a low-carb diet with more saturated fat, corresponded with an increase in the particle size of low-density lipoproteins (LDL). Larger LDL size is associated with a lower risk of cardiovascular disease. Lead researcher, Dr. R. M. Krauss, reported, "It's the carbohydrate that appears to have most of the effect when it comes to dietary influences. Increasing saturated fat does not appear to reduce the benefits of limiting carbohydrate."[10]

There were many other fallacies in the Seven Countries Study. Keys based his studies on an earlier one that tracked the eating patterns and heart disease mortality in 22 counties. The graph published with the original study showed no correlation between saturated fat and heart disease. Keys picked 7 countries out of the original 22 that supported his hypotheses and ignored the ones that did not. For example, Finland and Mexico had similar rates of fat consumption, but Finland had seven times as many coronary deaths as Mexico. Finland was selected for his study; Mexico was not. Subsequent studies have also found enormous differences in heart disease rates within countries, despite consistent cholesterol levels.[11]

Over the next 20 years, the National Institutes of Health spent millions of dollars trying to prove the hypothesis put forth by Keys, the man who was nicknamed "Mr. Cholesterol." Five major studies failed to show any connection between dietary fat and heart disease.

---

10   Krauss, R.M.; Blanche, P.J.; Rawlings, R.S.; Fernstrom, H.S.; Williams, P.T. "Separate effects of reduced carbohydrate intake and weight loss on atherogenic dyslipidemia." Am J Clin Nutr 2006;83:1025–31.

11   Uffe Ravnskov, M.D., Ph.D., *The Cholesterol Myths: Exposing the Fallacy that Saturated Fat and Cholesterol Cause Heart Disease*, 2003.

When a 6th study did seem to show that a reduction in cholesterol led to fewer heart attacks, *Time Magazine* trumpeted the news on the cover of its March 26, 1984, issue with a frowning face made of two eggs and a strip of bacon. Inside, an article titled, "Hold the Eggs and Butter," declared, "Cholesterol is proved deadly, and our diet may never be the same." The study that led to this conclusion was not a diet study at all, but a study of a cholesterol-reducing drug.[12] The 10-year study of 3,806 middle-aged men with high cholesterol showed that those who ate a low-fat diet and took a cholesterol-lowering drug had slightly fewer heart attacks than those on the same low-fat diet without the drug. However, there was no significant reduction in the number of deaths, as more participants taking the drug died of strokes, cancer, suicide, and violence than those in the placebo group.

Basil Rifkind, the project director for the NIH study that prompted the 1984 *Time* article, was quoted as saying he "believed" the research indicated that lowering the cholesterol and fat in your diet would reduce your risk of heart disease. It was his belief, nothing more. The nine-page article laid out the low-fat orthodoxy that continues to this day. You can read it online at: http://www.time.com/time/magazine/article/0,9171,921647,00. html#ixzz1B96rh7k4.

(Ironically, one of the conditions now suspected as being linked to low cholesterol is Parkinson's Disease.[13] Basil Rifkind died of Parkinson's Disease in 2008 at the age of 72.)

In January of 1977, a Senate committee, (The Select Committee on Nutrition and Human Needs) headed by George McGovern, officially endorsed the unproven lipid hypothesis when it published its *Dietary Goals for the United States,* advising that Americans should reduce their fat intake. The decision was made, not by scientists or researchers, but by a handful of politicians who chose to ignore the conflicting evidence they heard in two days of testimony and assigned the task of deciding what Americans should eat to a staff member. Gary Taubes, after reviewing the tapes of the hearings, exposed the lack of scientific evidence and the absence of consensus behind the Senate's guidelines in his March 2001 article in the journal *Science*, "The Soft Science of Dietary Fats,"[14] and in a 2002 article in *The New York Times*, "What if It's All Been a Big Fat Lie?"[15] You can read a blow-by-blow account of exactly how it all unfolded in *Good Calories, Bad Calories.*[16]

The press reported the government recommendations as if they were based on scientific proof and initiated a major change in the eating habits of the nation. Manufacturers picked up on the demand for low-fat products and seized on the opportunity to sell processed foods that bore little resemblance to the originals. As long as the label said, "fat-free," we ate it up.

There were many dissenters to the Senate recommendations. Among them, E. H. "Pete" Ahrens, chairman of the Diet-Heart Review Panel of the National Heart Institute, and his

---

12   *JAMA*. 1984 Jan 20;25;251(3):351-64. The Lipid Research Clinics Coronary Primary Prevention Trial results. I. Reduction in incidence of coronary heart disease. Read more on *Pub Med* at: http://www.ncbi.nlm.nih.gov/pubmed/6361299.

13   Huang, X.; Abbott, R.D.; Petrovitch, Mailman, R.B.; Ross, G.W. *Mov Disord*. 2008 May 15,23(7):1013-8. Low LDL cholesterol and increased risk of Parkinson's disease: prospective results from Honolulu-Asia Aging Study. Department of Neurology, University of North Carolina School of Medicine, Chapel Hill, North Carolina 27599-7025, USA. xuemei@med.unc.edu. Read about this study on Pub Med at: http://www.ncbi.nlm.nih.gov/pubmed/18381649.

14   Gary Taubes, "The Soft Science of Dietary Fats," *Science*, March 2001.

15   Gary Taubes, "What if It's All Been a Big Fat Lie?" *The New York Times*, July 7, 2002.

16   Gary Taubes, *Good Calories, Bad Calories; Fats, Carbs, and the Controversial Science of Diet and Health,* Anchor Books, 2007, 2008.

panel of ten experts who feared that changing the ratio of fats in the human body could have negative consequences. They warned, "The brain, for instance, is 70% fat, which chiefly serves to insulate neurons. Fat is the primary component of cell membranes. This could conceivably change the membrane permeability, which controls the transport of everything from glucose, signaling proteins, and hormones to bacteria, viruses, and tumor-causing agents into and out of the cell. The relative saturation of fats in the diet could also influence cellular aging as well and the clotting ability of blood cells."[17]

The testimony also included this comment from British researcher and surgeon, Peter Cleave: "I don't hold the cholesterol view for a moment. For a modern disease to be related to an old-fashioned food is one of the most ludicrous things I have ever heard in my life. If anybody tells me that eating fat was the cause of coronary disease, I should look at them in amazement. But, when it comes to the dreadful sweet things that are served up ... that is a very different proposition."

It is the sugar and starch in the diet that determine what happens to the fat we eat. If the diet is low in fat and high in carbohydrates, the body will make its own supply of saturated fat, and the sugars will provide the insulin to put it into storage. When the carbs are low, the fat is burned for energy, not stored in the arteries or anywhere else.[18]

Dr. Malcolm Kendrick, author of *The Great Cholesterol Con*,[19] cites a study done by the World Health Organization called, *Multinational Monitoring of Trends in the determinants in Cardiovascular Disease*.[20] The study found that the Swiss have the highest average cholesterol levels of any population or country in the world, yet their heart disease rate is one-third that of the United Kingdom. Australian aboriginals have the high-

> "...What right has the federal government to propose that the American people conduct a vast nutritional experiment, with themselves as subjects, on the strength of so very little evidence that it will do them any good?"
> — *Phillip Handler, President of the National Academy of Sciences, on the report by the Senate Select Committee that advised Americans to reduce fats and increase carbohydrates in their diets.*

est rate of heart disease in the world currently, but they have the lowest cholesterol level of any population studied. He says: "The French consumed three times as much saturated fat as was consumed in Azerbaijan, and had one-eighth the rate of heart disease. *Every single country in the top eight of saturated fat consumption had a lower rate of heart disease than every single country in the bottom eight of saturated fat consumption. And still we are told that a high saturated fat diet causes heart disease. Thank you and goodnight.*"

---

17   Gary Taubes, "The Soft Science of Dietary Fats," *Science*, March, 2001.

18   Lisa Cooper Hudgins, Marc Hellerstein, Cynthia Seidman, Richard Neese, Jolanta Diakun, and Jules Hirsch, "Human Fatty Acid Synthesis Is Stimulated by a Eucaloric Low Fat, High Carbohydrate Diet," *J. Clin. Invest.*, May, 1996, 97: pp. 2081–2091.

19   Malcolm Kendrick, *The Great Cholesterol Con*, John Blake; 1 edition, October 1, 2008.

20   http://www.youtube.com/watch?gl=GB&hl=en-GB&v=i8SSCNaaDcE.

Mark Twain tells of overhearing a conversation between two unscrupulous salesmen, one from Cincinnati and one from New Orleans, through a transom on a Mississippi riverboat. One was boasting about selling fake butter, the other fake olive oil.

"'Why, we are turning out oleomargarine NOW by the thousands of tons. And we can sell it so dirt cheap that the whole country has GOT to take it—can't get around it you see. Butter don't stand any show—there ain't any chance for competition. Butter's had its DAY—and from this out, butter goes to the wall. There's more money in oleomargarine than—why, you can't imagine the business we do....'

Then New Orleans piped up and said: 'Yes, it's a first-rate imitation, that's a certainty; but it ain't the only one around that's first rate...we turn out an olive oil that is just simply perfect—undetectable! We are doing a ripping trade, too—as I could easily show you by my order book for this trip. Maybe you'll butter everybody's bread pretty soon, but we'll cottonseed his salad for him from the Gulf to Canada, and that's a dead certain thing." – Mark Twain, *Life on the Mississippi*, 1883

Many fortunes have been made when entrepreneurs discovered that they could turn worthless waste byproducts into something that looked and tasted like food.

In 1837, candle maker, William Proctor, and his brother-in-law, James Gamble, a soap maker, founded Proctor & Gamble. Traditionally, both products were made of animal fats. With the help of a German chemist named E. C. Kayser, they developed the process of hydrogenation to solidify cottonseed oil so it could be used instead of lard and tallow for making soap and candles. They bought eight cotton mills in Louisiana to free them from dependence on the meat packers for their raw material. When they noticed how much the hardened cottonseed oil resembled lard, they decided to sell it as food, and in 1911 they introduced Crisco, named after the *crystallized cottonseed oil* used to make it. They promoted this new fat as a cheap, healthful, clean (and kosher), replacement for both butter and lard. [21] [22] [23] [24]

"It seems strange to many that there can be anything better than butter for cooking, or of greater utility than lard, and the advent of Crisco has been a shock to the older generation, born in an age less progressive than our own, and prone to contend that the old fashioned things are good enough."

– The Story of Crisco; 250 Tested Recipes, *by Marion Harris Neal, published by Procter & Gamble, 1913.*

---

21 McLagan, Jennifer, *Fat; An Appreciation of a Misunderstood Ingredient*, 2008, Ten Speed Press, p.85.

22 Schisgall, Oscar, *Eyes on Tomorrow: The Evolution of Proctor & Gamble*, J.G. Ferguson Pub Co., Distributed by Doubleday, 1981.

23 Pendleton, Susan C, "Man's Most Important Food is Fat: The Use of Persuasive Techniques in Proctor & Gamble's Public Relations Campaign to Introduce Crisco, 1911-1913," *Public Relations Quarterly*, March 22, 1999.

24 Enig, Mary G and Sally Fallon, "The Oiling of America."

How to Use This Book

Ingredients

FATS AND OILS

Can you afford to buy good quality fats and oils? Can you afford not to? The kind and quality of fats and oils you include in your diet is probably the most important diet-related decision you will ever make. This is not the place to skimp; saving money on cheap vegetable oil, shortening, and margarine may eventually cost you more in medicine and doctor bills, in addition to costing you your health and quality of life.

Sorting it all out: All fats contain a mixture of saturated, monounsaturated, and polyunsaturated fatty acids. They are usually classified by the one that predominates. We need the proper balance of all three for optimum health.

SATURATED FATS:

Saturated fats come mainly from animal sources and tropical plants like coconut and palm, and they are made in the body from carbohydrates. Saturated fats are very stable: they don't go rancid easily; they don't break down at cooking temperatures; and they don't form free radicals, which cause damage by stealing atoms from other molecules. They transport fat-soluble vitamins and minerals, and they are needed for proper utilization of calcium in the bones. Saturated fats have anti-microbial and anti-fungal properties, and they stimulate the immune system.[25] Saturated fats like butter and coconut oil contain short- and medium-chain fatty acids, which can be used for quick energy and are less likely to cause weight gain than the long-chain fatty acids like olive oil and the omega-6 polyunsaturated vegetable oils.

Archeological evidence shows that early man did not have access to a plentiful supply of polyunsaturates or grains. I doubt that you can find a single anthropologist who refutes the evidence that the diet of our ancient ancestors was high in animal products, including saturated fat. How could these foods suddenly become poison to modern humans?

But many studies show that saturated fat clogs arteries and causes heart disease and strokes, right? We constantly hear this stated as fact, as if it is a foregone conclusion that needs no supporting evidence. Actually there are many studies that show just the opposite. Gary Taubes catalogs all the controlled trials on nutrition and metabolism that have been done in the last 150 years in his book, *Good Calories, Bad Calories*.[26] Taubes, an award-winning science writer and relentless researcher, lets the evidence speak for itself. (His meticulously documented book has 115 pages of endnotes and references.) An objective overview of the science reveals the lack of any substantial evidence in support of the fat hypothesis of heart disease.

Part of the problem is that most people believe the lipid hypothesis, and like Tinker Bell, it is believing that keeps it alive. When a study is designed and interpreted and when it is reported by the media, it passes through the filter of the researcher's and the writer's preconceived

---

25   Stephen Byrnes, Ph.D., R.N.C.P., "The Myth of Vegetarianism," *Nexus Magazine*, Volume 9, Number 2, April-May, 2002.

26   Taubes, Gary, *Good Calories, Bad Calories; Fats, Carbs, and the Controversial Science of Diet and Health*, Anchor Books, 2007, 2008.

ideas. When confronted with new evidence, it is human nature for people to look for a way to reconcile it with what they already "know" to be true. We all do it. The phenomenon is called, "confirmation bias."[27]

A couple of examples: An article whose headline proclaimed, "Red meat causes cancer," reported the findings of a study in which researchers sorted through computerized data looking for correlations. (Correlations may suggest a relationship between bits of data, but they do not prove causation, and sometimes they are due to random chance.) One line in the article tells the story: "The numbers for the consumption of red meat were the same as that for the consumption of oranges, but everyone knows eating oranges doesn't cause cancer." Right.

> "...Until recently, saturated fats were usually lumped together with trans fats in the various U.S. databases that researcher use to correlate dietary trends with disease conditions. Thus, natural saturated fats were tarred with the black brush of unnatural hydrogenated vegetable oils."
>
> – *Sally Fallon*, Nourishing Traditions

And everyone *knows* that red meat does, so the study was accepted as confirmation of what they already believed, and the headline warned against red meat but not oranges.

In another case, a military-funded study conducted at the University of North Dakota discovered that pilots who ate the most fatty foods, such as butter or gravy, had the quickest response times in mental tests and made fewer mistakes when flying in tricky conditions. The researcher who conducted and reviewed the tests said, "We wound up analyzing the data every which way but upside down. It came out consistent every time." As usual, they kept looking for some way to make the findings fit what they already "knew" to be true. If the study had shown the fat-eaters to be mentally less capable, with slowed reflexes, I dare say, they wouldn't have given it a second thought.[28]

It is always wise to do a little research of your own before accepting what you read. Many studies are available on Pub Med and other free online sites. When a study is cited in an article or a book, look it up. The actual study may be difficult for non-scientists to understand, but most of them include an abstract written in plain English. You still need to be aware that the abstract may reflect the bias of the person interpreting the study, but most of them will describe how the study was done and give the actual results. One example that comes to mind is the recent study that compared four diets with Atkins coming out on top. The lead scientist, a vegetarian, was clearly surprised and dismayed by the outcome, but he was professional enough to tell the truth about how it turned out.[29]

Although the medical establishment is belatedly admitting that fat is essential to health, one last shred of the hypothesis remains, the invective against "artery-clogging" saturated fat and

27   Tavris, Carol and Aronson, Elliot, *Mistakes Were Made (but not by me)*, 2007, Harcourt Books.

28   Associated Press, 2009/10/06/hold_the_mayo_not_when_it_comes_to_astute_pilots/.

29   Christopher D. Gardner, et al., "Comparison of the Atkins, Zone, Ornish, and LEARN Diets for Change in Weight and Related Risk Factors Among Overweight Premenopausal Women," *Journal of the American Medical Association* 297, no. 9 (March 7, 2007), http://jama.ama-assn.org/cgi/content/abstract/297/9/969.

the belief that it causes high cholesterol and heart disease, but even that has taken a beating in recent studies. One, conducted by Dr. Jeff Volek and a team of researchers at the University of Connecticut,[30] tested the various components of metabolic syndrome, comparing a carbohydrate-restricted diet to a low-fat diet for overweight men and women over a 12-week period. The low-carb faction ate slightly more calories than those in the low-fat arm of the study.

The researchers discovered that those eating two-thirds less saturated fat than those on the low-carb diet, had an increase in the saturated fat in the bloodstream, despite the reduction in the amount they ate. The more saturated fat they ate, the less they had in their blood. They also reported that the markers for inflammation were dramatically reduced on the low-carb diet. You can read about the actual study on Pub Med at: www.ncbi.nlm.nih.gov.

> "The deleterious effects of fat have been measured in the presence of high carbohydrate. A high fat diet in the presence of high carbohydrate is different than a high fat diet in the presence of low carbohydrate."
>
> *– Richard Feinman, Ph.D.; R.D.; Biochemistry, State University of New York, NY.*

The conventional wisdom that predicts that an increase in saturated fat consumption would lead to more inflammation and an increase in the markers for the risk of metabolic syndrome, diabetes, and heart disease, was proved to be wrong. Dr. Volek explained, "This clearly shows the limitations of the idea that 'you are what you eat.' Metabolism plays a big role. You are what your body *does* with what you eat."

A study from the Harvard School of Public Health published in the *American Journal of Clinical Nutrition* analyzed the results of 21 studies with follow-up of from 5 to 23 years involving 347,747 subjects. The researchers came to the following conclusion: "A meta-analysis of prospective epidemiologic studies showed that there is no significant evidence for concluding that dietary saturated fat is associated with an increased risk of coronary heart disease or cardiovascular disease."[31]

> "When the facts change, I change my mind. What do you do, sir?"
>
> *– John Maynard Keynes, British economist*

A second study from the same issue of the *Journal of Clinical Nutrition* fingers the real culprits as refined carbs and being overweight. The conclusion ends with this statement, "…dietary efforts to improve the increasing burden of CVD risk associated with atherogenic dyslipidemia should primarily emphasize the limitation of refined carbohydrate intakes and a reduction in excess adiposity (fat)."[32]

---

30   Forsythe, C.E.; et al; Department of Kinesiology, University of Connecticut, *Lipids.* Comparison of low fat and low carbohydrate diets on circulating fatty acid composition and markers of inflammation, 2008 Jan;43(1):65-77, Epub 2007 Nov 29.

31   Patty W. Siri-Tario, Qui Sun, Frank B. Hu, and Ronald M. Krauss," Meta-analysis of prospective cohort studies evaluating the association of saturated fat with cardiovascular disease," American Journal of Clinical Nutrition, Vol. 91, No. 3, 535-546, March 2010.

32   Patty W. Siri-Tario, Qui Sun, Frank B. Hu, and Ronald M. Krauss, "Saturated fat, carbohydrate, and cardiovascular disease," *American Journal of Clinical Nutrition* Vol. 91, No. 3, 502-509, March 2010.

BUTTER:

Butter was a staple food in India and Ireland and other herding societies. It contains mostly saturated fat (66 percent saturated, the rest monounsaturated), but as it turns out, it is the trans fats that are the real villains and butter is actually good for us. It contains fat-soluble vitamins A (retinol), E, K, and D, and it is rich in minerals, including manganese, zinc, chromium, iodine, and especially selenium. It is a source for antimicrobial, anti-fungal, and anti-carcinogenic fatty acids; it strengthens the immune system and provides protection from heart disease, osteoporosis, and mental illness. It has been suggested that the alarming increase in osteoporosis in this country is the result of replacing butter with margarine.[33]

Nothing can compare with the taste of real butter, but it tends to burn easily. It can be combined with other oils to raise its smoke point, or clarified to use for sautéing and frying, although it will lose some flavor in the process.

Note: Salt serves as a preservative in butter. Unsalted butter's only advantage is that it lets you control the amount of salt in your recipe more carefully. Unsalted butter can be stored in the refrigerator for a month or frozen for six months. Butter wrapped in foil will not absorb off-flavors.

"For my mother, who always knew butter was better for you than margarine."

— Michael Pollan's dedication for Food Rules; An Eater's Manual

"I prefer butter over margarine because I trust cows more than chemists."

— Joan Gussow, author of The Feeding Web: Issues in Nutritional Ecology, *1978*

---

33   Sally Fallon with Mary G. Enig, Ph.D., *Nourishing Traditions*, ProMotion Publishing, San Diego, CA, 1995.

Researchers at Harvard's Joslin Diabetes Center found that the brains of those with diabetes suffer from a LACK of cholesterol.[34] The brain contains more cholesterol than any organ in the body. It is essential for normal brain function and most of it is made within the brain. According to C. Ronald Kahn, M.D., it is a lack of cholesterol that leads to the neurologic and cerebral complication of diabetes, including cognitive dysfunction, depression, and an increased risk of Alzheimer's disease.

The discovery came from a study of insulin-deficient, diabetic mice. The researchers found changes in many genes involved with cholesterol metabolism in the brain. These changes reduced the production of cholesterol and lowered the amount in cell membranes that play an important part in communication between brain cells. Dr. Kahn said that for those with diabetes, "This is another reason to think that keeping good control over blood sugar might make a difference." He added that these results raise the prospect that cholesterol-lowering statin drugs, some of which can cross the blood-brain barrier, "...might have unintended consequences for brain function."

---

34   Ryo Suzuki, Kevin Lee, Enxuan Jing, Sudha B. Biddinger, Jeffrey G. McDonald, Thomas J. Montine, Suzanne Craft, and C. Ronald Kahn. "Diabetes and Insulin in Regulation of Brain Cholesterol Metabolism," *Cell Metabolism*, Volume 12, Issue 6, 567-579, 1 December 2010.

CLARIFIED BUTTER AND GHEE:

Clarified butter is butter with the water and milk solids removed so that it can be stored at room temperature without spoiling and heated to higher temperatures without burning. Ghee is the Indian version; it is cooked until the milk solids are browned, giving it a nutty taste. Ghee can be found on the shelf at Indian markets. Clarified butter can be found in the dairy case at regular grocery stores. Both are easy to make:

Cut unsalted butter into pieces and melt in a saucepan over low heat. Raise the heat until it bubbles and let it cook until the water boils off. For Ghee, cook for about 10 minutes until fragrant and the solids start to brown. Skim off the foam that rises to the top and let stand until cool. Pour the clear liquid through a fine strainer into a glass jar. Use the milk solids left in the pan for flavoring vegetables or eggs.

COCONUT OIL:

Coconut oil was once a common ingredient in commercially produced foods. (It was what made movie popcorn smell so good.) The fear of saturated fats caused tropical oils to be replaced by polyunsaturated and hydrogenated oils, but coconut oil has recently regained popularity for cooking and as a nutritional supplement. Even unrefined, virgin coconut oil is extremely stable and can be stored at room temperature for over a year because of its high levels of natural antioxidants. It contains large quantities of lauric acid, which has antibacterial, antiviral, antifungal, and anti-protozoal properties. It reduces your chances of suffering a heart attack, improves cholesterol ratios, and raises the levels of antioxidant reserves n the cells. It is ideal for people who have trouble digesting fats and for athletes who need quick energy. [35] [36]

According to Bruce Fife, author of *The Coconut Oil Miracle*, coconut oil promotes weight loss; protects against cancer, diabetes, arthritis, and many other degenerative diseases; prevents premature aging of the skin; strengthens the immune system; and improves digestion.[37]

Is there already a cure for Alzheimer's disease and no one knows? Coconut oil "is a potential treatment for Parkinson's disease, Huntington's disease, multiple sclerosis and amyotrophic lateral sclerosis (ALS or Lou Gehrig's disease), drug resistant epilepsy, brittle type I diabetes, and diabetes type II...Ketone bodies may help the brain recover after a loss of oxygen in newborns through adults, may help the heart recover after an acute attack, and may shrink cancerous tumors."

– *Dr. Mary Newport*

http://www.coconutketones.com/whatifcure.pdf, July 22, 2008.

---

35   G. L. Blackburn, et al., "A reevaluation of coconut oil's effect on serum cholesterol and atherogenesis," *The Journal of the Philippine Medical Association*, 1988, 65: pp. 144-152. Second

36   I. A. Prior, F. Davidson, et al., "Cholesterol, coconuts, and diet on Polynesian atolls: a natural experiment: the Pukapuka and Tokelau island studies," *American Journal of Clinical Nutrition*, Aug., 1981, 34(8): pp. 1552-61.

37   Bruce Fife, C.N., N.D., *The Coconut Oil Miracle*, Avery, New York, 1999, 2000, 2002, 2004 Previously published as *The Healing Miracles of Coconut Oil*.

Coconut oil also shows promise for preventing and treating Alzheimer's disease. (Fifteen million people in the U.S. are predicted to have Alzheimer's disease by 2050.) When the brain is deprived of glucose due to a lack of insulin or to insulin resistance, it starts to atrophy. Ketone bodies provide an alternate energy source for the brain that could potentially keep brain cells alive and functioning. The body produces ketones when it converts fat into energy and a ready source of ketones are medium chain triglycerides (MCTs) like those found in coconut oil.[38]

Notes: Coconut oil is solid below 76º F and liquid at higher temperatures. It's called coconut oil when it is liquid and coconut butter when it is solid. It can be used like butter or shortening in its solid state and like oil in its liquid state.

Coconut oil and coconut milk provide quick energy and speed up the metabolism, so people who have problems sleeping may want to limit it to the morning hours.

TALLOW:

Tallow is the solid fat of beef and lamb. It is about half saturated, although half of that amount is stearic acid, which is converted to oleic acid (as in olive oil) once ingested. (Even the USDA's latest guidelines admit stearic acid is not harmful.) The other half is palmitic acid, which is believed to lower LDL cholesterol. Tallow also contains monounsaturated fats (again, like olive oil) and only small amounts of pro-inflammatory, polyunsaturated fat. It is very stable and can be used on high heat without becoming rancid or burning, making it one of the best choices for frying. Note: The fat from pastured animals contains more essential omega-3 fatty acids (the kind in fish) and more CLA (conjugated linoleic acid), both of which have health benefits.

TRANS FATS:

Avoid any product that lists "partially hydrogenated" oil as an ingredient. Trans fats are liquid oils that have been chemically altered to make them solid at room temperature and to prolong their shelf life. They were once considered an improvement over the natural fats in butter, tallow, lard, and coconut oil but are now widely recognized as a danger to health. They have been linked to cancer, atherosclerosis, osteoporosis, diabetes, obesity, stroke, problems with the immune system, and many other diseases.[39]

After years of warnings from scientists and consumer protection agencies about the dangers of artificial trans fats, The National Academy of Sciences conducted a government-funded study on them. In 2002, they released their finding that, "…the only safe intake of trans fat is zero." The FDA then ruled that nutrition labels on packaged foods must disclose the amount of the artificial fat they contain—the ruling was to go into effect in 2006 (four years after the conclusion of the study and 12 years after The Center for Science in the Public Interest petitioned the FDA to require such labels). There is a higher level of awareness about the trans fats now, but they are still ubiquitous in the food supply, especially in breads, cakes, cookies, crackers, pie crusts, chips, fried foods, cooking oils, and butter substitutes and spreads.

---

38   Veech, Richard L., et al.," Ketone Bodies, Potential Therapeutic Uses," *International Union of Biochemistry and Molecular Biology*, 1 April, 2001.

39   Sally Fallon and Mary G. Enig, Ph.D., *Nourishing Traditions: The Cookbook that Challenges Politically Correct Nutrition and the Diet Dictocrats*, New Trends Publishing, 2000.

There are a couple of loopholes in the disclosure laws. Product labels may legally say the level of trans fats is "zero" if it has 0.5 grams or less per serving. Some labels now say, "no trans fats," when the only thing that has changed is the serving size. You must diligently read the labels to see if any partially hydrogenated oils are listed.

There is also another loophole; the new rules do not cover foods served in restaurants. The Board of Health in New York City took matters into their own hands and voted to phase out trans fats by 2008, after first trying a voluntary campaign, which had no effect. The *Annals of Internal Medicine* reported that by July of 2008 restaurant use of trans fats had declined from 50% to less than 2% in the city, proving that it can be done.[40]

Note: There is an exception to the zero-tolerance rule for trans fats: dairy products and meat from ruminant animals contain *natural*, beneficial trans fats. One is conjugated linoleic acid (CLA), which has been shown to raise HDL cholesterol, increase insulin sensitivity, and to help with weight loss.[41]

It is the manufactured trans fatty acids that are linked to disease. So ditch the margarine; keep the butter.

MONOUNSATURATED FATS:
Monounsaturated fats are found in abundance in olive oil, avocados, macadamias, almonds, and peanuts, and most of the fat in lard and poultry is monounsaturated. They are relatively stable. The body can make monounsaturated fats out of saturated fats.

CANOLA OIL:
Canola contains about 60% omega-9 oleic acid and 10% omega-3 polyunsaturated fatty acids, so it is often recommended as an inexpensive alternative to olive oil, but it may not be any better than the other refined vegetable oils. It is made from rapeseed, originally used as furniture polish rather than food because it contained a toxin called erucic acid.[42] (Hats off to the marketing genius who realized that you couldn't sell something called *rapeseed* oil and renamed it *canola*, by combining the words *Canada* and *oil*.) Canola oil is made from hybridized rapeseed, and must be extracted with high-temperature mechanical pressing and chemical solvents. It must then be bleached, de-gummed, and deodorized. Some studies indicate that much of its omega-3 fatty acid content is converted into trans fats in the process.[43]

LARD:
You may be surprised to see lard listed here. It is not a mistake. Lard does contain saturated fat, but it contains mostly monounsaturated fat, the kind found in olive and nut oils.

Lard was a staple food in American until it was supplanted by shortening made from hydrogenated cottonseed oil. In 1940, the average consumption of lard hit a high of 14.4 pounds per capita. A steep decline followed as Crisco captured the market.

---

40 Sonia Y. Angell, M.D.; M.P.H.; Lynn Dee Silver, M.D., M.P.H.; Gail P. Goldstein, M..H.;. Christine M. Johnson, M.B.A.; Deboral R. Deitcher, M.P.H.; Thomas R. Frienden, M.D., M.P.H.; and Mary T. Bassett, M.D., M.P.H., *The Annals of Internal Medicine*, July 21, 2009, vol. 151 no. 2 129-134.

41 *Obesity* (Silver Spring) 2008;16(5):1019-24. Epub 2008 March 6.

42 Fran McCullough, *The Good Fat Cookbook*, 2003.

43 Sally Fallon and Mary Enig, Ph.D., "The Great Con-ola," *Nexus Magazine*, Aug/September, 2002.

A word of caution: most of the lard that is currently on store shelves is partially hydrogenated. That means that it has been treated with hydrogen so it contains the same trans-fats as the unnatural fats like shortening and margarine. To purchase natural lard, look for it in the cooler rather than on the shelf, and it should be refrigerated after you get it home.

OLIVE OIL:

Even the low-fat camp has conceded that some fat is necessary, and the one they endorse is olive oil. It would be hard to find fault with something that has been a staple food in many cultures for thousands of years. It can be used with little processing, and in addition to its high oleic acid content (up to 75%), it also contains small amounts of both the essential fatty acids, omega-6 and omega-3. Expeller pressed, extra-virgin olive oil is an excellent choice for flavoring, for dipping, for low-temperature cooking, and for dressing salads. Refined olive oil *extra light* can be heated to higher temperatures, but it will have lost some of its healthful compounds. Now for the bad news: the primary fatty acids in olive oil are the long-chain variety, which are more easily stored as body fat than medium- or short-chain fatty acids, such as those found in butter and coconut oil.

POULTRY FAT:

Duck, goose, and chicken fat are mostly monounsaturated. Jennifer McLagan attributes the low rate of heart disease exhibited by the French (the *French Paradox*) to their fondness for duck and goose fat. She gives the ratios for poultry fat as follows:

- Duck…saturated—33%; monounsaturated— 50%; polyunsaturated—13%
- Chicken…saturated—30%; monounsaturated—45%; polyunsaturated—21%
- Goose…saturated—28%; monounsaturated—57%; polyunsaturated—11%

Duck fat is often called "French butter" because it is the preferred fat for many uses in France. You can have a supply of excellent cooking fat with little extra effort by pouring off and straining the rendered fat from the pan when roasting a whole duck or searing duck breasts in a skillet. Score the duck skin in a diamond pattern before cooking, cutting through the skin but not into the meat, to render more fat and make the skin crisper. Store the duck fat, covered, in the refrigerator.

Chicken fat (schmaltz) was the primary fat for Jewish cooking, especially in northern Europe, since lard is prohibited by religious laws and oil was not commonly available.

The Secret of Olive Oil

In an article in the September 2005 issue of the *Journal Nature*, a group of scientists reported that freshly pressed olive oil contains a natural non-steroidal anti-inflammatory called oleocanthal, which has the same medicinal effect as ibuprofen. Only the freshest, extra-virgin olive oil contains the compound, since it is destroyed by heat, light, and time. Inflammation has been linked to many chronic diseases, including coronary heart disease.[44]

---

44 Gary K. Beauchamp, Russell S. J. Keast, Diane Morel, Jianming Lin, Jana Pika, Qiang Han, Chi- Ho Lee, Amos B. Smith, and Paul A. S. Breslin, "Phytochemistry: Ibuprofen-like activity in extra-virgin olive oil," *Journal Nature*, Sept, 2005, p. 45.

RICE BRAN OIL:

Rice bran oil, an omega-9 oil traditionally used in Japanese cooking, is high in monounsaturates, relatively inexpensive, and neutral in taste. It can be heated to high temperatures (490° F) without breaking down or absorbing flavors. Asian markets should have it in stock.

POLYUNSATURATED OILS

Polyunsaturated oils are less stable than monounsaturated and saturated oils. They are easily damaged by heat, light, and oxygen if they are refined and again if they are heated for cooking. When ingested, these altered fats form free radicals, highly reactive molecules linked to a great many health problems.

The authors of a study at the Wynn Institute for Metabolic Research in London, in which the content of human aortic plaque was analyzed, reported that, "No associations were found with saturated fatty acids. These findings imply a direct influence of dietary polyunsaturated fatty acids on aortic plaque formation and suggest that current trends favoring increased intake of polyunsaturated fatty acids should be reconsidered."[45]

> "Fats higher in saturated and monounsaturated fatty acids resist oxidation the best and are the slowest to turn rancid. Fats high in polyunsaturated fatty acids oxidize easily. If we eat oxidized fat, it not only makes us ill, but it also damages the cells in our bodies."
>
> — *Jennifer McLagan*

Polyunsaturated oils include the two essential fatty acids (EFAs): omega-3 and omega-6. They are called "essential" because they cannot be made in the body and must come from the diet. The ratio of EFAs is important because they are used to make substances, similar to hormones, that regulate many reactions in the body. Omega-6 oils promote blood clotting, muscle contraction, and inflammation, while omega-3s promote the opposite reactions: blood thinning, muscle relaxation, and an anti-inflammatory response. A high intake of omega 6, coupled with a low intake of omega-3, has also been associated with increased levels of depression, suicide, and bi-polar and explosive rage disorders.

To get the maximum benefits from polyunsaturates, use oils that are cold pressed, not extracted with heat and chemicals. Unrefined oils retain more essential fatty acids. They should be stored in the refrigerator in opaque containers, and they should not be used for cooking.

OMEGA-6 OILS:

Omega-6 oils include the heavily refined vegetable oils made from seeds and grains (soy, safflower, sunflower, corn, and cottonseed) that are found in most commercial products. Most of us get too much omega-6, which is usually highly processed, so we may still be deficient in this essential nutrient. Our reliance on oils made from soy and grains and on soy- and grain-fed livestock has upset the *yin and yang* relationship of EFAs (essential fatty acids) by greatly increasing our consumption of omega-6 in proportion to omega-3. Typical supermarket beef has a ratio of up to 13 parts omega-6 to one part omega-3, compared

---

45   C. V. Felton, D. Crook, M. J. Davies, M. F. Oliver, *Lancet*, 1995 Jan 28; 345(8944):256-7; author reply 257.

to a two- to one-ratio for wild game and pastured cattle.[46] Eggs from chickens fed on grain have up to 19 times the amount of omega-6 found in eggs from chickens eating a natural diet of plants, worms, and insects.

OMEGA-3 OILS

Omega-3 oils are found in eggs, in the meat, fat, bone marrow, and organs of animals, in fatty fish, and in krill. Linseed (flax), chia seed, walnuts, and a wild plant called purslane are among the few plant sources for omega-3s, and they contain only the precursor to the kind that can be used by the body. Omega-3 oils protect against cardiovascular disease, diabetes, and arthritis, but too much can increase the risk of strokes.

"High carbohydrate diets cause large releases in insulin, which sets up the scene for excess body fat storage. Fat does not. This is a fact of science – we don't get to vote."

– Fred Hahn, author of
The Slow Burn
Fitness Revolution

SWEETENERS

The decision to eliminate sugar is more important than just avoiding a few extra carbs. Sugar is a prime contributor to the epidemic of obesity, diabetes, and the cluster of diseases called the metabolic syndrome that have devastated this country for the last 40 years. Even the American Heart Association, while still clinging to the lipid hypothesis, has started to tell people that they need to cut down on sugar. Most people already know that, but the goodies and snacks that constantly surround us are hard to resist. If we can have food that satisfies our cravings without harming us, we are less likely to give in to temptation. If you have an iron will and are always in control of your impulses, eliminate sweets altogether and more power to you! But if you are subject to human frailties like me, then try the next best thing.

The landscape has changed dramatically in the last few years in regard to sugar substitutes, with many new ones now available. I take that as a positive sign, an indication that there is at last an awareness of the destructive nature of sugar and a demand for good alternatives. It remains to be seen which of the new products will become popular, readily available, and as a result, less expensive.

Below is a list of some of the choices. Some have been part of the traditional diets of humans for thousands of years, while some are recent inventions whose long-term effects are not known. We do, however, know the outcome of eating large amounts of sugar, and it is hard to imagine that anything could be worse, especially for those who can't properly metabolize it. (The white, granular substance we call sugar today hasn't been around that long either. Returning Crusaders brought cane sugar to Europe, but it was very expensive and reserved mainly for medicinal uses. Columbus took sugar cane plants to America in 1493, but it was grown primarily for making rum. It wasn't until fodder beets used as animal food were selectively bread to increase their sugar content in the late 1800s that sugar became more widely available.[47]

---

46   Bruce Watkins and Loren Cordain, M. Kehler, L. Rogers, "Fatty acid analysis of wild ruminant tissues: evolutionary implications for reducing diet-related chronic disease," *European Journal of Clinical Nutrition*, 2002, Mar; 56(3):181-91.

47   Kenneth F. Kiple, *The Cambridge World History of Food*, 2000.

Fructose is one of the sugars found in fruit, and it makes up half the sugar in common table sugar. Fructose has little effect on blood glucose and was once thought to be an ideal sweetener for diabetics. Not a good idea, as fructose has been implicated as contributing to nearly all of the classic manifestations of the insulin resistance syndrome, which leads to heart disease, diabetes, and hypertension.[48]

Fructose is not digested, absorbed, or metabolized like other sugars. It stimulates the formation of fat cells and bypasses the body's regulatory processes that reduce appetite.[49] Gary Taubes explains how fructose also causes gout in a chapter that was edited out of *Good Calories, Bad Calories*[50] for lack of space. Tim Ferriss published the missing chapter on his blog at: www.fourhourworkweek.com, October 5, 2009.

According to Dr. Michael Eades, fructose "... is a driving force behind the development of insulin resistance and all attendant problems. When researchers want to give lab animals insulin resistance, they feed the animals high doses of fructose."[51] And if that isn't enough, fructose also increases the formation of advanced *glycation end products*, known by the acronym AGEs, because they promote the cross-linking of proteins and speed up the aging process.

In the late 1960s manufacturers developed a way to make high fructose corn syrup by treating cornstarch with enzymes. HFCS is very similar to table sugar in composition, about half glucose and half fructose, but it was cheaper and its liquid form made it easier to use so it was added to nearly all processed foods. Most people were already eating a marginal diet, one significantly different from the diet of our ancient ancestors. The addition of huge amounts of fructose, along with a reduction in natural fats, may well have been the final insult that sent us over the edge.

> "Your body doesn't handle large amounts of fructose well. You can maintain life with intravenous glucose, but not with intravenous fructose; severe derangement of liver function results. There's also evidence that a high intake of fructose elevates levels of circulating fats, increasing the risk of heart disease."
>
> *— Dr. Andrew Weil*

If you only make one change in your eating habits, eliminating sweet drinks would be the most beneficial. Not only do they supply unnecessary calories and sugar, the consumption of a sweet beverage with every meal resets your "sweet meter" to a higher level. I was surprised to find how much sweeter everything tasted to me after I replaced sweetened beverages with water and tea.

A large survey conducted by Tufts University[52] discovered that the number-one source of calories in the diet of American adults is high-fructose sweetened drinks.

---

48   Sharon S. Elliott, et al, "Fructose, weight gain, and the insulin resistance syndrome," *American Journal of Clinical Nutrition*, Vol. 76, Nov. 2002.

49   George A. Bray, Samara Joy Nielson, and Barry M. Popkin, "Consumption of high-fructose corn syrup in beverages may play a role in the epidemic of obesity," *American Journal of Clinical Nutrition*, April, 2004, Vol. 79, No.4, pp. 537-543.

50   *Good Calories, Bad Calories; Fats, Carbs, and the Controversial Science of Diet and Health*, by Gary Taubes, Anchor Books, 2007, 2008.

51   Dr. Michael Eades: "Unclear on the Fructose Concept," www.proteinpower.com, September 23, 2007.

52   1999-2000 National Health and Nutrition Examination Survey.

HIGH INTENSITY SWEETENERS

ACESULFAME K

Acesulfame K (acesulfame potassium), sold as *Sunette*, is chemically similar to Saccharin, but it holds up to heat and can be used for cooking and baking; however, it has the same bitter aftertaste as saccharin. It is often blended with other sweeteners to enhance and sustain the sweet taste. When combined with sucralose, the synergy between the two gives a more natural flavor. It is the sweetener in Sweet One and in DiabetiSweet, which contains isomalt, a sugar alcohol, as a bulking agent and carries a warning that excessive consumption may cause stomach upset.

ASPARTAME

Aspartame is known as Equal in the little blue packets and as NutraSweet. One packet of Equal has four calories and 0.9 grams of carbohydrate. It is not heat-stable, so it cannot be used for cooking and it is not safe for people who suffer from a condition known as phenylketonuria. There are some concerns about safety with this sweetener, possibly involving brain and nerve damage, although the FDA considers it safe.[53] The bulking agents in aspartame products are dextrose and maltodextrin, sugars made from corn, and lactose (in the tablets), made from milk.

> "Two generations of physicians have been weaned on the knowledge that fats are bad and carbohydrates are good. ...in recent years randomized clinical trials have been undertaken to assess the effectiveness and the safety of low carbohydrate diets. Early results from these studies have been surprisingly positive... common wisdom has it that Dr. Atkins' untimely demise occurred just as his 30-year quest was about to be vindicated."
>
> *– Richard N. Fogoros, M.D., Heart Health guide on about.com.*

LO HAN GUO

Lo Han Guo is a natural sugar alternative made from a Chinese melon called monk fruit. It is 300 times as sweet as sugar and has zero calories.

NEOTAME

Neotame is a newer sweetener made by the Nutrasweet Company. It is similar to aspartame, but much sweeter (30 to 40 times as sweet as aspartame and 7,000 to 13,000 times as sweet as sugar), so only a tiny amount is needed. Neotame has the ability to enhance other flavors, especially mint, and it is heat stable. It is said to be metabolized quickly and fully eliminated from the body. The FDA approved its use in 2002 after reviewing more than 100 studies and declared it to be safe for general use and for children and pregnant women. It has also been approved for use in Australia and New Zealand. Sucralose and Neotame are the only two artificial sweeteners approved as safe by the CSPI.

Neotame is being marketed to manufacturers of soft drinks, dairy products, and chewing gum rather than to the general public.

---

53   Drs. Michael and Mary Dan Eades, Protein Power Lifeplan, 2000, pp. 166-167.

SACCHARIN

Saccharin is the artificial sweetener in *Sweet'N Low* in the pink packets and *Sugar Twin*. (One teaspoon of Sugar Twin Brown Sugar Replacement has 0.4 carbs and one calorie.) It has a bitter aftertaste that becomes more pronounced when it has been heated. For many years, the FDA required saccharin products to carry a label warning that it was a possible carcinogenic, but that requirement was removed in 2000.

STEVIA

Stevia, an all natural, no-calorie sweetener, was granted GRAS (generally recognized as safe) status in 2008, allowing it to be sold as a sweetener as well as a supplement without going through the normally required testing. Stevia is a South American herb that has been used by the indigenous people of Brazil and Paraguay for thousands of years as a sweetener and as a folk remedy for diabetes. It is 600 times as sweet as table sugar, but in its original form it has a bitter aftertaste that some people find objectionable. Many of the new stevia products that are now available, such as Truvia, Nuva, and PureVia, use only the sweet-tasting part of the leaf and combine it with erythyritol as a bulking agent. Stevia is also available as a liquid and as a blend with fructooligosaccharide (FOS), a sweet fiber that comes from chicory root or Jerusalem artichokes. FOS is prebiotic, meaning it promotes the growth of beneficial microbes in the digestive system.

> "...It is probably safe in moderate doses. However, until we have more research, women who are pregnant or breast-feeding should probably avoid using stevia. Similarly, people taking diabetes or blood pressure drugs should use stevia with caution because of the risk that it might cause hypoglycemia or hypotension when combined with these drugs."
>
> *— Katherine Zeratsky, R.D., L.D., Mayo Clinic Nutritionist*
>
> www.mayoclinic.com/health/stevia/AN01733MayoClinic.com

Stevia can cause hypoglycemia in some people, and it may increase insulin sensitivity and delay the absorption of glucose from the intestines. As a result, it can change the effectiveness of diabetes medications and interfere with the timing of injected insulin, making it essential for those with diabetes to consult with their doctors before using it. It is also said to lower blood pressure, so those on medication for hypertension should seek medical advice about using stevia.

Note: A study published in Denmark in 2000 demonstrated that stevia has the ability to stimulate insulin secretion via a direct action on beta cells. The researchers concluded that it may have potential as an anti-hyperglycemic agent in the treatment of type 2 diabetes.[54]

---

54   Jeppesen, P.B.; Gregersen, S.; Poulsen, C.R.; Hermansen, K., "Sevioside acts directly on pancreatic beta cells to secrete insulin: actions independent of cyclic adenosine monophosphate and adenosine triphospate-sensitive K+-channel activity," *Metabolism* 2000 Feb; 49(2):208-14. Abstract at: www.ncbi.nlm.nih.gove:80/entrez/query/fcgi?cmd=Retrieve&db=PubMed&list_uids=10690646&adopt=Abstract

TAGATOSE

Tagatose is a new synthetic sweetener chemically related to fructose but poorly absorbed by the body, so it yields only about one-third the calories. When used in large amounts (20 grams or about 5 teaspoons or more) it can cause digestive upset.

SUCRALOSE

Sucralose is a high-intensity sweetener that is made from sugar (sucrose) by altering it so that it is not broken down by our digestive enzymes. Sugar is converted into sucralose by substituting three chlorine atoms for three hydroxyl groups on the sugar molecule. Is it a natural product? Not really, but it has been used in Canada since 1991 and in Australia since 1992 and is not required to carry any warning labels. It is even considered safe for nursing mothers and pregnant women. It was originally marketed as Splenda, which comes in several forms: the now familiar yellow packets for tea or coffee; the granular form that is fluffed up with bulking agents so it can be substituted, measure for measure, for sugar; and tablets, which come in a dispenser. The latest additions to the product line are flavored blends for coffee and blends that combine equal parts of Splenda granular with regular or brown sugar. (I don't know why anyone would buy the last two, when it would be easy to make your own mixture.)

Sucralose is heat stable, so it can be used for cooking, but it is 600 times sweeter than sugar, so the volume is much smaller. Both the granular form and the packets of Splenda that are sold retail contain a small amount of real sugar, either maltodextrin or dextrose, as a bulking agent. The labels say "no calories and no carbohydrates," but that is not strictly true. Government regulations allow products below a certain count to make that claim. Each packet, which replaces two teaspoonfuls of sugar, contains 0.9 grams of carbohydrate and four calories. One teaspoon of granular Splenda contains 0.5 grams of carbohydrate and two calories. That doesn't sound like much, but one cup of granular Splenda adds 24 grams of carbohydrate and 96 calories when used in recipes. Splenda in packets adds the same amount for the equivalent of one cup of sugar. Even so, that is only one-eighth the amount in regular sugar. It continues to be popular because it is convenient to measure, it is readily available, it tastes good, and it seems to be safe.

The nutrition panel for Splenda Mini Tabs in the yellow dispenser gives the carb count as "less than one gram," which is the same as that for a teaspoon of Splenda granular. I contacted Mc Neil Nutritionals to find out what the tabs really contain—each tab equals the sweetness of one teaspoon of sugar and contains 0.2 calories and 0.04 carbs, so just a trace. You can crush the tablets and use them in recipes instead of the granular or packet forms of Splenda to reduce the amount of bulking agent, but the dispenser makes that a bit expensive since it would take 48 tabs to replace 1 cup of sugar. They work well for those times when you don't want to add any liquid to your recipe, but don't want the sugar contained in the bulking agents in the other dry forms.

Liquid sucralose is now being marketed by several companies who hope to go mainstream. It is just sucralose diluted with water, so it is truly calorie and carb free. (Pure sucralose is so sweet that the volume would be too small to measure as a dry powder.) The main difference among the brands is the concentration and the kind of dispenser they come in—some are easier to use than others. Most are currently only available online, but that may change soon. See Sources for more information.

Some of the sugar-free syrups, the kind used to flavor coffee, such as Atkins, Torani, and DaVinci, are another option for zero-carb sucralose. They are much more diluted than the liquid sucralose formulas above, so there must be enough liquid to replace when using them in recipes. They come in many flavors, and DaVinci makes an unflavored one to use as a sweetener. Any time you can substitute liquid sucralose or one of the syrups for Splenda granular or packets, there is an significant advantage in doing so.

SUGAR ALCOHOLS
These are the sweeteners that end in "-itol," like sorbitol, maltitol, and xylitol, that have been used for many years to make products for people with diabetes.

Most sugar alcohols have an unfortunate side effect called osmotic diarrhea, since they are only partially digested, and that's the reason they carry a warning against excessive consumption. Many low-carbohydrate products, like meal replacement shakes and bars, candies, and cereals contain sugar alcohols, the most common one being maltitol.

Sugar alcohols may be used alone or to boost the sweetening power of more expensive sweeteners like sucralose. The sugar alcohols are often excluded when figuring the net carb counts for foods because they were thought to have little or no effect on blood sugar levels. This may not be true for all of them, and some may have as much as half the carbohydrate in regular sugar.

DIABETISWEET
Diabetisweet is a combination of the sugar alcohol, isomalt, and acesulfame potassium. I use the brown sugar version of Diabetisweet in a few recipes because it tastes better than the other readily available, non-nutritive brown sugar substitutes. (Just Like Sugar Brown or LC Sweet, Brown are probably better choices, but they may have to be ordered online.)

ERYTHRITOL
Erythritol has a higher digestive tolerance than the other sugar alcohols, and foods containing substantial amounts are unlikely to cause any problems because it goes into the bloodstream and is then totally excreted. It has a glycemic index of zero and almost no calories. Since 1990 it has been added to commercially produced foods and beverages to provide sweetness and to improve taste and texture. The FDA granted GRAS (generally recognized as safe) status to erythritol in 1997.

Erythritol has gained widespread popularity with the introduction of several new steva blends, such as Nuva, PureVia, and Truvia. Since erythritol is only 70% as sweet as table sugar, combining it with stevia boosts the sweetness by 30% so that it can be substituted measure for measure for sugar. Because both erythritol and stevia come from natural sources, they can say "all natural" on the containers and in advertising. Erythritol is heat stable so it can be used for cooking, but the granular form does not dissolve well. It is available as a powder, like powdered sugar, which works better for baked goods than granular. (Powdered erythritol should be measured by weight rather than volume.) It is a powerful freezing depressant, which has benefits for making frozen desserts. It has two major disadvantages: if more than a relatively small amount is used, it has an unpleasant "cooling" sensation on the tongue, like a very strong minty taste, and it has a powerful tendency to crystallize out after cooling. Combining it with another sweetener helps with both problems.

MALTITOL

Maltitol is the most widely used sugar alcohol in commercial products because it can be substituted measure for measure for sugar in recipes. It has a glycemic index of 36 and half the calories of sucrose. However, it causes more digestive problems than most of the sugar alcohols, and although it is often counted as having zero carbs, it does seem to have an impact on blood sugar levels.

SORBITOL

Sorbitol has a glycemic index of 9 and 2.6 calories per gram. It is only about half as sweet as sucrose, meaning it is used in larger amounts and causes more digestive distress than most of the other sugar alcohols. It doesn't affect blood glucose or insulin levels, but it has no redeeming qualities like those in xylitol.

XYLITOL

Xylitol, also called *wood* or *birch sugar*, is a sugar alcohol found naturally in the inner bark of some trees and in some fruits and vegetables. A small amount is regularly made in the body. Xylitol has the same sweetness and bulk as regular sugar with 40% fewer calories and 75% less carbohydrate. It has no effect on insulin levels and little on blood glucose. It is produced commercially from hardwood trees or vegetable fibers. It has some health benefits, although it also has the laxative effect of some of the other sugar alcohols. Studies have shown that chewing gum sweetened with xylityol can prevent ear infections and tooth decay.[55] Its similarity to sugar attracts and then "starves" harmful microorganisms, allowing for the re-mineralization of tooth enamel. It also has potential as a treatment for osteoporosis. Xylitol can be used measure for measure like table sugar but it has a low glycemic index of 13. It produces a cooling mouth sensation like some of the other polyols.

I used a small amount of xylitol-sweetened artificial honey in a few recipes and listed xylitol as an option in others. The xylitol-sweetened honey is better than the ones made with maltitol, in both the amount of digestible carbohydrate and unpleasant side effects. (The Spice Barn gives it a carb count of 0.05 carbs per 100 grams.) Honey flavor is independent of the sweetener, so it could be made with other sugar substitutes. Netrition and Low-Carb Connoisseur sell Nature's Sweet xylitol honey, and they show a nutrition panel that gives it either 7 or 8 grams of sugar alcohol and a net carb count of zero.

Warning: Xylitol is poisonous to dogs.

SWEET FIBERS

These are sugar substitutes that have the bulk and physical characteristics of common sugar and actually offer some health benefits. Inulin, oligofructose (fructooligosachide), and polydextrose are in this category. Most of them are currently only available in health food stores and online, and some are expensive. They contain prebiotic, soluble plant fibers that are not broken down by human digestive enzymes. Most of them are only slightly sweet and they are usually combined with another sweetener, such as sucralose, stevia, or one of the sugar alcohols to boost the level of sweetness.

Note: Intestinal bacteria are necessary for digestive health. A *prebiotic* is a non-digestible food ingredient that selectively nourishes the friendly bacteria in the digestive tract and inhibits the harmful ones. You may notice that some indigestible sugars have a small number

---

55   K. K. Makinen, et al., "Xylitol chewing gums and caries rates: a 40-month cohort study," *Journal of Dental Research*, vol. 74, 1904-1913, 1995.

of calories listed on their nutrition panels. The calories come from the butyric acid, a beneficial fatty acid, produced by the bacteria in the digestive tract that feed on the fiber. Sweet fibers are said to aid digestion, enhance absorption of vitamins and minerals, and help eliminate toxins. Many commercial products, such as fiber-enriched yogurts, use one of these. A 2009 study from Pakistan showed that diets supplemented with oligofructose and polydextrose improved metabolic control in Type-2 diabetes and also reduced blood pressure and improved blood lipid profiles.[56]

OLIGOFRUCTOSE AND INULIN

Oligofructose, sometimes called fructo-oligosaccharide (FOS) or inulin, is synthesized from sucrose or extracted from chicory roots or jerusalem artichokes. It consists of chains of fructose molecules linked end to end and it is resistant to digestion by humans. Blends that use oligofructose or Inulin include Sweet*perfection*, *Just Like Sugar*, *SomerSweet Baking Blend*, and *LC Sweet*. See Sources for more information.

POLYDEXTROSE

Polydextrose consists of long chains of double glucose molecules, a small amount (10%) of sorbitol (a sugar alcohol), and citric acid. Studies have shown that most of it passes through the digestive tract unchanged, like soluble fiber. It is widely used in commercial products to allow a reduction in the amount of sugar or fat needed and to add beneficial fiber. (Inulin and oligofructose are similar sweet fibers made up of fructose molecules that can be used in a similar way, but polydextrose is much, much cheaper.)

A combination of polydextrose and sucralose makes an excellent replacement for sugar for some applications. While polydextrose has only a slight sweetening effect, it provides many of the properties that are missing in high intensity sweeteners like Splenda. It has the texture and mouth feel of sucrose and adds the missing bulk. It also thickens, stabilizes, caramelizes, and aids in moisture retention, while having little effect on insulin levels, and although it contains a large amount of indigestible carbohydrate, it is better tolerated than other polyols.[57] It is a common ingredient in commercial low-carb and low-calorie products, and it can be purchased for home use.

Polydextrose dissolves best in warm or hot liquids, as it tends to form a gel when mixed with cold liquid. It has a total of 27 grams of carbohydrate and 25 grams of fiber for a net carb count of 2 grams per ounce. It was approved by the FDA in 1981 and is generally considered safe.

YACON

Yacon (smallanthus sonchifolius), a member of the sunflower family, has been cultivated in Peru for hundreds of years. According to the venders, yacon is very low in carbs and low on the glycemic index. The edible part is a tuber, which looks like a sweet potato. It can be eaten fresh like a fruit or cooked and eaten as a vegetable. It can also be cooked down to make a syrup, which can be used like honey, maple syrup, or molasses. One-quarter

---

56   Cicek, B.; Arslan, P.; Kelestimur, F. "The effects of oligofructose and polydextrase on metabolic control parameters in Type-2 diabetes." Pak J Med Sci 2009;25(4):573-578.

57   Flood, M.T.; Auerback, M.H.; Craig, .S.A, "A Review of the clinical toleration studies of polydextrose in food," *Food Chem Toxical*, 2004 Sep;42(9):1531-42.

teaspoon of the syrup is equal to one teaspoon of sugar or honey in sweetness, so even if it were totally digestible, it would have only one-fourth the carbs and calories.

I think this new (to me) food has possibilities, but I have not been able to find reliable nutrition information for it. The labels give the counts as if it is all sugar and no fiber, so I am using it only in small amounts as an alternative to molasses and for the reasons given above. If most of it is, indeed, metabolized like soluble fiber, it should be an improvement. (The sugar in yacon would be fructose, so checking your blood glucose levels after eating it would not tell you how much of it is being absorbed.) One interesting thing I learned: yacon bubbles exactly like sugar when used to proof yeast. That could mean the yeast can digest yacon and we can't, or that it contains enough regular sugar to react with yeast. I made very good molasses cookies with it and would like to develop more recipes if I can find an accurate net carb count for it. If I do, I'll post them online.

> "Yacon root is considered the world's richest source of fructooligosaccharide (FOS), a unique type of sugar that can't be absorbed by the body. FOS acts as a prebiotic, serving as food for the "friendly" bacteria in the colon, and may help increase bone density and protect against osteoporosis."
>
> *– From the Live Super Food website*
> http://livesuperfoods.com/search/LSF060.html.

SUGARS
MOLASSES

Molasses is not a low-carb sweetener, but I'm including it on the list because I used a small amount as an option to add moistness and brown sugar flavor to a few of my recipes. Black strap molasses is the darkest and strongest kind, so you get more flavor with less. (I used fructose syrup for the same purpose in my first book, but low-carb expert and cookbook author, Dana Carpender, says she prefers molasses because it contains more glucose than fructose, and I have to agree with her on that point.) See Yacon, p. xxxix, for another alternative.

WHEY LOW

Whey Low is a blend of three kinds of natural sugar: sucrose (table sugar), fructose (fruit sugar), and lactose (milk sugar). The manufacturer claims that two of the sugars cancel each other out and also prevent some starch from being metabolized so that it has one-fourth the calories and impact carbs and one-third the glycemic index of sucrose. Fructose is said to interfere with the absorption of lactose, and lactose with the absorption of sucrose, leaving just the fructose. (See p. xxxiii about the dangers of fructose.)

"NATURAL" SWEETENERS

I frequently get questions about why I don't use some of the all-natural sugar alternatives, like brown rice syrup, agave nectar, and date sugar. I don't use most of them because they offer no advantage over common table sugar. (Stevia is the exception, as it has no calories and no carbs, and it is an option for use in my recipes.)

Let's look at some of those "healthy, all-natural, minimally-processed" sweeteners:

Agave nectar is touted as a wholesome, natural alternative to sucrose because it has a very low glycemic index, so it doesn't cause a spike in blood sugar or raise insulin levels. However, the dangers of fructose are well known, and agave nectar is almost pure fructose.

High fructose corn syrup contains 45% to 55% fructose; agave syrup may be up to 90% fructose, the most dangerous of all the sugars. The reason fructose doesn't provoke an insulin response is that it does not enter the blood stream but is metabolized in the liver where it is converted directly into triglycerides (fats). It promotes fat storage, especially around the midsection and the organs. It has been implicated as a major contributor to obesity, diabetes, heart disease, hypertension, and metabolic syndrome.

Succanat is sugar cane juice with the water removed. It retains trace amounts of vitamins and minerals that may be lost in the refining process, but it is still concentrated sucrose.

Date sugar is simply ground up dates. It is more than 96% sucrose. It contains some fiber and some trace minerals and vitamins, but it is essentially the same as common table sugar and causes a similar rise in blood sugar and insulin levels. It does not dissolve and is not a useful substitute for sugar for baking or cooking.

Maple syrup is made from the sap of maple trees, which is 2 to 3 percent sucrose. It is collected in buckets and boiled down to make a concentrated syrup. It takes 40 gallons of sap to make one gallon of syrup. Most of the sugar is sucrose (like common table sugar). Maple syrup contains traces of vitamins, especially the B vitamins and minerals.

Brown rice syrup is made by fermenting brown rice with enzymes to break down some of the starch into sugar and then cooking it until it is thickened. It is only half as sweet as table sugar. It contains 45% maltose (the kind of sugar in beer) and 3% glucose. The rest is starch. Maltose has a glycemic index of 110, higher than pure glucose (glucose or blood sugar has a GI of 100) and will provoke a very high insulin reaction. It contains 34 net grams of carbohydrate and 132 calories in a serving of 2 tablespoons.

Note: Brown rice syrup is one of several malt sugars made from grain that include barley malt, barley/corn malt, and rice syrups. Malt sugars are used in making beer, which is why beer is sometimes called "liquid bread."

GRAINS, STARCHES, FLOURS, AND THICKENERS

Why did humans abandon a hunter/gatherer lifestyle to embrace agriculture? Some have suggested that it was the addictive nature of grains that lured us away from an idyllic, if precarious, life to one of back-breaking toil. (Beer made of grain was invented before bread, which lends some credibility to the theory.)

Prehistoric men hunted, fished, engaged in games and competitions, and painted on cave walls. Prehistoric women gathered wild plants and small creatures such as snails, lizards, and crustaceans; tended the babies; and kept the home fires burning. (We haven't changed that much—the men did guy things; the girls went shopping.)

Grains have only recently become part of the diet of humans. Wild grains were not edible, and it was only after they were domesticated (probably for feeding livestock) that they entered the picture as food for humans. They contain chemicals to defend themselves from being eaten by pests (like us), such as enzyme blockers that prevent the digestion of proteins, and phytates that bind with minerals in the digestive tract, making them bio-unavailable. They also contain lectins that mimic proteins in the human body and trigger autoimmune responses.

Epidemiologists tell us that multiple sclerosis—an autoimmune disease in which the body attacks its own nerve sheaths—is most prevalent in cultures where wheat and rye are staple foods. Archeological evidence in skeletal remains reveals that rheumatoid arthritis followed wheat and corn around the world. Celiac disease is caused by cereal grains, and celiac sufferers are at risk for other autoimmune diseases. They are thirty times more likely to be schizophrenic.[58]

Even the book of Genesis describes agriculture as a curse:

"Cursed is the ground because of you;
through painful toil you will eat of it
all the days of your life.
It will produce thorns and thistles for you,
and you will eat the plants of the field.
By the sweat of your brow
you will eat your food
until you return to the ground…"

—Genesis 3, 17 –19.

---

58   Lierre Keith, *The Vegetarian Myth, Food, Justice, and Sustainability, 2009.*

"…if your average unhealthy person were to ask for the top three things to avoid in order to get healthy, I would tell them to stop smoking, to stop drinking their calories (as soda or juice), and to stop eating grains. Period. Full stop. They really are that bad."

– *Mark Sisson, author of*
The Primal Blueprint

GLYCEMIC INDEX AND GLYCEMIC LOAD:

The glycemic index is the ranking of carbohydrates by the effect they have on blood sugar levels. Glucose is generally used as the standard and given a value of 100; other foods are given a numeric value to show how they compare to glucose. (Some systems use white bread rather than glucose to represent 100.) Carbohydrates that break down rapidly have the highest glycemic index; those that break down slowly have the lowest.

While the *glycemic index* compares foods on a gram-for-gram basis to describe their potential to raise blood glucose levels, the *glycemic load* factors in the amount of carbohydrate in a standard serving. The glycemic index number, multiplied by the amount of carbohydrate in grams, divided by 100, gives the glycemic load.

However, it is not as simple as it sounds. Many factors affect the GI and GL of the same food, for example, mashed potatoes will be higher than cubed, because the digestive enzymes have contact with more surface area. Ripe fruit will rank higher than less ripe fruit, and cooked food will be higher than raw. The ranking will also be affected by other foods that are eaten at the same time; fiber, fat, and protein slow down the digestion of carbohydrates and lower their number. Another problem with rating foods by GI or GL is that it allows fructose to slip under the radar since it has little effect on blood glucose.

Turning to grains for food has been called the worst mistake humans ever made.[59] But what can we do? We LIKE them!

Note: Some people are better able to tolerate grains than others. I have included a few recipes that use a small amount of wheat flour, gluten flour, oats, or barley. If you are sensitive to these ingredients, you should not use them. Another concern is that even a small amount of grain can trigger carb cravings for some people, and they should also avoid them.

AGAR AGAR
Agar agar is a kind of seaweed. I used it as a thickener in my jelly recipes. It is similar to gelatin, but it melts at a higher temperature so it is more like jelly made with sugar when used on hot muffins or breads. It is a very powerful gelling agent, so you have to be careful not to use very much.

BARLEY
Sustagrain barley is a natural, waxy, hull-less variety that was developed through a conventional breeding program at Montana State University. It is available as flour or flakes, both of which are whole grains. It has 2 to 3 times the fiber and about half the starch compared to other common grains. One serving of ½ cup of Sustagrain barley flakes has 29 grams of carbohydrate and 14 grams of fiber for a net carb count (digestible carbohydrate) of 15 in ½ cup (45 grams) compared to rolled oats which have 27 grams of carbs and only 4 grams of fiber for a net of 23 in ½ cup (41 grams). It contains a relatively small amount of gluten.

COCONUT FLOUR
Coconut flour is coconut meat that has been ground into a powder. It is fairly low in carbs and high in fiber, but it makes very dry baked goods unless combined with a lot of eggs. Bob's Red Mill brand lists ¼ cup of coconut flour as having 16 grams of carbohydrate and 10 grams of fiber for a net count of 6 grams. It also contains 4 grams of coconut oil, a saturated fat that is prized for its healthful properties. **Note:** Coconut flour contains a lot of fiber. It is best to increase the amount of fiber in your diet gradually to prevent digestive distress.

KONJAC FLOUR
Konjac flour is made from the same plant used to make shiritaki noodles. In powdered form, it can be used as a thickener.

OAT FLOUR
Oat flour is whole grain flour containing the germ, the oil, and the fiber of the oat kernel. It has 48 grams of carbohydrate per cup compared to 88 for wheat flour and does not contain gluten (except when contaminated during processing). It tastes good and can be substituted in recipes that don't depend on gluten to rise, but it is still too high in starch to be used in more than small amounts.

PECTIN
Pectin is a plant fiber used to thicken jams and jellies. I use a small amount in frozen desserts to keep them from freezing too hard.

---

59   Jared Diamond, *"The Worst Mistake in the History of the Human Race,"* May 1987, Discover pp.64-66.

POTATO FLOUR

Potato flour is made from whole potatoes, as opposed to potato starch, which is just the extracted starch. Some manufacturers label their product as "potato starch flour," but here the word "starch" is just a milling term, and it is the same as potato flour. Potato flour is higher in carbs than wheat flour, but you need only one-third the amount for thickening. It is also higher than cornstarch, but you need only one-half as much. It has the advantage that it is totally gluten free.

Potato flour makes delicious sauces, compared to some of the other low-carb thickeners, which give the proper consistency but add no flavor.

VITAL WHEAT GLUTEN FLOUR

Vital wheat gluten flour, also called high-gluten flour or gluten flour, is wheat flour that has had most of the starch removed. The stretchy, gluten proteins trap the gas bubbles generated by yeast. A small amount of gluten flour is often used in low-carb recipes and products so they will rise and taste like yeast breads when made with ingredients that have less starch than wheat flour. **Note**: Some of the recipes in this book call for gluten flour. Those who are sensitive to gluten or who have celiac disease should not use them.

CELIAC DISEASE

Frozen blood samples taken from Air Force recruits in the 1950s showed that celiac disease, the intolerance of gluten, is four times more common today than it was 50 years ago. The finding demonstrates that the sharp increase in the condition is not just the result of greater awareness and detection.

Dr. Joseph Murray, the Mayo Clinic gastroenterologist who led the study, said, "Fifty years is way too fast for human genetics to have changed, which tells us it has to be a pervasive environmental influence." He believes that rapid changes in eating habits and food processing might be responsible for the increase.[60]

A survey from the Gluten Intolerance Group (GIG) showed that celiac in the United States has increased from 1 person in every 133 in 2003 to 1 in every 100 in 2009, an increase of 12 percent in 6 years.

People who cannot digest gluten, a protein found in wheat and other grains, develop "leaky gut syndrome" when the undigested protein triggers the body's immune system to attack and damage the lining of the small intestine.

Those who are gluten intolerant are at higher risk of having other autoimmune disorders, especially type 1 diabetes and thyroid disease, but also lupus, scleroderma, Sjogren's syndrome, and others (Information from GIG.)

Type 1 diabetes, a disease in which the body attacks its own insulin-producing cells, may also be tied to the consumption of grains. The August 9, 2009, issue of *Scientific American* suggests that "leaky gut" syndrome may play a role in all auto-immune diseases, and grains, especially those that contain gluten, are implicated in its development.[61]

---

60   Josephine Marcotty, "Study confirms increase in wheat gluten disorder," *Star Tribune*, July 1, 2009 – 9:27 AM. www.startribune.com/lifestyle/health/49558522.html.

61   Alessio Fasano, "Surprises from Celiac Disease; Study of a potentially fatal food-triggered disease has uncovered a process that may contribute to many autoimmune disorders," *Scientific American*, August 2009, pp. 54-61.

WHEY PROTEIN POWDER

Whey protein powder is dried milk protein. It is useful for protein shakes and in baked goods as a flour substitute. It can also make up the missing bulk when replacing sugar in recipes. It is available sweetened with sugar or artificial sweeteners or unsweetened. Check the label to be sure it has only one or two grams per serving of ¼ cup. Whey protein powder may contain a small amount of lactose. Those who are lactose intolerant can use egg protein powder instead. Another alternative is pea or rice protein powder, but I haven't tried those.

WHITE WHOLE-WHEAT FLOUR

White whole-wheat flour is made from white winter wheat. Regular whole-wheat flour is made from red winter wheat and has a distinctive, earthy flavor. The white variety has the same nutrition values as the red, with the bran and germ intact, but it tastes more like white flour. Both are slightly lower in starch than all-purpose flour, but still too high to be used in more than tiny amounts. **Note:** All-purpose flour has 22 net carbs per ¼ cup. Whole-wheat has from 18 to 21.

XANTHAN

Xanthan is a thickener, stabilizer, and emulsifier derived from a microorganism called *Xanthomonas camestris*. It is composed of indigestible simple sugars, similar to peanut shells. It can be used to replace flour or cornstarch to thicken soups and gravies, to add volume and texture to foods, and to give a cake-like texture to cakes and cookies. **Guar, Carob, and Acacia** gums are similar to xanthan. All are commonly used in commercial products.

General Tips

HIDDEN SUGAR AND STARCH

Choose no-sugar or no-added-sugar ingredients when possible. Canned tomatoes, chicken or beef stock, peanut butter, and many other products come either with or without added sugar. Always choose the brand with the fewest carbohydrates.

We all like to buy prepared, convenience foods, but hidden sugar and starch and deceptive labels can sabotage our efforts to eat a healthful diet. We must be constantly watchful about what we buy; we may not be getting what we think we are. Some examples:

- The label on a small roast chicken from the deli listed two grams of carbohydrate per serving, but the chicken was listed as having 11 servings. Who is going to eat just a wing? The whole bird had 22 grams of carbs. Careful reading of the label revealed five different sugars in a chicken that would naturally have none.
- When inquiring about the nutrition information of surimi (artificial crabmeat), I discovered that it contained wheat starch, sugar, cornstarch, tapioca starch and yam flour. It had 16 grams of carbohydrate in one-half cup.
- A gourmet ice cream store added a sugar-free option to its menu. The regular ice cream had 18 grams of carbs per scoop, but the "sugar-free" ice cream had 20 grams. The reason – the cream had been replaced with skim milk, which has lactose or milk sugar.
- I discovered that a package of fresh pork chops from the meat case had been injected with a sugar solution. A spokesperson for this major retailer suggested that

if I didn't want sugar in my meat, I should buy only their products labeled as "all natural pork" because they routinely added sugar to everything else.

READING LABELS

Food labels can be confusing and misleading. Here are some tips to help you navigate the minefield of food choices you will encounter on every shopping trip.

- Foods consist of three things: protein, fat, and carbohydrate. Anything that is not protein or fat is classified as carbohydrate on the label, even indigestible fiber. Subtract the grams of fiber from the carb total on the label to find the "true" carb count, which may be called the *net* or *effective* carbohydrate count. When searching online for products, some nutrition panels will have a button to click for the net carb count.
- The order in which the ingredients are listed on the label reflects the amount of each substance contained in the product from most to least. Manufacturers will frequently use more than one kind of sugar so that it will not be listed as the first ingredient. When added together, the different kinds of sugar may constitute the main ingredient.
- A product can legally claim that it has "zero grams of sugar" if it has less than 0.5 grams per serving. Check to see if a portion is unrealistically small. A reduction in serving size allows the manufacturer to state that it has no sugar when there may actually be a substantial amount in a more realistic serving.
- Sometimes a label will say "no sugar," when it should say, "no sucrose." Sugar has many names. Check the carbohydrate counts to be sure. (The second ingredient given for "sugar-free" Cool Whip on the Kraft foods website is corn syrup!)
- Product labels usually give amounts in grams. A gram is not a familiar unit of measure to most of us. It is easier to visualize ounces and pounds, so remember that 28.4 grams equal one ounce. A serving of snack foods or candy is usually one ounce, which equals about 14 potato chips or 8 chocolate kisses.
- Look for foods with the fewest ingredients. None of those chemicals and fillers is necessary. I currently have two brands of tomato sauce in my pantry: one lists "tomato puree (water, tomato paste), water, salt, citric acid, spice, tomato fiber, and natural flavor" as ingredients. (Natural flavor is usually double-speak for MSG.) The second one, an Italian brand, lists "tomatoes." I rest my case.

NUTRITION DATA

All nutrition counts should be considered as rough estimates only. There are many different databases, and they do not always agree. Additionally, manufacturers are allowed to be off by 20% in their package disclosures.

Many factors can influence the results in evaluating the content of foods; one fruit or vegetable may vary from another depending on size, variety, climate, location, moisture content, sugar content, storage conditions, and ripeness. It is not possible to test every one.

I've learned from experience that nutrition information on the labels of commercial products is sometimes wrong, especially for items that are not widely sold. Big companies can afford to invest in having their products individually tested; small ones have to depend on what is already available in the various databases. For example, I have two different brands of powdered erythritol that state the weight as being the same as that for granular erythritol. When I weigh it, it weighs twice as much. I suspect that the manufacturers, who are required to provide the information, took the numbers from some approved chart that only listed the weight for one form, so that is what they used. I can relate. I've had similar problems finding accurate information.

The databases are all rounded and generic. Most of them use either the most common numbers or a generic average of all the different brands rather than specifying a particular product. The rules are far from precise:

Any food that contains less than 0.5 grams of carbohydrate can legally say it contains none.

Any food that contains 0.5 grams may say "1 gram," or "<1 gram" (less than one).

When the serving size is small, as it is for something like cream, this presents a problem. The labels for most brands of organic cream say, "zero carbs" for a serving of one tablespoon, while the labels on non-organic cream, which usually contains milk, thickeners, and stabilizers, say, "1" or "<less than 1." At 1 gram per tablespoon, cream would have 16 grams of sugar per cup—or MORE than milk! (Milk has 11 or 12 grams per cup.) I often use cream by the cupful, so I assumed that organic cream had no carbohydrate, since 0 x 16 = 0. Right? Wrong.

The rep for Organic Valley told me that their cream, labeled as having zero carbs, actually contains 0.37 grams of carbs per tablespoon, but because that is less than 0.5 per serving, they are allowed to call it zero. That works out to 5.92 grams per cup—less than milk, but far from zero!

The moral of the story is that you can never know for sure exactly what you are getting. Nutrition counts are approximate at best, which makes keeping your consumption of carbohydrates to a minimum very, very important, espe-cially for those with diabetes—the smaller the number, the smaller the mistake you can make.

> "Big inputs make big mistakes; small inputs make small mistakes."
> – *Kanju Ishikawa, the oldest surviving type 1 diabetic in Japan.*

Another caveat for those who must use insulin: there is always some variation in how much insulin is actually absorbed and the body's sensitivity to it can be different from one day to the next. The less insulin you need, the smaller the variation will be.[62]

Note: Be vigilant in reading the labels on products you buy. Something that may have been low in carbs or sugar-free in the past can change at any time. Even some of the items listed in the Sources for this book may be different by the time you are reading about them.

The USDA defines carbohydrate in food as anything that is not fat or protein. This means that indigestible fiber must be included in the carbohydrate counts on labels. The Net Carb Count is a term that designates the number of grams of carbohydrate contained in a food after subtracting the metabolically inactive grams of fiber.

---

62   Dr. Richard Bernstein, *The Diabetes Solution*, 3007, Little, Brown and Company.

Drs. Michael and Mary Dan Eades, authors of the *Protein Power* book series used the term *Effective Carbohydrate Count* or *ECC*;[63] Dr. Robert Atkins used the term *Net Carbohydrate Count*;[64] it means the same thing: carbohydrate minus indigestible fiber. Dr. Richard Bernstein uses his own system to determine the amount of carbohydrate in foods based on testing to see how the various foods affect blood sugar levels. (I used the Net Count because it is the system I am most familiar with.)

Sugar alcohols are often excluded from the net counts or noted separately, although they vary from one to the other. See the chapter on Sweeteners for information about specific sugar alcohols.

Poldextrose and inulin are largely indigestible. They are often included in the carb counts on labels as if they were sugar, but they are metabolized like soluble fiber. They may be listed as having a few calories because they feed the beneficial microbes in the intestinal tract, and the microbes in turn produce butyrates (beneficial fats).

Customizing Menus

I designed the menus in this book to add up to roughly 20 to 50 net grams of carbohydrate per day. A menu may total more or less than the ideal amount for you, as the carbohydrate tolerance will be different for every individual. You will need to determine what is right for you by conferring with your doctor. It is important to remember that some protein can be converted into sugar and will also have to be taken into consideration and discussed with your doctor.

The holiday menus are slightly higher than most of the dinners, but if your family is similar to mine, these meals are usually eaten over a longer period of time and one mid-afternoon meal may serve as both lunch and dinner. They are frequently multiple-course meals, which are divided into an early appetizer course, a main course, and a dessert that comes later in the day and replaces the traditional third meal.

If the carb total for a menu exceeds your personal limit, you may substitute a similar item for one in the original plan. On pages 325 and 326 you will find lists for items by category that can be used as alternatives for pasta, bread, rice, and potatoes grouped together so you can compare the choices. The carbohydrate content per serving is given for each. Simply choose one that corrects the total carb count as necessary and use it as a replacement in the chosen menu. For example, **Faux Duchess Potatoes**, at 2.2 net grams, can be used instead of **Celery Root Puree**, at 8.2 grams, to lower a menu total by 6 net grams. It can also work the other way for those who can tolerate a higher intake, in which case a higher numbered item can replace a lower one, or extra dishes can be added. Another option is to alter the serving size to decrease or increase the total count, or to omit a dish.

Optional snacks are given as a separate index. Some have no carbs, so there will always be snacks that can be added to any day's menu combination.

---

63   Michael R. Eades, M.D. and Mary Dan Eades, M.D., *Protein Power*, Bantam, 1996.

64   Robert Atkins, M.D., *Dr. Atkins New Diet Revolution*, Avon, New York, 1992.

Note: Some people may need to omit or limit desserts, especially if sweets set off cravings or if they have a significant insulin response to any sweet taste, even in foods that contain no sugar.

A Note About Salt: Low-carb diets effectively reduce blood pressure for many people, making across-the-board salt reduction necessary only for those who are salt sensitive or who have been advised by their doctors to reduce their intake. *Some low-carb experts warn that it is possible for individuals to experience adverse reactions if sodium levels fall too low and that some people will actually need supplemental salt when eating 50 grams of carbohydrate or less per day.*

Drs. Michael and Mary Dan Eades, authors of the *Protein Power* book series, warn that if you feel light-headed or dizzy after starting a low-carb regimen, you may need more salt. They suggest adding more salt to your food or eating half a dill pickle twice a day. (Dr. Eades drinks dill pickle juice in order to supplement his salt intake. There is a picture of him drinking from his dedicated pickle jar on his blog.)

Dr. Mary C. Vernon tells her patients that if they experience dizziness or feel ill before they are fully adapted to a low-carb diet, they should add ½ teaspoonful of salt daily. She explained that typical high-carb diets cause water retention; when the body switches from burning sugar to burning fat, stored sugar is released, and retained water and minerals are lost with it, which can result in ion imbalances.

Those who need to reduce dietary salt can cut the amount in the recipes by half or use a salt substitute.

Before You Start

MISE EN PLACE:

I recommend that you use a technique called *mise en place* (French for "put in place"). This means you measure out all the ingredients and line them up in the proper order before starting. That way, if you are interrupted, you will know where you left off and what has or has not been added. Also, put out all the utensils, appliances, bowls, pans, etc., that will be needed.

PREPARATION TIMES:

Preparation and cooking times are approximate. People work at different speeds, and cooking equipment and conditions vary.

Note: The prep times given are for ingredients as they are listed in the recipe. For example, if a recipe calls for "**Marinara Sauce**," the estimated time assumes the sauce is already prepared and ready to use. Likewise, if "½ cup of onion, chopped," is listed, the time spent chopping the onion is not included, only the time needed to add the pre-chopped onion. If the list were to say only, "½ cup onion," and the directions said, "chop the onion," then the time would be counted.

"Life is not just being alive, but being well."

– Roman poet, Martial

EGGS:
Eggs are assumed to be large.

OPTIONAL INGREDIENTS:
Ingredients marked as "optional" are not included in the nutrition data totals, but the additional carb content is usually given.

MEASURES:
Whisk or stir dry ingredients like flours before measuring to fluff them up in case they have settled, and spoon them into the measuring container until overfilled, then level off with the straight edge of a knife or spatula. If you dip your measuring utensil and then press it against the side of the bag or box, you compress the contents, and you may have too much.

The volume of dry ingredients will vary depending on their moisture content. Sifting and whether they are sifted before or after measuring can also give different results. The most accurate way to measure dry ingredients is by weight, so for recipes where an accurate measurement is important, I have included the weight, as well as the amount in cups. Package labels give you an accurate weight for a stated volume, so with a little math you can always figure out the weight for the amount called for. A scale that can be reset to zero after each addition is useful, as it allows you to add the correct amount of each ingredient using just one container.

There are two kinds of measuring cups. Dry measures are designed to be filled to the top so you can level the contents with a straight edge. Liquid measures are marked to show the amount but include a little extra space at the top so the contents won't overflow. If you fill a liquid measure to the top with a dry ingredient, you will have too much.

RECIPE VARIATIONS:
For convenience, variations for recipes are listed under the original version rather than following the menu where they appear. This prevents your having to flip back and forth to follow the directions. When a menu calls for a variation of a recipe, in most cases, the page number for the variation will be given rather than the actual recipe.

A NOTE ABOUT SWEETENERS:
Cookbook authors try to use ingredients that are readily available and not too expensive. They must taste good, be easy to use, and have no issues with safety. When I wrote my first book, deciding what sugar substitute to use was easy. Splenda was really the only one that came close to meeting those requirements. That is no longer the case. There are now so many that it is difficult to choose one and impossible to include directions for using them all. My compromise solution is to list the amount of regular sugar (sucrose or table sugar) that would normally be used in a given recipe and let you make your own decision about which sweetener to use. (See p. xxxi for information about sugar substitutes.) The equivalents are given on the packaging of the different brands. That way, if you want to use an all-natural sweetener, for example, you can choose one such as stevia or erythritol; if you prefer the taste or convenience of another one, you can use that instead.

Any high-intensity sweetener can replace another since the volume is small and it will have little effect on texture or function in cooking (with the exception of some chocolate recipes in which you can't use even one drop of liquid sweetener.) This is not true for sweeteners that have bulk and do more than simply sweeten a dish. In those cases, I have specified a particular one or combination, for example, the sweeteners in the ice cream recipes are necessary to provide the proper texture and to keep it from freezing too hard. An additional high-intensity sweetener of your choice is used to adjust the sweet taste, but you still need the others or something similar to get the best results with the recipe.

Menus and Recipes

In order to make it easy to customize and combine daily meals, each menu is featured in the sidebar on the page with the first recipe listed. Carb counts are shown under each recipe and the total for the whole menu is given at the bottom. Recipes will follow in the order in which they are listed. When a recipe is used in more than one menu, the title of the dish will appear in the proper place, in the sidebar menu along with the page number where the recipe can be found.

Nutritional Information was calculated primarily using the Computer Planned Nutrition Analysis program from Nutritional Computing Concepts. Some data was taken directly from the USDA Release SR22 nutritional database. In a few cases, involving specific brands or unusual ingredients, data was taken directly from the manufacturer.

Important: If you use blood sugar-lowering medications or insulin, you should not change your diet without consulting your physician. ***Most people experience a dramatic drop in postprandial blood sugar levels when they switch to a low-carbohydrate diet. It is necessary to reduce your medications to prevent your blood sugar from dropping to dangerously low levels.***

"On days when warmth is the most important need of the human heart, the kitchen is the place you can find it..."

– *E.B. White*

Breakfasts

MENU 1

Protein Shake

MENU 2

Chocolate Avocado
Smoothie

MENU 3

Berry Protein Shake

MENU 4

Huevos Rancheros
with Tomatillo Salsa
and Crème Fraîche
or Sour Cream

MENU 5

Chocolate Granola

"Milk"

MENU 6

Hot Cereal
with Cream, Berries,
and Toasted Walnuts

Oven Bacon

MENU 7

Corned Beef Hash
with Poached Eggs

MENU 8

Scrambled Eggs
with Kippered Herring
or Smoked Salmon

Broiled Tomato
with Herbs

MENU 9

Fluffy Omelet
with Cherry Jelly
and Whipped Cream

Pork Sausage

Toasted Whole Grain
Bread and Butter

MENU 10

Poached Eggs
with Artichokes
and Hollandaise

Toasted Whole Grain
Bread with Butter

MENU 11

Greek Yogurt
with *Honey* and
Toasted Walnuts

Hard Cooked Egg

Barley Rusks
and Hot Tea

MENU 12

Eggs with Nopales,
Chorizo Sausage, and
Grilled Tortilla

Hot Cocoa

MENU 13

Eggs en Cocotte
with Ham
and Gruyère

Cheddar Cheese Muffin
with Butter and
Cherry Jelly

Protein Shake

I like MRM All Natural whey protein powder. It tastes good and dissolves easily in plain water. It is also the brand recommended by Drs. Michael and Mary Dan Eades (authors of the *Protein Power* book series). It comes in Dutch chocolate or vanilla, and it is sweetened with stevia. Two scoops have 3 grams of carbohydrate and 1 of fiber for a net count of 2 grams of carbohydrate and 36 grams of protein. If you are allergic to dairy products, Jay Robb sells both a whey and an egg white protein powder, also recommended by the Drs. Eades. See Sources.

Some protein powders contain thickeners; add more water if needed for a thinner texture.

Protein Shake

The breakfast dilemma: what is convenient, quick, tasty, portable, low in carbs, and high in nutrition? The answer is a meal-replacement shake. A shake can be made in advance and stored in a travel mug ready to grab and go on your way out the door. Vary the flavoring to keep it interesting.

2 scoops (usually ¼ cup each) sugar-free, vanilla protein powder
6 ounces (¾ cup) water
1 ounce (2 tablespoons) coconut milk
1 to 2 ounces (2 to 4 tablespoons) any flavor sugar-free syrup (such as DaVinci, Torani, or Ambiance) or to taste
¼ cup (4 tablespoons) kefir or yogurt with live cultures (or omit and add an additional ¼ cup water or coconut milk)
1 cup of ice

TO MAKE WITH A BLENDER:
Put ingredients in a blender container and blend on high for 30 to 60 seconds or until smooth or put in a large glass and use an immersion blender. Add more water for a thinner shake.

TO MAKE WITHOUT A BLENDER:
Put protein powder in a large glass or a shaker container. Add about 3 tablespoons of the water and stir to make a smooth paste. Slowly add remaining water while stirring. (If you use a mix that dissolves easily, you won't need to make a paste first—just put it all in and shake or stir.) Stir in other ingredients (except ice) until smooth. Add ice to container or pour over ice. (Ice will not be crushed, so drink will not be slushy.)

MAKES 1 SERVING OR 1½ CUPS (BEFORE ADDING ICE).

Per serving—Net carbohydrate: 3.8 grams (excludes 2 grams eaten by live culture in kefir); Protein: 46.4 grams; Fiber: 0 grams; Fat: 10.2 grams; Calories: 303

Total weight and weight per serving: 12 ounces or 340 grams (without ice)

Preparation time: 5 minutes active and total

NOTES:

Recipe was tested with MRM Whey Protein powder, which has a slightly larger scoop than the standard ¼ cup and a carb count of 1.5 grams per scoop. Two scoops of MRM equals a little more than ½ cup and increases the total carb count for the shake to 4.8 net grams.

This shake recipe calls for a "cup" of ice. Since ice cubes vary in size and volume, I'm not sure how to quantify the amount. It really doesn't matter, since it's just water, but a cup of ice cubes from my freezer melted to make a little over 10 ounces of water, so you can check yours for comparison.

Kefir is liquid yogurt. Look for one made with whole milk that contains live cultures. Both yogurt and kefir are probiotics that provide "good" bacteria for the digestive tract and enhance the immune system by keeping the bad guys out. But while both yogurt and kefir contain friendly bacteria, kefir also contains beneficial yeast cultures.

Fermented dairy products with live cultures must list the same number of carbohydrates as the milk that goes into them, but, according to Drs. Jack Goldberg and Karen O'Mara, authors of the *Go-Diet,* most of the sugar has been converted to lactic acid. That is why milk tastes sweet but buttermilk and yogurt taste sour. The amount of carbohydrate remaining is about 4 grams per cup.[65]

Many people with dairy allergies can tolerate milk, yogurt, and kefir made from goat's milk.

Protein Shake

---

65   Jack Goldberg, Ph.D., and Karen O'Mara, D.O., *GO-Diet: The Goldberg-O'Mara Diet Plan, the Key to Weight Loss & Healthy Eating,* Go Corp, 1999.

Chocolate Avocado Smoothie

Menu total: 4.9 net carbs

To keep the unused avocado from turning brown, at least for a little longer, do not remove the peel from the unused portion and leave the seed in place. (There's no magic in the seed; it just protects part of the avocado from contact with air.) Coat the cut surfaces with oil or cooking spray, wrap the avocado in plastic film, and refrigerate.

Avocado shakes made with chocolate syrup and sweetened, condensed milk are sold by street venders in Thailand and Vietnam, where they are popular as a mid-day snack.

MAKES 1 SERVING OR 3 CUPS (WHEN MADE IN A BLENDER).

Per serving—Net carbohydrate: 4.9 grams (5.9 grams with MRM brand whey protein powder scoops); Protein: 46.3 grams; Fiber: 5 grams; Fat: 23.3 grams; Calories: 431

Total weight and weight per serving: 1 pound 1¼ ounces or 489 grams

Preparation time: 5 minutes active, 6 minutes total

Chocolate Avocado Smoothie

Bananas are frequently used in smoothies to make them rich and creamy. Avocado is a perfect low-carb alternative, and they are also a better source of potassium. With chocolate and coconut, it creates a unique flavor that just might become your new favorite.

> 2 ounces of ripe avocado pulp (about half the yield from a 6-ounce avocado)
> 2 scoops (usually ¼ cup each) chocolate sugar-free protein powder
> 1 teaspoon Dutch cocoa powder, optional
> 6 ounces (¾ cup) water
> 2 ounces (¼ cup) coconut milk
> 1 to 2 ounces (2 to 4 tablespoons) chocolate or coconut sugar-free syrup, such as DaVinci, Torani, or Ambiance, or to taste
> 1 cup of ice

Cut avocado in half around the seed. Twist to separate halves. Reserve the half with the seed for another use. Peel the seedless half.

TO MAKE WITH A BLENDER:
Put avocado and other ingredients in a blender container and blend on high for 30 to 60 seconds or until smooth. Add more water for a thinner smoothie, more ice for a thicker one.

TO MAKE WITHOUT A BLENDER:
Mash avocado with a fork or puree until smooth and put into a large glass or a shaker container. Add protein powder and about 3 tablespoons of the water and stir to a smooth paste. Slowly add the rest of the water while stirring. Stir in other ingredients (except ice) until smooth. Add ice to container or pour over ice. (Ice will not be crushed, so this shake will not be slushy.)

VARIATION:

Chia and flax seed contain beneficial fiber and the precursors for essential Omega-3 oils. One or two tablespoons of whole or ground chia seed or freshly-ground flax seed can be added to a shake or smoothie, with the following cautions: both produce a gelatinous material when hydrated that may entrap oral medications in capsule or tablet form and prevent them from dissolving. If you must take a pill in the morning, it might be wise to wait until lunch to have chia or flax or any other high fiber food (including Sustagrain barley).

Also, flax seed contains phytoestrogens, estrogen mimics, which may disrupt the endocrine system and have been linked to breast cancer and thyroid problems. Soy foods and many common pollutants also contain chemicals that are similar to estrogen, so the effect may be cumulative. Flax seed must be ground before its nutrients can be utilized, and it is highly perishable, especially after it is ground, so use only freshly-ground flax. Chia does not contain phytoestrogens and does not go rancid easily. Additionally, it can be digested in both whole and ground form.

TIPS:

I prefer to buy natural coconut milk, not the kind with additives to keep it homogenized. It may have a thick layer of coconut cream on top. Stir the coconut cream back into the coconut milk. Shaking the can before opening will help homogenize the contents.

Make your shake with carbonated water for a special treat.

Berry Protein Shake

Menu Total: 6.3 net carbs

Resveratrol, a compound found mainly in red wine, has been called the *longevity molecule* for its antioxidant and anti-inflammatory properties. Not all red wines contain this natural fungicide produced by grapes. Grapes grown in a dry climate and those that have been sprayed to prevent fungal infection will contain very little. Muscadine grapes have more resveratrol because they have thicker skins and more seeds where the compound is concentrated. It is also found in lesser amounts in cocoa, dark chocolate, raspberries, and Spanish peanuts.[66]

_____

Those who are lactose intolerant may not have a problem using whey protein powder, which contains the protein from milk but very little milk sugar or lactose.

Berry Protein Shake

I added a little red wine for the resveratrol, but I got a big flavor boost as a bonus. I made it optional in the recipe, but do try it.

> 2 scoops (usually ¼ cup each) sugar-free protein powder
> 6 ounces (¾ cup) water
> 1 ounce (2 tablespoons) coconut milk
> 1 ounce (2 tablespoons) red wine or berry-flavored, sugar-free syrup, optional
> ½ cup (62 grams) unsweetened frozen raspberries or mixed berries
> ½ cup ice cubes

Put ingredients in a blender container and blend on high for 30 to 60 seconds or until smooth or put in a large glass and blend with an immersable blender. Add more water for a thinner shake.

MAKES 1 SERVING OF 2⅛ CUPS.

Per serving--Net carbohydrate: 6.3 grams; Protein: 44.9 grams; Fiber: 4 grams; Fat: 8.2 grams; Calories: 297

Total weight and weight per serving: 14 ounces or 397 grams

Preparation time: 5 minutes active, 6 minutes total

_____

66   *The FASEB Journal.* 2009; 23:2412-2424.) Resveratrol attenuates C5a-induced inflammatory responses *in vitro* and *in vivo* by inhibiting phospholipase D and sphingosine kinase activities Priya D. A. Issuree, Peter N. Pushparaj, Shazib Pervaiz, and Alirio J. Melendez.

Huevos Rancheros with Tomatillo Salsa and Crème Fraîche or Sour Cream

Huevos Rancheros
with Tomatillo Salsa
and Crème Fraîche
or Sour Cream

Menu total: 6.9 net carbs

If you have a large griddle, you can make more than one serving at a time. Use extra pan lids to cover the eggs or cook eggs separately and place on tortillas.

FOR EACH SERVING:

1 small, low-carb tortilla (about 6-inch diameter, about 3 net carbs)

½ cup (2 ounces) shredded Jack or Cheddar cheese

1 egg

Salt and pepper to taste

2 tablespoons **Tomatillo Salsa**, p. 10, or tomato salsa

Crème Fraîche, p. 297, sour cream, or plain, Greek-style yogurt

2 slices (1 ounce) of avocado for garnish, optional (Adds 1.2 net grams.)

Heat 1 teaspoon of oil in a medium skillet on medium-high. Fry tortilla, turning a few times, until puffed and just starting to brown on the bottom, about 2 minutes. Turn tortilla and reduce heat to medium. Cover almost to edge with shredded cheese. Break an egg on top. Season egg with salt and pepper to taste and cover pan. Cook for 5 minutes or until egg whites are set but yolks are still soft. Continue to cook a few minutes longer if you like harder yolks. Transfer to a plate and top with salsa. Add a dollop of **Crème Fraîche,** sour cream, or plain yogurt. Garnish with slices of avocado.

MAKES ONE SERVING.

Per serving—Net carbohydrate: 6.9 grams; Protein: 25.7 grams; Fiber: 7.5 grams; Fat: 24.9 grams; Calories: 349

Total and per serving weight: 4¾ ounces or 133 grams (tortilla, cheese, and egg only); 5⅓ ounces or 152 grams with salsa

Preparation time: 10 minutes active, 15 minutes total

Tomatillo Salsa

Salsa is always a carb bargain, but salsa verde, *made with* tomatillos, *the little green tomato-like fruits encased in a papery lantern, is even more so. Here's a fresh, colorful, crunchy, tomato-less, salsa that will add zest to any menu.*

5 or 6 tomatillos (12 ounces total as purchased; 10 ounces or 2 cups, chopped)
½ of a medium red bell pepper (½ cup or 4½ ounces, chopped)
½ a medium red onion (1 cup or 4½ ounces, chopped)
2 (3-inch) jalapeño chilies (1½ ounce or ¼ cup, seeded and minced), use more or less to taste
½ teaspoon salt
A dash of black pepper
2 tablespoons lemon juice
2 tablespoons chopped fresh cilantro or parsley

Remove husks from tomatillos and rinse to remove sticky residue. Chop tomatillos, pepper, and onion into small dice. Remove seeds and membranes from jalapeños. Mix vegetables together and stir in salt, pepper, lemon juice, and fresh cilantro or parsley. Chill for at least an hour before serving.

TIPS:

Wear rubber gloves when working with hot peppers and be especially careful not to touch your face or eyes.

———————

Chop the vegetables in a food processor, and the salsa can be made very quickly.

———————

Much of the fire of hot chilies comes from the membranes around the seeds. Leave them in if you like the heat.

MAKES 3¾ CUPS OR 30 SERVINGS OF 2 TABLESPOONS EACH.

Per serving--Net carbohydrate: 1 gram; Protein: 0.2 grams; Fiber: 0.3 grams; Fat: 0.1 grams; Calories: 6

Total weight: 1 pound 4⅛ ounces

Weight per serving: ¾ ounces or 28 grams

Preparation time: 25 minutes total, if chopped by hand, 10 minutes total if chopped in food processor.

Tomatillo Salsa, p. 10

Chocolate Granola

I can't resist an occasional visit to Molly Wizenberg's blog,
Orangette, *even though it makes me long to be young and*
perky and witty and full of joie de vivre, *but mostly it makes*
me wish I still had the metabolism to eat like her. On my last
foray into her world, I found the inspiration for something that
I can actually eat rather than just envy. It needed quite a few
changes, as carbs and calories and such have not yet intruded
into her consciousness, but her granola has chocolate and so does
mine, and that's really all that matters.

Chocolate Granola

4.9 net carbs

"Milk"

¼ cup "Milk" (p. 14)
1.8 net carbs

Menu total: 6.7 net carbs

2 tablespoons (10 grams) of Sustagrain barley flakes, or use rolled oats
and add 3.7 net carbs to total recipe

½ cup (30 grams) of unsweetened, flaked coconut

½ cup (52 grams) sliced almonds

¼ cup of pumpkin seeds (30 grams), or use part sesame, chia, or flax seeds

Sugar substitute equal to 2 tablespoons sugar

A pinch of salt

1 egg white from large egg

½ cup (2½ ounces) **Chocolate Chips**, p. 43,[67] or purchased chocolate chips

¼ cup (11 grams) of sugar-free **Dried Cranberries**, p. 12

Preheat oven to 300° F. Combine barley or oats, coconut,
almonds, seeds, sweetener, and salt and stir until blended.
Beat the egg white until fluffy and stir into the mixture
until evenly coated. Spread granola in a shallow baking pan.
Bake for 15 minutes, then stir and break apart any lumps.
Continue to bake for an additional 15 to 20 minutes or
until golden brown. Let cool completely. Stir in the chocolate and cranberries. Store granola in an airtight container.

To serve, top with ¼ cup **"Milk,"** p. 14, or cream and add
additional sweetener, if desired.

MAKES 5 SERVINGS OF ½ CUP.

Per serving—Net carbohydrate: 4.9 grams; Protein: 6.4 grams; Fiber: 13.1 grams;
Fat: 16 grams; Calories: 219

Total weight: 7½ ounces or 143 grams

Weight per serving: 1.5 ounces or 43 grams

Preparation time: 15 minutes active; 45 minutes total

---

67   You may use my recipes for sugar-free **Dried Cranberries** (p.12) and **Chocolate Chips** (p.
43) or use purchased, sugar-free cranberries and chocolate chips or chopped chocolate bars (see
Sources). Recipe was tested with chopped Choco*perfection* chocolate bars. One and one-third
Choco*perfection* bars make ½ cup of chocolate chunks.

Dried Cranberries

Unsweetened cranberries are too tart to be edible. Most packaged, dried cranberries contain about 4 teaspoonfuls of sugar in every one-quarter cup of berries. However, you can make your own sugar-free, dried cranberries. I dry lots of them when they are available fresh in the fall and winter since they keep extremely well.

> 3 cups fresh or frozen cranberries (one 12-ounce package)
> ¾ cup of water
> ½ cup (100 grams) of polydextrose
> High-intensity sugar substitute equal to ½ cup sugar or 12 packets of preferred sweetener (recipe was tested with 12 drops of EZ-Sweetz liquid sucralose)

Rinse and pick over cranberries, removing any that have soft spots. Cut each berry in half (you can line them up and cut 2 or 3 at a time.) Place cranberries in a saucepan or skillet just large enough to hold them in one layer. Add water and stir in polydextrose and sugar substitute. Bring to a boil, reduce heat to a simmer, and cook on low heat, stirring, occasionally at first, and more often as the syrup thickens, until the water is evaporated and the fruit is very sticky and glossy, about 30 to 40 minutes. Let berries cool in the pan. Lift out with a slotted spoon and spread on a nonstick baking sheet or one that has been sprayed with nonstick cooking spray or lined with a nonstick mat.

Preheat the oven to 350º F.

Put cranberries in oven and immediately reduce the temperature to 135º F. Bake, stirring and separating berries occasionally, until dry. A convection oven speeds up the process or you can use a dehydrator, if you have one, according to its directions. When dry, the cranberries should be glossy, shriveled, and only slightly sticky. If they are not dry enough, continue to bake until they are. (They take about 2½ hours in my convection oven.)

CRANBERRIES:
When the first European settlers arrived in North America, they discovered three unfamiliar fruits: blueberries, Concord grapes, and cranberries. Native Americans taught the colonists to use them for food, dye, and medicine.

Cranberries are naturally sour and contain mouth-puckering tannins. The addition of sweeteners or fats is necessary to make them palatable. The indigenous tribes of the East Coast mixed them with the dried meat, fat, and bone marrow of wild game to make *pemmican,* a staple food that could be stored as winter provisions and carried as "trail cake" when traveling. Pacific Coast peoples made a similar compound from fatty fish and local berries.

ALTERNATE METHOD:
Preheat the oven at 350º F for ten minutes. Place pan of berries in oven and turn off heat. Leave until oven is cool or overnight. Remove berries, preheat oven and repeat until berries are dry.

Dried cranberries can be refrigerated for up to two years or frozen indefinitely. Use them as a substitute for raisins. The fresh berries will be reduced to a little more than half their original weight and to ⅜ of their original volume.

MAKES 1⅛ CUPS OR 9 SERVINGS OF 2 TABLESPOONS.

Per serving—Net carbohydrate: 3.2 grams; Protein: 0.1 grams; Fiber: 11.4 grams; Fat: 0 grams; Calories: 26

Total weight: 5¼ ounces or 148 grams

Weight per serving: 1¼ ounces or 32 grams

Preparation time: 20 minutes active; total varies

TIPS:
You may use frozen cranberries for this recipe. Let them thaw before cooking.

Fresh cranberries are readily available in the fall and winter. They are beautiful and tart to use in sauces and desserts and, when sweetened, they can be substituted for cherries. When dried, they can be used as low-carb raisins.

Chocolate Granola, p. 11

"Milk"

NOTE:

If you use a sweetened vanilla whey protein powder, omit or reduce the sweetener.

Lactose, or milk sugar, tastes less sweet than other forms of sugar, but each 8-ounce serving of milk, including low-fat and non-fat milk, contains the equivalent of 3 teaspoonfuls of table sugar. By using the protein and cream components of real milk and replacing just the sugar, you can make your own low-carb milk.

2 tablespoons plain whey protein powder (2 net grams of carbohydrate or less per serving)
3 tablespoons heavy cream
1 cup water
Sugar substitute equal to 1 tablespoon sugar
A few grains of salt

Stir the whey powder and salt into the cream and mix to form a paste. Add the water and sweetener and whisk until smooth or mix in a blender. Chill until very cold or add ice to the glass.

MAKES 1 (8-OUNCE) SERVING.

Per serving—Net carbohydrate: 1.8 grams; Protein: 11.9 grams; Fiber: 0 grams; Fat: 17.6 grams; Calories: 210

Total weight: 8 fluid ounces

Preparation time: 5 minutes active and total

Chocolate "Milk"

2 teaspoons Dutch-process cocoa powder

2 tablespoons plain whey protein powder (2 grams of carbohydrate per serving or less)

A few grains of salt

3 tablespoons heavy cream

1 cup water

Sugar substitute equal to 2 tablespoons sugar

Stir together the cocoa powder, whey protein powder, and salt until well blended. Add 3 tablespoons of cream and mix to form a paste. Add the water and sweetener and whisk until smooth or mix in a blender. Chill or add ice.

MAKES 1 (8-OUNCE) SERVING.

Per serving—Net carbohydrate: 2.5 grams; Protein: 12.6 grams; Fiber: 1.3 grams; Fat: 17.6 grams; Calories: 223

Total weight: 8 fluid ounces

Preparation time: 5 minutes active and total

TIP:

If you prefer, you can use a pre-sweetened vanilla whey protein powder and eliminate or reduce the sugar substitute

Hood Calorie Countdown makes a milk substitute with only 3 net carbs per cup. They originally made a whole-fat version when it was called Carb Countdown, but they discontinued it when they changed the name to emphasize calories rather than carbs. The 2% tastes convincingly like real milk. They also make chocolate milk (4 net carbs per cup). Calorie Countdown uses Splenda and acesulfame K to replace the milk sugar (lactose). See Sources.

LC Foods For Low Carb Living sells a dry milk powder with zero net carbohydrates. Add cream to make whole milk. See Sources.

Hot Cereal with Cream, Berries, and Toasted Walnuts

Cereal with cream, 4.6 net carbs; 2 tablespoons dried cranberries, 3.2 net carbs; 2 tablespoons walnuts, 1.5 net carbs

Oven Bacon

0 net carbs

Menu total: 4.6 net carbs for cereal and cream; 9.2 net carbs including cranberries and walnuts

Since the advent of agriculture, man has been "improving" grain crops to make them starchier, sweeter, less perishable, and easier to grow and to harvest. Now that we are seeing the consequences, scientists are starting to reverse-engineer some food crops to more closely resemble their ancient predecessors. Sustagrain barley is one of the first to become available to the consumer. See Sources.

Hot Cereal with Cream, Berries, and Toasted Walnuts

If you really miss that bowl of hot cereal in the morning, try Sustagrain barley. It tastes like oatmeal but it isn't as soupy. It has more protein, 3 times the fiber, and half the starch of "healthful" oatmeal.

1 cup water
¼ cup (¾ ounce or 23 grams) Sustagrain barley flakes
A few grains of salt
Sugar substitute to taste
A sprinkle of cinnamon
¼ cup heavy cream or low carb "**Milk**," p. 14

OPTIONAL MIX-INS AND TOPPINGS:
2 tablespoons chopped walnuts
2 tablespoons sugar-free **Dried Cranberries**, p. 12, or other berries
1 tablespoon chia seeds or freshly-ground flax seeds, (adds zero carbs)

STOVETOP DIRECTIONS:
Bring water to a boil in a medium saucepan. Add barley flakes and salt. Cover, reduce heat to low, and cook for 15 to 20 minutes or until water is absorbed. Sweeten to taste, sprinkle with a dash of cinnamon, and serve hot with a splash of cream. Top with walnuts, chia or flax seeds, if desired. If using dried berries, add them halfway through the cooking time so they will plump.

MICROWAVE DIRECTIONS:
In a 6-cup, microwave-safe bowl, combine water, barley, and salt. (Don't use a small cup or bowl or it will boil over.) Microwave on high power for 3 minutes. Stir. Continue to microwave on high for 3 minutes longer or until water is absorbed and cereal is thick. Cool slightly and serve with sweetener and cream. Top with walnuts, **Dried Cranberries**, and chia or flax seed, if desired. If using dried cranberries, add them halfway through the cooking time so they will plump.

MAKES 2 SERVINGS of about ⅓ cup each for basic recipe

Per serving (including cream, excluding add-ins)—Net carbohydrate: 4.6 grams; Protein: 2.6 grams; Fiber: 3.5 grams; Fat: 11.9 grams; Calories: 148.5

Total weight: 6¼ ounces or 179 grams

Weight for each of 2 servings: 3¼ ounces or 90 grams

Preparation time: 5 minutes active, 25 minutes total on stovetop, 5 minutes active, 10 minutes total for microwave

"...I'm sticking with Michael Pollan's rule: Don't buy anything you've ever seen advertised. Although I offer up a slight variation: Don't eat anything that has its own cartoon character."

— *Sarah Gilbert*

Hot Cereal

General Mills has been advertising that Cheerios have been "proven to reduce cholesterol," based on the amount of soluble fiber they contain. Here are some comparisons of a ¾ cup (22.5 grams raw weight) serving of Sustagrain barley and a ¾ cup (22.5 grams) serving of whole-grain Cheerios. Note that the numbers below are for *plain* Cheerios, not the sweetened ones:

22.5 grams of plain Cheerios (¾ cup) have:
- 14 net grams of carbohydrate
- 2.5 grams total fiber
- 0.75 grams of soluble fiber

22.5 grams of Sustagrain barley flakes (about ¾ cup cooked) have:
- 7 net grams of carbohydrate
- 7 grams total fiber
- 2.5 grams of soluble fiber

TIP:
TO TOAST NUTS:
Preheat oven to 325º F. Spread nuts in a shallow baking pan and toast for about 10 minutes, stirring once or twice, until lightly browned and fragrant. Let cool. Alternately, put them in a dry skillet and heat on medium, stirring, for a few minutes.

Oven Bacon

Here's an alternative to the convenient, but expensive, packaged micro-wave-ready and pre-cooked bacon—and it comes with a bonus. Cooking a pound at a time is an efficient way to render this most flavorful of all fats. Bacon fat is an excellent, stable fat for frying at high heat; it can replace shortening or lard in baking, and nothing can match its smoky, savory taste. It's a must for frying okra and for flavoring green beans.

1 pound bacon (choose one that lists zero carbs)

Preheat oven to 350° F.

Place bacon strips on a greased rack in a large, open roasting pan. Bake for 30 to 35 minutes or until bacon is almost crisp. Let cool, wrap, and refrigerate. When needed, microwave strips for a few minutes until crisp or finish cooking in a frying pan.

Strain cooled bacon fat into a container, cover, label with date, and refrigerate.

A pound of regular bacon makes between ½ and ⅔ cup of bacon fat, depending on how lean it is.

———

Bacon is mostly monounsaturated (like olive oil). Both bacon fat and lard are 45% monounsaturated, 39% saturated, and 11% polyunsaturated fat.

MAKES 8 SERVINGS OF 2 SLICES.

Per serving—Net carbohydrate: 0 grams; Protein: 5.9 grams; Fiber: 0 grams; Fat: 6.7 grams; Calories: 87

Total weight: 6 ounces or 168 grams

Weight per serving: ¾ ounce or 21 grams

Preparation time: 5 minutes active; 35 to 40 minutes total

"I eat it (bacon) every day. Last time my blood pressure was checked (last week, when I went for a physical), it was 111 over 64. From eating bacon, eggs, sausage, cheese, hamburgers, chicken with the skin on it, and green vegetables swimming in butter…The dietary science that's based in evidence, not just passed-down hearsay, says sugar is what's really toxic, and carbohydrates, including starchy carbohydrates, are what causes the insulin reaction that puts on fat…."

—*Amy Alkon, AKA The Advice Goddess, syndicated columnist, journalist, and blogger.*

Corned Beef Hash with Poached Eggs

One corned beef brisket can provide enough for several delicious meals. Make Corned Beef and Cabbage for dinner, use some to make this tasty hash for breakfast, then polish off the rest in **Reuben Sandwiches** *(see Sidebar) for lunch. If you prefer, you can buy corned beef from the deli or even (gasp!) in a can to make your hash.*

Rutabaga *Faux* Potatoes (p. 285) made with about 1 pound of
    rutabaga
1 pound corned beef, cooked and cut into chunks (left over from **Corned
    Beef and Cabbage** recipe, p. 232, or purchased)
2 tablespoons olive oil, coconut oil, butter, or bacon fat
¾ cup onion (3½ ounces), diced
¾ cup red bell pepper (3½ ounces), diced
1 teaspoon Worcestershire sauce
¼ cup heavy cream
4 eggs
Salt and pepper to taste (for eggs)

Make **Rutabaga *Faux* Potatoes** according to recipe on p. 285; cut in ¼-inch dice and set aside. Pulse corned beef in a food processor with the metal blade until roughly chopped or chop by hand.

Heat fat in a large skillet and sauté onion and bell pepper over medium-high heat, stirring occasionally, until softened, about 5 minutes. Add rutabaga and continue to cook and stir until browned, about 5 minutes more. Stir in corned beef and cook, stirring occasionally, until it is browned. Add Worcestershire and cream and cook, stirring, for another minute.

Make 4 depressions in the hash with a large spoon and break an egg into each. Season eggs with salt and pepper to taste. Reduce heat to medium-low, cover pan, and cook for 5 minutes or until egg whites are set but yolks are still soft. Cut into 4 portions. Garnish with fresh parsley, if desired, and serve hot with low-carb **Ketchup**, p. 294, on the side (optional).

**MAKES 4 SERVINGS
OF 1½ CUPS EACH.**

Per serving—Net carbohydrate: 9.9 grams; Protein: 22.8 grams; Fiber: 2.4 grams; Fat: 31.8 grams; Calories: 424

Total weight: 33.8 ounces or 2 pounds 1.8 ounces

Weight per serving: 8½ ounces or 960 grams

Preparation time: 15 minutes active, 30 minutes total, excluding time to prepare *faux* potatoes.

Scrambled Eggs with Kippered Herring or Smoked Salmon

0.8 net carbs

Broiled Tomato with Herbs

4 net carbs

Menu total, 4.8 carbs

"Kipper" comes from the Old English word for "copper," a reference to the color of the cured fish.

———————

The expression "red herring" comes from the practice of pulling a kipper across the trail of a fox to distract the hounds and disrupt the hunt.

Scrambled Eggs with Kippered Herring or Smoked Salmon

4 eggs
1 (8-ounce) **Kippered Herring**, following recipe, or
    one 6½ ounce tin of kippered herring filets (5 ounces drained) or
    5 ounces smoked salmon
1 tablespoon butter
Fresh pepper to taste

Break eggs into a bowl and stir with a fork until mixed. Reserve. Remove bones and skin from kippered herring or use canned filets or smoked salmon. You should have about 5 ounces of boneless fish after preparation. Separate fish into flakes. Heat butter in a large skillet and add fish. Cook on medium-high heat for 1 minute. Reduce heat and pour eggs over fish. Cook and stir for a minute or two until eggs start to set. Continue to cook until eggs are done to taste. Grind fresh pepper over dish (taste before adding salt as the fish is already salty.)

PER SERVING

Net carbohydrate: 0.8 grams; Protein: 40.5 grams; Fiber: 0 grams; Fat: 29.7 grams; Calories: 440

Total weight: 11⅛ ounces or 315 grams

Weight per serving: 5½ ounces or 157 grams

Preparation time: 10 minutes active and total

"A good kipper is one of this country's worthy contributions to fine food."

– *English author, Jane Grigson*

Smoked Salmon with Scrambled Eggs

Use 5 ounces of smoked salmon in place of kippered herring.

"Your rainment, O herring, displays the rainbow colors of the setting sun, the patina on old copper, the golden-brown of Cordoba leather, the autumnal tints of sandalwood and saffon. Your head, O herring, flames like a golden helmet, and your eyes, are like black studs in circlets of copper."

— Joris Karl Huysmans (1848-1907)

GOOD EGGS:

Obesity plays a central role in the development of metabolic syndrome. Fat tissue is now known to be an active organ that secretes hormone-like substances called cytokines (proteins that carry signals between cells) that contribute to the systemic inflammation seen in chronic conditions associated with metabolic syndrome, such as atherosclerosis, diabetes, cancer, strokes, and Alzheimer's. Inflammation levels can be determined by measuring the amount of C-Reactive Protein (CRP) in the blood.

In a study published in *Nutrition and Metabolism* in February 2008[68] two groups of overweight men were given the same diet except that half of them ate about 3 eggs a day, while the other half had no eggs. Both groups were allowed unlimited calories as long as the proportion of carbs, fats, and protein stayed the same. At the end of the study, the men's blood was tested for markers for inflammation (CRP) and for adiponectin, a beneficial compound that is known to help regulate insulin sensitivity and fat metabolism. The men eating eggs had significantly less CRP and more adiponectin than the men eating no eggs. The researchers speculated that eggs moderate inflammation in two ways—the cholesterol in the eggs increases HDL ("good" cholesterol), and the antioxidant Leutein from the egg yolks lowers inflammation.

---

68 Joseph C. Ratliff, Gisella Mutungi, Michael J. Puglisi, Jeff S. Volek, Maria L. Fernandez, Eggs modulate the inflammatory response to carbohydrate restricted diets in overweight men, *Nutrition & Metabolism*, Vol. 5 (20 February 2008), 6.

Kippered Herring

Imagine bacon made of fish; that's kippered herring. The whole fish are split from head to tail, soaked in brine then smoked. Scrambled eggs and broiled tomatoes are traditional accompaniments.

If kippered herring is purchased frozen, follow thawing and cooking directions on package. Recipe can be halved or doubled using appropriately sized pan.

MAKES 4 SERVINGS OF ½ KIPPER EACH.

Per serving—Net carbohydrate: 0.8 grams; Protein: 40.5 grams; Fiber: 0 grams; Fat: 29.7 grams; Calories: 440

Total weight, including skin, bones, and tail: 13 ounces or 369 grams

Weight per serving: 3¼ ounces or 92 grams

Preparation time: 5 minutes active, 10 minutes total

2 kippered herring, about 1 pound total
1 tablespoon butter
4 slices lemon

Preheat broiler. Rinse herring and pat dry. Leave tail intact to facilitate boning, but head can be removed if it is included. Place butterflied herring, skin-side-down, on well-greased broiler pan. Dot with butter. Broil about 5 inches from heat source for 2 to 3 minutes or until brown. Turn skin-side-up and broil for an additional 2 to 3 minutes or until brown, for a total of 4 to 6 minutes. Cut each fish in half to make 4 servings and top each with a slice of lemon, if desired.

Broiled Tomatoes

A fabulous side dish anytime, but especially good with eggs and sausage for breakfast. Prepare them in advance and just tuck them under the broiler when you put the kettle on.

2 ripe tomatoes, about 10 ounces total, as purchased
Dash salt
1 tablespoon olive oil
1 (1/8 ounce) clove garlic, peeled and minced
2 tablespoons white wine
More salt to taste
Dash black pepper for each tomato half
4 teaspoons grated Parmesan cheese
Fresh basil, shredded, optional

Grease a small broiler-safe pan. Cut tomatoes in half vertically. Cut out stem button and make several slashes across the core but not into the wall of the tomato. Sprinkle lightly with salt. Invert on paper towels and let drain for 10 minutes. Heat oil in a small skillet over medium heat. Place tomatoes, cut-side-down, in the hot pan. Let tomatoes cook without moving for about 5 minutes or until brown. (You can tell when they are brown by looking at the edges.) Remove tomatoes from skillet and place cut-side-up in prepared pan. (Can be prepared to this stage in advance and refrigerated. Broil just before serving.)

Preheat broiler. Put minced garlic in the hot skillet and cook, stirring, for a few seconds. Add white wine and cook and stir for about 3 minutes or until most of the wine has boiled off. Pour liquid from skillet over tomatoes. Sprinkle with additional salt to taste and fresh black pepper. Top with grated Parmesan. Place tomatoes under broiler for about 5 minutes or until top is brown. Transfer tomatoes to serving dish and spoon drippings from pan over them. Garnish with fresh basil, and serve hot.

A broiled or grilled tomato is part of a full English breakfast (a fry-up), which might also include fried eggs, fried mushrooms, fried potatoes, rashers (that's Canadian bacon to Americans—American-style bacon is streaky bacon to Brits), kippered herring, sausages, baked beans, and fried bread, served with hot tea. If you want it all, order a *Full Monty*.

MAKES 2 SERVINGS.

Per serving—Net carbohydrate: 4 grams; Protein: 2.6 grams; Fiber: 1.6 grams; Fat: 8.2 grams; Calories: 110

Total weight: 8½ ounces or 237 grams

Weight per serving: 4¼ ounces or 118 grams

Preparation time: 5 minutes active; 25 minutes total

Fluffy Omelet with Cherry Jelly (p. 302) and Whipped Cream (p. 312)

Omelet, 1.1 net grams;
jelly, 0 net grams;
2 tablespoons whipped cream,
0 net grams

Pork Sausage

0 net grams

Toasted Whole Grain Bread and Butter (p. 290)

1 slice from 1-loaf recipe
without flax, 4.9 net grams

Menu total, 6 net carbs

MAKES 1 SERVING.

Per serving—Net carbohydrate:
1.1 grams; Protein: 12.7 grams;
Fiber: 0 grams; Fat: 15.7 grams;
Calories: 195

Total weight: 3¼ ounces or 94
grams

Preparation time: 10 minutes active
and total

Fluffy Omelet

As good as a Danish or a donut in the morning for fewer than 2 grams of carbohydrate. It also makes a quick bedtime snack.

> 2 large eggs
> A pinch of salt
> Sugar substitute equal to 1 tablespoon sugar (recipe was tested with
>   1 tablespoon powdered erythritol plus 3 drops Sweetz-free)
> Dash of cinnamon
> 1 teaspoon lemon juice
> Grated lemon zest, optional
> ½ tablespoon butter
> **Cherry Jelly**, p. 302, or fresh berries, optional
> **Whipped Cream,** p. 312, optional

Have ready a 7- to 8-inch nonstick skillet with sloped sides and ½ tablespoon butter. Place eggs in warm water for a few minutes so they are not ice cold.

Break eggs into a mixing bowl. Add salt, sweetener, cinnamon, lemon juice, and zest. Beat for about 3 minutes with an electric mixer or by hand with a balloon whisk (the kind with lots of wires) for about 5 minutes or until texture changes from large bubbles to fluffy. (You won't get stiff peaks unless you separate the whites from the yolks before beating.) Heat butter in skillet on medium-high heat until melted. As soon as the foam subsides, but before the butter starts to brown, pour in the egg mixture. Stir the center of the eggs for about a minute until slightly thickened. Reduce heat and cook for 2 to 3 minutes. Loosen edges of omelet with a rubber spatula—it should move freely in the pan. Using two spatulas, fold omelet in half. Let cook for a minute or so longer and turn to let other side cook for a minute or two more or until firm. Slide out onto a plate, sprinkle with more sweetener and cinnamon, and top with jelly or fruit and whipped cream, if desired. Serve at once.

Pork Sausage

It is nearly impossible to buy sausage that does not have sugar, MSG, preservatives, and fillers, but it takes only a few minutes to season plain ground pork to make your own fresh sausage. Cook it immediately or place patties in a single layer, separated with waxed paper, and freeze.

    1 pound of fresh ground pork
    1 teaspoon of salt
    ½ teaspoon of rubbed sage
    ¼ teaspoon of dried summer savory (optional)
    ½ teaspoon of freshly ground black pepper or to taste

Mix together well. Shape into patties. Heat 2 tablespoons of water in a skillet on low and add sausage patties. Cover and cook for five minutes. Remove cover and raise heat to medium. Cook until well browned, then turn and brown other side. Pour off fat as it accumulates and press sausage down with a spatula to ensure even browning. Total cooking time will be about 15 minutes.

MAKES 6 SERVINGS.

Per serving—Net carbohydrate per serving: 0 grams; Protein 12.8 grams; Fiber: 0 grams; Fat; 16 grams; Calories: 199

Total weight: 12¼ ounces or 348 grams

Weight per serving: 2 ounces or 57 grams

Preparation time: 5 minutes active; 20 minutes total

Notes: About 1 tablespoon plus 1 teaspoon of fat stays in the pan.

Don't use lean pork. Pork with a high fat content makes breakfast sausage that is juicy and flavorful.

"Everything in a pig is good. What ingratitude has permitted his name to become a term of opprobrium?"
— Grimod de la Reynière (1758-1838)

Poached Eggs with
Artichoke Bottoms
and Hollandaise

8.8 net carbs plus 0.3 for Hollandaise

Toasted Whole
Grain Bread with
Butter (p. 291)

1.9 net grams for 1 slice from 2-loaf
recipe with flax

Menu total, 11 net carbs

When eating eggs in a restaurant, you can reduce your chances of getting that rare bad egg if you order them cooked one at a time, such as poached, over-easy, or in the shell. Food service workers frequently mingle many eggs together (a practice called pooling) for making omelets or scrambled eggs, and if one is contaminated, the bacteria will quickly spread to the whole batch.

Poached Eggs with Artichoke Bottoms and Hollandaise

I was thinking of including Eggs Sardou, *the classic French-Creole recipe from Antoine's in New Orleans, in this collection, when Dr. Richard Bernstein offered to share this recipe from* The Diabetes Diet.[69] *I decided it was a much better choice, equally delicious, and equally low in carbs. (The original required two sauces plus truffles and anchovies.)*

> ½ cup **Hollandaise Sauce**, p. 28
> 1 tablespoon olive oil
> 4 ounces zero-carb Canadian bacon, in 4 slices
> 4 prepared artichoke bottoms
> 2 cups baby spinach leaves (about 3 ounces)
> Salt and black pepper to taste
> 4 eggs
> 1 teaspoon vinegar

Make **Hollandaise Sauce** according to following recipe. Keep warm over a water bath.

Heat olive oil in skillet. Sauté Canadian bacon, browning on both sides. Remove from pan and keep warm. Add artichoke bottoms to pan and sauté, stirring artichokes to absorb meat flavor. Add spinach leaves and stir until wilted. Season with salt and pepper. Remove from pan and keep warm with Canadian bacon.

---

69   Bernstein, Richard K., M.D. 2005. *The Diabetes Diet.* Little, Brown, and Company.

POACHED EGGS:

Put 2 inches of water into a skillet. Add 1 teaspoon vinegar. Bring to a rolling boil. Turn down heat slightly to a lively simmer. Crack 1 egg into a bowl. Holding bowl as close to water level as possible, slide egg into water. Repeat with other eggs. Cook about 3 minutes, or until pink on top. Remove with slotted spoon and season with salt and pepper.

To serve, divide spinach and artichoke bottoms between two plates. Top each artichoke bottom with a slice of Canadian bacon and a poached egg. Spoon 2 tablespoons **Hollandaise Sauce** over each egg.

MAKES 2 SERVINGS.

Per serving before adding sauce—Net carbohydrate: 8.8 grams; Protein: 31 grams; Fiber: 17.9 grams; Fat: 21.5 grams; Calories: 406

Total weight: 10½ ounces or 298 grams

Weight per serving: 5¼ ounces or 148 grams

Preparation time: 35 minutes active, 40 minutes total, including time for making sauce

If poaching eggs in a pot of water makes you nervous, there are many gadgets that can help you poach like a pro. Most electric egg cookers include a poaching insert. There are egg poachers that work in the microwave as well as egg holders on legs that fit in a pan of boiling water to steam your eggs to perfection.

Hollandaise Sauce

3 egg yolks
1 tablespoon cold water
Salt and pepper to taste
2 sticks butter, cut into small cubes
1 tablespoon lemon juice

Heat 1 or 2 inches of water in bottom half of a double boiler. Bring to a simmer, then reduce heat. In top half of double boiler, combine egg yolks, 1 tablespoon cold water, and salt and pepper. Place the pan over the hot water and whisk egg yolks until they begin to thicken. Do not let the mixture get too hot or the eggs will cook and the sauce will become lumpy. Whisk in butter a few pieces at a time until it is all incorporated. Whisk until thick and creamy. Whisk in lemon juice.

Recipe developed by Marcia Miele, of the Peter Herdic House in Williamsport, Pennsylvania. Reprinted by permission from the Diabetes Diet *by Dr. Richard Bernstein.*

MAKES ABOUT 1½ CUPS OR 6 SERVINGS OF ¼ CUP.

Per serving—Net carbohydrate: 0.3 grams; Protein: 1.7 grams; Fiber: 0 grams; Fat: 33.2 grams; Calories: 301

Total weight: 12 ounces or 341 grams

Weight per serving: 2 fluid ounces or 57 grams

Preparation time: 15 minutes active and total

"Our study showed further evidence that a number of bioactive peptides may be generated while digesting egg proteins, which would provide additional benefits for reducing another well-identified risk of heart disease…. Egg has been part of human diets for centuries and therefore it is safe to consume eggs."[70]

— *Jianping Wu*

70   Kaustav Majumder and Jianping Wu, "Angiotensin I Converting Enzyme Inhibitory Peptides from Simulated in Vitro Gastrointestinal Digestion of Cooked Eggs," Department of Agricultural, Food and Nutritional Science, University of Alberta, Edmonton, Alberta, Canada, published in *J. Agric. Food Chem.*, 2009, 57 (2), pp 471-477.

Greek Yogurt with "Honey" and Toasted Walnuts

½ cup (4 ounces) Greek-style plain yogurt with live cultures, made from whole milk

1 tablespoon (¾ ounce or 20 grams) artificial honey, such as Nature's Hollow, made with xylitol

2 tablespoons (½ ounce or 16 grams) chopped walnuts

MAKES 1 SERVING.

Per serving—Net carbohydrate: 3.1 grams (count excludes 4 grams eaten by the yogurt culture and 8 grams sugar alcohol); Protein: 6.8 grams; Fiber: 1 gram; Fat: 13.8 grams; Calories: 205

Weight per serving: 5¼ ounces or 150 grams

Preparation time: 4 minutes

Greek Yogurt with Honey and Toasted Walnuts

3.1 net carbs (excludes 4 grams eaten by the yogurt culture and 8 grams sugar alcohol)

Hard Cooked Egg (p. 278)

0.6 net carbs

Barley Rusks (p. 237) and Hot Tea

2 thin rusks—2 net carbs

Menu total: 5.7 net carbs

The carbs are in the whey in fermented and aged dairy products. Aged, dry cheese and concentrated yogurt will have lower counts than ones with higher moisture content. Traditional Greek yogurt is thicker and richer and contains less sugar and more protein than standard yogurt. Drain off any liquid that rises to the top of soft cheese and yogurt to keep the count as low as possible.

Brands of traditional Greek yogurt include: Fage, Oikos, and Chobani. Greek Gods is also good, but it contains pectin for thickening, so it is not totally authentic.

Eggs with Nopales,
Chorizo Sausage,
and Grilled Tortilla

6.4 net carbs

Hot Cocoa

3.2 net carbs

Menu total: 9.6 net carbs

Eggs with Nopales, Chorizo Sausage, and Grilled Tortilla

4 ounces bulk pork or beef chorizo sausage or links taken out of casings
½ cup (2½ ounces) prepared nopalitos
¼ cup (1¼ ounce) chopped onion
4 large eggs, lightly beaten
½ cup (1 ounce) shredded Jack or Cheddar cheese
2 (6- or 7-inch) low-carb tortillas
Crème Fraîche, p. 297, or sour cream and salsa, optional

Heat a medium skillet over medium-high heat. Add chorizo, breaking it up with a spatula, and cook for about a minute. Add onion and nopales and sauté till onions are translucent, an additional 5 minutes or so. Remove pan from heat and let cool for 5 minutes. Add the eggs and stir over medium heat until cooked to your taste. Sprinkle cheese over the top and cover pan for a minute or until cheese melts.

Heat tortillas on a greased griddle or skillet, turning frequently, until puffed and brown. Spoon eggs over tortillas and serve with **Crème Fraîche** (p. 297) or sour cream, and salsa, if desired.

MAKES 2 SERVINGS

Per serving—Net carbohydrate: 6.4 grams; Protein: 26.3 grams; Fiber: 4.6 grams; Fat: 32.3 grams; Calories: 425

Total weight: 13¼ ounce or 374 grams

Weight per serving: 6½ ounces or 187 grams

Preparation time: 10 minutes active and total

NOPALITOS:

Nopalitos are prepared prickly pear cactus pads. You may find them fresh, frozen, or packed in jars. To use fresh ones, you must cut away the spines and slice or chop the pads. The spines will have been removed from frozen nopales. To prepare fresh or frozen nopales, cover with water and bring to a boil, then drain and rinse. Nopalitos from a jar are already cooked but still need to be drained and rinsed. See page p. 139 for more information.

CHORIZO:

Chorizo is a spicy Mexican-style sausage. It is often sold as links rather than in bulk, but it can be removed from the casings.

The clerk at my local Mexican grocery warned me away from the chorizo sold there because, she said, it would cook down to almost nothing. It was very soft and was made of glandular tissue and fat. No meat was listed on the label. I eventually found chorizo links that listed pork and beef as the first two ingredients and chorizo in bulk at other stores. It's a good thing to always check the label. (When I asked for nopales, the same helpful clerk volunteered that her grandmother ate a fresh nopal cactus pad every morning and never needed medication to control her diabetes. "Her doctor was amazed," she said. That's just one anecdotal story, but nopal cactus is a folk remedy for diabetes in Mexico.)

"…The prickly pear cactus demonstrates the ability to decrease blood glucose levels as well as the hyperglycemic peak during glucose tolerance testing. In addition, Opuntia has demonstrated the ability to control experimentally induced diabetes."

— *Miguel Angel Gutierrez,* Medicinal Use of the Latin Food Staple Nopales: the Prickly Pear Cactus.

Hot Cocoa

Some brands of cocoa powder list 1 net gram of carbohydrate; some list two. If you use a cocoa with one net gram of carbs and a zero-carb sweetener, a rich, creamy, cup of cocoa is almost a *freebie!*

According to Greek mythology, the gods feasted on ambrosia *and* nectar, *which imparted immortality. The native people of Mexico called this heavenly food* xocolatl (bitter water). *The Aztec believed their god of the air, Quetzalcoatl, shared this magical substance with man. The botanical name for the cacao tree is* Theobroma cacao, *which means "drink of the gods." The Aztec used chocolate only for beverages, but for us it is truly both ambrosia and nectar.*

1 tablespoon Dutch cocoa (Use a brand with 1 net gram of carbs
    per tablespoon.)
Sugar substitute equal to 2 teaspoons of sugar or to taste
²/₃ cup of water
¹/₃ cup heavy cream
A few grains of salt
Optional flavorings:
    A dash of cinnamon
    A dash of chipotle and/or ancho chili powder
    A dash of allspice
    1 drop of orange oil
¼ teaspoon sugar-free vanilla extract

Combine the cocoa with a small amount of the water and mix to a smooth paste in a microwave-safe cup or a small saucepan. Stir in the rest of the water, the cream, sweetener, salt, and choice (or choices) of optional flavorings. Heat in the microwave for about 1½ minutes or on cooktop until hot. Stir in vanilla. Garnish with sugar-free **Whipped Cream**, p. 312, and dust with cocoa powder or sprinkle with orange zest, if desired.

MAKES 1 SERVING OF 1 CUP.

Per serving—Net carbohydrate: 3.2 grams; Protein: 2.6 grams; Fiber: 2 grams; Fat: 30 grams; Calories: 285

Total weight and weight per serving: 8 ounces or 227 grams

Preparation time: 3 minutes active; 4½ minutes total

Replace cream and water with **"Milk,"** p. 14, LC Foods Milk, or use Hood Calorie Countdown Milk.

If you prefer marshmallows in your cocoa, try the variation under my recipe for **Raspberry Marshmallow Squares** on p. 140. Alternately, see Sources for La Nouba sugar-free marshmallows.

The Aztecs added vanilla and chili to their chocolate beverages, but no sweetener. Modern Mexican hot chocolate is made from disks of coarsely ground cocoa nibs, sugar, and cinnamon, which are heated together with milk and the seeds from a vanilla bean. The drink is beaten to a froth by spinning a tool called a *molinillo* between the palms of the hands. This turned wooden tool was actually invented by the Spanish colonists in about 1700. Before that, the chocolate beverage was poured from one cup to another until aerated and foamy.

Stir, stir, chocolate,
Your nose is a peanut,
One, two, three, CHO!
One, two, three, CO!
One, two, three, LA!
One, two, three, TE!
Chocolate, chocolate!
Stir, stir, the chocolate!
Stir, stir, stir, stir!
Stir, stir, chocolate!

English translation of a rhyme repeated by children
when making hot chocolate with a molinillo.
— Texas State Library and Archives Commission

Molinillo

Eggs en Cocotte with Ham and Gruyère

0.9 net carbs

Cheddar Cheese Muffin (p. 46) with Butter and Cherry Jelly (p. 302)

Muffin, 3 net carbs; 1 tablespoon jelly, 0.1 net carbs

Menu total: 4 net carbs

Eggs en Cocotte

A cocotte is a small casserole dish used in France for baking eggs. You can use ramekins, custard cups, or even squat canning jars. Scale up the recipe and you can serve breakfast or brunch for eight, twelve, or more and have every egg perfectly cooked at the same time.

8 large eggs

4 teaspoons butter for ramekins

4 ounces (1 cup) diced sugar-free ham, such as Cure 81

4 tablespoons (¼ cup or 1 ounce) grated Gruyère cheese, plus an additional 4 teaspoons for top

4 teaspoons heavy cream

Salt and fresh back pepper to taste

A sprinkle of nutmeg for each serving

2 tablespoons chopped fresh parsley for garnish, optional

Remove eggs from refrigerator and place in warm water for 10 minutes to warm up. Preheat oven to 425° F. Bring a kettle of water to a boil. Line a large roasting pan with a folded kitchen towel or a double layer of paper towels. Place roasting pan on stovetop over low heat and add an inch or so of boiling water. (Water should come one third of the way up the sides of the baking dishes when all four are in pan.)

Butter 4 eight-ounce ramekins, cups, or small, wide-mouth, 8-ounce canning jars (do not use lids). Put ¼ cup of diced ham in each buttered ramekin, add 1 tablespoon of grated Gruyère cheese, and set in water bath. Heat for 5 minutes.

Break 2 eggs over ham and cheese in each dish, being careful not to break the yolks. Spoon 1 teaspoon of heavy cream over whites of eggs, leaving yolks exposed. Put 1 teaspoon grated Gruyère over egg whites (but not yolks). Sprinkle with salt, pepper, and nutmeg. Transfer to middle oven rack and bake for 10 to 15 minutes or until whites are opaque and set but yolks are still liquid. (Test egg whites with the tip of a spoon to see if they are firm.) Leave in oven for longer time for firmer yolks. Garnish with parsley, if desired, and serve hot. (Dishes can be kept warm in water bath for 10 minutes or so, if necessary.)

MAKES 4 SERVINGS.

Per serving—Net carbohydrate: 0.9 grams; Protein: 22.6 grams; Fiber: 0 grams; Fat: 20 grams; Calories: 276

Total weight: 22½ or 634 grams

Weight per serving: 5½ ounces or 159 grams

Preparation time: 15 minutes active; 30 to 35 minutes total

"We don't need to eat less cholesterol; we need to eat *more*, even those of us trying to lower our blood cholesterol and especially those of us trying to lose middle-body fat…Keeping the yolk intact during cooking and minimizing the cooking time to just long enough to solidify the white helps preserve the quality of the cholesterol. By not cooking the egg at all, however you'll get the cholesterol in its purest and most beneficial form."

– Drs. Michael and Mary Dan Eades

Eggs en Cocotte

Lunches

MENU 1

Peanut and Chicken Soup

Roasted Okra

Chocolate Chip Cookies

MENU 2

Creole Gumbo

Cheddar Cheese Muffin
with Butter

Lemon Frozen Yogurt

Almond Crisp Cookies

MENU 3

Poached Chicken with
Coconut Curry Sauce

Chayote Chutney

Broccolini Salad

Italian Cream Soda

MENU 4

Easy Chili

Cheese Quesadilla

Mexican Cole Slaw

Fruit Gelatin

MENU 5

Mystic Pizzas

Mixed Green Salad with
Red Wine Vinaigrette

Caramel Pecan Sundaes

MENU 6

Carnitas Soup
with Tomatillo Salsa,
Tortilla Strips,
and Toppings

Fresh Fruit Platter

MENU 7

Ham and Bean Soup
with Chana Dal

Whole Grain Bread
and Butter

Fresh Raspberries
with Cream

MENU 8

Roasted Red Pepper
and Tomato Soup

Cheese Puffs

Peanut Butter Cookies

"Milk"

MENU 9

Tacos with Salsa
and Toppings

Crème Caramel

MENU 10

Antipasto Salad

Easy Biskmix Crackers

Strawberry Rhubarb Parfait

MENU 11

Chicken A La King

Whole Grain Bread
Toast Points

Mixed Green Salad with
Red Wine Vinaigrette

Oops, It's Strawberry Shortcake!

MENU 12

Wrap Sandwich with
Poached Chicken

Stuffed Egg

Protein Bar

Peanut and Chicken Soup

8 net carbs

Roasted Okra

2.5 net carbs

Chocolate Chip Cookies

1.8 net carbs for 2 cookies

Menu total: 12.3 net carbs

TIPS:

For a smooth soup, puree in a food processor or with a stick blender before adding basil and chicken.

Use the kind of peanut butter that lists just peanuts or peanuts and salt as ingredients. It usually says, "stir before using." If it is refrigerated after stirring, it will not separate.

Look for tomatoes with the lowest carb count. Some have up to 9 grams in a ½ cup serving.

Peanut and Chicken Soup

Fragrant, earthy, and spicy, with echoes of exotic places.

2 tablespoons peanut oil
½ cup chopped onion (2½ ounces)
2 teaspoons minced garlic (¼ ounce)
¼ teaspoon red pepper flakes
2 tablespoons yellow curry powder
3 cups chicken stock (from **Poached Chicken** or zero-carb canned stock)
1 can (14½-ounce) diced tomatoes, without added sugar
2/3 cup natural peanut butter, creamy style
1 cup (8 ounces) canned coconut milk
¼ teaspoon salt or to taste
2 cups (10 ounces) cut up **Poached Chicken** (p. 277)
6 large fresh basil leaves, shredded (¼ cup), extra for garnish
Chopped peanuts and /or toasted coconut flakes, optional
Chicharones, optional

Sauté onion in peanut oil in a large saucepan on medium heat until softened. Add garlic, pepper flakes, and curry powder and cook and stir for two minutes more. Add chicken stock and tomatoes, including juice, and bring to a boil. Stir in peanut butter and simmer for about 15 minutes. Add coconut milk, salt, chicken, and basil. Stir over low heat until smooth and hot. Top with shredded basil. Garnish with chopped peanuts and toasted coconut flakes and serve with chicharones (pork rinds) on the side. (They make great croutons, if eaten immediately so they don't get soggy.)

MAKES 6 SERVINGS OF 1¼ CUPS

Per serving—Net carbohydrate: 8 grams; Protein: 24.5 grams; Fiber: 3.8 grams; Fat: 30 grams; Calories: 402

Total weight: 3 pounds 15 ounces or 1.79 kilograms

Weight per serving: 10½ ounces or 298 grams

Preparation time: 20 minutes active; 45 minutes total

Peanut Chicken Soup

Roasted Okra

Start with the smallest, freshest okra you can find. Leave the pods whole and cook them quickly. They will be creamy inside, not slimy, with seeds that pop when you bite into them.

Frozen okra can be used for soups and stews, but for this recipe, only fresh will do. Choose small okra and store it in a plastic bag in the vegetable bin of the refrigerator for no more than 3 days. Okra may be easier to find in an Asian specialty market, but when it is in season (June, July, and August), many supermarkets and farmers' markets will have it.

Use non-reactive pans, like ceramic or stainless steel, to prevent okra from discoloring. It won't change the taste or make it hazardous; it is just unattractive.

½ pound (about 38 to 40 pods) small, young okra pods, 2-to 3-inches long or less
2 tablespoons olive oil or bacon fat
Coarse salt to taste
Freshly ground black pepper to taste
2 tablespoons freshly grated Parmesan cheese

Preheat oven to 500º F.

Rinse okra and blot dry on paper toweling. Trim ends of caps but try not to puncture the pod capsule. Place oil or melted fat in a bowl; add okra and toss to coat. Lay pods on a rimmed baking sheet and sprinkle with coarse salt. Place pan on center rack in preheated oven and bake for 10 to 12 minutes or until crisp and brown, turning once or twice. (Use convection mode if your oven has it; watch the timing because it may brown more quickly.) Grind black pepper over okra, sprinkle with Parmesan, and serve hot or at room temperature as a side dish, an appetizer, or a snack.

MAKES 4 SERVINGS.

Per serving—Net carbohydrate: 2.5 grams; Protein: 2 grams; Fiber:1.3 grams; Fat: 7.7 grams; Calories: 91

Total weight: 4 ounces or 115 grams

Weight per serving: 1 ounce or 29 grams

Preparation time: 8 minutes active; 18 to 20 minutes total

Note: 1 teaspoon or more of the oil or fat included in the count will be left over.

"Okra: Devine Slime"

— Jane Tunks

Favorite Chocolate Chip Cookies

My friend, Jennifer Efoff, generously shared this recipe from her best-selling book, Splendid Low-Carbing for Life.

  Sugar substitute equal to 1½ cups sugar
  1 cup (8 ounces or 226.8 grams) butter, softened
  1 egg
  1 teaspoon molasses
  2½ cups (11 ounces or 310 grams) **Low-Carb Bake Mix**, p. 287.
  1 teaspoon baking soda
  ½ teaspoon salt
  2 cups (14 ounces or 400 grams) sugar-free **Chocolate Chips**, p. 43, or use purchased, sugar-free chips
  1 cup (4 ounces or 116 grams) chopped pecans or walnuts, or mixed nuts

In a food processor or in a bowl with an electric mixer, combine sugar substitute, butter, egg, and molasses; process. In a medium bowl, combine **Low-Carb Bake Mix**, baking soda, and salt. Sift into wet ingredients (dough will be fairly stiff). Stir in chocolate chips and nuts.

Drop by rounded tablespoonfuls onto ungreased cookie sheets.

Bake 8 to 10 minutes in 375° F oven or until light brown underneath. Cool slightly. Place cookies on wire rack to cool completely. Keep these cookies refrigerated and they will remain crunchy. Alternately, they may be frozen and defrosted one at a time in the microwave oven for about 15 seconds on high power.

Recipe from Splendid Low-Carbing for Life, *by best-selling cookbook author, Jennifer Eloff (www.low-carb.us). Used by permission.*

JENNIFER'S HELPFUL HINTS:
I made these cookies with ½ teaspoon salt and they were wonderful, in my opinion however, it is possible to reduce the salt by half, if desired.

_____

Netrition.com sells sugar-free chocolate chips by Sensato. They taste good, however, they are sweetened with maltitol, which may cause digestive upset. Carb Smart sells sugar-free chocolate chips without sugar alcohols. See Sources. Some people use a Lindt, Extra Fine Dark Chocolate bar (70% or 85% cocoa) chopped into small chunks instead of chips. Lindt's bars are low sugar, but not sugar-free. These cookies will definitely be affected by the quality of the chocolate chips used.

MAKES 52 COOKIES.

Per cookie—Net carbohydrate: 0.9 grams (1.59 grams with Splenda granular); Protein: 3.1 grams; Fiber: 2.8 grams; Fat: 8.5 grams; Calories: 101

Total weight: 37½ ounces or 1065 grams

Weight per cookie: ¾ ounces or 20.5 grams

Preparation time: active; 20 minutes; 30 minutes total

Favorite Chocolate Chip Cookies p. 41

Chocolate Chips

Adding liquid to melted chocolate is a big no-no. After years of making my chocolate chips with powdered, dry sweetener, I hit on a better solution. It lets me use one of the zero-carb liquids as the primary sweetener without causing the chocolate to seize and turn into a hard, dry lump.

1 teaspoon no-trans-fat shortening, such as Spectrum
High-intensity liquid sweetener equal to ½ cup sugar
A few grains of fine salt
4 ounces unsweetened chocolate, chopped

Line a baking sheet with parchment, waxed paper, or foil and place in the refrigerator to chill.

Place liquid sweetener and salt in a small saucepan. Add shortening and place over very low heat until shortening melts. Cook and stir for 1 minute more to let the liquid evaporate. Stir in chocolate and continue to stir until almost smooth. Remove from heat and let cool, stirring frequently, until it is about 80° F. (The slow cooling tempers the chocolate so it is smooth and shiny.) Pour it out on the chilled sheet pan and tilt the pan to spread the chocolate to a thickness of about ⅜ inch. Return pan to refrigerator until chocolate is cold. Peel off the paper or foil and chop into chips. Store away from heat in a covered container.

MAKES 1 CUP OR 8 SERVINGS OF 2 TABLESPOONS EACH.

Per serving—Net carbohydrate:
1.9 grams; Protein:1.9 grams; Fiber: 2.4 grams; Fat: 8.1 grams;
77 Calories:

Total weight: 4 ounces

Weight per serving: ½ ounce

Preparation time: 10 minutes active; 20 minutes total

VARIATION:
Mix in chopped nuts, coconut, or chopped, dried cranberries and drop by teaspoonfuls to make nut and/or fruit clusters. Pour melted chocolate into candy bar molds to make sugar-free chocolate bars.

NOTE:
The combination of sucralose and chocolate can be bitter. Adding a small amount of another sweetener gives a more natural sweet taste. Acesulfame K works well with sucralose to eliminate the problem. See Sources for brand names.

TIP:
Salty is the opposite of bitter. If your coffee is bitter, add a little salt. It also takes away some of the bitterness in chocolate. Use only fine salt so chocolate won't be grainy.

Creole Gumbo

6.1 net carbs

Cheddar Cheese Muffin with Butter

3 net carbs

Lemon Frozen Yogurt

3.5 net carbs

Almond Crisp Cookies (p. 305)

0.6 net carbs in 3 cookies

Menu total: 13.2 net carbs

N O T E :
Filé is the dried and ground young leaves of the sassafras tree. It has a mild, sweet flavor similar to thyme. It will become stringy and tough if boiled, so add it after the pot is removed from the heat.

———————

Gumbo may contain whatever meats and seafoods are fresh and available: shrimp, crab, oysters, crawfish, red snapper, turtle, and alligator. It often includes andouille sausage, tasso ham, and chicken, but it will always have the trio of aromatic vegetables so essential to the regional cuisines that it is called "the trinity:" onion, bell pepper, and celery.

Creole Gumbo

Gumbo is the perfect metaphor for New Orleans: a rich, steamy, spicy, mélange of diverse ingredients that combine into an experience that is unique to this place, a place that feels distinctly foreign, while at the same time epitomizing the melting pot that is America. French, Italian, Native American, Creole, Cajun, and African—all share a part in the history of the Louisiana bayou region, intersecting, interacting, and blending into a one-of-a-kind, savory stew.

A traditional gumbo starts with a dark roux made of flour and fat. Most recipes use either okra or filé powder to further thicken the stew; I used both in order to get the rich, thick texture of an authentic gumbo without using a floury roux.

Gumbo would normally be served over rice. I opted to keep the carb count as low as possible, but it could be served over my **Faux Rice**, *p. 284, made from Mexican-style hominy for only 2 more net carbs.*

½ pound of raw, shell-on shrimp (small or medium)
4½ cups of water or chicken broth
1 Turkish bay leaf
¼ cup cooking oil or bacon fat, more or less as needed
1 pound of chicken pieces, including skin and bones
2 teaspoons salt, divided
1 teaspoon of cayenne pepper
1 teaspoon black pepper
1 cup chopped onion (5½ ounces)
2/3 cup chopped red or green bell pepper (4 ounces)
3 cups fresh or thawed frozen okra, rinsed, trimmed, and sliced (10 ounces)
2/3 cup celery, chopped (1½ ounces)
2 garlic cloves, peeled and minced (2 teaspoons or ¼ ounce)
2 cups fresh, chopped tomatoes or one 14½-ounce can
10 ounces andouille or other spicy, smoked sausage, sliced
6 ounces ham, cubed (1¼ cups)
3 green onions, green tops only, chopped
3 tablespoons fresh parsley, chopped
Filé powder to taste

Peel shrimp. Put shells in a large stockpot and add water or broth, 1 teaspoon salt (omit salt if using canned broth), and bay leaf and bring to a boil. Reduce heat, cover, and simmer while preparing chicken.

Mix together the additional 1 teaspoon of salt and the cayenne and black pepper. Heat fat in a skillet. Coat chicken with some of salt and pepper mixture and brown on all sides in the hot fat. Add chicken to the stock pot. Reduce heat to low, cover pot, and simmer for 30 minutes.

Meanwhile, sauté onion, bell pepper, and celery in the fat left in the skillet until softened, about 5 minutes. Add garlic and sauté for a minute or two longer. Remove vegetables with a slotted spoon. Put half the okra in the skillet, turn the heat to low, and cook and stir until it starts to brown, about 10 minutes, adding more fat if needed. Add the rest of the okra, increase the heat to medium-high, and continue to cook and stir, uncovered, until the first okra is well browned but the second batch is still partly green.

Remove chicken from pot, remove meat from bones, and chop into bite-sized pieces. Discard skin and bones. Remove shrimp shells with a slotted spoon and discard. Return the chicken meat to the pot. Add sautéed vegetables, okra, and tomatoes. Add sausage and ham and any remaining salt and pepper mixture. Cover and simmer for 15 minutes. Just before serving, sauté shrimp in remaining fat in skillet. Add shrimp, green onions, and parsley to gumbo. Remove from heat and stir in filé powder or pass it at the table to be added to individual bowls. The gumbo will thicken after a few minutes.

MAKES 10½ CUPS OR 7 SERVINGS OF 1½ CUPS.

Per serving—Net carbohydrate: 6.1 grams; Protein: 27.6 grams; Fiber: 3 grams; Fat: 23.5 grams; Calories: 361

Total weight: 5 pounds 5 ounces or 2.4 kilograms

Weight per serving: 12 ounces or 340 grams

Preparation time: 1 hour active; 1 hour 15 minutes total

Creole Gumbo

Cheddar Cheese Muffins

This muffin recipe comes from my friend Jennifer Eloff, who says they are lovely served warm with sugar-free jam.

Note: *You will need two batches of **Biskmix,** to make these muffins.*

MAKES 12 MUFFINS.

Per serving—Net carbohydrate: 3 grams (3.9 grams with Splenda Granular); Protein: 14 grams; Fiber: 2 grams; Fat: 27.8 grams; Calories: 317

Total weight: 26 ounces or 736 grams

Weight per serving: 2¼ ounces or 61 grams

Preparation time: 15 minutes active; 30 minutes total

2 eggs
3¾ cup (15 ½ ounces or 440 grams) Biskmix, p. 288
1²/3 cups (3 ½ ounces or 100 grams) grated Cheddar cheese, divided
Sugar substitute equal to ½ cup sugar
½ cup water
¼ cup heavy cream
3 tablespoons olive oil

In large bowl, whisk eggs. Stir in **Biskmix,** 1 cup Cheddar cheese, sugar substitute, water, cream, and olive oil. Fill 12 greased muffin cups ¾ full. Sprinkle top of dough with remaining ⅓ cup Cheddar cheese.

Bake in 400º F oven 15 to 17 minutes. Remove from pan immediately. Serve warm. Microwave day-old muffins for 15 seconds.

Recipe from *Splendid Low-Carbing for Life, Vol. 2,* by best selling cookbook author, Jennifer Eloff (www.low-carb.us). Used by permission.

Cheddar Cheese Muffin

Lemon Frozen Yogurt

I really love this light, refreshing, and healthful frozen dessert, loaded with calcium and vitamin C. Another plus, the microbes in the live culture will have eaten some of the sugar in the yogurt, lowering the carb count considerably.

3 cups (one 24-ounce container) plain, whole milk, Greek-style yogurt, such as Fage or Greek Gods brand

2 teaspoons grated lemon zest (amount from one 5-ounce lemon)

¼ cup fresh lemon juice (amount from one 5-ounce lemon)

½ cup (56 grams or about 2 ounces) powdered erythritol

½ cup (104 grams or 3.6 ounces) polydextrose (plain, not with sweetener added)

Sugar substitute equal to 3 tablespoons sugar, such as liquid sucralose or stevia, or to taste

2 tablespoons sugar-free honey (with xylitol, preferred), such as Nature's Hollow brand

3/8 teaspoon powdered citric acid, such as Fruit-Fresh

¼ teaspoon lemon extract

Pinch salt

Pre-freeze the canister if using a counter-top machine or have ice and kosher salt ready for tub-style machine. Whisk ingredients together. Taste mixture and add more sweetener or more citric acid or Fruit-Fresh to adjust tartness if needed. Chill mixture for 1 hour. Freeze in ice cream maker according to manufacturer's instructions. Scrape into shallow container and place parchment, waxed paper, or plastic wrap directly on top of yogurt and then cover with a tight-fitting lid or a piece of foil. Place in freezer to ripen for an hour before serving. After longer storage, remove from freezer and place in refrigerator to soften before serving; time will vary depending on depth of yogurt, size of container, and temperature of refrigerator, but it may take an hour or so to reach the proper consistency.

TIP: Citric acid powder can be purchased at a pharmacy or in some specialty stores. You may also use Ball Fruit-Fresh, which is used to prevent fruit from darkening (it will add a tiny amount of sugar to the total). It can be found on the aisle with home-canning and jam-making supplies. Another option is to crush a vitamin C tablet and use as a powder. Check amount by tasting the mixture.

MAKES 1 QUART OR 8 SERVINGS OF ½ CUP.

Per serving—Net carbohydrate: 3.5 grams (count excludes 3 grams eaten by the yogurt cultures and 8 grams of sugar alcohol); Protein: 3.4 grams; Fiber: 11.2 grams; Fat: 3 grams; Calories: 80

Total weight: 1 pound 13 ounces or 820 grams

Weight per serving: 4 ounces or 117 grams

Preparation time: 10 minutes active, plus chilling and freezing time

Poached Chicken with Coconut Curry Sauce

Chicken, 0 net carbs;
sauce, 2.1 net carbs

Hominy *Faux* Rice (p. 284)

Chayote Chutney

1.4 net carbs

Broccolini Salad

4.7 net carbs

Italian Cream Soda (p. 213)

0.8 net carbs

Menu total: 13 net carbs

Poached Chicken with Coconut Curry Sauce

Poached Chicken, p. 277
Coconut Curry Sauce, p. 48

Divide **Poached Chicken** into 4 portions. Top each with ¼ cup of **Coconut Curry Sauce**. Serve hot over **Hominy *Faux* Rice,** p. 284, with **Chayote Chutney**, p. 50, on the side.

MAKES 4 SERVINGS OF ABOUT 1 CUP EACH.

Per serving (chicken and sauce only)—Net carbohydrate: 2.1 grams; Protein: 33.8 grams; Fiber: 0.6 grams; Fat: 12 grams; Calories: 268

Total weight: 16¾ ounces or 473 grams

Weight per serving: 4 ounces or 118 grams

Preparation time: 20 minutes active and 50 minutes total

Poached Chicken with Coconut Curry Sauce

Coconut Curry Sauce

A delicious way to add the health benefits of coconut and curry to your diet.

1 cup (8 ounces) canned coconut milk

1 tablespoon yellow curry powder

Sugar substitute equal to 1 tablespoon sugar

¼ teaspoon salt

¼ teaspoon crushed red pepper flakes or Sriachi hot sauce to taste

2 teaspoons lime juice

1 tablespoon shredded, fresh Thai basil

Bring the coconut milk and curry powder to a boil in a small saucepan. Simmer, while stirring, for 4 minutes. Add the other ingredients and simmer for 1 minute more. Serve over **Poached Chicken,** p. 277, or **Roast Lamb,** p. 244.

MAKES ABOUT 1 CUP OR 4 SERVINGS
¼ CUP EACH.

Per serving—Net carbohydrate: 2.1 grams; Protein: 1 gram; Fiber: 0.6 grams; Fat: 8.6 grams; Calories: 97

Total weight: 7½ ounces or 214 grams

Weight per serving: 2 ounces or 53.5 grams

Preparation time: 15 minutes active and total

Light coconut milk has been thinned with water. If you want thin coconut milk, it is more economical to buy the real thing and add water to it.

Chayote Chutney

Chayote was a staple food for the Aztec and Mayans. It has dozens of names around the world: it is called cristophene in France, mirliton in New Orleans, choco in Australia, zucca cenetaria in Italy, xuxu in Brazil, and chow chow in India. Another common name is vegetable pear. It is a hard, green, pear-shaped summer squash with a puckered seam along the bottom. The whole fruit is edible, but the seed has a different texture from the flesh, and the peel can be tough. To make it taste like soft-cooked apples, remove the seed, peel the fruit, and cook until tender before adding any acid, such as lemon juice.

A giant sculpture of a chayote squash adorns the dining room of the elegant Chayote's restaurant in San Juan, Puerto Rico. Chayote stuffed with prosciutto is one of many dishes on the menu that celebrates this staple of Caribbean cuisine.

Here's a zesty, crunchy, fruit condiment to use like pickle relish or to add some spark to grilled or roasted meats and curry dishes.

1 tablespoon coconut or peanut oil
¼ cup (1½ ounces) finely chopped onion (about ¼ of an 6-ounce onion)
¼ teaspoon red pepper flakes
3 tablespoon cider vinegar
1¼ cup (5 ounces) finely diced chayote squash
2 tablespoons (¼ ounce) chopped **Dried Cranberries** (p. 12)
1/8 teaspoon grated lemon zest
2 teaspoons whole mustard seed
1 ounce (about ¼ cup) fresh ginger root, peeled and finely chopped
6 tablespoons water, more if needed
Sugar substitute equal to ½ cup sugar
Pinch of salt

Heat oil in a small saucepan and cook onion until softened. Add red pepper flakes and cook for a minute longer. Add other ingredients and simmer for 15 minutes, stirring occasionally. Add more water if needed. Let stand for 15 minutes. Store in refrigerator. Serve at room temperature.

MAKES 10 SERVINGS OF 2 TABLESPOONS.

Per serving—Net carbohydrate: 1.5 grams; Protein: 0.4 grams; Fiber: 1.6 grams; Fat: 1.6 grams; Calories: 25

Total weight: 9¼ ounces or 263 grams

Weight per serving: 1 ounce or 26 grams

Preparation time: 10 minutes active (if ingredients are already chopped); 40 minutes total

Broccolini Salad

Crisp vegetables combine to make a sprightly chopped salad that will compliment any Asian menu. If you can find them, the kelp noodles add textural excitement.

3 ounces red bell pepper (1/3 cup, chopped)

4 ounces celery (3 stalks or 1 cup, cut up)

1 bunch broccolini (8 ounces)

2 teaspoons rice wine vinegar

Sugar substitute equal to ½ teaspoon sugar

½ teaspoon salt

½ teaspoon chili oil or to taste

1 teaspoon sugar-free soy sauce, such as Kikkoman

3 teaspoons sesame oil

2 tablespoons extra virgin olive oil

1 cup kelp noodles, rinsed and cut into 3-inch pieces (optional)

Remove seeds and membranes from pepper and remove strings from celery. Dice pepper and celery into ½-inch pieces. Reserve. Bring a large pot of water to boil over high heat.

Cut off tops of broccolini and separate into small florets. Chop stems into ½-inch pieces. Blanch both the stems and the florets in rapidly boiling water for 1 minute. Drain and place in a bowl of cold water to stop the cooking. Drain and set aside.

Place the rice-wine vinegar, sweetener, salt, chili oil, soy sauce, sesame oil, and olive oil in a large bowl and whisk until blended and thickened. Taste, and adjust seasonings with additional salt, chili oil, or sweetener to taste. Add celery, red pepper, cooled broccolini, and kelp noodles, if using, and toss until well coated. Refrigerate for 1 hour.

MAKES 4 SERVINGS OF 1 CUP.

Per serving—Net carbohydrate: 4.7 grams; Protein: 2.4 grams; Fiber: 1.5 grams; Fat: 11 grams; Calories: 128

Total weight: 1 pound 2½ ounces or 525 grams

Weight per serving: 4½ ounces or 128 grams

Preparation time: 25 minutes active; 1 hour 25 minutes including chilling time

Kelp noodles are made of kelp and sodium alginate, a salt derived from brown seaweed. These glossy, transparent noodles have a distinctive crunch, a neutral taste, no calories, no fat, and a net carbohydrate count of zero, but they are rich in vitamins and trace minerals, such as calcium, iron, vitamin K, and iodine. They can be rinsed and eaten raw straight out of the package without cooking.

Kelp Noodles stay fresh in the refrigerator for up to six months or at room temperature for a week. After opening the package, store them in water to prevent dehydration. They can be found with the Korean foods in some groceries or in stores that specialize in Asian foods. They can be ordered from the Sea Tangle Noodle Company in San Diego. (See Sources.)

Easy Chili

Easy Chili
4.5 net carbs for 1 cup

Cheese Quesadilla
3.1 net carbs

Mexican Cole Slaw (CAROLINA COLESLAW (p. 112.)
3.8 net carbs

Fruit Gelatin
0 net carbs

Menu total: 11.4 net carbs

For a few more carbs you can add 1 cup Mexican-style hominy (see p. 111) to your chili. (It will add 1.3 net grams of carbohydrate per serving.)

Foods packed in glass would be preferable to those in metal cans, especially cans with plastic liners, although they are often more expensive, and some things don't come that way yet. Frozen is also a good alternative to fresh.

Here's the solution for an easy meal when you're short on time and energy. This has been one of the most popular recipes from my first book, Carb Wars; Sugar is the New Fat.

> 1 pound lean ground beef or buffalo
> 1 cup water or broth (8 ounces)
> 1 (14.5-ounce) can enchilada sauce, mild, medium, or hot
> 2 cups or 16 ounces Pomi Chopped Tomatoes or 1 (14.5-ounce) can sugar-free, chopped tomatoes, including liquid*
> Salt, pepper, and chili powder (optional)

Brown ground meat in a large saucepan and drain off fat. Add water or broth, enchilada sauce, and tomatoes with their liquid to the saucepan. Simmer for 30 minutes. Taste and add salt, pepper, and chili powder, if desired. Serve with shredded Cheddar cheese, chopped green onion or chives, and sour cream or **Crème Fraîche** (p. 297) for topping, if desired.

> **MAKES 6 SERVINGS** of 1 cup each as side dish, 4 servings of 1½ cups as main dish
>
> Per serving of 1 cup—Net carbohydrate: 4.5 grams; Protein: 15.3 grams; Fiber: 2.9 grams; Fat: 9.2 grams; Calories: 173
>
> Total weight: 2 pounds 14 ounces or 852 grams
>
> Weight per serving: 8 ounces or 226 grams for 6 servings, 12 ounces or 340 grams for 4 servings
>
> Preparation time: 5 minutes active, 40 minutes total

* Many brands of canned tomatoes contain added sugar. (The average used by the USDA database is 9 grams of carbohydrate and 2 grams of fiber for a net of 7 grams in ½ cup.) Read the labels and choose one that comes out to 3 or fewer net carbs per ½ cup. Better yet, use Pomì tomatoes. They are imported from Italy and have a net carb count of one gram.

Quesadillas

Quesadillas are Mexican grilled cheese sandwiches, made with tortillas instead of bread. They make a perfect side dish to accompany a bowl of soup or scrambled eggs. They also make a quick snack. Small ones can be served as appetizers.

    2 low-carb tortillas (about 6 inches or 36 grams)
    ¼ cup (1 ounce) shredded Monterey Jack or Cheddar cheese
    1 tablespoon chopped, green chilies from a jar or can, optional
    1 teaspoon oil for frying

Place one tortilla on a microwaveable dish and cover with the cheese. Sprinkle with the optional chilies, if using, and place a second tortilla on top. Heat in the microwave until the cheese is melted and the tortillas stick together, about 1 minute on high. Cut the tortilla sandwich into six wedges. Fry the wedges in oil in a skillet until crisp and brown, then turn and fry the other side, about 1½ to 2 minutes total.

MAKES 2 SERVINGS OF 3 WEDGES EACH.

Per serving—Net carbohydrate: 3.1 grams; Protein: 8.5 grams; Fiber: 7 grams; Fat: 8.5 grams; Calories: 122

Total weight: 3½ ounces or 97 grams

Weight per serving: 1¾ ounces or 48.5 grams

Preparation time: 5 minutes active; 6 or 7 minutes total

Easy Chili and Quesadillas

Fruit Gelatin

Purchased, ready-to-eat gelatin desserts have fewer carbohydrates than the kind you make at home from a boxed powder, which contains sugar (maltodextrin) as a bulking agent. Making your own gelatin dessert is better yet, since most prepared jelled desserts contain aspartame.

Sugar-free Jell-O contains aspartame, one of the most controversial sugar substitutes. When you make your own gelatin dessert with plain gelatin, you can choose your sweetener.

2 envelopes (1 tablespoon or 7 grams each) of plain gelatin powder
½ cup cold water
2 cups boiling water
1 envelope of unsweetened Kool-aid, any flavor
1½ cups ice water
Sugar substitute equal to 1 cup sugar (recipe was tested with 24 drops of EZ-Sweetz liquid sucralose)
Sugar-free jam or fruit and **Whipped Cream**, p. 312, for garnish, optional

Stir gelatin powder into cold water and let stand for about 5 minutes until softened. Add boiling water and Kool-aid powder and stir until gelatin is dissolved. Add ice water and sweetener. Pour into mold or dishes. Refrigerate until firm, about 1½ hours. Garnish with a dab of sugar-free jam or a bit of sliced fruit and top with **Whipped Cream**, if desired.

MAKES 8 SERVINGS OF ½ CUP

Per serving—Net carbohydrate: 0 grams; Protein: 2 grams; Fiber: 0 grams; Fat: 0 grams; Calories: 9.5

Total weight: 2 pounds 3¼ ounces or 1 kilogram

Weight per serving: 4 ounces or 119 grams

Preparation time: 5 minutes active, 1 hour and 35 minutes total

Strawberry Rhubarb Parfait

Gelatin recipe, above, made with strawberry-flavored Kool-aid, divided
1 cup plain, Greek-style yogurt
Sugar substitute equal to 2 teaspoons of sugar or to taste
¾ cup **Rhubarb Sauce**, p. 162
Whipped Cream, p. 312, for garnish, optional

Make gelatin recipe above and let mixture cool. Place 1 cup of yogurt in a small bowl. Add 1 cup of the cooled but still liquid gelatin mixture and the additional sugar substitute and whisk until smooth. Divide yogurt mixture into 5 parfait glasses. Refrigerate until set, about 1½ hours. Spread 1 tablespoon **Rhubarb Sauce** over yogurt layer and pour remaining gelatin mixture over rhubarb. Refrigerate until set, about 1 more hour. Spoon a second tablespoon of **Rhubarb Sauce** on each parfait and garnish with a dollop of **Whipped Cream** if desired.

For an attractive presentation, use stemmed glasses. Make a thick pad over one side of a loaf pan with a folded kitchen towel and wrap the stems with more towels. Lean the glasses at an angle in the pan with the tops braced against the side of the refrigerator until the first layer sets up.

MAKES 5 SERVINGS OF 1 CUP EACH.

Per serving—Net carbohydrate: 1.8 grams (excluding sugar eaten by the yogurt culture); Protein: 4.3 grams; Fiber: 0.6 grams; Fat: 4.5 grams; Calories: 69

Total weight: 2 pounds 11¼ ounces or 1.2 kilograms

Weight per serving: 8½ ounces or 245 grams

Preparation time: 10 minutes active, 2 hours and 40 minutes total

Strawberry Rhubarb Parfait

Mystic Pizzas

4.2 net carbs

Mixed Green Salad
with Red Wine
Vinaigrette

1.4 net carbs

Caramel Pecan
Sundaes

4.7 grams

Menu total: 10.3 net carbs

Mystic Pizzas

*I can't pinpoint the creative genius who came up with an egg-
and-cheese pizza crust, but many variations have been circulating online in the low-carb community. Whoever you are, take
a bow!*

*My version includes an easy sauce and my favorite toppings. I
cut the crust into portions before assembling the pizza so every
slice has crispy, brown edges. It is amazing how much like real
pizza this is.*

CRUST:
  4 ounces cream cheese, softened at room temperature for 30 minutes
  2 large eggs
  2 egg whites (4 tablespoons)
  Pinch of black or cayenne pepper
  Sugar substitute equal to ½ teaspoon sugar
  ¼ cup (1 ounce) grated Parmesan cheese
  1 cup (4 ounces) shredded mozzarella cheese or Italian cheese blend
  2 tablespoons almond flour for pan

Preheat oven to 375° F and grease a 9- by 13-inch baking
dish or pan and a large baking sheet.

Beat cream cheese with an electric mixer until smooth. Beat
in eggs one at a time. Beat in egg whites, pepper, and sugar
substitute. Add mozzarella and Parmesan cheese and stir
until moistened. Sprinkle almond flour evenly in baking
pan. Pour egg and cheese mixture over almond flour and tilt
pan or use a spatula to spread evenly. Bake crust in preheated oven for about 25 minutes or until browned. Use a
wide spatula to loosen crust from pan and let cool for a few
minutes. Cut into 6 pieces and place on baking sheet, leaving space between slices.

PIZZA SAUCE:

    1 (8-ounce) can tomato sauce without added sugar

    2 garlic cloves (1/8-ounce each), peeled and minced (2 teaspoons)

    ½ teaspoon dried oregano

    ¼ teaspoon dried basil

    Ground black pepper to taste

Mix together. Recipe makes about 1 cup. (There will be extra sauce.)

PIZZAS:

    1 recipe of pizza **Crust**

    1/3 cup **Pizza Sauce** (5 to 6 tablespoons), from recipe above

    1½ cups (6 ounces) mozzarella cheese

    ¼ cup (1 ounce) Parmesan cheese, shredded or grated

    ¼ cup (1½ ounces) thinly sliced onion

    ¼ cup (1 ounce) thinly sliced red or green bell pepper

    ½ cup (2 ounces) sliced black olives

    2 ounces sliced pepperoni (about 28 slices)

TO MAKE PIZZAS:

Spread pizza sauce on crusts, leaving a ⅜-inch edge. Scatter onions, peppers, and olives over sauce. Top with cheeses. Microwave pepperoni on paper toweling for 30 to 40 seconds to render some of the grease, but do not let it become crisp. Distribute pepperoni slices evenly over pizzas. Bake at 375° F for about 15 to 20 minutes or until brown and cheese is bubbly.

MAKES 6 SERVINGS.

Per serving—Net carbohydrate: 4.2 grams; Protein: 21.2 grams; Fiber: 1 grams; Fat: 28.4 grams; Calories: 359

Total weight: 1 pound 8¾ ounces or 703 grams

Weight per serving: 4 ounces or 114 grams

Preparation time: 25 minutes active; 65 minutes total

TIPS:

A clear glass baking dish will make it easier to judge when the crust is brown.

————

The volume of grated cheese may change depending on whether it is compacted or fluffy, so I have given the amount in both cups and ounces.

Mixed Green Salad with Red Wine Vinaigrette

MAKES 4 SERVINGS OF 2 CUPS EACH.

Per serving with vinaigrette—Net carbohydrate: 1.4 grams; Protein: 0.7 grams; Fiber: 0.7 grams; Fat: 10 grams; Calories: 101

Total weight: 11½ ounces or 82 grams for salad and vinaigrette

Weight per serving: 2¾ ounces or 20 grams for salad and vinaigrette

Preparation time: 5 minutes active and total

8 cups (8 ounces) mixed salad greens, washed and dried
Red Wine Vinaigrette, p. 300
Coarse salt and freshly ground pepper to taste

Toss greens with dressing. Serve on chilled plates. Sprinkle with salt and pepper.

Caramel Pecan Sundaes

FOR EACH SERVING:
Put one scoop (½ cup) **French Vanilla ice Cream,** p. 308, in a serving dish. Top with 2 tablespoons **Caramel Sauce,** opposite, and 2 tablespoons chopped, toasted pecans.

NOTE:
I tested the **Caramel Sauce** recipe with Diabetisweet Brown for the caramel taste and because I needed something granular to mix with the poly-d to keep it from clumping. Diabetisweet contains isomalt, a sugar alcohol, and acesulfame potassium (Ace-K). You may substitute regular Diabetisweet or another granular sweetener, since the caramel syrup also provides caramel flavor. If you use Splenda Granular, it will add about 3 grams of carbohydrate to the total recipe.

MAKES 1 SERVING.

Per serving—Net carbohydrate: 4.7 net grams; Protein: 5.2 grams; Fiber: 19 grams; Fat: 38.2 grams; Calories: 389

Weight per serving: 4.4 ounces or 125 grams

Preparation time: 5 minutes active and total

Caramel Sauce

Everyone, including me, hates having to special order unusual ingredients, but, let's face it, caramel is sugar. To make it without sugar, we have to resort to something not normally used for the purpose. Many ingredients, like polydextrose and erythritol, that are common in foods we buy, are not readily accessible to the home cook and must be ordered. Hopefully, if we create a demand for a product, it will become more available and not seem so exotic.

½ cup (3¼ ounces or 92 grams) of polydextrose

2 tablespoons of caramel-flavored sugar-free syrup, such as DaVinci or Torani

2 tablespoons water

2 tablespoons brown sugar replacement, such as Diabetisweet Brown, Just Like Sugar Brown, or LC Sweet Brown

1 teaspoon powdered erythritol, optional

A pinch of salt

1½ tablespoons of butter, cut into pieces or part coconut oil

1/3 cup heavy cream

Mix polydextrose, brown sugar replacement, and salt together until <u>thoroughly</u> blended. Heat water and caramel syrup in medium-size bowl in microwave until hot. Stir in polydextrose mixture. Microwave on high for 4 to 5 minutes until dissolved and it becomes a thick, clear syrup. You will see a film on top that wrinkles when you move the bowl after the first minute or two. When all the water is evaporated and the bubbles become big and stretchy, add the erythritol, if using, and the butter and stir until melted. Whisk in the cream. Serve warm or at room temperature as a sauce for ice cream or desserts.

MAKES ¾ CUP OR 6 SERVINGS OF 2 TABLESPOONS EACH.

Per serving—Net carbohydrate: 1.8 grams; Protein: 0.3 grams; Fiber: 13.4 grams; Fat: 11 grams; Calories: 88

Total weight: 7¾ ounces or 222 grams

Weight per serving: 1⅓ ounces or 37 grams

Preparation time: 8 minutes active; 15 total

POLYTEXTROSE AND INULIN:

Polydextrose (also called poly-d, polyD, polyd, or PDX) is made up of chains of glucose molecules. Inulin is similar, but it is made of long chains of fructose molecules. (Ordinary table sugar, sucrose, is half glucose and half fructose.) Both are essentially indigestible by human enzymes and so are counted as fiber. They are, however, broken down into butyrates, a kind of short- chain fatty acid, by the bacteria that live in the digestive tract. (Because of this fat, there will be a few calories listed on nutrition panels for the fiber.)

Both poly-d and inulin are pre-bioic, meaning they selectively feed the friendly microbes and inhibit the harmful ones. Poly-d is most often made from corn and is less expensive than inulin, which is extracted from chicory root or Jerusalem artichokes. Whenever you see an ad for a product that claims to contain "healthful fiber," chances are that fiber is polydextrose or inulin.

Carnitas Soup with Tomatillo Salsa, Tortilla Strips, and Toppings

5.6 net carbs, including all condiments

Fresh Fruit Platter

6.1 net carbs

Menu total: 11.7 net carbs

I estimated the amount of each item used per person, but you should prepare extra "just in case" and so the bowls won't look skimpy for the last guests.

Carnitas Soup

I often serve this when I host a meeting or workshop at my house. I make tacos for dinner the night before the event and put the extra **Carnitas** *back into the pot with the cooking liquid and refrigerate it overnight. Everything but the avocado can be prepped ahead of time. I set it up buffet-style, so everyone can choose the add-ins they like. A platter of chilled fruit completes the meal.*

SOUP:

4 cups **Carnitas** from recipe on p. 276.

8 cups cooking liquid from **Carnitas**, use part chicken broth if desired

ADD-INS AND TOPPINGS:

1 cup (5.2 ounces or 149 grams) chopped red bell pepper (2 tablespoons per serving)

1 cup (3.5 ounces or 100 grams) chopped green onion, green and white (2 tablespoons per serving)

2 cups (5 ounces or 144 grams) shredded lettuce

2 ripe Hass avocados (7-ounces each, as purchased, 9.6 ounces for 2, peeled and seeded), diced

Lemon wedge (juice only, to squeeze over avocados to prevent darkening)

1 cup (6 ounces or 180 grams) chopped fresh tomato (2 tablespoons per serving)

1/3 cup (2.6 ounces or 74 grams) sliced black olives (2 teaspoons per serving)

1/3 cup (1½ ounces or 46 grams) diced, canned chilies, mild and/or hot (2 teaspoons per serving)

1 cup (4 ounces or 113 grams) shredded Monterey Jack cheese (1/4 cup per serving)

½ cup (4 ounces or 115 grams) real, cultured sour cream (1 tablespoon per serving)

1/3 cup (1.8 ounces or 51 grams) hot and/or mild salsa: **Tomatillo Salsa,** p. 10, and/or tomato salsa, fresh or from a jar (2 teaspoons per serving)

3 approximately 6 inch (3.8 ounces for three or 36 grams each) low carb tortillas, cut into strips and fried until crisp

Have ready **Carnitas** recipe from p. 276. Skim fat from reserved cooking liquid and heat on low. Add 4 cups of meat from **Carnitas** to pot and heat through. Set out dishes of vegetables and Jack cheese to be spooned into soup. Serve with sour cream and mild and hot salsas. Ladle soup into large, heated bowls and let guests add any or all of the fresh vegetables and toppings to their individual bowls. Tortilla strips can be added to soup or served on the side like chips.

MAKES 8 SERVINGS OF ABOUT 1½ CUPS SOUP, BEFORE ADDING VEGETABLES AND CONDIMENTS.

Per serving, including all condiments—Net carbohydrate: 5.6 grams (excluding 0.7 grams of sugar eaten by sour cream cultures); Protein: 26 grams; Fiber: 7.4 grams; Fat: 20 grams; Calories: 334

Weight per serving for 3 ounces (½ cup) of carnitas plus 1 cup broth: 10½ ounces or 298 grams; Weight per serving if all toppings and condiments are used: 1 pound and ½ ounce or 469 grams

Preparation time: 15 minutes active; 20 minutes total, not counting time to chop vegetables or prepare carnitas.

SOUR CREAM:
It can be difficult to find sour cream made from just cream. Most commercial brands have 2 grams of carbohydrate per tablespoon because they include milk or skim milk and thickeners. **Crème Fraîche**, p. 297, is a good alternative, but expensive if purchased. Plain yogurt is another option—the label may say 11 or 12 grams per cup, but if it has live cultures, most of the sugar will have been converted into lactic acid. (The same holds true for sour cream, if you can find one that contains live cultures.)

See Sources for Daisy brand sour cream.

Fresh Fruit Platter

The nutrition counts below are based on a combination of sliced cantaloupe and whole fresh strawberries, but raspberries, star fruit, papaya, blackberries, blueberries, cherries, and other melons are also possible choices. (Casaba melon is slightly lower in carbs than cantaloupe; honeydew is a little higher.) Black grapes are another option—see p. 270 for a way to reduce their carb count.

10 ounces (288 grams or about 2 cups) fresh strawberries with caps
　　attached
1 small (4¼-inch diameter, 441 gram or about 1 pound) ripe cantaloupe
Mint leaves for garnish

Rinse and drain berries. Peel cantaloupe and remove seeds; cut into 16 thin wedges. Arrange fruit attractively on serving plate, garnish with fresh mint if desired, and chill.

MAKES 8 SERVINGS.

Per serving—Net carbohydrate: 6.1 grams; Protein: 0.7 grams; Fiber: 1.2 grams; Fat: 0.1 grams; Calories: 30

Total weight: 1¾ pounds or 478 grams

Weight per serving: 3¾ ounces or 60 grams

Preparation time: 10 minutes active and total

Fresh Fruit Platter

Ham and Chana Dal Soup

14.6 net carbs

Whole Grain Bread (p. 290) and Butter

1 slice from 2-loaf recipe with flax, 1.9 net carbs

Fresh Raspberries with Cream

Raspberries, 3.4 net grams; cream, 1.6 net carbs

Total menu: 21.8 net carbs

MAKES 8 CUPS OR 6 SERVINGS OF 1¹⁄₃ CUPS.

Per serving—Net carbohydrate: 14.6 grams; Protein: 34.2 grams; Fiber: 5.5 grams; Fat: 11.3 grams; Calories: 327

Total weight: 4 pounds 8½ ounces or 2044 grams

Weight per serving: 12 ounces or 341 grams

Preparation time: 25 minutes active; approximately 1 hour and 25 minutes total

Ham and Chana Dal Soup

This makes a big pot of soup, but luckily, it's even better the next day (and the next).

Note: Chana dal is not low in carbs, but it is very low on the glycemic index and some people find it useful, so I included a couple of recipes for those who might want to try it. Read more about it on p. 66.

1 cup (8 ounces) chana dal, rinsed and picked over (weight may vary from 7 to 9 ounces depending on size of beans)
1 ham bone with at least a pound of meat or 3 pounds of meaty, smoked ham shanks
Water to cover meat
½ cup (2½ ounces) finely chopped onion
2 tablespoons butter
Salt, if needed
Fresh black pepper to taste

Cover the meat with water in a deep pot and simmer for 1 hour or until very tender. Remove meat from bones and cut into pieces. Discard bones, skin, and gristle. Strain the cooking liquid. Measure 6 cups and return to the pot along with the meat. Skim off the fat (or you can refrigerate the broth until the fat solidifies and lift it off after it is cold). Return the meat to cooking liquid, add the beans, and simmer, covered, for about an hour or until the beans are tender. The cooking time will vary depending on the size and freshness of the beans. Start checking them after 30 minutes so they don't become mushy.

Meanwhile, melt the butter in a skillet and sauté the onion for 3 or 4 minutes or until softened and slightly browned. When beans are cooked, stir onion and butter into soup and heat through. Add pepper. Taste and adjust the seasoning; salt may not be necessary depending on the saltiness of the ham. Serve in heated bowls.

This is a good way to use up the rest of a ham after the neat slices are gone. You need a ham bone with some meat left on it or you can use a ham hock plus 1 pound of diced ham. Another option is to use 3 pounds of ham shanks, which have more meat than hocks.

NOTES:
Data sources do not agree on the carbohydrate and fiber counts for chana dal. However, there have been a number of studies[71] [72] [73] that confirm that it has a minimal effect on blood sugar levels.

Most ham hocks and shanks have a small amount of sugar. There are a few brands of boneless hams that have no carbs and fewer still that have no carbs but include the bone. (See Sources.) You can make soup with boneless ham, but a lot of the flavor comes from the bone and marrow. A pound of zero-carb, boneless ham, such as Cure 81, plus one ham hock will minimize the sugar if you can't find sugar-free hocks or shanks. Also, check out Canadian bacon to use as ham; sometimes it is sugar free.

It's a miracle food for me now. It keeps my glucose readings so steady and reliable! In fact, last week I ran out of the chana dal I had cooked and in two days' time my glucose readings were all over the chart.

— Alef Grey, a diabetic vegetarian

71   Dilawari, Jang B., et al. "Reduction of postprandial plasma glucose by Bengal gram dal and Rajmah." *The American Journal of Clinical Nutrition,* Vol. 34, Nov 1981.

72   Dilawari, J.B., et al. "Exceptionally low blood glucose response to dried beans." *British Medical Journal,* Vol. 281, Oct 1980.

73   Walker, A.R.P., and B.F. Walker, "Glycaemic Index of South African Foods Determined in Rural Blacks—a Population at Low Risk of Diabetes." *Human Nutrition: Clinical Nutrition,* Vol. 38C, 1984.

Chana Dal

Plain, cooked chana dal can be used anywhere you would normally use beans, lentils, or whole-kernel corn. You can also spice them up for many delicious Indian or Middle Eastern dishes.

1 cup (almost 7 ounces) chana dal (weight varies with size of beans from under 7 ounces to 8 ounces in a cup)
2½ cups water
¼ teaspoon baking soda
Salt to taste

Rinse and pick over beans to remove any debris, or bad beans. Place water in saucepan and heat to boiling. Add beans and baking soda. Reduce heat and simmer for 35 to 45 minutes or until beans are soft. Add salt to taste and serve as a side dish or use in soup or chili.

MAKES 4 SERVINGS OF ½ CUP.

Per serving—Net carbohydrate: 21.1 grams; Protein: 9 grams; Fiber: 8.1 grams; Fat: 2.9 grams; Calories: 171

Total weight: 1½ ounces or 495 grams

Weight per serving: 4⅓ ounces or 124 grams

Preparation time: 5 minutes active, 40 to 50 minutes total

Chana dal are split, baby garbanzo beans. They are not are not a different variety or species, but they have a much lower glycemic index (GI) and load (GL) than garbanzos. Garbanzos have a GL of 8; chana dal's DL is 1! chana dals have a sweet flavor and they taste a bit like creamed corn. They are not low in carbohydrate, but they are digested very slowly so they help stabilize blood sugar.

They have become a diet staple for many vegetarians with diabetes. David Mendosa, www.mendosa.com, is the go-to-guy for everything about chana dal.

Some companies sell yellow split-peas as chana dal. They are not the same. Buy from an Indian store where they will know the difference.

Sally Fallon, author of *Nourishing Traditions*, recommends that garbanzos be soaked before cooking to make them more digestible and to neutralize the phytic acid and enzyme inhibitors they contain. To soak chana dal: Cover with boiling water, add 2 tablespoons of lemon juice, and let stand in a warm place for 24 hours before cooking. Acids prevent the cell walls of plants from breaking down. Baking soda is alkaline, so it does the opposite. The small amount in this recipe makes the beans cook in about one -third the time

Fresh Raspberries with Cream

½ cup fresh raspberries
¼ cup heavy cream
Sugar-free sweetener to taste, optional

Sweeten chilled berries to taste and serve with cream.

MAKE 1 SERVING

Per serving—Net carbohydrate:
5 grams; Protein: 2 grams;
Fiber: 4 grams; Fat: 22.4 grams;
Calories: 237

Total weight: 4¼ ounces or
122 grams

Preparation time: 5 minutes active
and total

Raspberries and Cream

Roasted Red Pepper and Tomato Soup

9.6 net carbs

Cheese Puffs

2 slices, 0.6 net carbs

Peanut Butter Cookies

1.8 net carbs for 2

"Milk" (p. 14)

1.8 net carbs

Menu total: 13.8 net carbs

Roasted Red Pepper and Tomato Soup with Artichoke Tapenade

Dr. Mary Dan Eades is a most remarkable woman. She has written and co-authored dozens of books, including the best-selling Protein Power *book series and* The Six Week Cure for the Middle Aged Middle, *with her husband, Dr. Michael Eades. She co-starred in the cooking series,* CookwoRX, *on PBS and co-authored* The Low-Carb Comfort Food Cookbook *and* Low-Carb Baking and Desserts Cookbook *with Ursula Solom. She is the president of the board and soloist for the Santa Barbara Choral Society, the mother of three, and an extraordinary cook. Her blog frequently features the beautifully photographed culinary creations and table settings that she prepares for her family and guests in her Southern California home. She agreed to share her recipe for this easy and delicious soup, served as part of a New Year's Eve dinner at the Casa de Eades.*

1 jar (12 ounces) roasted red peppers
1 can (about 15 ounces) fire-roasted diced tomatoes
1 can (14 ounces) zero-carb chicken broth with salt and spices
1 ($1/8$ ounce) garlic clove, peeled and smashed
1 cup vegetable broth
¼ teaspoon garlic powder
¼ teaspoon onion powder
¼ teaspoon sea salt
¼ teaspoon freshly ground black pepper
1 dash cayenne pepper
1 (6-ounce) jar Trader Joe's Roasted Red Pepper and Artichoke Tapenade (or other prepared tapenade), optional, adds 1 net carb per tablespoon

In the blender, combine all ingredients, except chicken and vegetable broth and tapenade, and blend until smooth. Pour into a large saucepan and stir in broth. You can do this as much as a couple of days ahead of time and store it, tightly sealed, in the refrigerator. Before serving, bring to a boil, reduce heat, and keep warm. Ladle into warm soup bowls, garnish with a healthy dollop of tapenade in the center, and serve.

Adapted and used with permission from Dr. Mary Dan Eades.

MAKES 6 CUPS OR 4 SERVINGS OF 1½ CUPS EACH.

Per serving—Net carbohydrate: 9.6 grams; Protein: 2.7 grams; Fiber: 2 grams; Fat 0.7 grams; Calories: 60

Total weight: 2 pounds and 15¼ ounces or 1.3 kilograms

Weight per serving: 2¾ ounces or 81 grams

Preparation time: 15 minutes active; 20 minutes total

TIPS:
Replace the tapanade with a dollop of **Crème Fraîche**, p. 297, sour cream, or plain Greek yogurt, if desired.

———

Dr. Eades developed this recipe as a way to get her boys to eat more vegetables by hiding them in their favorite soup. This is a "grown-up" version. You might want to tone down the spices a bit for the kids.

Roasted Red Pepper and Tomato Soup with Artichoke Tapenade

Cheese Puffs

NOTE:
A lot of fat will ooze out when using Cheddar instead of American cheese, so you will need to cut the parchment large enough to contain it. The fat loss means I can't give you accurate nutrition counts for fat or calories for these, but they are delicious and easy. (Fat or calories don't mean much anyway; when you limit the carbs, you limit insulin, so you can't store fat.)

EACH SLICE OF CHEESE MAKES 1 LARGE OR 4 SMALL PUFFS.

Per serving—Net carbohydrate: 0.3 grams; Protein: 4.6 grams; Fiber: 0 grams; Fat: 6.6 grams; Calories: 79

Total weight and weight per slice: ½ ounce or 13 grams

Preparation time: 2 minutes active; 3 minutes total

The idea of using slices of cheese for bread came from one of Dr. Richard Bernstein's books. Cut them into smaller pieces before cooking and they are like Cheez-its.

> 1 slice American or Cheddar Cheese, whole or cut into four pieces (Recipe was tested with Kraft Deli Deluxe American Cheese and Tillamook Medium Cheddar.)

FOR WHOLE SLICE:
Place one slice of cheese on a piece of parchment paper or a greased, microwave-safe plate. Microwave on high for about 1 minute or until puffed. Let cool for a minute or so. It should be firm enough to pick up, if it is not, microwave it for a few seconds more. (Be careful—it will be hot.) If it is still a little soft in the center, turn it over and cook a little longer. It is done if it breaks without bending. If American cheese is very dark inside, it is overdone. Note how long it takes in your microwave.

FOR FOUR PUFFS:
Cut each slice of cheese into 4 pieces. Place a few inches apart on a piece of parchment paper. Continue as above.

Cheese Puffs

Peanut Butter and Honey or Jelly Sandwich

1 **Cheese Puff**, p. 70
1½ tablespoons natural peanut butter
½ teaspoon artificial honey or **Jelly**, p, 201

Spread puff with peanut butter and drizzle with artificial honey or sugar-free **Jelly,** p. 201.

MAKES 1 OPEN-FACED SANDWICH.

Per serving—Net carbohydrate: 3.3 grams; Protein: 10.6 grams; Fiber: 1.5 grams; Fat: 18.6 grams; Calories: 234

Weight per serving: 1½ ounces or 44 grams

Preparation time: 2 minutes active; 3 minutes total

NOTE:

Gaiam makes a gadget with a crank that fits on the jar to stir your natural peanut butter if stirring is too tedious for you and your fridge space is maxed out. It is: Grandpa Witmer's Old Fashioned Natural Peanut Butter Mixer. It is available at www.Gaiam.com.

"Poets have been mysteriously silent on the subject of cheese."

– *C.K. Chesterton*

Peanut Butter Cookies

TIPS:

If you refrigerate natural peanut butter after stirring, the oil will not separate.

———

Use the kind of peanut butter that lists just "peanuts" or "peanuts and salt" as ingredients. It may be displayed with the organic foods and it will probably say, "stir before using." Smooth or crunchy is your call.

Flour-less peanut butter cookies have been around since the 1930s. The classic recipe was featured in a 2003 edition of Food and Wine Magazine *and repeated as one of their best recipes in a 30th Anniversary Issue in 2008. Paula Deen featured the recipe in one of her books and introduced a sugar-free version on her Food Network television show,* Paula's Home Cooking.

> 1 large egg
> 1 cup natural peanut butter, crunchy or plain, brought to
>   room temperature
> High intensity sugar substitute equal to ¾ cup sugar (recipe was tested
>   with 9 drops of EZ-Sweetz liquid sucralose)
> ¼ cup plus 2 tablespoons of brown sugar replacement, such as Diabetisweet, Just Like Sugar Brown, or LC Sweet Brown
> 1 teaspoon vanilla extract
> ½ teaspoon baking powder
> ½ teaspoon baking soda
> ¼ cup **Chocolate Chips** (optional)

Preheat oven to 350º F. Grease a large baking sheet.

Beat the egg with a fork until smooth. Add peanut butter, sweetener, vanilla, baking powder, and baking soda and mix well. Stir in chocolate chips if using. Shape tablespoonfuls of dough into 34 balls and place 2 inches apart on baking sheet. Flatten the balls with a fork, making a crosshatch design on each cookie. (Cookies will have a diameter of about 2 inches and will not spread much.) Bake for about 15 minutes or until firm and browned. Let cool for a few minutes before removing from pan.

MAKES 34 COOKIES.

Per cookie—Net carbohydrate: 0.9 grams, made with a zero-carb sweetener; Protein: 2.1 grams; Fiber: 0.5 grams; Fat: 3.9 grams; Calories: 47

Total weight: 13 ounces or 381 grams

Weight per cookie: ⅓ ounce or 11.2 grams

Preparation time: 10 minutes active, 35 minutes total

Peanut Butter Cookies

"Arachibutyrophobia" is the fear of getting peanut butter stuck in the roof of your mouth.

Tacos with Salsa and Toppings

6.7 net carbs

Crème Caramel

4.5 net carbs

Menu total: 11.2 net carbs

Always check the label when buying tortillas to be sure the brand is made without trans fats. Even though the package may proclaim "no trans-fats," if partially hydrogenated oil is listed in the ingredients, it has trans fats. (Legally, if a product has less than 0.5 grams per serving it can say it has none. Depending on the serving size, it can add up to quite a lot— and the only safe level of trans fats is zero.)

Tacos

Low-carb tortillas have been consistently available for at least 10 years (that's how long I've been buying them) and they are quite good. They can be used for enchiladas, fajitas, wrap sandwiches, and all your favorite Mexican dishes. Small ones (6- or 7-inch) have about 3 net grams of carbohydrate.

FOR EACH TACO:

  1 six- or seven- inch diameter (36 grams each) low-carb tortilla, such as La Tortilla Factory or Mama Lupe's

  1/3 cup (2 ounces) shredded **Carnitas**, p. 276, heated

  2 tablespoons (½ ounce) shredded Jack or Cheddar cheese

  2 teaspoons **Tomatillo Salsa**, p. 10, or prepared tomato salsa from a jar

  ¼ cup (about ¼ ounce) shredded lettuce

  2 tablespoons (½ ounce) chopped green onion, green and white

  2 tablespoons (1 ounce or ½ a small plum tomato) chopped tomato

  1 tablespoon (½ ounce) sliced black olives

  1 tablespoon diced mild or hot green chilies, optional

  2 tablespoons (1 ounce) sour cream, **Crème Fraîche**, p. 297, or plain yogurt, optional

  2 slices (1 ounce) avocado, optional, (adds 1.8 net grams of carbohydrate)

Fry tortilla in a greased skillet on medium-high heat until puffed and brown, turning several times so it puffs evenly. It should be slightly crisp but still flexible. When preparing more than one, stack them on a plate, separated by paper towels.

Place tortilla on a plate and put warm **Carnitas** in a strip down the center. Top with cheese, salsa, and additional toppings. Fold up tortilla to enclose fillings and serve.

MAKES 1 TACO. ALLOW 1 TO 2 PER PERSON.

Per serving of 1 taco including cheese, salsa, lettuce, onion, tomato, and olives—
Net carbohydrate: 6.7 grams (7.8 grams with tomato salsa rather than **Tomatillo Salsa**); Protein: 25 grams; Fiber: 8.7 grams; Fat: 14.8 grams; Calories: 269

Total weight per taco: 6 ounces or 170 grams without optional green chilies or **Crème Fraîche**
Preparation time: 5 minutes active and total

Tacos, p. 74

Crème Caramel

Prepare **Baked Custards,** p. 221, without nutmeg and chill.
Prepare **Caramel Sauce**, p. 59. Let sauce cool until just
warm. Pour 2 tablespoons of sauce over each chilled custard
and serve.

To make ahead, refrigerate the sauce and the custards
separately. Reheat sauce in the microwave on low setting
for about a minute or in the top of a double boiler until
just warm. Don't overheat. Pour 2 tablespoons of **Caramel
Sauce** over each custard and serve.

**MAKES 4 SERVINGS
OF ½ CUP.**

Per serving—Net carbohydrate:
4.5 grams; Protein: 5.8 grams;
Fiber: 13.4 grams; Fat: 44.1 grams;
Calories: 416

Total weight: 24½ ounces or
293 grams

Weight per serving: 6 ounces or
173 grams

Preparation time: 18 minutes
active, 1 hour 10 minutes total for
custards and sauce

Antipasto Salad

6 net carbs for 1½ servings

Easy Biskmix Crackers (p. 289)

½ batch, 0.8 net carbs

Strawberry Rhubarb Parfait (Variation under Fruit Gelatin, p. 54)

1.8 net carbs

Menu total: 8.6 net carbs

TIPS:

Smaller olives and tiny grape tomatoes work better than large ones for this salad. If necessary, cut the olives, tomatoes, and artichoke hearts in half so they are similar in size.

When serving whole cherry or grape tomatoes, prick each one with a knife or fork to protect bystanders from getting squirted with juice.

Antipasto Salad

Everything for the antipasto can be purchased ready-made in jars or from the deli, but I like to roast the peppers myself so they are just tender-crisp. Once you see how easy it is, you may never buy them again.

> 8 ounces salami, cut into ¾-inch dice
> 8 ounces aged Gouda cheese, cut into ¾-inch dice
> 2 cups (10 ounces) grape tomatoes (small cherry tomatoes)
> 1⅔ cups (6 ounces) pitted, black olives, drained
> 1 cup (6 ounces) pimento-stuffed green olives, drained
> 2 cups (10 ounces) marinated, quartered artichoke hearts, drained
> 1 cup (7 ounces) **Roasted Red Peppers**, p. 78
> ¼ cup (1¾ ounces) **Red Wine Vinaigrette,** p. 300
> 8 to 10 leaves Romaine lettuce (1 ounce each)

Place salami, Gouda, tomatoes, black and green olives, and roasted peppers in a large bowl. Add vinaigrette and toss to coat. Refrigerate for at least 1 hour or up to 2 days. Remove antipasto from refrigerator 30 minutes before serving.

Discard outer leaves from head of Romaine. Break lettuce into pieces and arrange in a large serving bowl or on individual plates. Toss antipasto and spoon onto lettuce leaves.

MAKES 10 SERVINGS OF 1 CUP.

Per serving—Net carbohydrate: 4 grams; Protein: 12.9 grams; Fiber: 1.9 grams; Fat: 20.6 grams; Calories: 255

Total weight: 3 pounds 7¼ ounces or 1.57 kilograms

Weight per serving: 5½ ounces

Preparation time: 25 minutes active and total

VARIATION:

Antipasto Appetizers

Omit lettuce and spear an assortment of tidbits on wooden picks to serve as appetizers or place antipasto mixture on a large platter, put wooden picks on the side, and let guests help themselves.

Roasted Red Peppers

2 red bell peppers, 7 to 8 ounces each as purchased

Cut about ½ inch off top of peppers. Make several cuts around the stem and pull it out. Cut ½ inch off bottom of peppers. Cut down through sides and open out into flat rectangles. Cut out seeds and membranes from all pieces. Flatten long side-wall pieces by breaking peppers where they naturally form segments, but leave the skin intact. Lay peppers, including top and bottom pieces, on a broiler pan. Place under broiler, 2 to 3 inches from heat source. Broil for 2 to 4 minutes, or until skin is blackened and blistered. Watch carefully and rotate pan for even heat, but do not turn the peppers over—you want the skin-side to be closest to the heat. (You may choose to cook the peppers on a grill; in which case you would keep the skin-side down.)

Put peppers in a bowl and cover with a plate or put in a plastic bag. Leave to steam for 15 minutes to loosen skins. Peel off skins. Cut into pieces and use in recipes or serve as an appetizer or side.

MAKES ABOUT 1½ CUPS OR 6 SERVINGS OF ¼ CUP.

Per serving—Net carbohydrate: 2.5 grams; Protein: 0.6 grams; Fiber: 1.2 grams; Fat: 0.2 grams; Calories: 16

Total weight: 8¾ ounces or 250 grams

Weight per serving: 1½ ounces or 43 grams

Preparation time: 15 minutes active; 34 minutes total

Chicken A La King

All it takes to elevate this old standby into a dish worthy of its name is a couple of egg yolks. Tender, moist, **Poached Chicken** *(p. 277) will produce the best result, but leftover roast chicken or turkey can also make a satisfying lunch or supper dish.*

2 tablespoons butter or olive oil

¼ cup (1½ ounces) chopped onion (¼ of a small, 2½-diameter, onion)

¼ cup (1½ ounces) chopped red and/or green bell pepper (one fourth of a 7- to 8-ounce pepper)

2 cups (5 ounces) fresh sliced mushrooms, quartered first, if large

2 teaspoons chicken base, such as Better Than Bouillon

2 egg yolks

1 cup heavy cream

¼ cup (zero-carb) chicken stock or water

2 cups (11.6 ounces) diced **Poached Chicken**, (p. 277)

Salt to taste (*Do not add salt* if using Better Than Bouillon brand chicken base.)

1/8 teaspoon fresh black pepper or to taste

Heat butter or oil in a large saucepan on medium heat. Add onion and pepper and cook and stir until softened, about 3 minutes. Add mushrooms and cook, stirring, for a minute or two longer. Stir in chicken base.

Mix egg yolks into ¼ cup of the cream in a small bowl and set aside. Add remaining ¾ cup cream and stock or water to pan and heat just until it starts to simmer. Reduce heat to low and cook for 5 to 10 minutes. Stir about ¼ cup of the contents of the pan into the reserved yolk and cream mixture to temper and then return to pan. Continue to cook and stir on low heat, not letting it boil, for about 5 minutes or until thickened. Add diced chicken and heat through. Add salt, if needed, and black pepper.

Serve over toasted low-carb bread points or cubes, p. 292, choice of pasta, p. 325, or rice substitute, p. 283-384.

NOTE:
You may substitute one 14-ounce can or jar of sliced mushrooms, drained, for fresh. Add with chicken.

Chicken A La King

5.5 net carbs

Whole Grain Bread (p. 291, toasted and cut into diagonal quarters or cubes.)

1 slice from 2-loaf recipe with flax, 1.9 net carbs

Mixed Green Salad with Red Wine Vinaigrette

2 cups, 1.4 net carbs

Oops, It's Strawberry Shortcake!

4.2 net carbs

Menu total: 13 net carbs

MAKES 3 SERVINGS OF A LITTLE MORE THAN 1 CUP EACH.

Per serving—Net carbohydrate: 5.5 grams; Protein: 32.7 grams; Fiber: 0.8 grams;
Fat: 44 grams; Calories: 551

Total weight: 1 pound 12 ounces or 793 grams

Weight per serving: 9⅓ ounces or 264 grams

Preparation time: 15 minutes active, 30 minutes total

Oops, It's Strawberry Shortcake!

When Jamie Van Eaton, who blogs as Cleochatra, accidentally used 3 ounces *instead of 3 tablespoons of cream cheese to make a batch of Revolution Rolls (from the* Atkins Diet Revolution*), she created an online sensation. The low-carb crowd was thrilled to have "bread" to hold their burgers. As oopsie mania spread through the forums and networks, they evolved into pancakes, waffles, corndogs, doughnuts, tiramisu, cream puffs, pizza, and much more, all with nary a speck of flour or sugar and less than one gram of carbohydrate each! This spongy puff also makes a great stand-in for cake.*

FOR STRAWBERRIES:

16 ounces fresh strawberries, about 2¾ cups, sliced

2 tablespoons (more to taste) vanilla sugar-free syrup, such as Da Vinci's, or use 2 tablespoons of water and sugar substitute equal to 2 tablespoons sugar

Rinse strawberries and remove caps. Slice and place in a bowl with the sugar-free syrup. Stir and refrigerate until needed.

FOR CAKES:

3 eggs, warmed up to room temperature

⅛ teaspoon cream of tartar

3 ounces (1 small package) cold cream cheese

1 teaspoon baking powder

4 packets Splenda, 6 packets stevia, or sugar substitute equal to 3 table-spoons of sugar, divided

½ teaspoon sugar-free vanilla

A few grains of salt, optional

FOR TOPPING:
Sugar-free Whipped Cream, p. 312, optional

Preheat oven to 300º F. Grease a muffin-top pan or a large, 6-cup muffin pan. Measure ingredients into prep bowls so you can work quickly.

William Lawrence of Chester, N.Y., accidentally invented cream cheese in 1872 while trying to reproduce a French cheese called *Neufchatel*. He wrapped his cheese in foil wrappers and sold it under the brand name *Philadelphia Cream Cheese*.

Separate eggs, putting whites and one half of the sugar substitute into a large bowl. Beat egg whites until foamy. Add cream of tartar and beat to stiff peak stage, about 5 minutes. Whites should be so stiff that they do not slip when the bowl is tipped.

In a second bowl, with the same beaters, beat cold cream cheese until creamy. Add egg yolks, baking powder, and remaining sugar substitute. Beat until smooth. (It would be better to beat the yolk mixture first, then the whites, but you would need to wash the beaters or use a second mixer. It's OK to get whites into the yolks, but if you get any of the oily yolks in the whites, they won't whip properly.)

Gently fold ½ the yolk batter into the whites, making a lazy sine wave through the batter once. Turn the bowl 90 degrees and repeat. Add second half of yolk mixture and repeat sine wave 2 more times.

Spoon batter into the muffin pan and smooth tops. Bake for 30 minutes. Cakes should be brown but slightly soft, not crumbly or dry. Remove pan from oven and let cakes cool in the pan for a few minutes. Transfer them to a rack until completely cool. When ready to serve, arrange cooled cakes in serving dishes. Put ¼ cup of strawberries on each cake and top with whipped cream, if desired, and serve.

Store cakes in a partially open plastic bag at room temperature for a day (so they breathe and don't get too moist). For longer storage, keep them in the refrigerator. Unwrap and set them on the counter for 15 to 30 minutes to dry out before using.

TIP:
Jamie says, if your Oopsie batter separates, just spoon the fluffy part onto the pan, make a slight depression in the center, and pour the liquid batter on top.

MAKES 8 SERVINGS.

Per serving for cake with ⅓ cup berries—Net carbohydrate: 4.2 grams; Protein: 3.8 grams; Fiber: 1.9 grams; Fat: 5.6 grams; Calories: 98

Total weight: 5 ½ ounces or 54 grams

Weight per serving: 2¾ ounces or 76.8 grams

Preparation time: 20 minutes active, 50 minutes total

"The concept of Revol-oopsie layers and whipped cream filling/frosting was a complete success!…The point is—Revoloopsie can become CAKE! Delicious CAKE! Beautiful CAKE! Do you hear me, people? CAKE that everyone will like!"

— *Jamie Van Eaton*

Oopsie Buns

If you want to try Jamie's Oopsie Buns, leave out the sweetener and vanilla in the cakes and spoon the batter into 6 mounds on a baking sheet. Otherwise the recipe is the same.

NOTE:

If your batter is too thin, you'll get pancakes rather than rolls. (They will be very nice pancakes, though.) Try using a muffin-top pan or pancake rings so they don't spread so much.

MAKES 6 BUNS.

Per serving—Net carbohydrate count: 0.9 grams; Protein: 4.2 grams; Fiber: 0 grams; Fat: 7 grams; Calories: 86

Total weight: 5⅞ ounces or 166 grams

Weight per serving: ½ ounce or 17 grams

Preparation time: 10 minutes active; 40 minutes total

Oopsie Eclairs

Make batter from shortcake recipe, but bake as for buns, making 12 long buns rather than six round ones. Put together in pairs using 2 tablespoons of **Whipped Cream**, p. 312, as filling. Drizzle with 1 tablespoon of **Chocolate Sauce**, p. 132.

MAKES 6 ÉCLAIRS.

Per serving—Net carbohydrate: 1.6 grams; Protein: 5 grams; Fiber: 2.6 grams; Fat: 13.8 grams; Calories: 191

Total weight: 7¼ ounces or 205 grams including **Whipped Cream** and **Chocolate Sauce**

Weight per serving: 1¼ ounces or 34 grams

Preparation time: 12 minutes active; 42 minutes total

Wrap Sandwich with Poached Chicken

1 small low-carb tortilla, 2 slices low-carb bread, or ½ a low-carb
    pita pocket

1 tablespoon **Mayonnaise**, p. 298, or use purchased real mayonnaise

2½ ounces sliced **Poached Chicken**, p. 277

1 slice (1 ounce) Cheddar cheese

1 leaf (½ ounce) lettuce

1 slice (1 ounce) tomato

1 (1 ounce) dill pickle, on the side

Spread Mayonnaise on tortilla. Layer other ingredients
except pickle on sandwich.

MAKES 1 SERVING.

Per serving—Net carbohydrate: 5.6 grams; Protein: 33.3 grams; Fiber: 8.1 grams; Fat: 23.8
grams; Calories: 396

Weight per serving: 6½ ounces 185 grams

Preparation time: 5 minutes active and total

Wrap Sandwich with Poached Chicken

5.6 net carbs

Stuffed Egg (p. 241)

2 halves, 0.8 net carbs

Protein Bar

3.3 net carbs

Menu total: 9.7 net grams

Part 1: Everyday Food: Lunches   83

Protein Bars

TIP:

Wrap bars in parchment paper
and then wrap in foil to make
a portable snack, much less
expensive than purchased
protein bars.

*Mark Sisson's Primal Energy Bar recipe was the starting point
for these yummy, convenient snack bars. Mark, author of* The
Primal Blueprint, *posted the original version on his blog at
www.marksdailyapple.com. They taste like granola bars, but
have nary a speck of grain.*

¼ cup plus 2 tablespoons (43 grams) almond flour or meal, divided

1 cup (about 4 ounces) of almonds, pecans, walnuts, or a mixture

½ cup (1 ounce) unsweetened, flaked coconut

¼ cup (2 ounces) of creamy nut butter, such as peanut or almond butter
    or seed butter, such as pumpkin butter or tahini paste

¼ cup coconut oil or use part butter

½ teaspoon salt

½ teaspoon cinnamon

1½ teaspoons sugar-free vanilla extract

¼ cup (3½ ounces) powdered erythritol plus a high-intensity sugar
    substitute, such as liquid sucralose or stevia equal to 2 tablespoons
    of sugar
    or:
    ¼ cup of xylitol, a sweet fiber, or a stevia blend with erythritol or
    oligofructose (use no additional sweeter with these)

¼ cup (1 ounce) sugar-free, vanilla whey protein powder

1 large egg, beaten with a fork

¼ cup **Dried Cranberries**, p. 12, or purchased, sugar-free dried
    cranberries, chopped or snipped into pieces

¼ cup (1 ounce) sugar-free **Chocolate Chips**, p. 43, or purchased chips
    such as Nevada Manna or sugar-free, chopped chocolate candy bar

Preheat oven to 325° F. Grease an 8- x 8-inch pan and
sprinkle with 2 tablespoons of the almond flour or meal.

Spread nuts and coconut on a shallow baking pan and toast
for about 10 minutes, stirring once, until golden brown.
Let cool.

While nuts are toasting, place nut or seed butter and coconut oil in a heat-safe bowl and microwave for about 30 seconds or heat in a small saucepan on stovetop until melted.

Remove from heat. Stir until smooth. Add salt, vanilla, and any liquid sweetener, if using.

Whisk or sift dry sweeteners, whey protein powder, and reserved nut flour or meal together until blended. Stir into nut butter and coconut oil mixture.

Place cooled nuts and coconut in bowl of food processer and pulse until roughly chopped, leaving some chunks for texture. Stir chopped nuts into batter. Add egg and mix thoroughly. Fold in cranberries and chocolate chips.

Press bar mixture evenly into pan. Bake at 325º F for about 15 to 20 minutes or until brown around the edges. Don't over-cook. Any oil standing on the top should be absorbed as the bars cool. Sprinkle with a little more almond flour if necessary. Let cool in pan and slice into 16 squares. For easier cutting, chill in refrigerator for 10 minutes. Store in an airtight container at room temperature or refrigerate for a firmer texture.

MAKES 16 SERVINGS.

Per serving—Net carbohydrate: 3.3 grams; Protein: 4.7 grams; Fiber: 4 grams; Fat: 12.8 grams; Calories: 149

Net carbohydrate per serving: 3.7 grams: Protein: 5.4 grams

Total weight: 1 pound or 453 grams

Weight per serving: 1 ounce or 29 grams

Preparation time: 20 minutes active, 45 minutes total

Protein Bars

Dinners

MENU 1

Cottage Pie

Sautéed Cabbage

Snow Pudding
with Custard Sauce

MENU 2

Oven Baked Fish Fillets

Caprese Salad

Jicama Shoestring Fries

"Apple" Cobbler

MENU 3

Japchae

Kimchi

Cauliflower *Faux* Rice

Coconut Ice Cream

MENU 4

Chicken with Spices
and Roasted Pumpkin

Lettuce Wedge Salad with
Blue Cheese Dressing

Lemon Icebox Pie

MENU 5

Pork Tenderloin with Fennel,
Onion, and Celery

Pasta with Alfredo Sauce

Pots de Crème au Chocolate

MENU 6

Barbecued Country-Style Ribs

Cheese Polenta

Carolina Coleslaw

Pumpkin Pound Cake

MENU 7

Spaghetti with Meat Sauce

Mixed Greens with Roasted Garlic
and "Balsamic" Vinaigrette

Lemon Cake with Lemon Glaze

MENU 8

Roast Chicken with
Mushroom Gravy

Cauliflower *Faux* Mashed Potatoes

Green Beans with
Red Wine Vinegar and
Extra Virgin Olive Oil

Yellow Cake with
Chocolate Butter Cream Frosting

MENU 9

Oven Fried Chicken

Ginger Pumpkin Purée

Slow Cooked Green Beans

Chocolate Sundaes

MENU 10

Eggplant Casserole

Greek Salad

Mocha Mousse

MENU 11

Meatloaf

Celery Root Purée

Nopalitos

Raspberry Marshmallow
Squares

MENU 12

Indian Butter Chicken
(Murgh Makhani)

Cauliflower *Faux* Rice

Roasted Okra

Rose Flavored Ice Cream with
Star Fruit in Anise Syrup

Cottage Pie

7 net carbs

Sautéed Cabbage

3.2 net carbs

Snow Pudding with
Custard Sauce

Snow Pudding, 0.9 net grams;
Custard Sauce, 1.4 net grams

Menu total 12.5 net carbs

**MAKES 6 SERVINGS
OF ⅛ CUP.**

Per serving—Net carbohydrate:
7 grams; Protein: 20.8 grams;
Fiber: 2.4 grams; Fat:18.5 grams;
Calories: 289

Net carbohydrate per serving:
7 grams; Protein: 20.8 grams

Total weight: 3 pounds 6½ ounces

Weight per serving: 9 ounces or
258 grams

Preparation time: 15 minutes active,
30 minutes total

Cottage Pie

This traditional English comfort food becomes **Shepherd's Pie**
if made with ground lamb. It is equally comforting topped with
Biscuit *dough (p. 220) and called a* **Pot Pie**.

4 cups (1 recipe) **Cauliflower** *Faux* **Mashed Potatoes** (p. 281)
1 teaspoon of oil
1 pound lean ground beef
1⅓ cups (6 ounces) chopped onion (one 7-ounce onion as purchased)
1½ cups (5 ounces) sliced fresh mushrooms
2 teaspoons potato flour
⅔ cup of beef stock or broth
1 teaspoon of Worcestershire sauce
¾ teaspoon salt or to taste
¼ teaspoon black pepper or to taste
1 tablespoon melted butter or use cooking spray
¼ teaspoon smoked or sweet paprika

Prepare **Cauliflower** *Faux* **Mashed Potatoes**, (p. 281).
Grease an 8- by 8- by 2-inch (2 quart), ovenproof baking
pan or casserole. Preheat oven to 400° F.

Heat a large skillet over medium-high heat. Add oil, heat for
a few seconds, and add ground beef. Cook and stir until meat
starts to brown. Add onions and mushrooms and cook until
onions are softened. Remove meat mixture from pan and reserve. Drain off all but 2 teaspoons of fat from pan. Add potato flour and cook and stir for a minute or two or until flour
is slightly browned. Add stock or broth, Worcestershire sauce,
salt, and pepper and cook and stir until slightly thickened.

Return meat mixture to pan and stir into gravy. Transfer
filling to baking dish. Spread **Cauliflower** *Faux* **Mashed
Potato** mixture evenly over top. Drizzle with melted butter or coat with cooking spray. Sprinkle with paprika. Bake
for about 15 minutes or until bubbly and brown. Use
convection heat if your oven has that option or broil for a
few minutes 6 to 8 inches from heat source if top does not
brown adequately. Serve hot.

Sautéed Cabbage

My two finicky kids loved cabbage cooked this way when they were little.

1 head of cabbage, about 2½ pounds (only half will be used for this recipe)
2 tablespoons butter
2 teaspoons sugar-free soy sauce, such as Kikkoman

Rinse cabbage and cut in half. Reserve half for another purpose. Remove white core. Place cut-side down on cutting board. Slice into shreds (as for coleslaw but not quite as fine). Melt butter in a large skillet over medium-high heat. Sauté cabbage for 5 to 8 minutes, stirring occasionally, until tender-crisp and slightly browned. Add soy sauce to pan and cook and stir for another minute or two. Serve hot.

MAKES 4 SERVINGS.

Per serving—Net carbohydrate: 3.2 grams; Protein: 1.4 grams; Fiber: 2.3 grams; Fat: 5.9 grams; 75 Calories;

Total weight: 1 pound ⅛ ounces or 454 grams

Weight per serving: 4 ounces or 114 grams

Preparation time: 10 minutes active, 15 minutes total

Snow Pudding with Custard Sauce

My recipe for this refreshing, old-fashioned dessert is adapted from one in The Fanny Farmer Cookbook, *originally published in 1896. The copy now on my shelf is one I found in an antique store after I wore out my first one. When I needed to know how to make ketchup or crackers or other things that no one makes from scratch anymore, I could always find it in Fanny Farmer's book. It is truly a treasure and a window into the past. (One edition is on-line at: http://www.bartleby.com/people/Farmer-F.html).*

1 tablespoon gelatin, a little less than 2 packets (7 grams each)
½ cup cold water
½ cup boiling water
Sugar substitute equal to 1 cup of sugar
A few grains of salt
¼ cup lemon juice, the amount from 1½ small lemons
½ teaspoon grated lemon zest (amount from ½ a small lemon)
3 egg whites, fresh or reconstituted from powdered egg white (Reserve yolks for custard sauce if using fresh egg whites.)
1 recipe of **Custard Sauce**, p. 91

Soften gelatin in ½ cup cold water in a large bowl for a few minutes. Heat ½ cup water to boiling. Pour over gelatin and stir until dissolved. Stir in sugar substitute, salt, lemon juice, and zest. Place in refrigerator to chill. Stir every 5 minutes at first, then as often as every minute until as thick as raw egg whites, which may take less than 10 minutes or up to an hour.

Beat gelatin mixture with an electric mixer for 2 or 3 minutes or until fluffy. Add egg whites and beat an additional 3 minutes or until it forms soft peaks that droop over when beater is lifted. Spoon into serving dishes. (Ms. Farmer would have used a mold that had been dipped in water.) Refrigerate until firm.

Make **Custard Sauce** while pudding chills. Top each serving with ¼ cup of **Custard Sauce**.

TIPS:

Pasteurized eggs in the shell do not work well for beating because the whites will not attain enough volume. Dried egg whites, such as Just Whites, can be used instead of raw egg whites in recipes that will not be cooked. To use Just Whites, mix 2 tablespoons with 6 tablespoons water. Stir gently for 2 minutes then continue to stir until dissolved (a tiny whisk works well for this, the kind intended for use as a bar tool).

Soft peak stage describes meringue that forms peaks that droop over when the beater is lifted. Stiff-peak means they stand straight up.

MAKES 6 SERVINGS OF 1 CUP.

Per serving—Net carbohydrate: 0.9 grams; Protein: 3.5 grams; Fiber: 0 grams; Fat: 0 grams; Calories: 17

Total weight: 12½ ounces or 356 grams

Weight per serving: 2 ounces or 59 grams

Preparation time: 15 minutes active and total

Custard Sauce

Fanny Farmer said, "A jar of custard in the refrigerator is a joy." How true!

1 whole egg
3 egg yolks
Sugar substitute equal to ¼ cup sugar
A few grains of salt
1 cup (8 ounces) heavy cream
1 teaspoon sugar-free vanilla extract

Heat water in the bottom of a double boiler until hot but not bubbling.

Beat the egg and the egg yolks until smooth. Place in the top of the double boiler with the sweetener, salt, and heavy cream. Place over, but not touching, the hot water in bottom pan. Cook and stir until the custard is thick enough to coat a spoon dipped into it, about 7 minutes. Add vanilla and chill.

MAKES ABOUT 1½ CUPS OR 6 SERVINGS OF 1.5 OUNCES OR ABOUT ¼ CUP EACH.

Per serving—Net carbohydrate: 1.4 grams; Protein: 3.3 grams; Fiber: 0 grams; Fat: 18.2 grams; Calories: 181

Total weight: 9½ ounces or 270 grams

Weight per serving: 1½ ounces or 45 grams

Preparation time: 10 minutes active and total

Fanny Farmer is credited with introducing the use of exact measurements in recipes. Older recipes would list *an average tumbler, a jigger,* or *a piece the size of a walnut* as amounts for ingredients.

Oven Baked Fish Fillets

1.2 net carbs

Jicama Shoestring Fries

4.9 net carbs

Caprese Salad

3.1 net carbs

"Apple" Cobbler

3.8 net carbs

Menu total: 13 net carbs

MAKES 3 SERVINGS.

Per serving—Net carbohydrate:
1.2 grams; Protein: 33 grams; Fiber:
0.1 grams;
Fat: 10.5 grams; Calories: 236

Total weight: 15½ ounces or 437
grams

Weight per serving: 4¾ ounces or
136 grams

Preparation time: 15 minutes active; 35 minutes total

Oven Baked Fish Fillets

1 pound (three 5- to 6-ounce) filets of firm, white fish, such as cod,
    snapper, tilapia, or haddock
1 teaspoon lemon juice
Salt and pepper to taste
2 tablespoons (1/8 cup) real **Mayonnaise**, p. 298
2 tablespoons (1/8 cup) plain Greek yogurt or real sour cream
2 green onions, green tops only, chopped or 2 tablespoons
    chopped chives
2 tablespoons (¼ ounce or 8 grams) grated Parmesan cheese

Preheat oven to 450º F. Grease a broiler pan.

Blot fish fillets dry and place on broiler pan. Sprinkle with lemon juice, salt, and pepper. Bake for about 12 minutes for each inch of thickness, or until fish is opaque and flakes easily. An instant-read thermometer should register an internal temperature 140º F when fish is done.

While fish cooks, mix mayonnaise, yogurt or sour cream, green onions or chives, and Parmesan in a small bowl.

Remove fish from oven and move oven rack to upper position. Turn on broiler to preheat. Spread topping over fish and broil for 1 to 1½ minutes or until golden brown. Serve at once.

TIPS:
Fish pieces need to be uniform in thickness so they will cook evenly. Thin pieces can be folded in half, or the thin sides of uneven fillets can be overlapped.

It takes only a few minutes to remove the bones from fish before cooking. I keep a pair of tweezers in my kitchen drawer for that purpose. Drape the filet over an up-side-down bowl so the bones will pop up; they are lined up neatly in a row, making them easy to remove.

Jicama Shoestring Fries

If the Jicama is cut very thin and fried very crisp, it tastes convincingly like shoestring potatoes. If not, it will stay soft, and its distinctive sweet taste will shatter the illusion. (It will taste a bit like sweet potato fries though, so you may still like it.)

12 ounces jicama root, about 5 cups sliced
Oil for frying
Salt to taste
Grated Parmesan cheese, garlic powder, onion powder, and/or
    smoked paprika, optional

Peel jicama and cut into thin slices, about ⅛-inch thick. Stack the slices and cut again into fine julienne strips (about ⅛-inch square) with a chef's knife or slice with the julienne disk on a food processor. Put an inch or two of oil in a deep skillet or deep fryer and heat to 360° F. Fry jicama in several batches for about 2 minutes each or until golden brown and crisp. Drain, sprinkle with coarse salt and other flavorings, if using. Put fries on a rack in a roasting pan and keep in a warm oven until all the jicama is fried. Serve hot as a side or snack or use to garnish steaks or burgers.

TIP:
You must peel away the tough, white fibers under the skin on jicama root, not just the thin brown layer.

MAKES 4 SERVINGS OF A LITTLE OVER ½ CUP.

Per serving—Net carbohydrate: 4.9 grams; Protein: 0.9 grams; Fiber: 6.1 grams; Fat 2.3 grams; Calories: 68

Total weight: 2½ ounces or 71 grams

Weight per serving: ½ ounce or 18 grams

Preparation time: 5 minutes active, 10 minutes total

"Americans were starting to eat more potatoes in the fifties, but at the beginning of the decade the per capita consumption was only about 6 pounds per person per year. Fifty years later...the average American was consuming about eighty pounds of potatoes per year. And french fries constituted almost 40 percent of that total."

– *Steven Gdula,*
The Warmest Room in the House, *2008*

Caprese Salad

NOTE:
You must use only top quality ingredients for a recipe as simple as this one.

TOMATOES:
Fully ripe, home grown tomatoes are the best choice for this classic salad if you are lucky enough to have them. Heritage tomatoes can also be excellent if you can find any that managed to make it to market undamaged and if you can afford the price. Tomatoes on the vine are also available and can be quite good. Be sure to pick those that are still attached to a fresh, green stem—the more stem, the better, because they continue to ripen after they are harvested by drawing nutrients stored in the stem. Tomatoes ripen from the stem end of the cluster to the tip, so use those first. And never, never, never put fresh tomatoes in the refrigerator!

The purists will tell you that a Caprese insalada has six ingredients, no more, no less, and balsamic vinegar is not one of them. However, Italians use slightly green tomatoes, which are much more tart than the ripe ones preferred by Americans.

I was surprised when I first visited a European marketplace; most of the produce looked wonderful—but they had both ripe tomatoes and hard, green tomatoes with just a slight blush. The green ones were labeled "salad tomatoes," and the ripe ones were, "sauce tomatoes." I'll take the American stand on this issue and say to use the sweetest, reddest, ripest, tomatoes you can find—and add a splash of vinegar if you want to. (Red-wine vinegar plus a little sweetener is a better choice than balsamic, which can be very high in sugar.)

3 (2½-inch diameter) ripe tomatoes (you will need sixteen ¼-ounce slices or about 10 ounces, sliced)
8 ounces fresh mozzarella cheese (twelve ¼-inch slices)
8 large, fresh, sweet basil leaves, shredded, plus 4 small sprigs for garnish
4 tablespoons extra virgin olive oil
Coarse salt and freshly ground, black pepper to taste

Rinse tomatoes. Cut about ¼ inch from each end and discard or use for another purpose. Cut center portion into ¼-inch thick slices. Slice the mozzarella into rounds that are similar to the tomatoes in size and thickness. Arrange on individual serving plates, alternating mozzarella and tomato in overlapping slices, beginning and ending with a tomato slice. Scatter shredded basil over the dishes and drizzle each serving with two tablespoons of olive oil. Season with salt and freshly ground pepper. Garnish with extra basil sprigs. Prepare as close to serving time as possible and keep cool.

MAKES 4 SERVINGS.

Per serving—Net carbohydrate: 3.1 grams; Protein: 12.8 grams; Fiber: 1.1 grams; Fat: 23.7 grams; Calories: 276

Total weight: 1 pound 2¾ ounces 532 grams

Weight per serving: 4¾ ounces or 133 grams

Preparation time: 15 minutes active and total

"As with many secular pleasures, Heaven and Hell are near each other….The tomato will need to taste like a tomato, the mozzarella will have to carry a label with a buffalo, the basil will need to have the scent of freshness, and the olive oil will have to be one of the finest varieties."

— Reinhardt Hess and Sabine Salzer,
Regional Italian Cuisine, *1999.*

BASIL:
Basil will turn dark if it gets too cold. Keep fresh basil in a vase of water on the counter, as if it were a bouquet of flowers. If you change the water every day, it will stay fresh longer.

To slice basil leaves, stack the leaves together and roll them up. Cut diagonally into thin strips. This is called a *chiffonade*. (*Chiffonade* is a noun; *chiffoner* is the verb. It's French for, "made of rags." Aren't you glad you know that?)

Caprese Salad

"Apple" Cobbler

Chayote is a summer squash, like cucumber and zucchini, but it has the texture of a hard fruit. Its bland taste makes it a chameleon, capable of taking on the character of apples, pears, peaches, or potatoes, depending on the context.

FRUIT LAYER:

2 or 3 chayote squash, about 1½ pounds, as purchased

¼ cup (3½ ounces or 48 grams) granular erythritol or xylitol, or a blend with bulk, such as Sweet*perfection* or Just Like Sugar

High intensity sugar substitute equal to ½ cup of sugar

½ teaspoon ground cinnamon

2 teaspoons applejack brandy or apple cider vinegar

3 tablespoons water

2 tablespoons lemon juice

1 teaspoon grated lemon zest (thin yellow part of rind)

¼ teaspoon xanthan gum

A few grains of salt

1 tablespoon butter

CAKE TOPPING:

¼ cup (1 ounce or 28 grams) almond flour or meal

¼ cup sugar-free vanilla whey protein powder

1 teaspoon baking powder

¼ teaspoon xanthan gum (optional)

1/8 teaspoon cinnamon

Dash of salt

3 tablespoons butter, melted

¼ cup cream

High intensity sugar substitute, such as sucralose or stevia, equal to ½ cup sugar

Butter an 8- by 4-inch, oven- and microwave-safe baking dish.

Cut chayotes into quarters and remove pits. Peel chayote pieces and cut crosswise into thin slices. Place in baking dish. Add sweeteners, cinnamon, applejack or vinegar, and water. Microwave on high for 20 to 25 minutes or until tender, stirring every 5 minutes. Remove from microwave, stir in lemon juice, lemon zest, xanthan gum, and salt.

Applejack is hard cider with a high alcohol content. It was first made by American colonists who distilled apple cider by leaving it out to freeze and then removing the ice to concentrate the alcohol, which did not freeze. This method of distillation is called "jacking."

MAKES 5 SERVINGS OF ABOUT ½ CUP.

Per serving—Net carbohydrate: 3.8 grams (count excludes 9.6 grams of sugar alcohol); Protein: 4.7 grams; Fiber: 3.6 grams; Fat: 17 grams; Calories: 193

Total weight: 1 pound 7 ounces or 646 grams

Weight per serving: 4½ ounces or 129 grams

Preparation time: 25 minutes active, 65 minutes total

Taste and add more sweetener if needed. Dot with 1 tablespoon butter.

Preheat oven to 375° F.

Whisk almond meal, whey protein powder, baking powder, xanthan gum (if using), cinnamon, and salt together in a bowl. Add melted butter, cream, and sweetener and stir until just blended. Spread topping evenly over hot chayote in pan (reheat chayote if necessary). Bake uncovered for about 20 to 25 minutes or until top is brown. Serve warm with heavy cream, **French Vanilla Ice Cream** (p. 308), or **Whipped Cream**, p. 312, if desired.

TIPS:
Xanthan gum is a thickener and an emulsifier. Almond flour or meal makes a topping with a cornbread-like texture; adding xanthan makes it more cake-like.

___

Chayotes exude a sticky juice that can be irritating to the skin. Rinse them after peeling and wash your hands or wear gloves.

Chayotes

Japchae
5.9 net carbs

Kimchi
Optional, see Sidebar
Sugar-free kimchi, 1 net carb

Cauliflower *Faux* Rice (p. 283)
1.1 net carbs

Coconut Ice Cream (p. 310)
2.3 net carbs

Menu total: 9.3 net carbs; add 1 for optional kimchi

Japchae

In a futile effort to stay low carb at a Korean restaurant where the menu listed only noodle and rice dishes, I chose one called japchae. The description said it was made with "yam" noodles so I took a chance, hoping they were like Japanese shirataki, which are sometimes called yam noodles, but are made from konjac, an entirely different plant. The noodles had a distinctly rubbery texture, similar to shirataki, but the waiter insisted they were made of sweet potatoes. I later consulted a few Korean cookbooks that confirmed that sweet potato starch was the main ingredient in dangmyeon *noodles used in japchae, so I reluctantly crossed it off my list and forgot about it.*

After I discovered kelp noodles and was looking for potential uses for them, The Seattle Times *Sunday magazine featured a recipe for japchae in a story by Matthew Amster-Burton. Ah ha! I gave it a try. My version is not authentic, but it is still delicious!*

½ bunch fresh spinach, about 4 ounces as purchased, rinsed and trimmed
6 ounces (½ package) kelp noodles or use shirataki noodles (see Sidebar)
2 garlic cloves, minced (2 teaspoons), divided
6 ounces beef sirloin, sliced into thin strips (about 2½-inches by 3/8-inch by ¼-inch)
1 tablespoon plus 1½ teaspoons sesame oil, divided
Dash of salt
2 tablespoons peanut oil or other cooking oil, divided
3 tablespoons plus 1 teaspoon naturally brewed (no sugar) soy sauce, such as Kikkoman, divided
¼ of a medium onion (2 ounces), sliced
3 or 4 shitaki mushrooms, about ¾ ounces or 21 grams as purchased, stems discarded, caps sliced
3 green onions (38 grams or 13/8 ounces), cut into 1-inch pieces
Sugar substitute equal to 1½ tablespoons sugar
Toasted sesame seeds for garnish

Heat a pot of water to boiling and blanch spinach for about 30 seconds. Rinse immediately in cold water. Squeeze the water from the leaves and form into a ball. Cut ball in half and place in a small bowl with ½ teaspoon of the sesame oil and a dash of salt. Set aside to marinate.

Rinse kelp noodles. Bring a pot of water to boiling and heat noodles for a few minutes while cooking beef, onions, and mushrooms. Drain noodles and keep warm.

Heat 1 tablespoon of the vegetable oil in a large skillet or wok over medium-high heat. Add beef, 1 teaspoon of the soy sauce, and 1 teaspoon of the sesame oil. Stir fry 3 to 4 minutes or until beef looses its pink color. Stir in the garlic and cook for a few seconds more. Transfer beef and garlic to a large bowl and set aside.

Add remaining 1 tablespoon of cooking oil to pan and add sliced onions and mushrooms. Cook until onion is translucent, about 3 minutes. Add the green onions and stir-fry for about 1 minute more. Transfer onions and mushrooms to bowl with beef. Add kelp noodles, reserved spinach, remaining 3 tablespoons soy sauce, remaining 1 tablespoon sesame oil, and sugar substitute to bowl. Combine thoroughly. Serve warm, garnished with toasted sesame seeds.

MAKES 2 SERVINGS.

Per serving—Net carbohydrate: 5.9 grams; Protein: 31.8 grams; Fiber: 3.3 grams; Fat: 28.8 grams; Calories: 431

Total weight: 8⁷⁄₈ or 246 grams

Weight per serving: 4½ ounces or 125 grams

Preparation time: 25 minutes active and total

Japchae is traditionally served with rice and a side of hot, pickled napa-cabbage (Kimchi) for dinner or alone as a snack. You may want to try it with Kimchi, which is available in jars at Asian groceries. (Choose one without sugar; it should have zero to one gram of carbs per serving.)

———

Shirataki noodles are made of konjac root and consist mainly of gelatinous fiber. They have zero carbs, zero fat, and zero protein. Plain shiratki is rubbery and tasteless, but it can support a tasty topping. Tofu shiratki has a small amount of tofu added which gives it a texture more like soft egg needles and adds a small amount of carbohydrate. They are available with the Asian foods in many groceries.

See p. 51 for information about kelp noodles.

TIP:

An 18-by-13-inch baking sheet with a 1- inch rim is best for this recipe. If you don't have a large, shallow baking sheet, use 2 smaller ones. Don't crowd the pan or the contents will steam rather than caramelize.

Chicken with Spices and Roasted Pumpkin

Pumpkin is very low in carbohydrates and high in fiber, but fresh pumpkins are only available from September to December. Butternut squash is also delicious in this recipe, and it is available both fresh and frozen year round. It will, however, cost you a few more carbs.

1 small pie pumpkin (about 2 pounds as purchased) or butternut squash
    (add 3 net carbs per serving if using squash)
6 bone-in chicken thighs or about 3 pounds
¼ cup light olive oil or other fat with a high smoke point, divided
2 teaspoons chili powder
1 teaspoon cocoa powder
½ teaspoon freshly ground black pepper
½ teaspoon ground cumin
½ teaspoon ground coriander
¼ teaspoon ground cinnamon
1½ teaspoons salt
Sugar substitute equal to ½ teaspoon sugar, optional

Preheat oven to 450° F.

Cut pumpkin or squash in half, remove seeds and stringy fibers, and peel. Cut into 1½-inch cubes or slice into ½-inch wedges. Set aside.

Blot chicken dry with paper towels. Place 2 tablespoons of the oil in a large bowl. Add chicken pieces and turn to coat. Mix spices and seasonings together in a small bowl. Reserve 2 teaspoons of the mixture. Sprinkle half of the remaining seasonings over chicken. Turn chicken and repeat with other half. Let stand for about 5 minutes.

Heat remaining 2 tablespoons of oil in a large (12- or 14-inch) skillet over medium-high heat until hot but not smoking. Arrange chicken in pan in a single layer and cook, turning once, until both sides are browned, about 6 to 8 minutes. Remove chicken to a plate.

Add pumpkin or squash to skillet. Sprinkle with reserved 2 teaspoons of spice mixture. Cook and stir in hot pan juices for 5 minutes or until it just starts to brown. Transfer pumpkin to a large, rimmed baking sheet. Place chicken, skin-side-up, on top of pumpkin and place in pre-heated oven. Roast for 25 minutes or until chicken is cooked through and skin is crisp. Remove chicken and pumpkin to a serving platter. To make a sauce, pour pan juices into a narrow container and let sit for a few minutes until the fat rises to the top. Skim off fat and serve sauce on the side.

MAKES 6 SERVINGS

Per serving—Net carbohydrate: 3 grams; Protein: 30.5 grams; Fiber: 1.4 grams; Fat: 11.5 grams;* Calories: 238*

Total drained weight: 2 pound 7 ounces or 1.2 kilograms;

Drained weight per serving: 6 2/3 ounces or 188 grams

Preparation time: 25 minutes active; 1 hour total

*Note: About half the fat will be drained or left over, so 11.5 grams of fat and 103.5 calories is excluded from the counts.

Pumpkin and red kuri squash have the lowest carbohydrate count and the most fiber in the winter squash family. Red kuri, a small, pear-shaped squash, available in late summer to mid-winter, can be used in this recipe instead of pumpkin or butternut squash. They are smooth, nutty, and delicious, but they have a hard rind making them difficult to peel. A few minutes in the microwave will soften them.

Chicken with Spices and Roasted Pumpkin

Lettuce Wedge Salad with Blue Cheese Dressing

The word "lettuce" used to be synonymous with "iceberg" in America. It has been out of vogue in recent years, perhaps because it was so overused. I can't argue that it has much in the way of nutrients, and it is a bit bland compared to Romaine or butter head, but you can't do justice to this classic salad without the dense, crisp texture of iceberg lettuce.

½ pound bacon (½ ounce per slice, cooked weight)
1 head (about 2 pounds, as purchased) iceberg lettuce,
  outer leaves removed
Coarse salt to taste
Fresh black pepper to taste
2 tablespoons chopped, fresh chives for garnish, optional
Blue Cheese Dressing, below

Cook bacon until crisp. Drain. Rinse lettuce and blot dry. Cut head vertically into 8 wedges. Remove core and place a lettuce wedge on each of 8 chilled salad plates. Top each serving with 3 tablespoons of **Blue Cheese Dressing** and crumble 2 strips of bacon on top. Sprinkle with coarse salt and freshly ground black pepper. Garnish with chopped chives, if desired, and serve.

BLUE CHEESE DRESSING

½ cup **Mayonnaise**, p. 298, or purchased no-trans-fat, real mayonnaise
½ cup Greek-style plain yogurt or sour cream
1 tablespoon lemon juice
2 ounces (½ cup) mild blue cheese, such as Gorgonzola
Salt and fresh black pepper to taste

Combine mayonnaise, yogurt or sour cream, lemon juice, and blue cheese in a medium bowl and whisk until combined, but not smooth; small lumps of blue cheese should remain. Add salt and pepper to taste and chill. Dressing can be made ahead and refrigerated.

MAKES 8 SERVINGS.

Per serving—Net carbohydrate: 1.3 grams; Protein: 3.5 grams; Fiber: 0.8 grams; Fat: 3.4 grams; Calories: 52

Total weight: 2 pounds 5¼ ounces or 1 kilogram

Weight per serving: 4⅔ ounces or 132 grams

Preparation time: 10 minutes active; 15 minutes total

MAKES 1½ CUPS OR 8 SERVINGS OF 3 TABLESPOONS.

Per serving—Net carbohydrate: 1.6 grams; Protein: 2.2 grams; Fiber: 0 grams; Fat: 13.3 grams; Calories: 134

Total weight, dressing only: 10 ounces or 284 grams

Weight per serving: 1¼ ounces or 36 grams

Preparation time: 10 minutes active and total

Lemon Icebox Pie

My mother used to make a lemon icebox pie that had just three ingredients plus a graham cracker crust: sweetened condensed milk, lemon juice, and egg yolks. It seemed like magic when the acid in the lemon juice made the egg yolks set up. Here's my super-easy version for the time-challenged. You don't even have to measure anything, just open the containers and combine. You can leave out the lemon zest if that's too much cooking for you!

Baked **Almond Pie Crust**, p. 168

16 ounces (two 8-ounce tubs) whipped cream cheese

1 eight-ounce container plain, Greek-style yogurt (full fat, if possible), with live cultures

3 packets of *Crystal Light On the Go* powdered lemonade mix or the equivalent amount of any sugar-free lemonade mix

2 teaspoons grated lemon zest, optional

Beat all ingredients together. Pour into cooled **Almond Pie Crust**. Refrigerate until set. Top with sugar-free **Whipped Cream**, p. 312, if desired.

MAKES 10 SERVINGS.

Per serving with crust—
Net carbohydrate: 4.2 grams (excludes 0.8 gram eaten by the yogurt culture); Protein: 6 grams; Fiber: 1.7 grams; Fat: 23 grams; Calories: 248

Total weight: 1 pound 11 ounces or 767 grams

Weight per serving: 2¾ ounces or 96 grams

Preparation time: 5 minutes total

"I prefer Hostess fruit pies to pop-up toaster tarts because they don't require as much cooking."

— *Carrie Snow*

Pork Tenderloin with Fennel, Onion, and Celery

1 pork tenderloin, about 1 pound
1 teaspoon fennel seeds
½ teaspoon salt (do not use salt if using Better Than Bouillon)
½ teaspoon pepper
2 tablespoons peanut or olive oil
1 fennel bulb (8 ounces), stalks removed and fronds reserved
¼ cup fennel fronds, fine green part only, chopped
1 medium (3.5 ounce) onion, peeled
2 stalks celery (3 ounces)
3 garlic cloves (3/8 ounce), peeled and crushed
¼ cup white wine
½ cup water or chicken stock
½ teaspoon chicken base, such as Better Than Bouillon, optional
2 tablespoons butter, softened
1 teaspoon fresh lemon juice

Preheat oven to 350° F with rack in middle position.

Rinse pork and pat dry. Crush fennel seeds with a mortar and pestle or with bottom of a heavy skillet. Sprinkle pork with crushed fennel seeds, salt, and pepper. Reserve some of fennel fronds for garnish. Cut fennel bulb and onion lengthwise into ½-inch wedges. Remove strings from celery with a vegetable peeler and slice into 2-inch lengths.

Place oil in a 12-inch, oven-safe skillet. Heat on medium-high heat until oil shimmers in the pan. Brown pork on all sides, about 6 minutes total, then transfer to a plate. In same pan, sauté fennel, onion, and celery for 4 minutes. Add garlic and sauté until garlic is softened and other vegetables are golden brown, about 2 minutes more. Add wine, stirring and scraping up brown bits, then stir in water or broth and butter. Put pork on top of vegetables and transfer skillet to oven. Roast for about 15 minutes or until an instant-read thermometer inserted into the thickest part of pork registers 145° to 150° F. Transfer pork to a cutting board, tent loosely with foil, and let rest for 5 to 10 minutes.

Meanwhile, transfer skillet with vegetables to stovetop and boil, stirring occasionally, until almost all the liquid has evaporated. Stir in lemon juice. Place vegetables on serving platter or plates. Thinly slice the pork, place over vegetables, and drizzle with pan juices. Garnish with chopped fennel fronds if desired.

Recipe adapted from *Gourmet Magazine,* February 2009

MAKES 4 SERVINGS.

Per serving—Net carbohydrate: 5.6 grams; Protein: 31 grams; Fiber: 2.3 grams; Fat: 17.3 grams; Calories: 324

Total weight for vegetables and pork: 1 pound 10 ounces or 735 grams

Weight per serving for vegetables and pork: 6½ ounces or 184 grams

Preparation time: 20 minutes active, 45 minutes total

NEW SAFETY GUIDELINES FOR PORK:
Today's pork is very lean and should not be overcooked. According to the new USDA guidelines, pork chops, roasts, and tenderloins can be safely cooked to medium-rare with a final internal temperature of 145° F, followed by three minutes of resting time. The lower cooking temperature will produce pork that's succulent and tender and will likely yield a finished product that is pinker in color than most of us are accustomed to.

Restaurants have been following this standard for nearly 10 years. The new temperature recommendation, announced on May 24, 2011, reflects advances in food safety and nutritional content for pork. Both the USDA and the National Pork Board suggest using a digital cooking thermometer to ensure an accurate final temperature.

NOTE:
Ground pork, like all ground meat, should be cooked to 160° F.

Dreamfields pasta is made of regular semolina flour (that's why it tastes so good), but it contains a fiber blend that protects most of the starch from being digested. It has 5 digestible grams of carbohydrate in a standard 2-ounce serving (dry weight) and a low glycemic index of 13. It should be cooked only to the *al dente* stage, which means it should feel slightly firm "to the tooth." If it is overcooked, it will become more digestible. It is also important that if it is reheated, it should be done so gently and only until warm.

Those with diabetes are advised to test for blood glucose spikes after eating Dreamfields. The Dreamfields website states, "Results do vary by person, so try Dreamfields and see what your glycemic results show. "Dreamfields comes as spaghetti, angel hair, rotini, penne, linguini, lasagna, and two sizes of macaroni. Company president, Mike Crowley, said in a recent interview that the company is developing a rice product using a similar technique to protect some of the starch from digestion.

See p. 325 for non-grain pasta alternatives, such as spaghetti squash, kelp noodles, or shirataki noodles.

Pasta with Alfredo Sauce

Classic Italian cooking can be summed up this way: the finest ingredients, simply prepared. Case in point:

FOR SAUCE:
    2 teaspoons minced garlic (¼ ounce)
    ¼ cup butter (2 ounces or ½ stick)
    1 cup heavy cream (8 ounces)
    1¼ cups (5 ounces) Parmesan cheese, finely grated
    Salt to taste (Parmesan is salty; you many not need more.)
    Freshly ground black pepper to taste

FOR PASTA:
    7.5 ounces Dreamfields pasta, prepared al dente, by package directions. (This is the amount for 5 servings of 1½ ounces each, which is 25% less than a standard 2-ounce serving)

Melt butter in a heavy saucepan over medium-low heat. Add garlic and cook until softened but not browned, about 1 minute. Stir in cream, salt and pepper. Simmer over low heat, stirring frequently, for about 30 minutes or until slightly thickened. Remove from heat and stir in cheese. Serve over Dreamfields pasta or pasta alternative of choice, p. 325. It also makes a delicious sauce for eggs or vegetables.

MAKES 1²/₃ CUPS OR 5 SERVINGS OF ¹/₃ CUP OF SAUCE.

Per serving, sauce only—Net carbohydrate: 2.5 grams; Protein: 10.2 grams; Fiber: 0 grams; Fat: 34.2 grams; Calories: 349

Per serving for sauce plus pasta, based on digestible carbs—Net carbohydrate: 6.25 net grams; Protein: 15.5 grams; Fiber: 3.75 grams; Fat: 34.5 grams; Calories: 493

Total weight for sauce only: 12¼ ounces or 348 grams;

Total weight for pasta only: 18¾ ounces or 533 grams

Weight per serving for sauce only: 2½ ounces or 71 grams;

Weight per serving for 1½ ounces dry pasta, cooked: 3¾ ounces or 107 grams

Preparation time: 5 minutes active; 35 minutes total

Pots de Crème au Chocolate

It's just pudding. Shhh, don't tell anyone.

3 ounces unsweetened chocolate
4 egg yolks
Sugar substitute to equal ½ cup sugar
1/8 teaspoon salt
1 cup heavy cream
2/3 cup water
2½ teaspoons sugar-free vanilla extract
2½ teaspoons Godiva chocolate liqueur or Kahlúa, optional
Whipped Cream, p. 312, and raspberries for garnish, optional

Cut chocolate into small pieces and place in medium heat-proof bowl. Have ready three or four 5- to 6-ounce custard cups or ramekins.

Whisk together yolks, sweetener, and salt in a second bowl. Whisk in cream and water. Place mixture in a medium saucepan and cook over medium-low heat, stirring constantly and scraping bottom and sides of pan with a flexible spatula until slightly thickened and an instant-read thermometer reads 175° to 180° F. This will take about 8 to 12 minutes. Do not let custard come to a simmer.

Pour hot custard over chocolate and whisk or stir until chocolate is melted and smooth. Whisk in vanilla extract and liqueur, if using. Pour into cups.

Let pots de crème cool to room temperature, then cover and refrigerate for at least 4 hours. Remove from refrigerator and let stand at room temperature for 20 minutes before serving. Garnish with sugar-free **Whipped Cream** and a raspberry, if desired.

NOTE:
When using sucralose in chocolate recipes, adding a small amount of another sweetener will give a more natural sweet taste. Replace the equivalent of 2 teaspoons sugar with one packet of Sweet One (Sunette), 2 teaspoons of DiabetiSweet, or an equivalent amount of stevia extract or stevia blend when using Splenda.

MAKES 2¼ CUPS OR 4 SERVINGS.

Per serving—Net carbohydrate: 5.2 grams; Protein: 6.7 grams; Fiber: 3.6 grams; Fat: 38.1 grams; Calories: 377

Total weight: 1 pound 2¾ ounces or 531 grams

Weight per serving: 4²/₃ ounces or 133 grams

Preparation time: 20 minutes active and total plus chilling time

Pots De Crème au Chocolate, p. 107

"Okay, first of all, here's how you do NOT pronounce *Pots de Crème:* "Pawts deh Creem." Here's how you DO pronounce *Pots de Crème:* "Po de Krehm", or, if you want to get really technical, "Po de k (insert phlegmy, back-of-the-throat crackly French sound) ehm."

— *Ree Drummond, www.thepioneerwoman.com*

Barbecued Country-Style Ribs

Country-style ribs come from the loin end of the pork shoulder or the shoulder end of the loin, depending on where the two cuts are divided. They are meatier than spareribs and they have more fat to make them succulent and tender. They are also a better buy. Compared to the more popular back ribs, they have about twice the meat at half the price.

1 teaspoon salt
3½ pounds boneless country-style pork ribs
Additional salt and pepper to taste
2/3 cup **Barbecue Sauce**, p. 293, or use purchased low-carb barbecue sauce (see Sources)
Nonstick cooking spray

Grease a large roasting pan and rack.

Bring a large pot of water to a boil. Add 1 teaspoon of salt. Add ribs to pot, turn heat to low, and cover. Cook for 30 minutes.

Preheat oven to 325° F. Drain ribs and place on rack in greased roasting pan. Sprinkle with salt and pepper; cover the pan tightly with a lid or with a sheet of parchment paper (to keep the foil from touching the meat) and then with aluminum foil. Bake at 325° F for 1½ hours. Uncover and drain off the pan drippings. Brush the ribs with sugar-free **Barbecue Sauce,** spray with non-stick spray, and continue to bake, uncovered, for another 15 minutes. Turn the ribs and baste the other side with barbecue sauce. Spray with non-stick spray and bake for 15 minutes more. Spray once more and serve hot.

MAKES 4 SERVINGS OF 8 OUNCES EACH.

Per serving—Net carbohydrate: 1.6 grams; Protein: 77 grams; Fiber: 0.5 grams; Fat: 48.6 grams; Calories: 774

Total weight: 2 pounds or 906 grams

Weight per serving: 8 ounces or 227 grams

Preparation time: 10 minutes active, 2 hours and 35 minutes total

---

Barbecued
Country-Style Ribs
1.6 net carbs

Cheese Polenta
5 net carbs

Carolina Coleslaw
3.8 net carbs

Pumpkin
Pound Cake
3.9 net carbs

Menu total: 14.3 net carbs

Modern pigs from factory farms, "the other white meat," are much leaner than old-fashioned porkers. Some producers, like Niman Ranch, raise hogs in open pastures without the use of antibiotics or growth hormones. Because the hogs live outdoors in the Midwest, they develop more fat for insulation from summer heat and winter cold, which promotes superior marbling, flavor, and tenderness. See Sources for more information about choices.

Barbecued Country-Style Rib (p. 109)s

Cheese Polenta

This is one of my favorite recipes using Mexican-style hominy. Serve it as a side dish for roast chicken, duck, ham, or pork.

2 cups Juanita's Mexican Style Hominy (13 ounces),[74] drained
¾ cup cream
1 tablespoon butter
2 ounces grated Gruyère cheese (about ½ cup), plus 5 teaspoons (3/8 ounce) more for tops
2 ounces grated Parmesan cheese (about ½ cup)
¼ cup sugar-free **Dried Cranberries**, p. 12, or purchased sugar-free cranberries (see Sources)
1/8 teaspoon nutmeg
Salt and pepper to taste

Butter six ½-cup baking dishes or a muffin tin and a shallow baking pan.

Plump the cranberries in hot water if they are very dry. Add a little sugar-free sweetener if they are unsweetened. (Blot them well or the polenta will be pink.)

Process the hominy in the bowl of a food processor until evenly chopped and similar in texture to rice. Place the hominy, cream, and butter in a heavy saucepan. Cook, stirring, until it bubbles and thickens. Stir in the ½ cup of Gruyère and all the Parmesan cheese, the cranberries, nutmeg, and salt and pepper. Cook and stir a few minutes more until it forms a smooth mass that pulls away from the pan. Press the mixture into the buttered baking dishes or muffin tin. Chill for a minimum of 15 minutes. It can be made ahead and refrigerated at this point.

Preheat the oven to 450° F. Loosen the edges of the polenta with a knife and unmold onto a greased baking pan. Place one teaspoon of Gruyère on top of each serving and bake for 5 to 10 minutes until golden brown on top. Run under the broiler briefly to brown, if necessary. Watch carefully so they don't burn. Serve hot.

---

74   The weight given on a large can of Juanita's Mexican Style Hominy is 29 ounces but that includes the liquid. After draining, the hominy weighs about 16 ounces.

MEXICAN-STYLE HOMINY:
Juanita's Mexican-style Hominy is surprisingly low in carbohydrates, just 4 net grams per one-half cup, considering that most corn products, and even other brands of hominy, have from 13 to 25 grams in the same amount.

Put it, straight out of the can, in soups instead of dumplings or noodles, and in chili instead of beans. Serve it with butter as a side dish or whirl it in the food processor and use it in place of rice, bulgur, barley, grits, or polenta. If you can't find Juanita's, there are other brands that are almost as low, just be sure it says "Mexican Style" on the label. They vary a great deal in carbohydrate content, so be sure to check the carb count.

NOTE:
The volume of grated cheese may vary depending on whether it is compacted or fluffy. Use weight for a more accurate measure.

SERVES SIX.

Per serving—Net carbohydrate: 5 grams; Protein: 9.2 grams; Fiber: 7.8 grams; Fat: 19.9 grams; 259 Calories

Total weight: 1 pound 3 ounces or 540 grams

Weight per serving: 3 ounces or 90 grams

Preparation time: 20 minutes active; 45 minutes total

Carolina Coleslaw

North Carolina-style coleslaw has a tangy, vinegar-based dressing without mayonnaise.

1 pound (5½ cups or about ½ a small head) finely shredded cabbage
2 ounces (½ cup) finely chopped green onion
3 ounces (½ cup) red bell pepper, cut into thin strips
⅓ cup plus 2 tablespoons cider vinegar
Sugar substitute equal to 2 tablespoons sugar
⅓ cup olive or peanut oil
½ teaspoon salt or to taste
¼ teaspoon fresh ground black pepper
1 teaspoon celery seed

MAKES 5 SERVINGS OF 1 CUP EACH.

Per serving—Net carbohydrate: 3.8 grams; Protein: 1.3 grams; Fiber: 2.5 grams; Fat: 13.2 grams; Calories: 145

Total weight: 1 pound 9½ ounces or 724 grams

Weight per serving: 5 ounces or 145 grams

Preparation time: 10 minutes active and total plus chilling time.

Note: About ¼ cup of dressing will be left in bowl.

Put vegetables in a large, heat-resistant bowl. Heat vinegar, sweetener, and oil to boiling in a small non-reactive pan (stainless steel, enamel, or ceramic). Pour hot mixture over vegetables in bowl and toss to coat. Add salt, pepper, and celery seed and toss again. Cover and refrigerate for 1 hour or overnight. Serve with a slotted spoon or pour off liquid.

VARIATION:

Mexican Coleslaw

Leave out the sweetener in the recipe for **Carolina Coleslaw** to make **Mexican Coleslaw.**

Carolina Coleslaw

Pumpkin Pound Cake

Television chef and cookbook author, George Stella, contributed this recipe.

It is hard to believe that this trim, energetic man, with the twinkling blue eyes, had given up on life at the age of forty. At 467 pounds, he was on disability, suffering from congestive heart failure, and was confined to a wheelchair because his spine could not support his weight. After his doctor told him he was going to die, he discovered low carb and lost over 250 pounds and found a new career, inspiring others with his success story and his food. His wife and two sons joined him in his new way of eating, and the Stella family lost a total of 560 pounds.

2 tablespoons wheat bran

2½ cups (9 ounces or 225 grams) almond flour

Sugar substitute equal to 1½ cups sugar

1½ teaspoons baking powder

1½ teaspoons pumpkin pie spice

¼ teaspoon salt

7 eggs

1½ cups canned pumpkin purée (not pumpkin pie filling)

1½ teaspoons sugar-free vanilla extract

Sugar-free **Whipped Cream**, p. 312, for garnish, optional

Preheat oven to 300° F. Grease a 5- by 9-inch loaf pan and sprinkle with wheat bran, shaking the pan to coat on all sides—this will prevent sticking.

In a bowl, whisk together the almond flour, sugar substitute, baking powder, pie spice, and salt. In another bowl, beat the eggs and then whisk in the pumpkin and vanilla. Combine the dry and wet ingredients and stir until combined. Pour batter into prepared pan.

Bake until golden brown and a wooden pick inserted in the center comes out clean, about 1½ hours. Cool completely before removing from pan. Slice into 16 portions.

Recipe from, Eating Stella Style; *used by permission*

Using Granular Splenda adds 2.3 net carbs per serving of cake. It contains sugar as a bulking agent, which adds 1 net gram of carbohydrate per 2 teaspoons (or 0.9 grams per packet, which is equal to 2 teaspoons of granular). Crushed Splenda tabs, the ones that come in a yellow dispenser, are an option for eliminating the sugar used in granular sweeteners, as it has only a tiny amount of maltose, but it requires counting out 36 tablets (to equal 1½ cups sugar) and crushing them to a powder. Liquid sucralose has zero carbs.

MAKES 16 SERVINGS.

Per serving—Net carbohydrate 3.9 grams (made with 0 carb sweetener) or 6.2 grams (made with granular Splenda); Protein: 9.1 grams; Fiber: 3.9 grams; Fat: 14.8 grams; Calories: 189

Total weight: 2 pounds ¾ ounces or 926 grams

Weight per serving: 2¾ ounces or 77 grams

Preparation time: 15 minutes active; 1 hour 45 minutes total

Spaghetti with
Meat Sauce

6.9 net carbs

Mixed Greens with
Roasted Garlic
and "Balsamic"
Vinaigrette

1.8 net carbs

Lemon Cake
(p. 116) with
Lemon Glaze

3.3 net carbs for cake,
0.9 net carbs for glaze

Menu total: 12.9 net carb

Spaghetti with Meat Sauce

FOR EACH SERVING:
1¾ ounces (slightly less than the standard 2-ounce serving)
 Dreamfields pasta or pasta alternative, see p. 325
1/3 cup **Meat Sauce**, p. 296
2 tablespoons grated Parmesan cheese or to taste.

Prepare Dreamfields pasta *al dente*, according to package directions, or see Pasta alternatives, p. 325. Top with sauce and sprinkle with Parmesan cheese.

MAKES 1 SERVING.

Per serving with 1¾-ounces Dreamfield's pasta—Net carbohydrate: 7.7 grams; Protein: 14.5 grams; Fiber: 5.5 grams; Fat: 0.67 grams; Calories: 252

Weight per serving: 9 ounces or 254 grams (including pasta, sauce, and cheese)

Preparation time: 5 minutes active; 15 minutes total, not including making **Meat Sauce**.

Mixed Greens with Roasted Garlic and "Balsamic" Vinaigrette

Balsamic vinegar can be very high in sugar. I have one that came in a fancy crystal decanter that has 10 grams of carbs per tablespoon (almost as much as pure sugar)! Red wine vinegar and a touch of sweetener is a better choice.

8 cups (8 ounces) mixed greens or mesclun, washed and dried
Roasted Garlic and "Balsamic" Vinaigrette, p. 301.

Place greens in a large bowl. Pour half of dressing over greens and toss until coated. Divide between 4 chilled salad plates and serve with remaining dressing on the side.

MAKES 4 SERVINGS OF 2 CUPS EACH.

Per serving—Net carbohydrate: 1.8 grams; Protein: 0.8 grams; Fiber: 0.8 grams; Fat: 16.9 grams; Calories: 164

Total weight: 2⅞ ounces or 82 grams for salad and dressing

Weight per serving: ¾ ounce or 20 grams for salad and dressing

Preparation time: 5 minutes active and total

Roasted Garlic

1 whole head of garlic, about 2½ ounces as purchased
1 or 2 teaspoons olive oil

TO PREPARE GARLIC:

Peel away the papery outer layer from a bulb of garlic, leaving the cloves intact. Cut off about ½ inch of the top of the head with a knife. Cut off the tips of any remaining individual cloves so that all are exposed. Pour the olive oil over the garlic bulb and rub to cover the entire head.

TO COOK IN MICROWAVE:

Place garlic on a small dish and microwave for 1 minute. Turn upside down and microwave for another minute. The garlic is done when it feels very soft to the touch. If it is still firm, continue to microwave it for 15 to 30 seconds at a time, until it is soft enough to spread easily.

TO ROAST IN OVEN:

Wrap garlic in foil. Bake at 400° F for 35 minutes or until very soft.

Let garlic cool for about 15 minutes. Squeeze the soft roasted garlic out of skins to use as a spread or as an ingredient in salad dressings, dips, and recipes.

MAKES ABOUT 3.5 TABLESPOONS GARLIC PULP.

Net carbohydrate per teaspoon of garlic pulp: 0.9 grams; Protein: 0.2 grams; Fiber: 0.1 grams; Fat: 0.02 grams; Calories: 4

Total weight: 1 ounce or 28 grams

Preparation time (microwave): 5 minutes active, 7 minutes total

Preparation time (regular oven): 5 minutes active, 40 minutes total

Tossed salads are a staple for dieters, but most commercial dressings contain high-fructose corn syrup, thickeners, and starch. Bottled cream dressings substitute milk and "modified food starch" for cream. Use real, organic cream or real, zero-carb mayonnaise and good oil to make your own salad dressings. When you eat in a restaurant, olive oil and vinegar are probably the safest choice. At home, indulge in some really special flavored vinegars and extra-virgin olive oil or macadamia, hazelnut, or walnut oil to dress your salads.

Lemon Cake, p. 125

Lemon Glaze

*A sweet, tart glaze, perfect over the **Lemon Cake** version of my **Yellow Cake**, p. 124. Docking the cake with a fork or wooden pick before glazing will make it extra moist.*

6 tablespoons (2¼ ounces or 67 grams) polydextrose, see Sources
2 tablespoons (¾ ounce or 24 grams) granular erythritol (erythritol crystals)
⅛ teaspoon salt
¼ cup lemon juice (amount from 1 large lemon)
High intensity sugar substitute equal to 2 tablespoons sugar or to taste
3 tablespoons butter, cut into small pieces
¼ teaspoon grated lemon zest

MAKES ½ CUP OR 10 SERVINGS OF 2½ TEASPOONS EACH.

Per serving (glaze only)—Net carbohydrate: 0.9 grams; Protein: 0.1 grams; Fiber: 5.7 grams; Fat: 3.5 grams; Calories: 39

Total weight: 5 ounces or 140 grams

Weight per serving: ½ ounce or 14 grams

Preparation time: 10 minutes active and total plus cooling time

Whisk polydextrose, erythritol, and salt in a microwave-safe bowl until well blended. Stir in lemon juice and high-intensity sweetener. Microwave on high for about 4 minutes or until it bubbles and forms a thick, clear syrup. (Can also be cooked in a small saucepan on the stovetop.) Add the butter and zest and stir until butter melts. Let cool and pour over whole cake or warm individual slices in microwave and glaze with 2½ teaspoons each when ready to serve. Dock cake with a fork or wooden pick before glazing, if desired.

Refrigerate glaze and reheat as necessary.

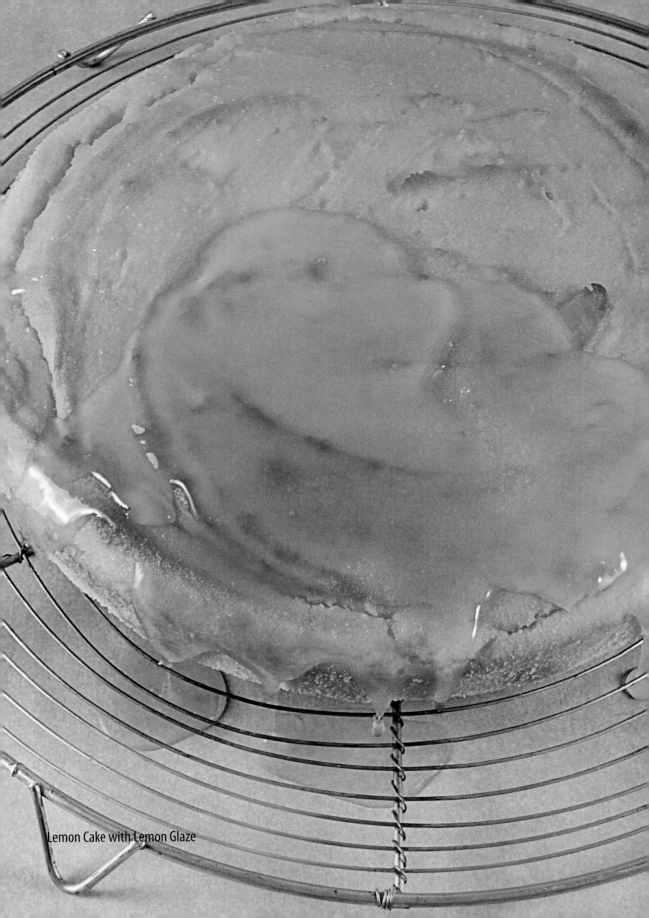

Lemon Cake with Lemon Glaze

Roast Chicken

Roast Chicken

0 net carbs

Mushroom Gravy

3.3 net carbs

Cauliflower *Faux* Mashed Potatoes (p. 281)

2.2 net carbs

Green Beans with Red Wine Vinegar and Extra Virgin Olive Oil

2.6 net carbs

Yellow Cake with Chocolate Butter Cream Frosting

Cake, 3.3 net carbs;
Frosting, 0.6 net carbs

Menu total: 12 net carbs

NOTE:
Air-chilled chickens are chilled with a blast of cold air rather than a water bath, so they absorb less water.

Roast Chicken

I'm not chef Joel Robuchon's grandmother, but his Grandmother's Roast Chicken *recipe is very similar to mine.*[75] *It requires turning the chicken from side to side and cooking it at a high temperature. Perhaps this was a classic French technique, perhaps his grandmother invented it herself, or perhaps she learned it as I did, way back when, from* American Home *magazine. (I have, however, adopted one part of chef Robuchon's recipe that was not originally in mine: I now rest my chicken upside down after cooking.)*

1 whole chicken, about 4½ pounds as purchased
2 to 3 tablespoons butter
1 teaspoon salt
½ teaspoon pepper
1 stalk celery, with some green top left on
½ a peeled onion
2 carrots
1 or 2 stems of fresh thyme or 1 teaspoon dried
Several leaves of fresh sage or 1 teaspoon dried

FOR THE ROASTING PAN:
1 stalk of celery, chopped
½ onion, chopped
1 carrot, chopped
2 garlic cloves, chopped
A stem of fresh thyme or ½ teaspoon dried thyme
Several fresh sage leaves or ½ teaspoon dried sage

Remove chicken and butter from refrigerator. If chicken has been frozen, be sure it is completely thawed. Unwrap chicken and remove neck and giblets from body cavity. Refrigerate liver. Let butter and chicken stand at room temperature for 30 minutes. Grease a roasting pan and a "V" shaped rack. Preheat the oven to 425° F.

Rinse chicken and pat dry inside and out. Remove and discard the deposits of fat usually found just inside the body

---

75   *Simply French: Patricia Wells Presents the Cuisine of Joel Robuchon,* 1991.

cavity and on the underside of the neck skin or use for another purpose. Sprinkle chicken with salt and pepper inside and out, including the neck cavity. Put giblets (except liver) and neck in the baking pan. Brush the entire bird with softened butter. Lay it on its side on the rack and place the pan in the preheated oven. Roast for 20 minutes.

Using potholders (waterproof is advisable) or several layers of paper towels, turn chicken to other side so the opposite wing and leg are up. Baste with pan drippings or butter and add ¼ cup water, chopped vegetables, garlic, and extra herbs to the pan. Return to oven. Reduce temperature to 375º F and roast for 20 minutes.

Turn chicken breast-side-up and baste with pan juices or butter. Roast for 20 minutes longer or until well browned. (Use convection mode if your oven has that option to aid browning. Convection may reduce cooking time.)

Baste again and add another ¼ cup of water to the pan. Continue to roast until juices run clear when thigh joint is pierced where it joins the body or until an instant-read meat thermometer inserted in the thickest part of the thigh, not touching bone, registers 170º F, about 10 to 15 minutes longer. The juices in the body cavity should have no trace of pink and the leg should move freely. (The temperature will continue to rise to about 180º F as the chicken rests.)

When the thermometer registers the correct temperature, remove pan from oven. Lift chicken, tipping it so the juices drain back into the pan, and place in a heat-resistant bowl that will hold it almost vertically, breast down, with the tail tilted up, so the juices flow down to bathe the white meat. Tent loosely with foil and let rest in a warm place 10 to 20 minutes while making gravy.

MAKES 4 SERVINGS.

Per serving—Net carbohydrate: 0 grams; Protein: 54.7 grams; Fiber: 0 grams; Fat: 27 grams; Calories: 479

Total weight, edible yield: 1 pound 12 ounces or 800 grams

Weight per serving: 7 ounces or 200 grams

Preparation time: 30 minutes active, 1 hour 45 min total

NOTE:
Even a "fresh" chicken may be partially frozen. A sign in one of my local stores explained that their "fresh" chickens may feel hard because they are required to hold them at 26º F, but that "technically" they are not "frozen." (?) If the giblets are icy when you remove them, you will need to wait until the chicken is completely thawed so it will cook evenly.

Trussing is not necessary and may result in uneven cooking, according to Christopher Kimball of America's Test Kitchen. He says it is just a hold-over from the time when poultry was spit roasted and needed to be tied into a neat package to keep it from falling into the fire.

Chef and author Charlie Palmer not only agrees, but recommends using a wooden dowel or metal skewer to hold the body cavity open so heat can circulate freely for more even cooking. He also drives a metal skewer through the thickest part of the thigh so it will cook in the same amount of time as the breast meat.[76]

---

76 *Chef's Secrets as Told to Francine Maroukian; Insiders Techniques from today's culinary Masters.*

Mushroom Gravy

TIP:

If you use chicken stock, you can reduce it while the chicken roasts. Add the de-fatted juices from the roasting pan and cutting board to the gravy and reheat before serving.

This recipe comes from George Stella, star of the Food Network show, Low-Carb and Lovin' It, *and his own cooking show on QVC. George is known for creating easy, tasty food using fresh, healthful ingredients that can be found on the outer aisles of the grocery store. He says, "There's more than one way to thicken a sauce or gravy! Since flour and cornstarch are out when you're eating low-carb, a classic French cream reduction is in order."*

2 cups defatted chicken or turkey juices from the roasting pan or
    homemade stock
½ cup heavy cream
3 tablespoons unsalted butter
10 ounces shitake mushrooms, rinsed, stemmed, and sliced
1 tablespoon chopped fresh thyme leaves
1 garlic clove, minced
¼ cup dry sherry
Salt and freshly ground black pepper to taste
½ teaspoon red wine vinegar

MAKES 1 ²/₃ CUPS OR 6 SERVINGS ABOUT ¼ CUP EACH.

Per serving—Net carbohydrate: 3.3 grams; Protein: 2.3 grams; Fiber: 1.3 grams; Fat: 7.6 grams; Calories: 103

Net carbohydrate per serving: 3.3 grams; Protein: 2.3 grams

Total weight: 13½ ounces or 385 grams

Weight per serving: 2¼ ounces or 64 grams

Preparation time: 10 minutes active; 35 minutes total

Bring stock to a simmer over medium-high heat in a wide, shallow pan and cook until reduced by half, about 15 to 20 minutes. Add cream and cook until reduced enough to coat the back of a spoon, about 8 to 15 minutes.

Heat the butter in a skillet over medium-high heat. Add the mushrooms, thyme, garlic, and sherry and cook, stirring occasionally, until mushrooms are tender and liquid is almost evaporated, about 6 minutes. Add mushroom mixture to the reduced stock and season with salt and pepper. Reheat if necessary and stir in vinegar. Transfer to a gravy boat and keep warm until serving time.

Recipe from *Livin' Low Carb: Family Recipes Stella-Style*, Simon and Schuster, 2005. Used by permission.

VARIATION:

Beef Mushroom Gravy

Make gravy with beef stock to accompany **Standing Beef Rib Roast** on p. 260.

Giblet Gravy

If giblet gravy is a hard sell at your house, the delicious, health-ful, sautéed liver makes a great cook's treat. (It's my husband's choice morsel, so I have to share it.)

Make gravy above, without mushrooms. Sauté the reserved liver in a skillet with a tablespoon of olive oil or butter. Chop the liver and the giblets into small dice and stir into gravy.

"Simple roast chicken is the test of a good cook."

— *Virginia Willis, author of* Bon Appétit, Y'all, *2008*

Giblet gravy once or twice a year may be the last source of organ meats included in the standard American diet. Organ meats were an important source of nutrients in most traditional societies. Even Ancel and Margaret Keys, who invented the Mediterranean Diet[77], advised eating liver once a week. (Contrary to the common perception that their diet was largely vegetarian, they also regularly ate beef, pork, lamb, chicken, Canadian bacon, and fish.)[78]

A trip to an ethnic grocery or foreign marketplace (Chinese, Japanese, Mexican, French— just about anywhere but here) will let you see how important organ meats are in the diet of most societies. *The Silver Spoon*,[79] the *Bible* of Italian cooking, devotes 28 pages to variety meats.

77   Ancel and Margaret Keys, *Eat Well, Stay Well*, 1959, *The Benevolent Bean*, 1967, and *Eat Well, Stay Well the Mediterranean Way*, Doubleday, *1975*

78   "The Fat of the Land," *Time Magazine*, January 13, 1961, Vol. LXXVII No.3.

79   *The Silver Spoon*, Phaidon, 2005.

Roast Chicken, p. 118

Green Beans with Red Wine Vinegar and Extra Virgin Olive Oil

The salt in the cooking pot keeps the beans bright green without adding significantly to the saltiness of the finished dish. Leaving the pot uncovered also helps them retain their bright color.

8 ounces fresh, small green beans *(haricots verte)*
Water
2 teaspoons salt
Additional salt to taste
2 tablespoons extra virgin olive oil
1 teaspoon red wine vinegar
Freshly-ground black pepper to taste

Rinse beans and snap off stem ends. Place in a large bowl of cold water and let soak for 10 minutes.

Bring a large pot of water to a full boil. Put 2 teaspoons salt into water. Add beans. When water returns to boil, reduce heat to keep beans cooking at an active simmer for 6 to 12 minutes. The time will vary depending on the size and freshness of the beans; very skinny, fresh beans will cook faster than larger, older ones. Taste one after the first 6 minutes and every 2 minutes or so afterwards and cook until they are tender-crisp and have lost their grassy taste. Remove beans from heat and drain. Place in a serving dish and toss with salt. Pour olive oil over beans and toss again until well coated. Add vinegar and a grating of black pepper and toss a third time. Serve warm or at room temperature.

TO COOK IN MICROWAVE:
Microwave on high for about 4 minutes (for 8 ounces of beans) or until tender-crisp.

NOTE:
Sometimes thin green beans come packaged in plastic with instructions saying to snip off a corner of the bag and microwave them in the package. As tempting as that is, many people are wary about eating foods cooked in plastic. I prefer to place such beans in a loosely covered dish or to wrap them in parchment paper and return them to the cooking bag before cooking in a microwave, so they are not in contact with the plastic.

MAKES 4 SERVINGS OF ABOUT ½ CUP.

Per serving—Net carbohydrate: 2.6 grams; Protein: 1.1 grams; Fiber: 1.8 grams; Fat: 6.9 grams; Calories: 80

Total weight: 8¾ ounces or 246 grams

Weight per serving: 2¼ ounces or 62 grams

Preparation time: 10 minutes active, 25 minutes total (15 for microwave-cooked beans)

Yellow Cake

A rich, moist, basic cake that can be varied by using different flavorings, frostings, and toppings. It is sugar-free, grain-free, gluten-free, and delicious.

Erythritol comes in granulated form (called *crystals*) or as a powder. Although all the packages I have seen say they weigh the same by volume, the powdered form really weighs about half as much as the granulated. If you start with powdered erythritol, it is better to measure by weight than by cups to get the proper amount. If you start with the granular form, you may measure by weight or cups, but you will need to grind it in a food processor or a coffee or spice grinder before using in baking, as it does not dissolve easily.

¾ cup (3 ounces or 85 grams) almond flour
¾ cup (3 ounces or 85 grams) coconut flour
¼ cup (2 ounces or 56 grams) granular erythritol, another sweetener with bulk, or a blend
1 teaspoon baking powder
A pinch of salt
½ cup (4 ounces or 1 stick) butter, softened to room temperature
4 ounces whipped or regular cream cheese, softened to room temperature
High-intensity sugar substitute equal to ¾ cup sugar, such as stevia or liquid sucralose (recipe was tested with 18 drops EZ-Sweetz)
6 eggs, at room temperature
2 teaspoons vanilla extract
1 teaspoon coconut, almond, lemon, or other extract
¾ teaspoon xanthan gum, for better texture, optional

Preheat oven to 350° F. Grease a 9-inch round cake pan, line with a circle of parchment paper, and grease the paper also. Dust with coconut flour and tap out the excess.

Put almond flour, coconut flour, erythritol and/or any other dry sweetener, baking powder, and salt in food processor. Process for about 2 minutes until well mixed and erythritol, if using, is very finely ground. Alternately, grind erythritol in a spice or coffee grinder and whisk with flours, baking powder, and salt. Reserve.

Beat the butter and cream cheese with an electric mixer until fluffy. Add one egg and beat until incorporated. Blend in extracts and any liquid sweetener. Sprinkle xanthan gum over butter mixture, a little at a time, and beat in. Add remaining eggs, one at a time, alternating with reserved flour mixture, and beating until smooth after each addition. Beat for an additional minute. Scrape batter into prepared cake pan and level the top. Bake at 350° F for 45 to 55 minutes or until golden brown and a wooden pick inserted near the center tests clean.

Set cake on a rack to cool for 10 minutes. Run a knife around the edge to loosen. Turn cake out of pan and place, right-side-up, onto a cake rack. Leave until completely cool. Frost with **Chocolate Butter Cream**, p. 126, or serve with **Whipped Cream**, p. 312, sugar-free **Ice Cream** (see Index), or follow directions for one of the variations below. For a two layer cake, double recipe or cut cake in half and stack layers with frosting between. (Double the nutrition counts per slice.)

Recipe adapted from Kent Altena at www.atkinsdietgeek.com.

MAKES 10 SERVINGS.

Per serving with zero-carb sweeteners—Net carbohydrate: 3.3 grams; Protein: 7.8 grams; Fiber: 4.2 grams; Fat: 21.6 grams; Calories: 249

Total weight: 1 pound 6 ounces or 715 grams

Weight per serving: 2½ ounces or 72 grams

Preparation time: 25 minutes active, 1 hour 5 minutes total

VARIATIONS:

Coconut Cake

Make **Yellow Cake** above, but use 1 teaspoon of vanilla extract plus 2 teaspoons coconut extract.

Microwave slices of cake until warm. Dock with a fork or wooden pick and douse each serving with 1 tablespoon of coconut-flavored sugar-free syrup (such as DaVinci's or Torani's). Top with grated coconut and **Whipped Cream** if desired.

Lemon Cake With Lemon Glaze

Make **Yellow Cake**, p. 124, using 1 teaspoon of vanilla extract and 2 teaspoons of lemon extract. Add 1 teaspoon grated lemon zest to batter. Spread **Lemon Glaze**, p. 116, over cake.

Toasted Cake with Ice Cream

Split cake slices horizontally and toast until lightly browned. Top with a scoop of **Ice Cream,** see Index.

A combination of sugar substitutes has advantages over any one alone. Erythritol has no calories or carbs, unlike most of the other sugar alcohols, however, it has two significant disadvantages. First, it has an odd, *cool* taste if used in quantity. Second it has a tendency to recrystallize, producing a grainy texture. Using a second sweetener, such as sucralose or stevia, helps; using a third would be even better. You may find that adding a packet of acesulfame K (Sweet One or Sunette) to the mix improves the taste.

Chocolate Butter Cream Frosting

No need to feel guilty when you indulge in this rich, chocolaty frosting. Double the recipe to fill and frost two layers.

¼ cup (1¾ ounces or 48 grams) of erythritol crystals, Sweet*perfection*, Just Like Sugar, or other sweetener with bulk

½ cup (4 ounces or 1 stick) butter, softened

5 tablespoons unsweetened cocoa powder

2 tablespoons cream or coconut milk, more if needed

1 teaspoon sugar-free vanilla extract

A pinch of salt

High-intensity sugar substitute to taste, such as liquid sucralose, stevia, or Splenda (Recipe was tested 6 drops EZ-Sweetz)

1 raw egg yolk, preferably from a pasteurized egg, optional (but good!)

If using granular erythritol, whirl it in a coffee or spice grinder or a food processor for a minute or two, until fine—let it settle before opening the top. Beat the butter in a medium bowl with an electric mixer or by hand until fluffy. Beat sweeteners into butter, then beat until smooth. Blend in the cocoa powder (slowly or it will escape). Beat in the vanilla, salt, and the cream or coconut milk and the egg yolk, if using. Add additional high-intensity sweetener to taste, starting with a small amount. Store frosting in the refrigerator, but let it warm up a bit before serving.

Recipe adapted from Lauren Benning of www.healthyindulgentcies.blogspot.com.

Yellow Cake, p. 124, with Chocolate Butter Cream Frosting, p. 126

Oven Fried Chicken

0.7 net carbs

Slow Cooked Green Beans

4.4 net carbs

Ginger Pumpkin Purée

7.1 net carbs

Chocolate Sundaes

3.4 net carbs

Menu total: 15.6 net carbs

NOTE:

About ½ cup of the cream and egg white mixture and ½ cup of pork rind and Parmesan mixture will be left over, so the carb count will actually be close to zero. Most of the fat will also stay in the pan, so the actual fat count will also be lower.

Oven Fried Chicken

Flour or bread crumbs can't produce a crisp, brown crust that compares to this.

> 3 pounds chicken parts, as purchased (8 pieces: breast halves, thighs, drumsticks, and wings)
> 4 ounces of pork rinds (about 1½ cups of crumbled rinds)
> ¼ cup (1 ounce) Parmesan cheese, finely grated
> Salt and pepper to taste
> 3 egg whites
> ¼ cup heavy cream
> ¼ cup peanut oil, light olive oil, lard, or bacon fat
> ¼ cup butter

Have ready a rack (for drying) and a large roasting pan. You may need a second pan to avoid crowding the chicken. For more uniform-sized pieces, cut each breast half crosswise into 2 pieces or have butcher cut it. Rinse chicken pieces and blot dry. Trim away any extra skin and fat. Sprinkle with salt and pepper and set aside. Process pork rinds in the bowl of a food processor until finely ground. Place pork rind crumbs on a dish; you will need about 1½ cups of processed crumbs. Stir in Parmesan. In a medium bowl, whisk egg whites until foamy. Whisk in the cream. Dip chicken in egg white and cream mixture and then roll in pork-rind mixture until evenly coated. Place on a rack to dry for 15 minutes.

Preheat oven to 425° F. Place the fat and oil in the roasting pan. Put the pan in the preheated oven until butter is melted, about 5 minutes. Place chicken in the pan, skin side down, and bake for 30 minutes. Turn the chicken and bake for an additional 30 minutes, or until well-browned and crisp. Serve hot or cold.

SERVINGS: 5 SERVINGS OF 2 PIECES EACH.

Per serving—Net carbohydrate: 0.7 grams; Protein: 48.9 grams; Fiber: 0 grams; Fat: 57.9 grams; Calories: 727

Total weight: 2 pounds 7 ounces or 1108 grams

Weight per serving of 2 pieces including bones: 7¾ ounces or 222 grams

Oven Fried Chicken

Slow Cooked Green Beans

The worst thing you can do to most green vegetables is over-cook them. Take broccoli, for example. Boil it for more than 15 minutes, and it becomes the mushy, stringy, bitter stuff that previous generations of kids surreptitiously fed to the dog. It bears little resemblance to the delightfully crisp, healthful, and popular *vegetable we know today. However, there is an exception to the rule. Don't get me wrong; I love fresh, crisp, brightly-colored, green beans, steamed for no more than three minutes in the microwave. But I also love the old-fashioned Southern green beans that I ate as a child, which are something altogether different. Mature beans, cooked down with a bit of bacon and a piece of onion until they turn Army-green, will no doubt lose some nutrients in the process, but they also become meltingly tender, rich, and indescribably delicious.*

MAKES 6 SERVINGS OF ½ CUP.

Per serving—Net carbohydrate: 4.4 grams; Protein: 2.4 grams; Fiber: 2.1 grams; Fat: 6.8 grams; Calories: 97

Total weight: 1 pound 2½ ounces or 526 grams

Weight per serving: 3 ounces or 85 grams

Preparation time: 10 minutes active; 2 hours 10 minutes total

3 slices (2.6 oz) bacon, chopped
½ cup (2½ ounces) chopped onion
1 (16-ounce) package frozen green beans
½ cup water
¼ teaspoon salt
Black pepper to taste

Fry bacon in large saucepan until it starts to brown, about 5 minutes. Add onion and fry until bacon is crisp and onion is soft, about 5 minutes more. Add water, frozen green beans, and salt and pepper. Bring to a boil, reduce heat to low, cover pan, and simmer for 2 hours. Stir occasionally, adding more water if necessary.

Ginger Pumpkin Purée

A delightful side dish for ham, pork, or poultry.

16 ounces cooked, pureed pumpkin or 1 can (some contain only 14½ or 15 ounces, but the difference is negligible)

6 ounces coconut milk or 1 small can (some contain only 5.6 ounces, also a negligible difference)

2 tablespoons butter, melted

Sugar substitute equal to ¼ cup sugar

1 teaspoon black strap molasses, brown sugar substitute, or yacon syrup, see Sources

2½ teaspoons ground ginger

¼ teaspoon salt or to taste

Dash of black pepper or to taste

1 egg, beaten with a fork, optional (for thicker consistency)

Mix pumpkin with coconut milk, butter, sweeteners, and ginger. Season with salt and pepper. Stir in beaten egg, if using. Place in a medium saucepan and set over low heat. Cook, stirring, until heated through and thickened, about 5 minutes. Serve hot as a side dish, with additional butter.

MAKES 2²/₃ CUPS OR 5 SERVINGS OF SLIGHTLY MORE THAN ½ CUP.

Per serving—Net carbohydrate: 7.1 grams; Protein: 1.6 grams; Fiber: 2.7 grams; Fat: 9.9 grams; Calories: 133

Total weight: 1 pound 6⁷/₈ ounces or 648 grams

Weight per serving: 4.6 ounces or 130 grams

Preparation time: 15 minutes active and total

NOTE:

In China, pumpkin is used as an herbal remedy for the treatment of diabetes. According to a paper published in the July, 2007, issue of the *Journal of the Science of Food and Agriculture*, researchers discovered that a molecule called D-chiro-inositol, found in pumpkin, can mediate insulin activity and may actually be able to regenerate damaged cells in the pancreas. In the study conducted at East China Normal University, rats with type 1 diabetes were given pumpkin extract. After 30 days, diabetic rats who were given the extract had only five percent less insulin in their blood than the healthy rats in the control group.

A chef told me, 'Ginger is a soft kiss from a girl who likes to bite.'

— *Alton Brown*

Chocolate Sundaes

½ cup **French Vanilla Ice Cream** (p. 308)
2 tablespoons **Chocolate Sauce**

Scoop ice cream into serving dishes. Top with 2 tablespoons
Chocolate Sauce just before serving

VARIATIONS:

Ganache: Frosting or Truffles

FOR GANACHE:
Chill until spreadable. Use to
frost or fill cookies or cakes or to
make **Chocolate Truffles.**

FOR TRUFFLES:
Chill ganache until firm and
scoop into teaspoon-sized
portions. Chill and roll in sifted
cocoa powder or finely chopped
nuts or coconut.

Chocolate Sauce

4 ounces unsweetened chocolate, such as Ghirardelli
2 tablespoons of butter
High intensity sugar substitute equal to 4 tablespoons sugar
½ cup heavy cream
A few grains of salt
1 teaspoon vanilla extract

Chop the chocolate into small pieces. Melt butter in a small
saucepan on low heat and stir until melted. Add cream, sugar substitute, and salt. Cook and stir until bubbles appear,
then reduce heat and stir for one minutes more. Remove
pan from heat and stir in vanilla. Sauce with solidify when
refrigerated but can be reheated on low in the microwave or
over hot water on stovetop until pourable. Add a little water
or more cream for a thinner sauce.

*If using liquid sucralose or Splenda, replace the equivalent
of 2 teaspoonfuls of sugar with a second sweetener, such as
acesulfame K or stevia.

Eggplant Casserole

If you love lasagna, you'll love this.

1 recipe of **Meat Sauce**, p. 296
2½ pounds of eggplant (about 6 Asian eggplants or 2 regular)
3 tablespoons oil
Salt to taste
¾ cup grated Parmesan cheese (3 ounces)
1 cup shredded mozzarella cheese (4 ounces)
¼ cup (1 ounce) shaved Parmesan cheese

Preheat broiler and grease a rimmed baking sheet. Cut ends off eggplant and peel if desired. (The dark skin looks pretty, but it may be tough. Cut eggplant into ½-thick slices. Salt both sides of the eggplant slices and place in a colander or a paper towel-lined bowl to draw out the bitter juices. Put a heavy dish on top to press out the liquid. Let stand for 1 hour. Rinse to remove the salt and blot dry with paper towels. Brush both sides of slices generously with olive oil and sprinkle with salt. Place on baking sheet. (It may need to be done in 2 batches.) Broil 5 to 6 inches from heat source for about 5 minutes or until it starts to brown. Turn over and broil for 5 more minutes or until second side starts to brown and eggplant is cooked but still firm. Alternately, bake at 450° for 20 minutes. Preheat oven to 350° F. Grease a 9- by 13-inch, oven-proof casserole dish.

TO ASSEMBLE: Place a layer of eggplant slices in the bottom of the casserole dish. Spread with a layer of **Meat Sauce** and sprinkle with half the mozzarella and half the Parmesan cheese. Repeat with remaining eggplant slices, sauce, and cheese to make 2 layers. Bake at 350° F for 30 to 40 minutes or until sauce bubbles and top is browned. Let sit for 5 minutes before cutting. Top with thin shavings of Parmesan cheese and serve hot.

MAKES 8 SERVINGS.

Per serving—Net carbohydrate: 8.3 grams; Protein: 21.6 grams; Fiber: 5.5 grams; Fat: 17.9 grams; Calories: 293

Total weight: 4 pounds 4 ounces or 1.9 kilograms

Weight per serving: 8½ ounces, 241 grams

Preparation time: 20 minutes active, 50 to 60 minutes total (not including time to prepare sauce)

Eggplant Casserole
8.3 net carbs

Greek Salad
4.3 net carbs

Mocha Mousse
1.4 net carbs

Menu total: 14 net carbs

EGGPLANT:
Small, skinny, Asian eggplants are preferable to the large Globe variety because they are firmer and less seedy. Chinese eggplants are lavender and have a curved shape; Japanese eggplants are straight and dark purple. If the big ones are all you can find, check the "belly button" on the blossom end. If it is round, the eggplant will be less meaty and it will have more seeds, which tend to be bitter, than the ones with an oval shaped dimple. Don't ask me why.

Greek Salad

A traditional Greek Salad does not include lettuce.

European cucumbers, also called English cucumbers, are milder, less seedy, and more digestible than the regular ones. They are usually sold in a protective plastic sleeve and are not waxed, so they don't need to be peeled.

Barley Rusks, p. 237, are part of a traditional Greek salad. Dip them in water, shake off the water, break them up, and toss with the salad. They will add 1.5 net grams of carbs for each thick rusk to the total per serving.

3 or 4 ripe tomatoes (11 ounces)
1 small red onion (4 ounces)
1 red or green bell pepper or some of each (5 ounces)
1 European cucumber (10 ounces)
2 Anchovy filets, optional
Dried Greek oregano to taste
Sea salt to taste
Freshly-ground black pepper to taste
2 tablespoons extra-virgin olive oil
1 cup of Greek feta cheese (4½ ounces)
16 Kalamata olives (2½ ounces)
1 lemon, cut into 8 wedges
Pepperoncini (hot peppers) or capers for garnish, if desired.

Cut tomatoes into wedges. Peel onion, cut into thin slices, and separate into rings. Remove seeds and membranes from pepper and slice into thin rings. Slice cucumber into ¼-inch slices. Crush anchovy filets with a fork in a large bowl, if using. Add vegetables to bowl and sprinkle with salt, oregano, and black pepper. Drizzle olive oil over salad and toss. Just before serving, crumble feta over salad and add olives. Garnish with hot peppers and/or a few capers, if desired. Serve with lemon wedges to be squeezed over salad.

MAKES 8 SERVINGS OF 1 CUP

Per serving—Net carbohydrate: 4.3 grams; Protein: 3.1 grams; Fiber: 1.3 grams; Fat: 7.5 grams; Calories: 99

Total weight: 2 pounds 6 ounces or 1.1 kilograms

Weight per serving: 4¾ ounces or 136 grams

Preparation time: 20 minutes active and total

Greek Salad, p. 134

Mocha Mousse

1 envelope (¼ ounce) plain gelatin
½ tablespoon Dutch cocoa
¼ cup cold water
½ cup hot decaffeinated coffee, brewed, instant, or made with a single serving packet
Sugar substitute equal to ½ cup sugar
½ cup heavy cream

Mix gelatin and cocoa until blended in a small bowl. Add water and let soak for 5 minutes. Pour hot coffee into bowl and stir to dissolve gelatin. Stir in sweetener and place bowl in refrigerator for 30 minutes to an hour, stirring frequently, until mixture is thick and syrupy. (Check it often so it doesn't set. If it sets up, you must re-melt it and start over, or it will be lumpy.) Transfer the mixture to a chilled bowl and beat with an electric mixer until light. Add the cream and beat till fluffy. Spoon into dessert dishes and chill until firm, about 15 minutes. Serve with **Whipped Cream**, p. 312, if desired.

A little something for the coffee and chocolate lovers.

MAKES 3 SERVINGS OF ABOUT ½ CUP EACH.

Per serving—Net carbohydrate: 1.4 grams; Protein: 3 grams; Fiber: 0.2 grams; Fat: 14.9 grams; Calories: 149

Total weight: 15⅝ ounces or 441 grams

Weight per serving: 5.2 ounces or 147 grams

Preparation time: 10 minutes active, 25 minutes total, plus 15 minutes to chill

Meatloaf

3.8 net carbs

Celery Root Purée

8.2 net carbs

Nopalitos

0.9 net carbs

Raspberry Marshmallow Squares

0.4 net carbs

Menu total 13.3 net carbs

MAKES 4 SERVINGS.

Per serving—Net carbohydrate: 3.8 grams; Protein: 29.6 grams; Fiber: 0.8 grams; Fat: 21.3 grams; Calories: 330

Total weight: 1 pound 4¾ ounces or 587 grams

Weight per serving: 5 ounces or 147 grams

Preparation time: 15 minutes active, 1 hour total

Meatloaf

Most meatloaf recipes include a filler like bread crumbs or rolled oats to retain moisture and lighten the texture. When you include the requisite onion, it adds up to a lot of carbs for a meat dish. Using green onions instead of regular ones and pork rinds instead of oats significantly reduces the count.

3 or 4 green onions, about ½ cup (1½ ounces), chopped
¼ cup (1¼ ounces) green or red bell pepper, chopped
2 garlic cloves (¼ ounce), peeled and chopped
1 tablespoon olive oil
1 pound ground beef, buffalo, or a mixture of beef, turkey, and/or pork
2 tablespoons **Barbecue Sauce**, p. 293, plus additional ¼ cup for top
2 teaspoons Worcestershire sauce
1 teaspoon salt
½ teaspoon black pepper
1 tablespoon cream
1 tablespoon water
1 large egg, beaten with a fork
½ cup (½ ounce) crushed pork rinds
¼ cup (½ ounce) grated Parmesan cheese
1 teaspoon dried or 2 teaspoons fresh, chopped chives, optional

Preheat oven to 350º F. Grease a roasting pan.

Chop the white part of the green onions and enough of the green tops to make ½ cup. Cook the white part of the onion, the bell pepper, and garlic in the oil until softened. Mix all ingredients together in a bowl. Shape into two oval mounds on a greased roasting pan. Spread the additional ¼ cup of **Barbecue Sauce** over the loaves and spray with non-stick spray. Bake at 350º F for 35 to 45 minutes or until brown.

Note: About 2 teaspoonfuls of the oil stays in pan.

VARIATION:
Meatballs

Shape the **Meatloaf** mixture into small meatballs, about 1 inch across. Fry in high-heat oil or fat, in several batches, for 3 to 4 minutes until brown and firm. Serve on wooden picks with warmed **Barbecue Sauce**, p. 293, for dipping or serve with **Marinara Sauce,** p 295, over your choice of pasta, p. 325

MAKES ABOUT 40 MEATBALLS.

Per meatball—Net carbohydrate per meatball: 0.38 grams; Protein: 3 grams; Fiber: 0.08 grams; Fat: 2.1 grams; Calories: 33

Total weight: 20¾ ounces or 588 grams

Weight per meatball: ½ ounce or 15 grams each

Preparation time: 20 minutes active; 1 hour 5 minutes total

Meatballs

Celery Root Purée

CELERY ROOT:

Scrub celeriac well to remove all the dirt that tends to cling to its hair-like roots. To prepare, slice it first and then peel it, so it is easier to get into all the convoluted spaces. Cut off the fibrous roots, but if some are large, you can peel and use them too. (Some stores sell celeriac without the roots and tops.)

———

Celery Root, also called celeriac or knob celery, comes from a variety of celery grown for its fleshy, white root rather than its stalks. It can be eaten raw, boiled, braised, deep-fried, puréed, sautéed, or steamed.

You would never suspect that the silky, white puree drizzled around an artfully arranged plate in a four-star restaurant started life as the ugly sibling of the humble celery plant.

1 pound celery root, trimmed (about 1 1/3 pounds as purchased, without roots and tops)
2 garlic cloves (1/8 ounce each), peeled
Water to cover
1/4 teaspoon salt
2 tablespoons cream
1 egg
1 tablespoon butter
Salt and pepper to taste

Wash the celery root well, peel it, and cut it into cubes. Cover it with water to which you have added 1/4 teaspoon salt and cook it with the garlic in a covered pan until very tender, about 20 to 25 minutes. Rinse and drain. Blot dry on paper towels, pressing out as much liquid as possible.

Purée the celery root and garlic in a food processor or with a stick blender until smooth. In a small bowl, beat the egg with a fork and blend in the cream. Add egg and cream mixture and butter to the processor bowl; scrape down the bowl with a spatula and process until blended. Return the mixture to the pan and cook and stir over low heat until the egg is cooked and the purée has the consistency of mashed potatoes, about 5 to 10 minutes. Correct the seasoning and serve, topped with a pat of butter or a pool of gravy.

MAKES 4 SERVINGS OF ½ CUP.

Per serving—Net carbohydrate: 8.2 grams; Protein: 3.4 grams; Fiber: 1.8 grams; Fat: 7.2 grams; Calories: 113

Total weight: 1 pound 2 ounces

Weight per serving: 4½ ounces

Preparation time: 30 minutes active; 50 minutes total

Nopalitos

You may find fresh prickly pear cactus pads displayed with the vegetables in the supermarket, especially in areas with large Hispanic populations. However, unless you are prepared to deal with viscous juices and treacherous spines, you might prefer to buy them packed in glass jars. They come plain or pickled in vinegar with onions and cilantro. Look for them with the Mexican foods.

1 (16-ounce) jar plain nopalitos (8¾ ounces drained)

Rinse nopalitos well under cold running water and drain. Heat on stovetop or in microwave until hot and serve as a green vegetable. Do not add additional salt.

MAKES 2 CUPS OR 4 SERVINGS OF ½ CUP.

Per serving—Net carbohydrate: 0.9 grams; Protein: 1 gram; Fiber: 1.5 grams; Fat: 0 grams; Calories: 11

Total weight: 8¼ ounces or 232 grams

Weight per serving: 2 ounces

Preparation time: 3 minutes active, 8 minutes total

NOPALES:

Nopal is the Spanish word for cactus. *Nopales* means, "cactus stem." *Nopalitos* are the cactus pads after they have been cut up and prepared for eating. They taste like green beans with a lemony tang, and their texture resembles roasted green peppers.

———

The prickly pear cactus (Opuntia Cactaceae) produces two food crops. The edible pads called noplales, used as a green vegetable, and the sweet fruit called prickly pear, cactus fig, Indian fig, or tuna.

———

Pickled nopalitos can be served cold or at room temperature as a relish or salad, or they can be added to omelets or heated and used as a side dish.

Raspberry Marshmallow Squares

This reminds me of the coating on one of my old junk food favorites, Hostess Snowballs, those marshmallow- and coconut-coated chocolate cakes with a "cream" center (actually a trans-fat and sugar center).

2 ounces frozen or fresh raspberries or strawberries or ¼ ounce dried

2 packets (7 grams each) powdered gelatin

½ cup cold water

½ cup boiling water

High-intensity sugar substitute equal to 1 cup sugar

4 teaspoons sugar substitute with bulk, such as erythritol, xylitol, Sweet*perfection*, or a stevia blend

A few grains of salt

1 teaspoon vanilla extract

3 egg whites, fresh or reconstituted from powdered egg whites

¼ to ½ cup of finely grated coconut (1 to 2 ounces or 30 to 60 grams)

Granular sugar substitute equal to 2 teaspoons of sugar, such as Sweet-*perfection*, Just Like Sugar, LC Sweet, or Splenda

Grease an 8- x 8-inch pan. Line with parchment paper and grease paper also. Chop berries into fairly large pieces. Reserve.

Soften gelatin in ½ cup cold water in a large bowl for a few minutes. Heat additional ½ cup water to boiling. Pour over gelatin and stir until dissolved. Stir in first 2 sugar substitutes, salt, and vanilla. Place in refrigerator to chill.

Stir every 5 minutes at first then as often as every 2 minutes until it becomes as thick as raw egg whites. This may take less than 10 minutes or up to an hour, depending on your refrigerator. If the gelatin accidentally sets up and becomes lumpy rather than syrupy, reheat it and start over.

Beat gelatin mixture with an electric mixer for 2 or 3 minutes or until fluffy. Add egg whites and beat for about 3 minutes more or until it forms soft peaks that droop over when the beater is lifted. Quickly stir in berries. Spoon into

NOTE:

Don't use pasteurized eggs in the shell for whipping. They have been heated too much to beat up properly. If you are concerned about safety, you can use reconstituted powdered egg whites.

pan and spread with a flexible spatula. Cover with plastic film and press down to level the top. Refrigerate until firm.

Turn out of pan, peel off paper and cut into 16 squares. Mix coconut and remaining sweetener in a small bowl and roll each marshmallow until coated on all sides. Eat them out of hand or garnish with a berry and a dab of **Whipped Cream**, p. 312, and serve with a fork.

MAKES 16 SQUARES.

Per serving—Net carbohydrate: 0.4 grams; Protein: 1.6 grams; Fiber: 0.4 grams; Fat: 1.2 grams; Calories: 20

Total weight: 12¼ ounces or 348 grams

Weight per serving: ¾ ounce or 22 grams

Preparation time: 15 minutes active; 25 minutes total plus setting time.

You may use only high-intensity sweetener to make marshmallows if you choose, but the small amount of bulk sweetener, such as erythritol, xylitol, Sweet*perfection*, or a stevia blend will give a texture more like marshmallows made with regular sugar. Plain ones (without raspberries) melt beautifully in a cup of hot cocoa. Without the bulk sweetener, they melt more quickly.

Raspberry Marshmallow Squares

Indian Butter Chicken (Murgh Makhani)

5.3 net carbs

Cauliflower *Faux* Rice (p. 283)

1.1 net carbs

Roasted Okra (p. 40)

2.5 net carbs

Rose Flavored Ice Cream (p. 310) with Star Fruit in Anise Syrup (p. 146)

ice cream, 2.3 net carbs;
2 ounces star fruit and syrup,
4.3 net carbs

Menu total: 15.5 net carbs

Indian Butter Chicken (Murgh Makhani)

I fell in love with this dish when I first had it at a local Indian restaurant. The chef declined to share the recipe, so I wrote down the name and looked it up online. The versions I found were many and varied, but all were long and complicated and used a lot of exotic ingredients. Here's a very simplified Butter Chicken—*not authentic, but very good and very easy.*

6 ounces (1 small) onion, cut into chunks
4 garlic cloves (½ ounce total), peeled
6 ounces (1 medium) red bell pepper, seeded and cut into chunks
2 tablespoons coconut oil or peanut oil
1½ tablespoons **Garam Masala**, purchased or made by following recipe, more to taste
2 teaspoon chili powder, more to taste
1 teaspoon turmeric
1½ teaspoons powdered ginger
½ teaspoon salt or to taste
16 ounces Pomi brand Strained Tomatoes or two 8-ounce cans tomato sauce
1 cup heavy cream
½ cup (1 stick) butter
3 tablespoons natural almond butter
Sugar substitute equal to 1 teaspoon of sugar
2 pounds boneless, skinless chicken breasts or chicken tenders, cut into bite-sized pieces
Additional cream and fresh coriander (cilantro) for garnish, if desired

Puree onion, garlic, and red pepper in a food processor or food mill until smooth. Heat oil in a large skillet over medium heat. Add pureed onion, garlic, and pepper and cook until water is evaporated. Add **Garam Masala**, chili powder, tumeric, ginger, and salt and continue to cook, stirring, until spices are fragrant and vegetables are cooked, about 5 minutes more. Stir in tomato sauce, cream, and butter and cook until heated through. Add chicken pieces to skillet. Cover and simmer on low heat for 20 minutes or until chicken is cooked, stirring occasionally. Stir in almond butter and sugar substitute. Serve in bowls garnished with a swirl of fresh cream. Sprinkle with chopped fresh coriander, if desired.

NOTE:

Use no-sugar-added tomato sauce to keep the carb count low. I used Pomi Strained Tomatoes, imported from Italy, which contain nothing but tomatoes and have 1 net gram of carbohydrate in ¼ cup. Pomi chopped tomatoes have 0.5 net carbs in ½ cup. Hunt's and Del Monte give the net count for ½ cup of tomato sauce as 4 grams. The USDA data base lists 7 net per ½ cup as the average, which would add an extra 28 carbs to the total recipe! Nutrition counts for **Butter Chicken** recipe were based on Pomi Strained Tomatoes (see Sources). Add the extra carbs if using another brand.

MAKES 6²/₃ CUPS OR 6 SERVINGS OF ABOUT 1 ¹/₈ CUPS EACH.

Per serving—Net carbohydrate: 5.3 grams (made with Pomi Strained Tomatoes); Protein: 24.8 grams; Fiber: 2.6 grams; Fat: 36 grams; Calories: 455

Total weight: 3 pounds 12 ounces or 1.7 kilograms

Weight per serving: 10 ounces or 284 grams

Preparation time: 11 minutes active, 40 minutes total (Remember that for ingredients such as, "garlic, peeled," the recipe prep time starts after the ingredients are prepared as they are listed.)

BUTTER:

Butter was a staple food in traditional herding societies, like Ireland and India. India uses more butter than any country in the world; however, some of the total is used ceremoniously in festivals and religious rites. (It was so vital to life that cows were revered as sacred animals—understandable, since killing a cow would have been like killing the goose that laid the golden egg.)

The Irish who lived in the area around Cork were said to have eaten an average of a pound of butter per person per day. The area was known for its rich, life-giving butter, churned from the milk of pastured cows eating lush green grass.

Ancient *bog butter* is frequently discovered in Irish bogs, where it had been packed in wicker baskets and buried to preserve it or to hide it from invaders. Some has been dated as being 3 thousand years old.

Butter making was mysterious and magical to the people in the region and as is the case with any chancy enterprise associated with survival, there were many superstitions about it. A horseshoe was nailed to the bottom of the churn because it was believed that metal would keep away fairies and witches who would "steal the butter" from the churn. While the butter was being made, bystanders would chant, "Come, butter, come; Peter stands at the gate waiting for a buttered cake," in Irish as a protective charm.

Information courtesy of the National Museum of Ireland and from Peter Foynes, curator of the Butter Museum in Cork, Ireland.

Garam Masala

GARAM MASALA:
Garam masala means *hot and spicy* in the Hindi language. This aromatic blend of roasted spices from northern India varies from one region and even one family to another. This is a basic recipe including all or most of the possible ingredients, but you can alter it to suit yourself. It's best when made from freshly ground, whole spices, but it is available ready-made at most Asian markets and many supermarkets. If using a purchased mixture, toast it in a dry skillet for a minute or two to bring up the flavor.

MAKES ABOUT 4 TABLESPOONS

Net Carbohydrate will be less than 1 gram per teaspoon.

Total weight: 7/8 ounces or 24 grams

Weight per teaspoon: 1/12 ounce or 2 grams

Preparation time: 15 minutes active and total

Use some or all of the spices on the list to make your own blend. When cooking with masala, add it to your dish toward the end of the cooking time.

1 tablespoon cardamom seeds
1 (2-inch) piece of stick cinnamon
1 teaspoon black cumin
1 teaspoon whole cloves
1 teaspoon black peppercorns
1 teaspoon cumin seeds
½ teaspoon coriander seeds
½ teaspoon mace powder
½ teaspoon fennel seeds
¼ teaspoon nutmeg
1 Turkish bay leaf
1 piece of star anise
A few saffron threads

Toast spices in a skillet over a low-flame for about 2 minutes or until fragrant, shaking pan or stirring a few times. Let cool and grind to a powder in a spice grinder or with a mortar and pestle. Stored in an airtight container in a cool, dry place, the **Garam Masala** will remain potent for several months.

Rose Flavored Ice Cream, p. 310

Rose Flavored Ice Cream, p. 310

STAR FRUIT:

Star fruit makes a low-carb and healthful treat, only 4.8 net carbs in a large (4½ inch) fruit. When buying star fruit, look for firm fruit without soft or brown spots. If it is green, ripen it at home until it is turns yellow, then use or refrigerate it. Although the outside may darken after it is cut, the interior flesh does not turn brown, like many fruits, and it retains its unique crunchy texture for days.

To prepare star fruit, slice crosswise into "stars" and remove the seeds. I have heard that the seeds are so toxic that they can be used as a pesticide, so be sure to remove them. If there is a tough brown ridge that runs along the edge of each rib, cut it away. This will be easier to do before slicing the fruit.

Star Fruit can be sweetened with a little sugar substitute and eaten fresh or used as a dessert topping, as a condiment, or in my recipes for **Star Fruit in Anise Syrup** or the variation under **Candied Fennel Tart**, p. 272.

Star Fruit in Anise Syrup

Beautiful, star-shaped fruit slices, flavored with star anise, taste as heavenly as they sound.

1 large or 2 small star fruit (also called carambola), about 6 ounces total
Sugar substitute equal to ¾ cups sugar, such as sucralose or stevia extract
¾ cup polydextrose
1 cup water
1 tablespoon grated lemon zest, the amount from ½ a medium (5 ounce) lemon
½ teaspoon anise seeds or 2 whole anise stars
A few grains of salt

Slice small star fruit into ¼-inch thick "stars." Slices from larger fruits can be divided into smaller pieces; see Tips. Remove the seeds that are found between the segments. Place fruit slices in a pan just big enough to hold them in a single layer. If using a granular or dry sweetener, stir together with polydextrose. If using a liquid sweetener, add with water. Put water into pan with star fruit and stir in sweetener and polydextrose, lemon zest, anise seeds or whole stars, and salt. Simmer for about 20 to 30 minutes, stirring occasionally, or until liquid bubbles, becomes shiny and thick, and is reduced to about ¾ cup. Serve as a condiment with curry dishes or as a topping for ice cream or desserts.

MAKES ¾ CUP OF FRUIT AND SYRUP OR ABOUT 4 SERVINGS AS A CONDIMENT OR TOPPING.

Per serving—Net carbohydrate: 4.3 grams; Protein: 0.4 grams; Fiber: 34.5 grams; Fat: 0.1 grams; Calories: 52

Total weight: 8 ounces or 227 grams

Weight per serving: 2 ounces or 57 grams

Preparation time: 7 minutes active, 37 minutes total

TIPS:

The star-shaped slices can be divided into smaller pieces. They naturally separate down the center of each point into v-shaped segments that resemble sets of wings or flying birds (more heavenly references!). For a stunning fruit tart, separate fruit into segments and arrange in concentric circles, using larger pieces on outer ring and progressively smaller ones toward center. See variation for **Candied Fennel Tart** on p. 272.

When uniform slices are needed, buy extra star fruit and use similar-sized stars. Match remaining slices for another batch or use for another purpose.

You can replace both the polydextrose and the hi-intensity sweetener with ¾ cup of PolyD Plus, which already includes sucralose.

POLYDEXTROSE:

Polydextrose has the texture and mouth feel of sucrose and adds missing bulk in recipes made with high intensity sweeteners. It also browns and caramelizes like regular sugar, but it behaves like soluble fiber when ingested. It is widely used in commercial products to allow a reduction in the amount of sugar or fat needed and to add beneficial fiber. It has a total of 27 grams of carbohydrate and 25 grams of fiber for a net carb count of 2 grams per ounce. See Ingredients for more information. My recipes were tested with Stay-lite III polydextrose from Honeyville Grain.

Star Fruit in Anise Syrup

PART 2

Special Occasions and Entertaining

Company's Coming

Special Occasions and Entertaining

MENU 1

Rumaki

Grilled Sesame Steak Skewers

Cauliflower *Faux* Rice

Sautéed Bok Choy

Snowball Sundaes
with Chocolate Sauce

MENU 2

Herb Roasted Olives
with Parmesan Fricos

Pan-Seared Wild Salmon

Rhubarb Sauce

Macaroni and Cheese
Custards

Simply Roasted Asparagus

Cheesecake

MENU 3

Egg Flower Soup

Pork in Peanut Sauce

"Noodles"

Sautéed Broccolini

Coconut Mousse
with Caramel Sauce

MENU 4

Baked Shrimp with Two Sauces:
Sweet and Spicy Sauce
and Cocktail Sauce

Vanilla Spice Broiled Chicken

Celery Root Gratin

Waldorf Salad

Chocolate Cheese Pie
with Almond Crust

Cantaloupe with Prosciutto

Chicken Parmesan

Eggplant and Sundried Tomato
Mini Pizzas

Caesar Salad

Chocolate Cupcakes with
Butter Cream Frosting

Jicama with Lime and Chili

Grilled Steak with
Herb and Spice Rub

Baked Red Peppers Caprese

Stuffed Zucchini Blossoms

Coconut Macadamia Pie

Rumaki

Rumaki

1 pound chicken livers
1 tablespoon naturally brewed (no sugar) soy sauce
1 (8-ounce) can whole water chestnuts, drained (5 ounces, drained)
9 slices bacon, partially cooked in microwave or oven (p. 18), cut in half

Preheat oven to 400° F.

Rinse chicken livers, cut into bite-size pieces, and remove connective tissue. Place in a bowl with soy sauce, turn to coat, and refrigerate for 15 minutes. Cut water chestnuts in half, crosswise. Wrap a piece of liver and a slice of water chestnut in each half-slice of bacon. Secure with a wooden pick. Place on broiler pan (to catch the drippings) and bake in preheated oven for about 20 minutes, or until the liver is cooked and the bacon is crisp. Serve hot. Plan to have 2 or 3 per person.

MAKES APPROXIMATELY 18 INDIVIDUAL SERVINGS OR 6 SERVINGS OF 3 EACH.

Per 1 piece—Net carbohydrate: 1 gram; Protein: 5.6 grams; Fiber: 0.3 grams; Fat: 2.7 grams; Calories: 54

Total weight: 1 pound 3¼ ounces or 545 grams

Weight per serving: 1 ounce or 30 grams

Preparation time: 10 minutes active; 45 minutes total, including marinating time

TIPS:

The bacon should be partially cooked so it will not shrink too much. Pre-cooking also renders some of the fat, reduces splattering, and prevents excess drippings from overflowing the broiler pan. Cook bacon by the method on p. 18 or microwave it for a few minutes. It needs to be flexible enough to wrap around the filling, so don't let it crisp.

You can also grill or broil the **Rumaki**, in which case it becomes even more important that most of the fat is rendered from the bacon before cooking to avoid flare-ups.

Grilled Sesame Steak Skewers

These are always a hit as a main dish or as an appetizer.

1½ pounds sirloin steak (1- to 1½-inches thick)

MARINADE:

¾ cup naturally brewed (no sugar) soy sauce

¾ cup water

2 tablespoons sesame oil

2 tablespoons red wine vinegar

2 teaspoons fresh ginger, peeled and grated

3 cloves garlic, peeled and crushed

Sugar substitute equal to 1 tablespoon sugar

4 tablespoons toasted sesame seeds

Soak 12 to 14 wooden skewers in water for an hour or more. Place the beef in the freezer for about 20 minutes or until partially frozen to facilitate slicing. Cut into ⅛-inch thick slices and thread onto skewers.

Combine the marinade ingredients in a large, non-reactive, rectangular dish. Add the meat skewers, turn to coat both sides with marinade, and cover dish with plastic wrap. Place in the refrigerator for three hours, turning or basting steak with marinade occasionally.

Preheat the grill or broiler.

Remove the beef skewers from the marinade and drain, reserving the liquid. Grill or broil them for 2 to 3 minutes on each side, brushing with the marinade and turning once. Bring the remaining marinade to a boil and serve as a sauce with the meat, if desired. Serve as a main dish or an appetizer.

TIP:
Thread the beef onto small skewers when making appetizers and serve 2 or 3 per person.

SESAME SEEDS:
You may be able to buy sesame seeds already toasted, but if not, put them in a dry skillet and heat, stirring, for a few minutes or until fragrant and lightly browned.

Sesame seeds from the bulk bins are usually a much better buy than the ones in the little jars on the shelves with the spices. Even better deals can be found online for larger quantities.

MAKES 4 MAIN DISH SERVINGS OF 3 SKEWERS EACH.

Per serving of 3 skewers—Net carbohydrate: 1.4 grams; Protein: 52.3 grams; Fiber: 0.4 grams; Fat: 28.6 grams; Calories: 488

Total weight: 1 pound 5 ounces or 600 grams

Weight per serving: 5¼ ounces or 150 grams

Preparation time: 20 minutes active; 4 hours and 40 minutes total, start to finish

Note: *Most of the marinade remains in the dish and is not included in the counts.*

Ramaki, p. 152, Grill Sesame Steak Skewers, p. 153, with Sautéed Bok Choy

Sautéed Bok Choy

10 ounces baby bok choy, about 6 small heads (4½ cups, cut up)
1 tablespoon cooking oil
2 teaspoons naturally brewed soy sauce

MAKES 2 SERVINGS OF ¾ CUP EACH.

Per serving—Net carbohydrate: 2.1 grams; Protein: 2.4 grams; Fiber: 1.4 grams; Fat: 7.3 grams; Calories: 83

Total weight: 7⅝ ounces or 216 grams

Weight per serving: 3⅝ ounces or 108 grams

Preparation time: 6 minutes active, 12 minutes total

Rinse bok choy and cut away and discard any bruised or damaged parts. Blot dry. Split the white, fleshy, stem-end on smallest heads; cut an "X" in larger ones. Cut stems crosswise into ½-inch horizontal slices. Cut the green leafy tops horizontally into 1-inch segments.

Heat oil in a large skillet on medium-high heat. Add bok choy stem pieces to pan and sauté for about 3 minutes while turning and stirring. Add leafy tops and continue to cook and stir for about 2 minutes more or until shiny and wilted. Add soy sauce to pan and cook for an additional minute. Serve hot.

Snowball Sundaes

Scoop balls (½ cup or 65 grams) of **Coconut Ice Cream,** p. 310, or **French Vanilla Ice Cream,** p. 308, onto a sheet pan. Return to freezer and freeze until hard. Roll in flaked, unsweetened, toasted or plain coconut, using about 2 tablespoons per ball. Top with 2 tablespoons **Chocolate Sauce,** p. 132, just before serving.

"Ice Cream is exquisite. What a pity it isn't illegal."

— Voltaire (1694-1778)

MAKES 1 SERVING WITH ½ CUP ICE CREAM, 2 TABLESPOONS COCONUT, AND 2 TABLESPOONS SAUCE.

Per serving—Net carbohydrate: 4.2 grams; Protein: 5.2 grams; Fiber: 9.6 grams; Fat: 31 grams; Calories: 344

Weight per serving: $3^2/_3$ ounces or 107 grams

Preparation time: 5 minutes, not including time to re-freeze ice cream.

Snowball Sundae

Herb Roasted Olives

Herb Roasted Olives

An Amuse Bouche is a flavorful, bite-sized appetizer that "entertains the mouth" as it awaits the main event. Set out dishes of assorted olives and nuts, and no one will complain, but roasting the olives makes them slightly chewy and concentrates the flavors in a way that is guaranteed to keep your bouche *amused. Serve them solo with skewers for spearing or with* **Barley Rusks**, *p. 237 or* **Almond Crisps**, *p. 304.*

1 cup (4 ounces) pitted black olives
1 cup (4 ounces) pitted Kalamata olives
1 cup (4 ounces) green olives, stuffed with garlic, almonds, or pimento
8 to 10 whole garlic cloves (1 ounce total), peeled
1 tablespoon *Herbes de Provence*, see p. 158
¼ cup olive oil

ADD AFTER BAKING:
¼ teaspoon freshly ground black pepper
1 teaspoon freshly grated lemon zest
Sprigs of fresh rosemary and/or thyme for garnish, optional

Preheat oven to 425° F.

Drain olives and place on a small, rimmed baking sheet with the garlic, *Herbes de Provence*, and olive oil. Toss together until well mixed. Bake for about 20 to 25 minutes, or until olives are sizzling and garlic is starting to brown, stirring after first 10 minutes. Cool on pan until just warm. Transfer to a bowl, grind fresh black pepper and grate fresh lemon zest over olives and toss. Garnish with sprigs of fresh herbs, if desired. Serve warm or at room temperature.

MAKES 8 SERVINGS.

Per serving—Net carbohydrate: 1.8 grams; Protein: 0.5 grams; Fiber: 1.1 grams; Fat: 10.5 grams; Calories: 103

Total weight: 10 ounces or 284 grams

Weight per serving: 1¼ ounce or 36 grams

Preparation time: 10 active; 30 to 35 minutes total

Herb Roasted Olives with Parmesan Fricos

Olives, 1.8 net carbs; Fricos 0.3 net carbs each

Pan-Seared Wild Salmon

0 net carbs

Rhubarb Sauce

3.2 net carbs

Macaroni and Cheese Custards

3.5 net carbs

Simply Roasted Asparagus

1.2 net carbs

Cheesecake

4.4 net carbs

Menu total 14.4 net carbs

TIP:
Garlic cloves often have a bitter green core. Unless you know the garlic is very fresh, split the clove, remove the green sprout in the center, and cut away any other green part before using.

Provençal Herbs

Herbes de Provence (Provençal herbs) *is an aromatic seasoning blend made form the plants that thrive on the rocky, sun-drenched, hillsides of Southern France. You can make your own custom mix using some or all of the following dried herbs listed below.*

Start with thyme, summer savory, rosemary, and either oregano or marjoram and choose which others to include. If you have one of those cute little terra-cotta clay pots with a cork, keep some of your herbs on the countertop. If you have extra, it makes a great gift.

MEASUREMENTS ARE FOR DRY HERBS.
   1 tablespoon each of thyme, chervil, rosemary leaves, and
      summer savory
   1 teaspoon each of lavender, tarragon, and marjoram
   ½ teaspoon each of oregano, mint, bay leaves, basil, fennel seeds,
      rubbed sage, and orange zest.

Put everything in a spice grinder or processor and blend until fine. Store in an airtight container. (To mix by hand, you will need to first chop or crush the bay and rosemary leaves and fennel seeds.)

MAKES ABOUT ⅓ CUP, GROUND.

Whole batch—Net carbohydrate: 4.3 grams; Protein: 1.8 grams; Fiber: 6.2 grams; Fat: 1.4 grams; Calories: 49

Parmesan Fricos

These wonderful, zero-carb cheese "crackers" can be served with soup or salad, used as an appetizer, or just for snacking. They can be crumbled over a Caesar salad in place of croutons or draped over the back of a cup to cool to make baskets to use like taco shells. Make small ones to use as a base for canapés or to top with sour cream and smoked salmon or Crème Frâiche and a dab of caviar.

1½ cups (4 to 5 ounces) coarsely grated Parmigiano-Reggiano cheese

Preheat oven to 350º F with oven rack in middle position. Line one or more baking sheets with parchment paper. (If you put 4 fricos to a pan, it will take 4 batches to make 16.)

Grate the cheese by hand into medium-fine shreds. Place cheese by about 2 tablespoonfuls on lined baking sheets, allowing 5 inches between the centers of the mounds—they won't spread when they bake. (The paper makes them easier to remove; they will pop off when you lift the paper.) Spread the cheese to make a 3½- to 4- inch circle. Neaten the edges and tap the mounds down slightly with your finger to even out the thickness. Don't make them too thick; they should be open and lacy. Bake for 6 to 8 minutes, or until golden. Do not overcook or they may become bitter. Let them cool for a few minutes on the pan, then lift the paper off the pan and set on a rack until completely cool. Carefully remove fricos from paper. Repeat until all cheese is used. Store in an airtight container, separated with sheets of parchment paper for up to 2 days.

VARIATIONS:

Make **Fricos** using other hard cheeses, like Asiago, Manchego, aged Cheddar, or aged gouda. Sprinkle with sesame seeds, poppy seeds, cumin, crushed fennel seed, cracked black pepper, or other seeds or spices, if desired. Also see recipe for **Cheese Puffs**, p. 70.

For small **Fricos**, make 32 mounds with 1 tablespoon of cheese each.

Frico is Italian for *little trifles.*

For small fricos , make 32 mounds with 1 tablespoon of cheese each.

To make appetizer baskets, make small fricos. Remove from baking sheet and shape over the bottom of mini muffin cups while still warm and flexible. Large ones can be shaped over the back of a cup or bowl.

FOR 16 PIECES.

Per serving—Net carbohydrate: 0.3 grams; Protein: 3.4 grams; Fiber: 0 grams; Fat: 2.7 grams; Calories: 37

Total weight: 4 ounces or 114 grams

Weight per serving: ¼ ounce or 7 grams

Preparation time: 15 minutes active; 30 minutes total

Caviar and Crème Fraîche Appetizer

MAKES 32 APPETIZERS.

Per each: Net carbohydrate: 0.5 grams (0.2 grams per frico plus 0.1 for caviar and 0.2 for **Crème Fraîche**); Protein: 1.8 grams; Fiber: 0.3 grams; Fat: 2; Calories: 28

Total weight: 11½ ounces or 330 grams

Weight per each: ⅓ ounce or 10 grams each

Preparation time: 5 minutes active and total

Make 32 small **Fricos** rather than 16 large ones. Spoon a teaspoonful of **Crème Fraîche,** p. 297, or sour cream onto each **Frico**. Top with ¼ teaspoon of caviar and serve immediately. (You can make them earlier if you use **Parmesan Almond Crisps**, p. 304, as the base.)

"The biggest mistake is wrapping cheese tightly in plastic—that doesn't allow the cheese to breathe. Instead, loosely wrap cheese in parchment paper, then store it in a cool area, like a wine cabinet or in the crisper section of your fridge."

– Terrance Brenner of Artisanal Bistro, Fromagerie, and Wine Bar in New York City, on the proper way to store cheese.

Pan-Seared Wild Salmon

One of the joys of life in the Northwest is our abundance of fresh wild salmon. There is a world of difference in the taste of wild salmon compared to farm raised, which are fed on grain products with artificial color and antibiotics added.

4 (6-ounce) skin-on wild salmon fillets
1 tablespoon of oil (light olive oil or peanut oil)
Salt and pepper

Sprinkle the salmon with salt and pepper. Heat a heavy skillet over high heat for about 3 minutes. Add the oil to the pan. When the oil starts to shimmer (but before it starts to smoke), add the fillets, skin side down, and cook without moving them for 30 seconds. Reduce the heat to medium-high and continue to cook until the skin side is well browned and the bottom half of each fillet is opaque, about 4 to 5 minutes. Turn and cook, again without moving, until the fillets are no longer translucent and they are firm, but not hard, to the touch, 3½ to 4½ minutes. Remove the fillets from the pan and let stand for a minute before serving.

MAKES 4 SERVINGS.

Per serving—Net carbohydrate: 0 grams; Protein: 36.2 grams; Fiber: 0 grams; Fat: 17.9 grams; Calories: 315

Total weight: 22 ounces or 625 grams

Weight per serving: 5½ ounces or 156 grams

Preparation time: 15 minutes active and total

Note: About 1 tablespoon of fat included in count remains in pan.

"Fish is the only food that is considered spoiled once it smells like what it is."

– P. J. O'Rourke

NOTES:
Fish and seafood have been staples in our diet since pre-historic times and continue to be important to a healthy diet today. One caveat: much of the world's supply of fish contains high concentrations of heavy metals and toxins. Because big fish eat little fish and the toxins add up, when it comes to fish, smaller is better. Wild fish from cold waters, like salmon, contain fewer toxins and more beneficial omega-3 fats.

———

Choose salmon filets from the large end of the fish so they will have the same thickness and cook in the same amount of time.

———

Wild salmon will retain its bright red color when cooked. Artificial colors fade to pale pink.

Rhubarb Sauce

TIP:

Frozen rhubarb can be used when fresh is not available.

Sorrel is a popular accompaniment to fish in French cuisine, but it is not well known in America. This sour/sweet sauce serves the purpose nicely as a condiment with salmon. You can also serve it like applesauce or cranberry sauce or use it as a topping for ice cream or desserts.

1 pound fresh rhubarb, rinsed and trimmed
¼ cup water, more if needed
1 teaspoon lemon juice
Sugar substitute equal to 1 cup sugar or to taste
A few grains of salt, optional

Cut rhubarb into ½-inch slices. Soak in cold water for 20 minutes to remove some of the astringency, if desired. Drain and place in a medium saucepan with water, lemon juice, and sweetener. Bring to a boil, reduce heat to low, and cover pan. Simmer for 10 minutes or until soft, stirring occasionally. Serve warm or cold.

MAKES 1½ CUPS OR 3 SERVINGS OF ½ CUP.

Per serving—Net carbohydrate: 3.2 grams; Protein: 0.9 grams; Fiber: 2.1 grams; Fat: 0.2 grams; Calories: 25

Total weight: 13¾ ounces or 392 grams

Weight per serving: 4²/₃ ounces or 131 grams

Preparation time: 5 minutes active, 35 minutes total

VARIATIONS:

Add a 2-inch piece of stick cinnamon, ½ teaspoon of anise seed, or a slice of fresh ginger to the rhubarb as it cooks for variety.

Macaroni and Cheese Custards

Calling this a "custard" doesn't prepare you for the beautiful, brown, cheesy crust. I could have called it Macaroni and Cheese Soufflé *(it tastes like one, but that makes it sound much harder to make than it is), or* Crustless Macaroni and Cheese Quiche *(no improvement over the first title), or* Cheese Puffs *(sounds too much like Cheetos). Whatever you call it, I know you are going to love this versatile dish: it can be served for breakfast; as the main course for brunch or luncheon; as an appetizer; or the one I like best, as a delicious, low-carb side dish.*

  2 ounces Dreamfields elbows (½ cup dry)
  1 cup grated Gruyère cheese (2½ ounces)
  ¼ cup grated Parmesan cheese (1 ounce)
  1 cup of heavy cream (8 ounces)
  3 large eggs
  ½ teaspoon salt
  1/8 teaspoon cayenne pepper

Bring a pot of salted water to a boil. Stir in macaroni and cook until just done, stirring once or twice. (Check for doneness one or two minutes before the time given in the directions on the pasta box. It should be slightly firm since it will be cooked again.) Drain immediately and rinse with cold water. Place on paper toweling to cool.

Preheat oven to 325º F. Butter 4 eight-ounce capacity ramekins. Stir together Gruyère and Parmesan cheese and pasta and place one fourth of the mixture in each buttered baking cup.

Heat the cream until just warm. (You should be able to comfortably touch the pan. If the cream is too hot, it will cook the eggs.) Whisk together cream, eggs, salt, and pepper until smooth. Pour the custard mixture over cheese and pasta, filling the cups almost to the top. Put ramekins on a baking sheet and place on middle rack in preheated oven. Bake for 35 to 40 minutes or until puffed and well browned. (Check progress by looking through oven window; do not open oven door until custards are well risen.) Remove to a rack and let cool for about 5 minutes. Custards will sink a bit as they cool. Serve warm.

NOTES:
Dreamfields pasta is made of regular semolina flour (that's why it tastes so good), but it contains a fiber blend that protects most of the starch from being digested. It has 5 digestible grams of carbohydrate in each 2-ounce serving (dry weight) and a low glycemic index of 13. It should be cooked only to the *al dente* stage, which means it should feel slightly firm "to the tooth." If it is overcooked, it will become more digestible. It is also important that if it is reheated, it should be done so gently and only until warm.

———————

The Dreamfield's website advises those with diabetes to test for blood glucose spikes after eating Dreamfields. "Results do vary by person, so try Dreamfields and see what your glycemic results show."

MAKES 4 SERVINGS.

Per serving—Net carbohydrate (count excludes 31 protected carbs in the pasta): 3.5 grams; Protein:15.5 grams; Fiber: 1.3 grams; Fat: 34 grams; Calories: 409

Total weight: 14 ounces 398 grams

Weight per serving: 3½ ounces or 99 grams

Preparation time: 15 minutes active; 50 minutes total

Macaroni and Cheese Custards, p. 163

Simply Roasted Asparagus

Simply Roasted Asparagus

*Serve it plain or topped with **Hollandaise**, p. 28, or **Browned Butter Sauce**, p. 263. It also makes great finger-food to serve cold with a dip.*

  1 pound (450 grams) fresh asparagus
  1 tablespoon (¼ ounce) extra virgin olive oil
  Freshly ground black pepper to taste
  Coarse salt to taste

Place oven rack in center position and preheat oven to 350° F.

Snap off the ends of asparagus stalks. They will naturally break at the point where they become tough. Use a vegetable peeler to pare away the triangular scales, which may have collected sandy soil as the shoots pushed up through the ground. (Many people omit this step. The asparagus is prettier unpeeled, but it may be slightly gritty. You can decide.) Rinse in cold water.

Spread asparagus in a single layer on a rimmed baking sheet and drizzle with oil. Roll stalks back and forth until completely coated with oil. Place pan on middle rack in oven and roast for 10 to 15 minutes or until just tender-crisp. (Longer cooking will make the asparagus limp and stringy.) Sprinkle with salt and pepper and serve.

MAKES 4 SERVINGS.

Per serving—Net carbohydrate:1.2 grams; Protein: 1.3 grams; Fiber: 1.1 grams; Fat: 3.5 grams; Calories: 42

Total weight: 8¾ ounces or 246 grams

Weight per serving: 2¼ ounces or 61.5 grams

Preparation time: 15 minutes active, 25 to 30 minutes total

NOTES:
Recipe can be doubled without increasing the cooking time.

_____

The size of the spear is not an indicator of tenderness, but of the age of the root; older plants will produce thicker shoots. Look for asparagus standing upright in a tray of water on the produce counter. It should be firm and bright green with tightly closed tips. When you get it home, break off the lower part of the stalks. Discard the lower stem or reserve to make puréed soup. Put the asparagus in a container of water as if it were a bouquet of flowers and use it within a day or two.

Cheesecake

CHEESECAKE:

Cheesecakes are believed to have originated in ancient Greece. They are first mentioned as being served to Olympic athletes on the isle of Delos in 776 B.C.E. Here is the earliest recorded recipe:

"Take cheese and pound it till smooth and pasty; put cheese in a brazen sieve; add honey and spring wheat flour. Heat in one mass, cool, and serve."
– Greek writer Athenaeus, 230 A.D.

Here's a Roman version from Cato:

"Libum to be made as follows: 2 pounds cheese well crushed in a mortar; when it is well crushed, add in 1 pound bread-wheat flour or, if you want it to be lighter, just ½ a pound, to be mixed with the cheese. Add one egg and mix all together well. Make a loaf of this, with the leaves under it, and cook slowly in a hot fire under a brick."
– Roman politician, Marcus Porcius Cato (234-149), *De Agricultura or De Re Rustica*

continued on next page…

My husband made this cheesecake for my birthday. I've included instructions for baking it in a water bath to minimize cracking, but he omitted this step; you can always pretty it up with some whipped cream, shaved chocolate, or berries on top.

1 recipe of **Almond Pie Crust**, recipe following
2 pounds cream cheese (four 8-ounce packages), at room temperature
Sugar substitute equal to 1½ cups sugar or 1½ cups granular Splenda
4 large eggs, at room temperature
Grated zest of 1 lemon (2 tablespoons)
2 tablespoons of heavy cream
1 teaspoon of sugar-free vanilla extract

Preheat oven to 375° F. Butter bottom and sides of a 9-inch springform pan. Line with parchment paper and butter the paper also. Wrap the outside of the pan with foil to prevent leaks. Place a folded dishtowel in the bottom of a roasting pan large enough to hold the springform pan.

Make **Almond Pie Crust** mixture and press into bottom of pan. Bake for 8 to 10 minutes until lightly browned and fragrant. Remove and let cool.

Lower oven temperature to 350° F. Put a kettle of water on to heat while making filling.

Beat the cream cheese with an electric mixer until smooth. Beat in the sweetener. Add the eggs one at a time, beating after each addition. Scrape down the bowl and beat in the remaining ingredients.

Pour the filling mixture over the baked crust and smooth the top. Set the larger pan on the middle oven rack and place the cheesecake pan inside. Carefully pour water into the outside pan until it comes about halfway up the sides of the springform pan. Bake for 10 minutes. Reduce the heat to 275º F and bake for 1 hour, or until the edges are lightly browned. Remove the cake from the oven and run a dull knife around the inside edge of the pan. Return to the oven and turn off the heat. Let cool for 1 hour in oven. When cool, remove cake from oven and run a knife around the edge again. Loosen the rim of the pan but leave in place. Cover with plastic wrap and refrigerate for several hours or overnight. Remove sides of pan and serve with berries and **Whipped Cream**, p. 312, if desired.

MAKES 12 SERVINGS.

Per serving, including crust—Net carbohydrate: 4.4 grams; Protein: 10 grams; Fiber: 1.4 grams; Fat: 34 grams; Calories: 387

Total weight: 2 pounds 11½ ounces or 1.2 kilograms

Weight per serving: 3½ ounces or 102 grams

Preparation time: 30 minutes active; 1 hour 40 minutes total plus 1 hour in oven to cool

Note: The cake will shrink as it cools. Loosening the edges from the sides of the pan will minimize cracking.

This one came from a mid-16th Century English cookbook: *"To make a tarte of Chese - Take harde Chese and cutte it in slyces, and pare it, than laye it in fayre water, or in swete mylke, the space of three houres, then take it up and breake it in a morter tyll it be small, than drawe it up thorowe a strainer with the yolkes of syxe eggs, and season it wyth suger and swete butter, and so bake it."* – A Proper newe Booke of Cokerye, declarynge what maner of meates be beste in season, for al times in the yere, and how they ought to be dressed, and serued at the table, bothe for fleshe dayes, and fyshe dayes, 1545.

———

Say Cheese! *Cheesecake* became synonymous with pin-up photos and calendar art in the 1930s. A magazine called *Cheesecake* featured Marilyn Monroe in a yellow bikini on its cover in 1953.

Almond Pie Crust

MAKES 12 SERVINGS AS CHEESECAKE CRUST; 8 TO 10 AS PIE CRUST.

Per serving of 12 servings as cheesecake crust—Net carbohydrate: 1.3 grams; Protein: 2.5 grams; Fiber: 1.4; Fat: 7.8; Calories: 86

Per serving of 8 servings as pie crust—Net carbohydrate: 2 grams; Protein: 3.8 grams; Fiber: 2.1 grams; Fat: 11.7 grams; Calories: 129

Per serving of 10 servings as pie crust—Net carbohydrate: 1.6 grams; Protein: 3 grams; Fiber: 1.7 grams; Calories: 103

Total weight: 5¾ ounces or 5.8 ounces or 165 grams

Weight per serving for 12 servings: ½ ounce or 14 grams;

Weight per serving for 8 servings: 21 grams

Weight per serving for 10 servings: 16.5 grams

Preparation time: 10 minutes active; 20 minutes total

If you use a regular pie pan, this tasty crust is excellent for any one-crust pie or tart.

- 1¼ cup almond meal (5 ounces)
- 2 tablespoons butter, melted
- 3 tablespoons of granular Splenda or equivalent in preferred granular sugar substitute

Preheat oven to 375° F. Butter bottom and sides of a 9-inch pie pan.

Mix crust ingredients together and press into pan. Bake for 8 to 10 minutes until lightly browned and fragrant. Remove and let cool.

Egg Flower Soup

Everyone loves this simple Chinese soup, especially kids. Some restaurants thicken it with cornstarch, but I think the consistency is better without it. In any case, use a good, rich chicken stock; the success of the soup depends on the quality of the stock.

    8 ounces (1 half breast) boneless, skinless chicken breast
    4 eggs
    4 cups **Chicken Stock**, homemade, p. 279, or purchased
    2 teaspoon grated fresh ginger root
    2 tablespoons naturally brewed soy sauce
    1 teaspoon sesame oil, more to taste
    2 tablespoons chopped green onion tops or fresh chives
    Pepper to taste
    Salt to taste or use more soy sauce

Poach the chicken as in recipe for **Poached Chicken** on p. 277. Drain and cut across grain into 1-inch pieces then shred. Break the eggs into a bowl and beat with a whisk until well blended but not foamy. Refrigerate until needed.

Place stock, ginger, soy sauce, and sesame oil in a large saucepan and bring to a boil. Turn off the heat just before adding the eggs. Stir soup to create a vortex and pour in eggs in a thin stream near the outside of the pan, while stirring (stir in one direction only). Add chicken and chives or green onions. Season with salt or more soy sauce and pepper, if desired. Serve the soup in heated bowls with additional soy sauce on the side.

SERVINGS: MAKES 5 CUPS OR 4 SERVINGS OF 1¼ CUPS.

Per serving—Net carbohydrate: 1 gram; Protein: 15.9 grams; Fiber: 1.1 grams; Fat: 7.1 grams; Calories: 139

Total weight: 1 pound 10⅛ ounces or 1.2 kilograms

Weight per serving: 5½ ounces or 156 grams

Preparation time: 10 minutes active, 12 minutes total

Egg Flower Soup

1 net carb

Pork in Peanut Sauce

2 net carbs

Sautéed Broccolini

3.7 net carbs

Coconut Mousse with Caramel Sauce

Mousse, 2.6 net carbs,
Sauce 1.1 net carbs

Menu total: 14.2 net carbs

CHIVES:

I planted a pot of chives in my flower bed years ago and they have returned every year. In fact, I have to weed them out to keep them from taking over. Not only do I have fresh chives much of the year, but also beautiful (and edible!) flowers.

I've included the option of using chives rather than green onions in my **Egg Flower Soup**, because chives are a better carb bargain.

Pork in Peanut Sauce

This is similar to an Indonesian satay, but without the tedium of threading skewers. One of my recipe testers said her husband actually licked his plate!

1 pound boneless pork loin or tenderloin
¼ cup sesame oil (2⅛ ounces)
2 tablespoons natural peanut butter
2 tablespoons naturally brewed soy sauce, such as Kikkoman
Sugar substitute equal to 4 teaspoons of sugar
4 teaspoons peeled and minced garlic (4 cloves, ⅛ ounce each)
½ teaspoon dried red pepper flakes or to taste
2 tablespoons peanut or olive oil

To serve:
1 ½ ounces Dreamfields linguini or pasta alternative, cooked (p. 325)
1 tablespoon toasted sesame seeds (optional)

Place the pork in the freezer for 20 minutes to make it easier to slice. Cut pork crosswise into 3 pieces. Cut lengthwise into narrow slices and then into strips. Reserve.

Place sesame oil, peanut butter, soy sauce, sweetener, garlic, and red pepper in a small bowl and whisk together until blended and thick. Reserve.

Heat wok or large skillet over medium-high heat. Add oil and heat until very hot but not smoking. Add pork in two batches; cook and stir for about 3 to 4 minutes or until browned but do not overcook. Remove from pan and reserve until all the pork is cooked. Return meat to pan and add reserved sauce mixture. Cook and stir for 30 seconds until bubbly and heated through. (Longer cooking may cause the sauce to separate.) Serve over pasta; garnish with sesame seeds. Serve at once.

TIPS:

Look for sesame seeds in the bulk bins at the grocery rather than in the small, expensive jars displayed with the spices. You may find sesame seeds that are already toasted.

To toast sesame seeds:
Heat a dry skillet over medium-high heat. Add sesame seeds and cook and stir until lightly browned and fragrant.

Use the kind of peanut butter that lists just "peanuts" or "peanuts and salt" as ingredients. You may find it with the organic foods and it will probably say, "stir before using." If you stir and refrigerate natural peanut butter, the oil will not separate. Smooth or crunchy is your call.

Kikkoman Naturally Brewed Soy Sauce has no sugar.

MAKES 4 SERVINGS OF ABOUT ¾ CUP.

Per serving, including pasta, based on digestible carbs—Net carbohydrate: 5.75 net grams; Protein: 24 grams; Fiber: 4.35 grams; Fat: 28.6 grams; Calories: 486

Total weight: 15¾ ounces or 443 grams

Weight per serving: 4 ounces or 111 grams

Preparation time: 20 minutes active and total

Sautéed Broccolini

Broccoli's sweet, tender little cousin has thin, edible stalks similar to asparagus and florets that are smaller and more open than those of broccoli.

1 bunch fresh broccolini (8 ounces)
½ teaspoon salt
2 tablespoons light olive oil or peanut oil
½ teaspoon dried, red pepper flakes or to taste
2 teaspoons minced garlic (2 cloves, 1/8 ounce each)
Additional salt and black pepper to taste

Wash broccolini and trim ends. Cut stems diagonally into ½-inch slices. Put 1 teaspoon salt into a large pot of water and heat to boiling. Blanch broccolini for 3 to 5 minutes until bright green. Drain and blot dry. Heat oil in a skillet over medium-high heat until hot but not smoking. Add broccolini, garlic, and pepper flakes and sauté for about 2 minutes. Add salt and black pepper, if desired. Serve hot.

MAKES 4 SERVINGS OF ½ CUP.

Per serving—Net carbohydrate: 3.7 grams; Protein: 2 grams; Fiber: 0.7 grams; Fat: 7 grams; Calories: 85

Total weight: 7 ounces or 199 grams

Weight per serving: 1¾ ounces or 49.7 grams

Preparation time: 7 minutes active; 15 minutes total

BROCCOLINI:
Broccolini, also called *baby broccoli* or *aspirations*, is billed as being similar to both broccoli and asparagus, but milder than either. This diminutive hybrid of broccoli and Chinese kale was developed in Japan in 1993. It is 100% usable. The thin, tender stems are actually side shoots off the main stalk so the plant can produce new ones, allowing multiple harvests per season.

Broccolini can be steamed, sautéed, or used fresh. Fresh Broccolini can be stored in the refrigerator for up to three weeks.

Coconut Mousse with Caramel Sauce

TIP:
Chocolate Sauce, p. 132, is equally good on this dessert.

1 tablespoon gelatin (1 packet or 7 grams)

2 ounces (4 tablespoons) water

2 egg yolks

Sugar substitute equal to 3 tablespoons sugar

¾ cup finely shredded, unsweetened coconut

1 teaspoon coconut extract or coconut rum or liqueur (adds 0.7 carbs)

2/3 cup heavy cream

1 recipe of **Caramel Sauce**, p. 59

A few shavings from a sugar-free chocolate candy bar for garnish, optional

Have ready 4 molds or custard cups. Chill a bowl and the beaters for an electric mixer. Put the gelatin in the water to soften for five minutes.

Place the coconut and coconut milk in a small saucepan and bring to a boil. Add softened gelatin and heat until gelatin is melted.

In a second bowl, beat together egg yolks and sweetener until thoroughly mixed and smooth. Strain hot coconut milk and gelatin mixture over egg yolk mixture, whisking constantly, and pressing out as much liquid from the coconut as possible. Reserve drained coconut. Stir in extract, rum, or liqueur.

In the chilled bowl, with chilled beaters, whip the cream to stiff peaks and gently fold into the cooled custard. Divide the mixture evenly among 4 cups or molds and refrigerate until set, about 2 to 3 hours.

Meanwhile, spread reserved coconut on paper toweling to dry or replace it with fresh coconut. Place on a rimmed sheet pan in a single layer and toast in a 350° F oven for about 10 minutes or until lightly browned. Stir every 5 minutes.

Pour 2 tablespoons of **Caramel Sauce,** p. 59, into each of 4 serving dishes. Unmold mousses and place on sauce. Top with the toasted coconut and drizzle with a little more Caramel Sauce. Using a vegetable parer, shave a few curls from a sugar-free chocolate candy bar over dishes to garnish, if desired.

MAKES A LITTLE OVER 2¼ CUPS OF MOUSSE OR 4 SERVINGS OF SLIGHTLY MORE THAN ½ CUP.

Per serving—Net carbohydrate: 2.6 grams; Protein: 5 grams; Fiber: 3 grams; Fat: 29 grams; Calories: 291

Total weight: 1 pound ¼ ounce or 460 grams

Weight per serving: 4 ounces or 115 grams

Preparation time: 25 minutes active; 3 to 3½ hours total

Baked Shrimp

If you want to be the toast of the party with minimal effort, take a platter of shrimp. Add a zesty sauce (or two) and you're sure to be invited back.

- 1½ pounds large- to jumbo-sized (21 to 35 count) raw shrimp (1 pound 4½ ounces, peeled weight)
- 1 tablespoon olive oil
- 1 teaspoon kosher salt
- ¼ teaspoon freshly ground black pepper
- 1 teaspoon Old Bay Seasoning

Preheat oven to 400° F.

Peel shrimp, leaving last segment and tail intact. Make a cut down the back and remove the black vein if shrimp are not already deveined. Place shrimp in a bowl and toss with olive oil until coated. Mix salt, pepper, and seasoning together, sprinkle over shrimp, and toss again. Place shrimp on a rimmed baking sheet and bake for 8 to 10 minutes or until just cooked through. (They are done when they curl up and turn pink.) Serve hot or cold. You can bake and chill the shrimp several hours or up to a day ahead. Serve with **Sweet and Spicy Sauce** (p. 174) and/or **Cocktail Sauce** (p. 175).

MAKES 10 APPETIZER SERVINGS OF 2 OR 3 SHRIMP EACH.

Per serving—Net carbohydrate: 0.5 grams; Protein: 10.8 grams; Fiber: 0 grams; Fat: 2.3 grams; Calories: 68

Total weight: 1 pound 3¼ ounces

Weight per serving: 2 ounces

Preparation time: 25 minutes active; 35 minutes total

TIP:
"Easy peel" shrimp have shells that have been split down the back to make peeling and deveining easier. You may also find peeled, cooked shrimp, but whether frozen or fresh, always buy raw shrimp; they will taste much better.

Baked Shrimp with Two Sauces: Sweet and Spicy Sauce and Cocktail Sauce

Shrimp 0.5 net carbs;
1 tablespoon Sweet and Spicy Sauce
or 1 tablespoon Cocktail Sauce,
0.8 net carb

Vanilla Spice Broiled Chicken

0.7 net carbs

Celery Root Gratin

6.6 net carbs

Waldorf Salad

2 net carbs

Chocolate Cheese Pie with Almond Crust

4.4 net carbs

Menu total: 15 net carbs

Sweet and Spicy Sauce

A little sass and a little bite make a lively dipping sauce for shrimp, grilled meats, and fried foods.

> Sugar substitute equivalent to ½ cup sugar
> ¼ cup rice vinegar
> ¼ cup water
> ½ teaspoon salt
> 2 cloves (¼ ounce) garlic, peeled and minced (2 teaspoons)
> ½ teaspoon crushed red pepper flakes
> 2 tablespoons sugar-free orange marmalade or apricot preserves (see Sources for brands with only 2 net carbs per tablespoon)

Place sweetener, vinegar, water, salt, and garlic in small saucepan. Bring to a boil, reduce heat to low, and simmer for 10 minutes. Add the pepper and marmalade or preserves. Heat and stir for a few minutes until melted. Serve at room temperature. Store, covered, in the refrigerator.

MAKES ABOUT ½ CUP PLUS TWO TABLESPOONS TOTAL OR 10 SERVINGS OF 1 TABLESPOON EACH.

Per serving—Net carbohydrate: 0.8 grams; Protein: 0.1 grams; Fiber: 0.1 grams; Fat: 0 grams; Calories: 4

Total weight: 4¾ ounces or 136 grams

Weight per serving: ½ ounce or 14 grams

Preparation time: 5 minutes active, 15 minutes total

TIPS:

Rubbing your hands on an object made of stainless steel will remove the odor of garlic. A spoon or a faucet will work as well as the gadgets sold for the purpose.

———

Jok'n'Al's jams and preserves have only 2 grams of carbs per serving. Waldon Farms is made without fruit and has zero carbs.

———

LIQUID SUCRALOSE:

Three drops of liquid sucralose from Sweetzfree equals the sweetness of 2 teaspoonfuls of sugar. One drop of EZ-Sweetz equals 2 teaspoons. Unlike sweeteners such as Splenda granular and Nutrasweet, which use sugar as a bulking agent, liquid sucralose is truly calorie and carbohydrate free.

"Make hunger thy sauce, as a medicine for health."

— *Thomas Tusser*

Cocktail Sauce

This super-easy, semi-homemade cocktail sauce contains no high-fructose corn syrup, often the main ingredient in commercial products.

1 (14½-ounce) can tomatoes, drained

½ cup prepared salsa (mild, medium, or hot)

1 tablespoon prepared horseradish

Sugar substitute equal to ½ teaspoon sugar

Dash of freshly ground black pepper

¼ teaspoon salt

Place tomatoes, salsa, horseradish, sweetener, salt, and pepper in food processor or blender and purée until smooth. Refrigerate until needed. Serve with **Baked Shrimp**, p. 173, or other seafood.

MAKES ABOUT 1 ¹/₈ CUPS OR 18 SERVINGS OF 1 TABLESPOON EACH.

Per serving—Net carbohydrate: 0.8 grams; Protein: 0.2 grams; Fiber: 0.3 grams; Fat: 0 grams; Calories: 5

Total weight: 12.8 ounces or 364 grams

Weight per serving: ¾ ounce or 20 grams

Preparation time: 8 minutes active and total

Baked Shrimp, p. 173, with Sweet and Spicy Sauce and Cocktail Sauce

Vanilla Spice Broiled Chicken

Ground vanilla is made by pulverizing dried vanilla beans. It can be used in liquid-sensitive recipes where the use of an extract would not be desirable. The flavor of ground vanilla is more intense and holds up to prolonged cooking, unlike extracts, which must be added at the end of the cooking time. Vanilla powder can be stored indefinitely in a tightly closed glass container in a cool, dry, dark place.

What could be more seductive than a combination of vanilla, lemon, and spices mingled with the smoky flavor of grilled chicken?

1 whole chicken, 4 to 5 pounds, cut into quarters
½ a lemon
¼ cup butter, melted
1 tablespoon **Vanilla Spice Rub**, opposite, divided

Cut whole chicken into quarters or have butcher do it for you. Reserve backbone, wing tips, and giblets for another purpose. Loosen skin from flesh of chicken pieces, being careful not to tear it. Sprinkle Vanilla-Spice Rub directly on meat underneath skin, using ¼ teaspoonful per piece. Refrigerate chicken for a several hours or overnight.

Grease a broiler pan. Adjust oven rack so chicken will be about 5 to 7 inches from the heat source. Preheat broiler to about 450º F. (If your broiler setting does not go that low, move rack farther away.) Remove chicken from refrigerator. Rub skin-side of each piece with cut lemon and coat with melted butter. Sprinkle ¼ teaspoon Vanilla Spice Rub over butter. Turn and rub other side with cut lemon and coat with butter. Sprinkle with another ¼ teaspoon of rub, making the total amount used on each chicken quarter about ¾ teaspoon (including amount already used under skin). Place chicken skin-side-down on rack of broiler pan. Broil for 35 to 45 minutes, turning and basting with more butter every 15 minutes. (You may need to adjust the heat—it should start to brown after 15 minutes. Turn down the heat or move pan farther from heat if it browns too quickly.) Skin should be very crisp and brown, but not black.

MAKES 4 SERVINGS.

Per serving—Net carbohydrate: 0.7 grams; Protein: 58 grams; Fiber: 0.3 grams; Fat: 58.4 grams; Calories: 472

Total weight: 3 pounds 5¼ ounce or 1.5 kilograms

Weight per serving (for 4 servings): 13⅓ ounces or 377 grams

Preparation time: 20 minutes active; 55 minutes total, excluding time for spices to infuse

Vanilla Spice Rub for Meat or Poultry

This sweet, spicy, savory seasoning mix introduces the intriguing flavor and seductive aroma of vanilla so, unlike other marinades, it doesn't get its kick from sugar and MSG.

- 1 teaspoon ground vanilla bean, made by directions below or purchased (see Sources)
- ½ teaspoon black pepper
- ½ teaspoon ground cinnamon
- ½ teaspoon allspice
- 1 teaspoon granular Splenda or equivalent in preferred dry sugar substitute
- 1 teaspoon smoked paprika or regular paprika
- 1 teaspoon kosher or coarse salt

To use a whole vanilla bean: If vanilla bean is moist, let it dry, uncovered, at room temperature for a few days before grinding. Cut bean into small pieces and grind in a coffee or spice grinder with other spices in ingredients list. Alternately, grind vanilla bean with a mortar and pestle or crush to a paste with the back of a spoon. Mix with other ingredients.

Use as a rub for meat or poultry. Rub mixture can be stored in an airtight container for up to three months.

Recipe adapted from the Singing Dog Vanilla Website, www.singingdogvanilla.com.

> **MAKES 1½ TABLESPOONS OF RUB.**
>
> Per serving of ¾ teaspoon—Net carbohydrate: 0.4 grams; Protein: 0.1 grams; Fiber: 0.3 grams; Fat: 0.1 grams; Calories: 3
>
> Preparation time: 10 minutes active and total

TIPS

Whole allspice berries, stick cinnamon, and black peppercorns can be freshly ground with the vanilla bean to increase the volume. Purchased, ground versions of the other spices called for in the recipe could be put in the grinder with the vanilla as well to add bulk, since it may be difficult to manage such a small amount.

One 6-inch vanilla bean makes 1 teaspoon of ground vanilla. One teaspoon of vanilla powder is equal to one teaspoon of extract.

Ground vanilla beans can be purchased as vanilla powder (see Sources), but be sure to get pure, ground vanilla beans, not a mixture containing sugar.

Celery Root Gratin

TIP:
Celeriac is esteemed by gourmands the world over, but it is unfamiliar to most Americans, so it tends to linger on the produce shelf. Make sure to choose one that is firm and heavy for its size, as it is not easy to judge its freshness by appearance.

Celery root tastes like potatoes with a hint of celery and parsley; it makes an elegant side dish for a special dinner party.

1 celery root (1 pound with roots and top trimmed)
1 teaspoon salt
Dash black pepper
Dash ground nutmeg
½ cup heavy cream (4 ounces)
1 tablespoon butter

Preheat oven to 375° F. Grease a 12- by 12- by 2-inch baking dish.

Wash the celery root well, using a brush if needed. Cut into quarters to make it easier to reach into convoluted spaces. Peel and trim away any brown parts. Cut into thin slices (⅛-inch thick). Place root in dish in three layers, seasoning each layer with salt, pepper, and nutmeg. Pour cream evenly over top. Dot with butter. Cover pan tightly with foil or a lid and bake for 30 minutes. Remove cover and bake for 30 to 35 minutes more or until celery root is tender and top is browned. Serve hot.

MAKES 2½ CUPS OR 5 SERVINGS OF ½ CUP EACH.

Per serving—Net carbohydrate: 6.6 grams; Protein: 1.7 grams; Fiber: 1.4 grams; Fat: 11.4 grams; Calories: 137

Total weight: 15¾ ounces or 449 grams

Weight per serving: 3⅓ ounces or 94 grams

Preparation time: 20 minutes active; 1 hour and 20 minutes total

Waldorf Salad

Jicama has all the crunch of a crisp, fresh apple with a fraction of the carbs. The cider vinegar provides the apple taste.

2 cups peeled and cubed jicama (9 ounces)

2 tablespoons of apple cider vinegar

Sugar substitute equal to 2 teaspoons of sugar, (use more if vinegar has more than 5% acidity)

1 cup sliced celery (3½ ounces)

⅓ cup of real **Mayonnaise**, p. 298

A few thinly sliced red grapes (optional)

A generous dash of nutmeg

⅛ teaspoon salt

Dash of black pepper

½ cup broken walnuts (2 ounces)

Toss the jicama with the vinegar and sugar substitute and let stand for 5 minutes. Mix with other ingredients. Add walnuts just before serving.

MAKES 9 SERVINGS OF ½ CUP

Per serving—Net carbohydrate: 2 grams; Protein: 1.4 grams; Fiber: 2 grams; Fat: 10.7 grams; Calories: 115

Total weight: 1 pound 6½ ounces

Weight per serving: 2½ ounces

Preparation time: 10 minutes active; 15 minutes total

Waldorf Salad

Chocolate Cheese Pie

MAKES 12 SERVINGS OF PIE.

Per serving—Net carbohydrate: 4.4 grams for crust and filling (2.1 net for filling only); Protein 5.8 grams; Fiber: 3.1; Fat: 29.9; Calories: 307

Total weight: 1 pound 10⅛ ounces or 742 grams

Weight per serving, filling only: 2¼ ounces or 62 grams

Weight per serving, filling and crust: 2¾ ounces or 76 grams

Preparation time: 10 minutes active; 15 minutes total

MAKES 28 SERVINGS OF 2 TABLESPOONS EACH AS CAKE FROSTING.

Per serving—Net carbohydrate: 0.9 grams; Protein: 1.3 grams; Fiber: 0.8 grams; Fat: 9.7 grams; Calories: 26

Net carbohydrate per serving: 1.3 grams

Total weight: 1 pound 10⅛ ounces or 26.2 ounces or 742 grams

Weight per serving: 0.9 ounces (Frosting only)

Preparation time: 10 minutes active; 15 minutes total

Serve this in small portions, as it is very rich. The filling also makes a delicious cake frosting.

Baked **Almond Pie Crust**, p. 168
4 ounces unsweetened chocolate, finely chopped
2 tablespoons Dutch-process cocoa
Sugar substitute equivalent to 2 cups sugar
½ cup brewed decaf coffee or water
8 ounces cream cheese
1 teaspoon sugar-free vanilla extract
2 teaspoons Kahlúa or crème de cacao liqueur, optional (adds 0.1 grams net carbs per serving)
A pinch of salt
1½ cups heavy cream

Heat one-half inch of water in the bottom of a double boiler to a simmer. Reduce heat so water is hot but not bubbling. Stir together the cocoa and 1 teaspoon of the coffee or water to make a smooth paste in the top of the double boiler. Gradually stir in the rest of the coffee or water. Stir in the chocolate. Set top pan over, but not touching, the hot water. Stir constantly until chocolate is melted and mixture is smooth. Let cool until barely warm.

Beat the cream cheese with an electric mixer until fluffy. Beat in vanilla, sweetener, chocolate liqueur (if using), and salt. Add chocolate mixture and beat in. Add the heavy cream and beat until mixture is fluffy.

Place in a baked, 9-inch **Almond Pie Crust**. Top with sugar-free **Whipped Cream,** p. 312, and a grating of chocolate or dust with cocoa powder, if desired.

To use as **CHOCOLATE CAKE FROSTING**, spread on completely cooled cake layers. Extra filling will keep for several days in the refrigerator.

Makes about 3½ cups, enough to fill a 9-inch pie shell or frost and fill a double layer cake.

Cantaloupe with Prosciutto

Casaba melon is actually a little lower in carbs than canta-loupe, if you can find one. Honeydew is a bit higher. For a few more carbs, you can try a different twist on this classic appetizer and use papaya.

This recipe serves 8, but you can buy a cut melon and use only the amount you need for fewer servings.

> 1 (2 pounds as purchased) ripe cantaloupe (1 pound, peeled and seeded)
> 8 ounces thinly sliced prosciutto (about 16 slices)
> 1 lime, cut into 8 wedges

Peel and seed the cantaloupe and cut into 24 thin wedges. Arrange 3 wedges in a fan pattern on each of 8 chilled plates. Divide the prosciutto into 8 portions and wrap a piece of prosciutto around each slice of melon or simply drape over melon on plate. Serve with lime wedges.

MAKES 8 SERVINGS.

Per serving—Net carbohydrate: 4.3 grams; Protein: 8.5 grams; Fiber: 0.5 grams; Fat:6.1 grams; Calories 90:

Total weight: 1 pound 8 ounces or 682 grams

Weight per serving: 3 ounces or 85 grams

Preparation time: 10 minutes active and total

HOW TO CHOOSE A RIPE MELON:

Follow your nose. A fragrant cantaloupe is ripe. It's a little trickier to judge a watermelon. The owner of my favorite local produce stand, Stocker Farms, gave me a quick lesson: First, check the stem end for a bit of sticky, black, dried juice; if it is there, it means the melon is sweet and ripe. Next, hold the watermelon in one hand with your arm outstretched so it is not touching your body. (That requires some muscle or a small melon.) Slap it with the other hand. If you feel vibrations, it means it is not over-ripe.

Cantaloupe with Prosciutto
4.3 net carbs

Chicken Parmesan
1.3 net carbs

Eggplant and Sundried Tomato Mini Pizzas
3.7 net carbs

Caesar Salad
3.4 net carbs

Chocolate Cupcakes
2.6 net carbs for cake;

Chocolate Butter Cream Frosting (see p. 126)
0.9 net carbs for frosting

Menu total: 16.2 net carbs

TIP:
A "standard" cantaloupe (477 grams or slightly over 1 pound) is listed as having 39.9 grams of carbohydrates in my database. The equivalent amount of casaba would have 31.4 carbs; papaya would have 46.8.

Chicken Parmesan

For best results, use authentic Parmigiano-Reggiano. The big box stores usually have the best prices on the good stuff—sometimes about half what it is in the regular grocery stores. Treat it like the treasure it is and don't waste a crumb—see quote, p. 160, for storage tip. (Trader Joe's stores have great prices on gourmet cheeses in smaller amounts.)

A combination of part finely-grated and part shredded Parmesan makes the best crust.

4 skinless, boneless chicken cutlets (1½ pounds total), about ¼-inch thick
¼ teaspoon salt
2 egg whites
2 tablespoons heavy cream
1 tablespoon dry mustard powder
1 tablespoon dried chives and/or parsley
½ teaspoon freshly ground black pepper
¼ cup (½ ounce) finely grated Parmesan cheese
1 cup (3 ounces) shredded Parmesan cheese
2 tablespoons light olive oil
2 tablespoons butter, cut into pieces
4 lemon wedges, optional

Rinse cutlets and pat dry. Sprinkle both sides with salt. Place egg whites and cream in a small bowl and beat with a fork until foamy. On a pie plate, stir together mustard powder, chives or parsley or both, pepper, and both grated and shredded Parmesan cheese. Dip chicken pieces in egg whites and cream, let excess drain away, and then place in cheese and seasoning mixture. Turn and coat other side, pressing down so coating will adhere. Place cutlets on rack to dry for 15 minutes.

Heat a large skillet over medium-high heat and add oil and butter. When foaming subsides, add chicken pieces. (Cook in two batches if necessary to avoid crowding pan.) If fat is hot enough, it should sizzle when cutlets are added. Do not move them until a golden-brown crust has formed on the bottom, which should take about 1 to 1½ minutes. Turn and repeat to brown other side for a total cooking time

NOTES:
Time and temperature are critical for moist, tender cutlets. They should be cooked to what the French call *à point (to the perfect point)*—the outside should be crisp and brown but the inside should be just cooked through, still slightly translucent rather than opaque white. The slices need to be uniform in thickness, so they cook evenly.

Many stores sell bulk packages of ice-glazed, thin chicken fillets, making it easy to remove and thaw only the number needed. You may also be able to purchase fresh chicken labeled as "cutlets" or "thin-sliced." If not, you can buy fresh, skinless, boneless chicken breasts and make your own cutlets.

of about 2 to 3 minutes for ¼-inch thick cutlets. (Do not overcook or meat will be dry.) Drain on absorbent paper. Serve with lemon wedges or see Variation below.

MAKES 4 SERVINGS OF 1 CUTLET

Per serving—Net carbohydrate: 1.3 grams; Protein: 46.5 grams; Fiber: 0.4 grams; Fat: 26.3 grams; Calories: 434

Total weight: 1 pound 11 ounces or 767 grams

Weight per serving: 6¾ ounces or 192 grams

Preparation time: 15 minutes active, 30 minutes total

Note: About ½ cup of cheese mixture and ¼ cup of egg white mixture will be left over, although they are included in the nutrition count.

VARIATION:

Spread 2 tablespoons of **Marinara Sauce** (p. 295) on each cutlet and top with a slice of mozzerella cheese before removing from pan. Place in preheated oven for a few minutes until cheese is melted.

FOR CHICKEN CUTLETS:

To facilitate cutting fresh fillets, freeze them for 15 minutes until firm but not completely frozen. Put fillet on cutting board with the smooth side up and place one hand on top. Hold knife parallel to cutting board and slice through center of meat horizontally, making two thin slices from each half-breast. Frozen fillets can be partially thawed and sliced in the same way.

"…the only cheese whose flavour underpins an entire cuisine."

— *Jeffrey Steingarten on* Parmigiano-Reggiano

Eggplant and Sun-Dried Tomato Mini Pizzas

TIPS:

For more uniform slices, choose a long, thin eggplant, rather than a fat, round one. A one-pound eggplant will yield about 18 (½-inch-thick) slices of varied diameter. Substitute 1 pound of small Chinese or Japanese eggplants to make appetizer-sized servings.

———

To substitute dry tomatoes for oil packed: place ¼ cup of chopped, dried tomatoes and 1 peeled and minced clove of garlic in a small saucepan or a microwave dish with enough extra-virgin olive oil to cover. Heat through. Mix with **Marinara Sauce** as directed in recipe.

VARIATION:

You may use a slice or two of pepperoni per pizza instead of bacon. Microwave pepperoni on paper towels for a few seconds to remove some of the grease before using.

This is no ordinary pizza! It makes a delicious and beautiful vegetable side dish for family meals or entertaining.

1 regular or 3 or 4 Asian eggplants, about 1 pound as purchased (peeled weight 14 ounces)
1 to 2 tablespoons olive oil
¼ teaspoon salt
¼ cup (2 ounces) sun-dried tomatoes packed in garlic-flavored olive oil (including about 1 tablespoon of the oil)
¼ cup (2 ounces) **Marinara Sauce** (p. 295) or purchased no-sugar-added marinara sauce
6 ounces (1½ cups) shredded mozzarella or provolone cheese
¼ cup (1 ounce) chopped red onion
4 slices (¼ pound raw) bacon, cooked until almost crisp and chopped
Freshly ground black pepper to taste

Preheat broiler and grease a rimmed baking sheet.

Cut ends off eggplant and peel if desired. (The dark skin looks pretty, but it may be tough.) Cut eggplant into ½-thick slices. Salt both sides of the eggplant slices and place in a colander or a paper towel-lined bowl to draw out the bitter juices and remove excess moisture. Put a heavy dish on top to press out the liquid. Let stand for 1 hour. Rinse to remove the salt and blot dry with paper towels.

Brush both sides of slices with olive oil and sprinkle with salt. Place in a single layer on baking sheet. Broil 5 to 6 inches from heat source for about 5 minutes or until starting to brown. Turn over and broil for an additional 5 to 6 minutes until second side starts to brown and eggplant is cooked but still firm.

If sun-dried tomatoes are not already cut into small pieces, cut them with kitchen scissors or knife, reserving garlic-flavored oil. Place in a medium bowl and add 1 tablespoon of the flavored oil and **Marinara Sauce**. Spread sauce on eggplant slices, dividing equally. Cover with cheese. Sprinkle chopped onion over cheese and top with bacon pieces. Broil for an additional 2 to 3 minutes or until cheese is bubbly and starting to brown. *Watch carefully so bacon doesn't burn.* Grind fresh black pepper over pizzas. Serve hot as a side dish, as an appetizer, or a snack.

MAKES 6 SERVINGS.

Per serving—Net carbohydrate: 3.7 grams; Protein: 8.5 grams; Fiber: 2.8 grams; Fat:11.5 grams; Calories: 161

Total weight: 1 pound 7¼ ounces or 658 grams

Weight per serving: 3⁷⁄₈ ounces or 109 grams

Preparation time: 25 minutes active, 70 minutes total

Eggplant and Sun-Dried Tomato Mini Pizzas

Caesar Salad

TIP:

Pasteurized eggs in the shell are available in many stores around the country. They can be used to make the coddled eggs for Caesar salad to eliminate the small risk of contracting a food-borne illness from raw eggs.

——————

To turn a **Caesar Salad** into a substantial main dish, top it with grilled salmon, shrimp, or chicken.

——————

See p. 292 for low-carb garlic **Croutons**.

In her book, From Julia Child's Kitchen, *Julia Child tells of eating at Caesar Cardini's restaurant in Tijuana, Mexico, as a child. Fifty years later, she contacted Cardini's daughter to ask about her father's recipe for his famous salad. The original contained neither anchovies nor egg yolks, she learned. Cardini preferred the subtlety of a dash of Worcestershire sauce to anchovies, and he broke whole coddled eggs over the finished salad. He served the romaine leaves whole, intending them to be picked up and eaten out of hand.*

2 heads of romaine lettuce, small inner leaves only (about 1 pound of leaves)
2 large eggs
3 garlic cloves (3/8 ounce), peeled
½ cup extra virgin olive oil
2 anchovy fillets, drained and mashed to a paste, or 2 teaspoons prepared anchovy paste, optional
¼ teaspoon Worcestershire sauce (use ½ teaspoon if omitting anchovies)
1½ teaspoons dry mustard
2 tablespoons lemon juice (amount from one small, 2-inch diameter lemon)
1½ tablespoons real **Mayonnaise**, p. 298, or purchased real, no-trans-fat mayonnaise
½ cup (1 3/8 ounce) freshly grated Parmesan cheese
Salt to taste
Freshly ground black pepper to taste

Remove any large leaves from lettuce heads and reserve for another use. Rinse and dry small leaves. Break into two or three pieces. Wrap in a towel and refrigerate for 30 minutes to crisp.

Place eggs in warm water for a few minutes so they are not ice cold. Bring 3 cups of water to a boil in a small saucepan. Add eggs and boil for exactly one minute. Place in cold water to halt cooking. Reserve.

Put garlic and the ½ cup olive oil in a blender. Mash the anchovies with a fork until they form a paste, or use prepared anchovy paste. Add mashed anchovies or prepared paste to the blender. Add mustard, lemon juice, and mayonnaise. Blend on high until emulsified. Add 2 tablespoons of the Parmesan cheese and blend again. Add salt and pepper to taste. (Makes about ¾ cup or 6 ounces of dressing.)

Place chilled lettuce leaves in a large bowl. Pour dressing over lettuce and toss until well coated. Break the eggs over the salad and toss again. Sprinkle with remaining Parmesan and toss once more. Grind additional pepper over salads and sprinkle with coarse salt to taste. Place salad on chilled plates and serve.

MAKES 4 SERVINGS OF 2 CUPS.

Per serving—Net carbohydrate: 3.4 grams; Protein: 9.4 grams; Fiber: 2.6 grams; Fat: 37.1 grams; Calories: 382

Total weight: 1 pound 6 ounces or 630 grams

Weight per serving: 5½ ounces or 157 grams

Preparation time: 15 minutes active and total, excluding chilling time for lettuce

"The only things I see again clearly are the eggs. I can see him break 2 eggs over that romaine and roll them in, the greens going all creamy as the eggs flowed over them. Two eggs in a salad? Two one-minute coddled eggs? And garlic-flavored croutons and grated Parmesan cheese? It was a sensation of a salad from coast to coast...."

– Julia Child, describing the salad made for her family by Caesar Cardini in 1925 or '26, From Julia Child's Kitchen.

There is a slight risk of food poisoning from salmonella bacteria in undercooked eggs. The risk is greater if the eggs are old or have been improperly refrigerated. The white is more likely to be infected than the yolk. The USDA estimated that 1 egg in 20,000 could be infected. Statistically, that means that if you eat two eggs a day you might encounter one infected egg every 27 years, and even then it would not be a health hazard unless it had been improperly stored or not completely cooked. Fresh, local eggs are unlikely to be a problem, but those who are vulnerable to food-bourne illness or those who have a compromised immune system may prefer to have their eggs thoroughly cooked or to use pasteurized eggs in the shell, available at many grocery stores.

Chocolate Cupcakes

NOTE:

Use the kind of coconut milk that comes in a can, not the thinner ones sold in the dairy case as a beverage.

Nut flours, like almond and coconut, make delicious, healthful replacements for wheat flour. They are more readily available now, due to the increasing demand for gluten-free products.

6 tablespoons butter

¼ cup (1 ounce or 28.4 grams) coconut flour

¼ cup (1 ounce or 28.4 grams) almond flour

½ cup (2 ounces or 80 grams) cocoa powder

½ cup (4 ounces or 113 grams) granular erythritol* (may be called crystals) or other sweetener with bulk

½ teaspoon baking powder

½ teaspoon salt

½ cup (4 ounces) coconut milk

4 large eggs

High intensity sugar substitute equal to 1 cup sugar, such as liquid sucralose, crushed Splenda minis, or stevia (recipe was tested with 24 drops EZ-Sweetz)

1 packet (equivalent to 2 teaspoons of sugar) of a third sweetener, such as acesulfame K (Sweet One), optional

½ teaspoon vanilla

Preheat oven to 400° F. Grease 10 cups of a 12-cup muffin pan and dust with sifted cocoa powder or use fluted paper liners.

Melt butter and let stand until cool but still liquid.

Place coconut flour, almond flour, cocoa powder, baking powder, salt, erythritol and/or any other dry sweetener in bowl of food processor. Process for a minute or two, scraping down bowl once or twice to be sure contents are thoroughly mixed and granular sweeteners, such as erythritol or xylitol, are ground to a fine powder. Alternately, grind such sweeteners in a spice or coffee mill and whisk with other dry ingredients.* Set aside.

Beat eggs in a large mixing bowl with an electric mixer or by hand until blended. Add melted butter, coconut milk, and vanilla and beat until well mixed. Add reserved dry ingredients, one third at a time, to bowl, beating until smooth after each addition. Spoon batter into muffin cups.

Bake for 16 to 18 minutes or until cakes are firm to the touch and a wooden pick inserted in the center comes out clean. Place pan on rack and let cool for 10 minutes. Remove cupcakes and place, right-side-up, on cake rack until completely cool. Frost with **Chocolate Butter Cream Frosting**, p. 126, or serve with **Ice Cream**, p. 308, or **Whipped Cream**, p. 312.

Recipe adapted from Cooking with Coconut Flour *by Bruce Fife, N.D.*

* Erythritol is available as a powder, but it is better to measure it by weight, not volume, as it varies a lot. (Even pre-powdered erythritol will be lumpy and may need to be ground or sifted.)

MAKES 10 CUPCAKES.

Per serving—Net carbohydrate: 2.6 grams; Protein: 5.1 grams; Fiber: 4 grams; Fat: 12.6 grams; Calories: 157

Total weight: 18 ounces or 511 grams

Weight per serving: 1¾ ounces or 51 grams

Preparation time: 25 minutes active and 45 total, not counting cooling time

Chocolate Cupcakes

Jicama with Lime and Chili

Cool, crunchy, juicy jicama slices, rubbed with lime juice and dipped in chili powder are a popular snack sold by street venders in Mexico.

1 pound of peeled jicama
2 limes
½ teaspoon sea salt or to taste
1 teaspoon chili powder or to taste

Use a knife to peel jicama or peel it twice with a vegetable parer to remove the tough fibers under the skin. Rinse and cut in half and then into ¼-inch thick slices. Place in a large bowl. Cut the limes in half, squeeze the juice over the jicama, sprinkle lightly with salt, and toss. Sprinkle with chili powder and toss again. Arrange on a platter and serve ice cold.

MAKES ABOUT 40 SLICES OR 10 SERVINGS OF 4 SLICES EACH.

Per serving of 4 slices—Net carbohydrate: 1.8 grams; Protein: 0.3 grams; Fiber: 2.2 grams; Fat: 0.1 grams; Calories: 17

Total weight: 1 pound or 454 grams

Weight per serving of 4 slices: 1²/₃ ounces or 45 grams

Preparation time: 8 minutes active and total

TIP:
Jicama roots range from the size of a baseball to almost as big as a basketball. If you must buy more than you need for this recipe, use the extra for **Jicama Shoestring Fries**, p. 93, or salads.

Grilled Steak with Herb and Spice Rub

This is my interpretation of steak with a South American rub.

4 tender steaks, such as rib eye or New York, 1- to 1-½ inches thick
Herb and Spice Steak Rub, below
Salt to taste

Remove steaks from refrigerator 30 to 45 minutes before cooking to bring almost to room temperature (70° F is ideal). Preheat grill on high.

Coat *one side only* of each steak with 1½ teaspoons of the rub mixture, below, pressing it in so that it adheres. Place steaks, rub-side-down, on grill and cook for about 3 minutes. Turn (use tongs, not a fork) and cook second (un-coated) side for 3 minutes or to desired doneness. (Cooking time will vary depending on thickness of steaks and distance from heat source.) Remove steaks to a warm plate, tent loosely with foil, and let rest for about 5 minutes to redistribute juices before serving.

HERB AND SPICE STEAK RUB:

   1 teaspoon fennel seed
   1 teaspoon freshly ground black pepper
   1 teaspoon dried chives or onion flakes
   1 teaspoon dried parsley
   1 teaspoon dried rosemary
   1 teaspoon cayenne pepper, or to taste

Crush fennel seed with a mortar and pestle or with the bottom of a heavy pan. Place in a small container. Add other ingredients and mix well. Store airtight until needed. (Rub can also be made in a spice grinder.)

"Red meat is not bad for you. Now, blue-green meat, that's bad for you."

—*American comedian, Tommy Smothers*

TIPS:

A one-inch-thick steak, 5 or 6 inches from hot coals, will take about 6 minutes total for rare or about 8 minutes for medium-rare. Use an instant-read thermometer, inserted into the side of the meat, not touching fat or bone, to check doneness: 130° F indicates rare; 135° F is medium rare. (Cook it to 140° or above and you've wasted your money buying good steaks. Make a pot roast instead.)

———

Steaks and chops should be close to room temperature before grilling, or they will not cook evenly.

MAKES 4 SERVINGS, STEAK WITH RUB.

Per serving (for one 8-ounce bone-less steak)—Net carbohydrate: 0.5 grams; Protein: 41 grams; Fiber: 0.6 grams; Fat: 46 grams; Calories: 591

Total weight, cooked: 1 pound 11⅝ ounces or 784 grams

Weight per serving, cooked: 6⅞ ounces or 196 grams

Preparation time: 5 minutes active, 10 minutes total plus standing time

Baked Red Peppers Caprese

MAKES 6 SERVINGS.

Per serving—Net carbohydrate: 4.9 grams; Protein: 5.8 grams; Fiber: 2.1 grams; Fat: 6.5 grams; Calories: 105

Total weight: 1 pound 11 ounces or 767 grams

Weight per serving: 4½ ounces or 128 grams

Preparation time: 10 minutes active; 45 minutes total

These beautiful peppers combine the flavors of a traditional Caprese salad with tender-crisp red peppers for a delicious and easy side dish.

1½ teaspoons olive oil
1½ teaspoon of red wine vinegar
Sugar substitute equal to ¼ teaspoon of sugar
1 clove garlic (1/8 ounce), peeled and minced (1 teaspoon)
1 cup mozzarella cheese, cut into ½-inch cubes (5 ounces)
8 ounces cherry tomatoes, cut in half or quartered if large (1½ cups)
Salt and black pepper to taste
¼ cup total fresh basil leaves, shredded, divided
3 medium red bell peppers (6 to 7 ounces each as purchased), cut in half lengthwise, seeds and membranes removed

Preheat oven to 375° F.

Mix together the olive oil, vinegar, sweetener, garlic, cheese, tomatoes, salt and pepper, and half the basil. Place pepper halves in shallow baking pan. Fill with tomato/cheese mixture and pour any remaining liquid over tops. Bake for about 35 minutes or until peppers are tender-crisp; scatter remaining basil on top and serve hot.

"When the diet is wrong, medicine is of no use. When the diet is correct, medicine is of no need."

— *Ancient Ayurvedic Proverb*

Baked Red Peppers Caprese

Stuffed Zucchini Blossoms

Fresh zucchini blossoms only last a day or two, so don't expect to find them in the supermarket. Zucchini is notoriously prolific, however, and very easy to grow. A few plants on a sunny patio should give you an abundant supply. Many farmers' markets sell them in season as well.

1 cup (8.5 ounces) fresh, whole milk ricotta cheese
2 egg yolks
6 fresh chives, green part only (2 tablespoons or 6 grams, chopped)
¼ cup (1 ounce) finely grated Parmesan cheese plus 2 tablespoons
½ teaspoon lemon juice
½ teaspoon salt or to taste
3 or 4 grinds of fresh black pepper or to taste
8 to 12 zucchini, squash, or pumpkin blossoms
2 tablespoons olive oil for frying

Place ricotta in a strainer set over a bowl to drain for 1 hour. Check inside blossoms and brush away any debris or small bugs. Submerge in cool water. Dip out and drain on paper towels. Gently blot dry and cut off stems. Remove pistils from male flowers with a pinch and twist motion or snip out with kitchen shears.

Put the ricotta, egg yolks, chives, Parmesan, lemon juice, salt, and pepper in a bowl and mix until smooth.

Scoop out tablespoon-sized portions of the cheese mixture and shape with your hands into ovals. (Larger flowers may need more.) Open petals and place filling in flowers. Carefully press petals back into shape to completely enclose filling. Dust stuffed blooms with more Parmesan cheese. Let rest on a double layer of paper toweling for 15 minutes.

Heat oil in a skillet. Place flowers about ½ inch apart in pan and fry for 2 or 3 minutes per side or until brown. Fry in batches if necessary. Sprinkle with additional grated Parmesan, if desired, and serve warm or at room temperature. **Marinara Sauce**, p. 295, for dipping makes a nice addition. Allow 2 large or 4 small stuffed blossoms per serving.

MAKES 8 TO 12 DEPENDING ON SIZE OF BLOSSOMS.

Per serving (counts exclude blossoms as no data is available)—Net carbohydrate: 1.7 grams; Protein: 5.4 grams; Fiber: 0 grams; Fat: 5.2 grams; Calories: 73

Total weight for 8 large blossoms: 8 ounces or 227 grams

Weight per serving for 2 large blossoms: 2 ounces or 57 grams

Preparation time: 15 minutes active; 20 minutes total, not counting draining time

Note: There will probably be some filling left over that is included in the nutrition count.

TIPS:

Large blossoms are gorgeous and easy to fill, but smaller, one-bite blooms are a bit more convenient for eating without cutlery.

Blossoms from any squash or pumpkin can be used for stuffing *IF* they have not been sprayed with unsafe chemicals.

Female flowers will have a tiny zucchini attached. Male blooms are preferable (and expendable as they have already served their purpose). The pistils are edible, but stuffing is easier if they are removed.

EDIBLE FLOWERS:

Roses, tulips, nasturtiums, marigolds, pansies, chives, hibiscus, banana blossoms, lily buds, and violets are popular edible flowers, but not all flowers that are edible should be eaten or used as garnish. Buy only those specifically marketed for use as food rather than flowers from a nursery or florist. Wild plants grown by the side of the road may have been sprayed with weed killer or they may have toxic or they may have absorbed toxins from car emissions. If you don't know the flowers are safe, don't eat them.

The most commonly eaten flowers are broccoli, cauliflower, artichokes, and capers.

Stuffed Zucchini Blossoms

NOTE:

It has been estimated that 1 in 133 people in the United States suffers from gluten intolerance, also known as Celiac disease. Strict adherence to a gluten-free diet for life is the only way to prevent serious complications from the disease. Many more people are sensitive to gluten, although most get better and some may even reverse the condition on a low-carb diet. More information is available at www.celiac.com.

Coconut Macadamia Pie

What could be better?

FOR THE CRUST:
½ cup (2 ounces) vital wheat gluten flour
½ cup (2 ounces) almond flour (or use ½ cup of finely chopped nuts)
½ cup (2 ounces) unsweetened, flaked coconut
Sugar substitute equal to 1/3 cup sugar
¼ teaspoon salt
4 tablespoons (¼ cup or half a stick) cold butter, cut into 4 pieces

FOR THE TOPPING:
1 egg white
Sugar substitute equal to ¼ cup sugar
2 cups unsweetened, large-flake, coconut

FOR THE FILLING:
1 packet (¼ ounce) unflavored gelatin
½ cup water
8 ounces cream cheese, softened to room temperature
Sugar substitute equal ¾ cup plus 1 tablespoon of sugar
1 teaspoon vanilla extract
1 teaspoon coconut extract
2 teaspoons rum or coconut rum, optional
1¼ cups (5 ounces) coarsely chopped, roasted Macadamia nuts
1 cup cold heavy cream

TO MAKE THE CRUST:
Preheat the oven to 350º F.

Combine crust ingredients in the bowl of a food processor and pulse to form coarse crumbs or cut butter into dry ingredients with a pastry blender. Press into the bottom and up the sides of a 9-inch pie pan. Bake for 10 to 15 minutes or until lightly browned. Remove from the oven and cool completely.

TO MAKE THE TOPPING:

Bake topping while crust cooks or reheat oven to 350° F.

With clean beaters, beat together the egg white and sweetener until stiff. Fold in the coconut. Spread the mixture on a nonstick or parchment-lined baking sheet and bake in preheated oven for about 10 minutes or until it starts to brown. Let cool until it can be handled. Turn the pieces over and break up the clumps. Continue to bake for another 5 minutes or until evenly golden brown. Remove from oven and cool completely.

TO MAKE THE FILLING:

Sprinkle gelatin over the water in a microwave-safe bowl or a small saucepan. Let sit for a minute or two until the gelatin is moistened. Heat in the microwave or on stovetop until the gelatin is dissolved. Let cool completely.

Beat together the cream cheese, sweetener, extracts, and rum, if using, until smooth and fluffy. In another bowl, with clean beaters, beat the heavy cream to soft-peak stage. Carefully fold in the cooled gelatin mixture, then the cream-cheese mixture with a flexible spatula. Fold in the chopped nuts. Pour into the pie shell and refrigerate for an hour or two or until firm.

TO SERVE:

Sprinkle the topping over the pie just before serving. It is very rich, so servings should be small.

TIP:
You'll have a gummy mess if you try to clean up spilled gluten flour with a wet towel. Vacuum it up or use a dry towel to wipe it away.

MAKES 10 SLICES.

Per serving—Net carbohydrate: 5.5 grams; Protein: 12.4 grams; Fiber: 6.1 grams; Fat: 51.7 grams; Calories: 547

Total weight: 2 pounds 2¾ ounces or 985 grams

Weight per serving: 3½ ounces or 99 grams

Filling only: 15 minutes active; 25 minutes total, excluding setting time

Preparation time for crust, filling, and topping: 30 minutes active; 1 hour and 10 minutes total, excluding 1 to 2 hours setting time

PART 3

Seasonal and Holiday Menus

Seasonal and Holiday Menus

MENU 1: OUTDOOR BARBECUE

Stuffed Celery

Bacon-Cheese Buffalo Burgers

French Fries (Fried Green Beans)

Coco-Choco-Chia Bars

MENU 2: HOT DOG PARTY

Meatballs with
Barbecue Dipping Sauce

Chicago Style Hot Dogs
with Tomato, Cucumber, Pickle,
Mustard, Onion, Sport Peppers,
and Sweet Relish

Ice Cream Sodas and
Ice Cream Floats

MENU 3: NEW YEAR'S DAY

Baked Ham

Bavarian Sauerkraut

Home Fries

Cheddar Biscuits
with Butter

Baked Custards

MENU 4: VALENTINE'S DAY DINNER

Steamed Artichokes with
Garlic Lemon Butter

Duck Breasts with
Raspberry Glaze

Cauliflower *Faux* Rice

Spinach Salad with Goat Cheese,
"Pear," and Fennel

Chocolate Dipped Strawberries

Coffee Mocha and/or
Dry Champagne

MENU 5: ST. PATRICK'S DAY

Corned Beef and Cabbage

Bannock Bread with
Tomatillo Jam and Butter

Rhubarb Ginger Fool

MENU 6: EASTER DINNER

Stuffed Eggs

Spring Radishes with Sweet Butter

Roast Leg of Lamb

Mint Jelly

Cheddar Biscuits with Butter

French Style Peas

Ambrosia Panna Cotta

MENU 7: THANKSGIVING DINNER

Stuffed Celery

Roast Turkey with Brown Sauce

Turkey Dressing

Cauliflower with Herbed Cheese

Cranberry Sauce

Fennel Citrus Salad

Pumpkin Pie with Whipped Cream

MENU 8: CHRISTMAS DINNER

Pumpkin Soup with
Parmesan Almond Crisps

Standing Beef Rib Roast

Brown Sauce

Faux Duchess Potatoes

Cranberry Jelly Mold

Steamed Broccoli with
Browned Butter Sauce

Christmas Puddings with
Cranberry Syrup and
Custard Sauce

MENU 9: NEW YEAR'S EVE SUPPER

Crème Fraîche and
Caviar Appetizers

Oyster Bisque

Cheese Puffs

Mixed Green Salad with
Red Wine Vinaigrette

Cheese Platter with Fruit

Candied Fennel Tart

Stuffed Celery

Smear some cream cheese on a celery stick and you've got a quick, low-carb snack; make this delightfully retro stuffed celery and you've got an impressive hors d'oeuvre.

4 ounces soft goat cheese, crumbled
4 ounces (half an 8-ounce package) cream cheese, brought to room temperature
1 ounce (2 tablespoons) plain whole-milk yogurt, such as Greek Gods or Fage brand
½ teaspoon Worcestershire sauce
1/8 teaspoon hot sauce
Salt and pepper to taste
2 tablespoons purchased olive tapenade or roughly chopped black olives
2 tablespoons chopped **Roasted Red Peppers**, p. 78, or purchased
1 bunch of celery
Dash of smoked paprika for olive-filled celery sticks
Minced fresh parsley for roasted-pepper filled sticks

Pureé goat cheese, cream cheese, yogurt, Worcestershire, and hot sauce in the bowl of a food processor and puree until smooth or mix by hand. Season with salt and pepper to taste. Divide cheese mixture in half. Stir tapenade or chopped olives into one half and roasted red peppers into other half. Set aside. Filling can be made ahead and softened to room temperature before using.

Peel celery with a vegetable parer to remove *all* the strings. Cut into 3- or 6-inch lengths. With a small spatula, fill each celery stalk with 1 to 2 tablespoons cheese mixture or pipe filling using a pastry tube with the star tip. Use olive filling for half the stalks and red pepper filling for the rest. Sprinkle half the appetizers with paprika and garnish half with snipped fresh parsley. Serve chilled.

Stuffed Peppers, Cherry Tomatoes, and Other Vegetables

Use the same filling for tiny fresh or pickled peppers, or cherry tomatoes, split snow peas, or marinated artichoke bottoms to make a colorful party platter that will look like it was a lot more work than it was.

Eliminate the goat cheese and use 8 ounces of cream cheese for a less expensive version.

MAKES 18 SERVINGS OF 1 SIX-INCH-LONG OR 2 THREE-INCH-LONG PIECES EACH.

Per serving—Net carbohydrate: 1 gram; Protein: 1.9 grams; Fiber: 0.6 grams; Fat: 3.7 grams; Calories: 50

Total weight: 1 pound 4½ ounces or 582 grams

Weight per serving: 1 ounce or 28½ grams

Preparation time: 25 minutes active and total

Stuffed Celery, Peppers, Peas, and Cherry Tomatoes

Bacon-Cheese Buffalo Burgers

Beef from grass-fed cattle is more healthful than that from feed-lot cows fed on soy and corn, but it is sometimes hard to find and usually more expensive. Grass-fed buffalo is quickly becoming a popular replacement for beef. Since buffalo is leaner than beef, I put the bacon in the burgers rather than on them, to keep them moist and flavorful. (Feel free to put it on them too.)

> "My reasoning for this is pretty simple: do all of that and you'll have meatloaf. And if you wanted meatloaf, well then you should just go make that instead."
> — *Bobby Flay on why he never mixes seasoning, herbs, spices, or onion into his burgers.*

1 pound ground buffalo
2½ ounces bacon (2 thick-cut slices), chopped
Salt and pepper to taste
4 slices Cheddar cheese
4 lettuce leaves or low-carb tortillas or buns (p. 325 for bread options)

Mix chopped bacon into buffalo meat. Divide into 4 balls and flatten into patties about ½-inch thick and 4 inches in diameter. Make the burgers thinner in the center so they will stay flat when they cook. Lightly grease a large skillet or grill and heat on medium. Add burgers and cook for about 5 to 6 minutes per side or until browned. (Do not press down on burgers with spatula—that will make them less juicy and cause them to splatter.) Sprinkle with salt and fresh black pepper. When burgers are almost done, cut or tear cheese slices to fit and put on hot burgers. Wrap in a lettuce leaf or simply put them on a plate to be eaten with a knife and fork. Alternately, place burger on warmed low-carb tortilla or bread of choice, see p. 325.

Serve with dill pickles, sliced tomatoes, sliced red onion, mustard, **Ketchup**, p. 294, and lettuce. (Condiments will add: 1 slice tomato: 0.6 net carbs; 3 slices dill pickle: 0.3 net carbs; 1 thin slice red onion: 0.6 net carbs.)

MAKES 4 SERVINGS OF ONE BURGER EACH.

Per serving (excluding bun and condiments) —Net carbohydrate: 0.4 grams; Protein: 29.2 grams; Fiber: 0 grams; Fat: 24.2 grams; Calories: 343

Total weight, excluding buns and condiments: 14⅓ ounces or 406 grams

Weight per serving: 3½ ounces or 101 grams

Preparation time: 10 minutes active; 15 minutes total

The primary food source for the Plains Indians was buffalo until millions were slaughtered and they came very close to extinction in the late 1800s. Buffalo are now being raised on private ranches, and the numbers are recovering. Grass-fed buffalo graze in open fields where they socialize in herds. They are usually hormone-free, antibiotic-free, and pesticide-free. They also have a healthful Omega-3 to Omega-6 fatty acid ratio, similar to wild game, unlike feed-lot animals.

In the 1830s, George Catlin traveled the West and painted hundreds of Native Americans while they were still living their traditional lifestyle. He reported that Osage warriors, who lived mostly on buffalo, averaged between 6'6" and 7' tall.[80]

"French explorers in North America referred to the new species they encountered as 'les boeufs,' meaning oxen or beeves. The English, arriving later, changed the pronunciation to 'la buff.' The name grew distorted as 'buffle,' 'buffler,' buffillo,' and eventually, 'buffalo.'"

— *J. Albert Rorabacher, author of*
The American Buffalo in Transition

80   George Catlin, "Letters and notes on the manners, customs, and conditions of North American Indians," Re-printed by Dover Inc, NY. Ny. 1973.

French Fries
(Fried Green Beans)

TIPS:

TIPS:
Skinny little green beans called *haricots vert* are usually specified for making *haricots frites*, but regular-sized beans are also good. If beans are large, you may choose to blanch them in boiling water before frying, but it really isn't necessary; you may prefer the slightly al dente texture of the larger ones.

TO BLANCH BEANS:
Heat a pot of water to boiling, add the beans, and cook for 2 minutes. Cool under cold water, drain, and blot dry before continuing with recipe.

The French have been frying green beans for a long time (longer than they've been frying potatoes it seems, as what we call french fries were actually invented in Belgium.) These seem comfortingly familiar alongside a steak or a burger.

6 ounces of *haricots vert* or any fresh green beans
3 tablespoons bacon fat, cooking oil, or lard
Coarse salt and freshly ground pepper to taste
Grated Parmesan cheese, optional

Rinse beans and snap off ends. If beans have strings, break the stem ends and pull them down with the strings still attached. (Some stores sell packages of small beans already washed and trimmed.) Break beans in half or leave whole if they will fit into the pan. Blot dry with paper towels.

Heat a medium skillet over medium-high heat and add oil. Add beans, in batches, to hot oil. (Use a splatter screen when adding beans and be careful!) Stir fry for 4 to 5 minutes or until brown and crispy. Dip out with a slotted spoon and drain on paper towels. Repeat with remaining beans. Sprinkle with crunchy salt and Parmesan, if desired, or serve with low-carb **Ketchup,** p. 294, or see Sources.

MAKES 2 SERVINGS OF A LITTLE OVER ½ CUP EACH.

Per serving—Net carbohydrate: 3.3 grams; Protein: 1.3 grams; Fiber: 2.3 grams; Fat: 6.6 grams; 83 Calories:

Total weight: 3 ounces or 85 grams

Weight per serving: 1½ ounces or 43 grams

Preparation time: 5 minutes active, 15 minutes total

Note: Most of the fat will be left in the pan.

FLAX:

Flax seeds are one of the few plant sources for Omega-3 fatty acids, the anti-inflammatory fat found in cold-water, fatty fish. Omega-3 oils are highly unsaturated and therefore very fragile. They quickly become rancid with exposure to air, heat, and light, so flax seed should be freshly ground and used promptly. Ground flax meal can be frozen, but it should be used within a few weeks. The whole seeds are much more stable and will keep up to a year if stored correctly. They contain both soluble and insoluble fiber, which promotes digestive function, however the nutrients are only available when the seeds are ground.

There are concerns about over-consumption of flax. Flax contains estrogen mimics, called lignans, which may act as endocrine disruptors. Also, flax seed, like cashews, some beans, almonds, and a few other foods, contain small amounts of cyanide. The USDA considers 3 tablespoons of ground flax a day to be a safe.

CHIA:

Remember chia pets? The Aztecs used chia seeds for food and spread chia seeds on vessels and animal shapes made of porous pottery to grow sprouts. Chia seeds are similar to flax, in that they also produce a gel, however, chia does not need to be ground in order for its nutrients to be utilized by the body. It contains complete proteins, which are rarely found in the plant kingdom and it is a rich source for Omega-3 oils (two-thirds of chia oil is Omega-3 essential fatty acids) and natural antioxidants that help keep the fragile oils fresh.

Coco-Choco-Chia Bars, p. 208

Coco-Choco-Chia Bars

Chocolate, coconut, walnuts, whey protein, chia, and butter are known to possess remarkably healthful properties. These moist, chewy bars could qualify as super-food candy; it's not an oxymoron.

NOTES:

You may substitute 6 table-spoons of ground flax seed for the chia seed or 3 tablespoons of each. They are interchange-able in the recipe, but they differ in nutrients. Chia has several advantages over flax: it contains no toxic substances, its nutrients are bioavailable from the whole seed, so it doesn't have to be ground, it contains no phytoestrogens (plant estro-gens), and it is more stable and less likely to become rancid. The downside is that it may be more expensive and more dif-ficult to find. See Sources.

___

Coconut oil and coconut butter are the same thing. It is liquid above 76° F and solid below.

___

I've specified two kinds of sweetener for this recipe. The first one is high intensity, such as liquid sucralose, Splenda, or stevia. The second sweetener should have some bulk, such as an oligofructose blend (Sweet-*perfection* or Just Like Sugar for example) or a stevia blend with inulin, oligofructose, or erythritol. Other sweeteners with bulk, such as powdered xylitol or erythritol will also work. See Sources.

1 cup (2 ounces) large-flaked, unsweetened, toasted coconut

½ cup (1 ounce) large-flaked, unsweetened, plain coconut

4 tablespoons water, divided

½ cup (about 2.4 ounces dry weight) sugar-free **Dried Cranberries**, see p. 12

High intensity sugar substitute to equal ¼ cup sugar (or to taste if cran-berries are already sweetened), such as sucralose, or stevia

2 raw egg whites[81] or equivalent amount of powdered, reconstituted egg whites

6 tablespoons (1¼ ounces or 34.5 grams) whole or ground chia seeds

1 cup chopped walnuts

1 cup sugar-free **Chocolate Chips**, p. 43, or purchased chocolate chips

½ cup plain whey protein powder (2 net grams of carbohydrate or less per serving)

¼ cup Sweet*perfection*, Just Like Sugar, powdered xylitol, or powdered erythritol (add 4 teaspoons extra if using erythritol)

A few grains of salt

4 tablespoons (¼ cup) butter

4 tablespoons (¼ cup) coconut oil

Line an 8- by 8-inch square pan with waxed paper, parch-ment, or foil, leaving overhang on two sides to facilitate removal. Grease the paper or foil with butter or coconut oil or use cooking spray.

Sprinkle ½ cup toasted coconut in bottom of prepared pan. Mix ½ cup plain coconut with 2 tablespoons water. Stir and let stand for a few minutes until moist.

___

81   Note: This recipe is not cooked. You may use reconstituted egg-white powder to avoid the slight risk of salmonella. See p. 187 for egg safety tips.

Roughly chop dried cranberries. Place in a small bowl with 2 tablespoons water and high-intensity sweetener. Cover and microwave for one minute. Stir and let stand for a few minutes until fruit is softened and liquid is absorbed.

Mix the moistened coconut and cranberries, the chia seeds, nuts, chocolate pieces, protein powder, second sugar substitute, and salt together in a large bowl. Add egg white or reconstituted egg-white powder and stir until blended. Melt butter and coconut oil together, let cool until slightly warm so it won't melt the chocolate, and stir into mixture in bowl, reserving about 3 tablespoons. Spread coconut, cranberry, chocolate, and walnut mixture over toasted coconut in pan and press firmly in place. Sprinkle remaining toasted coconut on top. Drizzle with reserved butter and oil mixture. Cover with a second sheet of paper or foil and press down firmly so coconut adheres to candy.

Chill for about 30 minutes or until firm; turn out of the pan and cut into 20 squares. Store in the refrigerator but let warm up for a few minutes before serving.

MAKES 20 SERVINGS OF 1 SQUARE.

Per serving—Net carbohydrate: 2.2 grams; Protein: 4.8 grams; Fiber: 7.3 grams; Fat: 16.6 grams; Calories: 192

Total weight: 1 pound 8½ ounces or 700 grams

Weight per serving: 2¼ ounces or 35 grams

Preparation time: 20 minutes active and total

TO TOAST COCONUT:
Spread coconut on a baking sheet and bake in an oven set to 325º F for about 10 minutes or until lightly browned, stirring occasionally. Alternately, stir coconut in a dry skillet over medium heat for a few minutes until just slightly colored.

NOTES:
Oligofructose, inulin, and polydextrose are indigestible fibers that preferentially feed the "good" bacteria in the digestive tract and enhance the immune system. In one study, rats fed oligofructose and inulin lived 30% longer than the controls. Only semi-starvation has produced a comparable effect. Sweet*perfection* is a blend of oligofructose made from chicory root with erythritol and stevia extract. It has a glycemic index of zero and only 5 grams of carbohydrate per cup. Just Like Sugar is another oligofructose blend, and LC Sweet is a blend of inulin and stevia. See Sources.

"Unlike flaxseed, chia seeds can be stored for long periods without becoming rancid and don't require grinding (whole flaxseed is tough to digest). Chia provides fiber (about 2 tablespoons—25 g—give you 7 g of fiber) as well as other important nutrients, including calcium, phosphorus, magnesium, manganese, copper, niacin, and zinc."

– *Dr. Andrew Weil*

HOT DOG PARTY

Meatballs (p. 137) with Barbecue Sauce for dipping (p. 293)

0.38 net carbs per meatball,
1.1 net carbs for a serving of 3

Chicago Style Hot Dogs

Hot dog, including all condiments,
9.4 net carbs; low-carb tortilla,
3 net carbs

Soft Drinks

0 net carbs

Ice Cream Sodas and Floats

2.3 net carbs

Menu total: 15.8 net carbs

MAKES 1 SERVING.

Per serving, with condiments, but no bun—Net carbohydrate: 9.4 grams; Protein: 8.3 grams; Fiber: 2 grams; Fat: 2 grams; Calories: 90

Weight for one 2-ounce hot dog with condiments but no bun: 4¾ ounces or 145 grams

Preparation time: 10 minutes active, 35 minutes total

The Chicago-style hot dog is thought to have originated at Fluky's on Maxwell Street in 1929. It was originally called a "Depression Sandwich."

Chicago Style Hot Dogs

Here are the rules: It must be an all-beef hot dog, steamed, but never boiled, served on a steamed poppy-seed bun. It must have the right toppings, applied in the proper order, to ensure that you taste every ingredient in each bite. And you are to dress the dog, not the bun. And don't ever, ever, EVER, let anyone from Chicago catch you using ketchup!

I'll give you some options for the bun, but it's also OK to just pile it all up on a plate and use a fork, in spite of what the Chicago hot dog police may say. Here are the necessities, in the correct order:

FOR EACH CHICAGO-STYLE HOT DOG:

1 all-beef hot dog, 8-to-a-pound size (2 ounces each) or larger
Choice of bun or substitute, p. 325
A sprinkle of poppy seeds
1 teaspoon yellow mustard
1 teaspoon sugar-free sweet pickle relish
1 tablespoon chopped onion (0.3 ounce)
2 tomato wedges (¼ of a small tomato or about 1 ounce)
1 fresh cucumber spear (about ½ ounce)
1 dill pickle (¼ of a 3 ounce pickle or ¾ ounce)
2 sport peppers (see Sidebar)
A dash of celery salt

Bring a pot of water to a boil. Turn down the heat until it stops bubbling and add the hot dogs. Cook uncovered for 20 minutes. Meanwhile, prepare bun of choice or a low-carb tortilla and sprinkle with poppy seeds. Add hot dog and top with condiments in the order given above. Alternately, put the hot dog on a plate, add the condiments, sprinkle with poppy seeds, and serve with a knife and fork.

"Nobody—I mean *nobody* puts ketchup on a Hot Dog!"

– from the Clint Eastwood movie Sudden Impact

BUT WHAT ABOUT NITRITES?

What contains the most nitrites? 467 hotdogs, 1 serving of arugula, 2 servings of butterhead lettuce, 4 servings of celery or beets, or the spit in your mouth?

Salivary nitrite accounts for 70 to 97 percent of our total exposure to nitrites. Our primary source from food is vegetables. Nitrites occur naturally in plants as a result of the nitrogen cycle where nitrogen is fixed by bacteria. To see if people could be getting too many nitrites from vegetables, the Scientific Panel on Contaminants in the Food Chain of the EFSA (European Safety Authority) compiled the analytical results from 20 member states and Norway on the nitrite levels in produce. The report was published in the June 5, 2008, EFSA Journal.[82] Here are some of the average levels they found: arugula, 4,677 ppm (parts per million); butterhead lettuce, 2,026 ppm; beets, 1,279 ppm; celery, 1,103 ppm; hot dogs or processed meat, 10 ppm. [83]

"A chemical is still the same chemical, regardless of where it comes from...."
—*Sandy Szwarc, B.S.N., R.N., C.C.P.*

A small study of rats done at MIT in the 1970s started the nitrites-cause-cancer scare. The National Academy of Sciences reviewed the scientific data in 1981 and found no link between nitrates or nitrites and human cancers. Since then, more than 50 studies have investigated a possible link between nitrates and cancer and found no association.

Even more surprising, scientific evidence is building that nitrates are actually good for us. They are produced in our bodies in greater amounts than we eat in food and nitrate is important for maintaining healthy immune and cardiovascular systems. It is being studied as a treatment for high blood pressure, heart attacks, sickle cell disease, and circulatory problems.

"The public perception is that nitrite/nitrate are carcinogens, but they are not. ...If nitrite and nitrate were harmful to us, then we would not be advised to eat green leafy vegetables or swallow our own saliva...."[84] [85]
—*Dr. Nathan Bryan, Ph.D., the University of Texas, Houston, whose research has unveiled many beneficial effects of nitrite*

---

82   Scientific Documents Nitrite in vegetables-Scientific Opinion of the Panel on Contaminants in the Food chain, 5 June 2008

83   Sandy Szwarc, B.S.N., R.N., C.C.P., Does banning hotdogs and bacon make sense? Junk Food Science, July 29, 2008.

84   Bryan, N.S.; Calvert, J.W.; Elrod, J.W.; Duranski, M.R.; Gundewar, S.; Ji, S.Y.; Lefer, D.J. (2007) "Dietary Nitrite Supplementation Protects Against Myocardial Ischemia-Reperfusion Injury." Proc Natl Acad Sci USA. Nov. 27;104(48):19144-9.

85   Elrod, J.W.; Calvert ,J.W.; Gundewar, S.; Bryan, N.S.; Lefer, D.J. (2008) "Nitric Oxide Promotes Distant Organ Protection: Evidence for an Endocrine Role of Nitric Oxide." Proc Natl Acad Sci USA. Aug. 12;105(32):11430-35.

Sweet Pickle Relish

SPORT PEPPERS:
Small, green, sport peppers
come packed in vinegar in a
jar. They are about 1 to 1½
inches long and medium-hot
in taste. Each Chicago style hot
dog should have two whole,
not sliced, peppers. *Vienna
Sport Peppers* and *Il Primo
Chicago Hot Dog Sport Peppers*
are two brands that claim to
be authentic. If you can't find
them, they can be ordered
online (see Sources), or you can
substitute any medium-hot
pickled pepper.

Instructions for making authentic Chicago-style hot dogs usually specify ten-to-the-pound
size hot dogs. Eight or fewer is
better. My husband, a baseball fan and the true hot dog
lover in the family, insists on
four-per-pound Knockwurst by
Hebrew National. Just be sure
to check the carb count on the
label when making your choice,
as most brands contain varying
amounts of corn syrup.

Some of info above from:
http://www.hotdogchicagostyle.com

There are several ways to go here. The easiest is to buy sugar-free, sweet pickle relish which you may find at stores or online (see Sources). Next option: buy sugar-free sweet pickles and chop them in a food processor. But while sugar-free relish and pickles are difficult to find, you can always use dill pickles to make into sweet relish.

1 (16-ounce) jar dill pickles, without garlic (Recipe was tested with Vlasic Stackers Kosher Dills.)
¾ cup cider vinegar
Sugar substitute equal to ½ cup sugar

Drain and rinse pickles. Cover with cold water and let stand for 15 minutes. Drain again. Wash pickle jar and lid and rinse with boiling water. Pulse pickles in food processor until evenly chopped or chop by hand into ¼-inch dice and return to pickle jar.

Combine vinegar and sweetener in a small saucepan and bring to a boil. Remove from heat and let cool for five minutes. Pour enough liquid over chopped pickles to cover and replace lid. Refrigerate for at least 48 hours before using.

Recipe adapted from Low Carb Luxury.

NOTE:
I lived in Chicago long enough to appreciate a good Chicago-style hot dog, but I still enjoy a dog with chopped onions, pickle relish, and sauerkraut or a chili dog with cheese. If you are entertaining a crowd, set up a condiment bar and let your guests choose from the toppings. (Just don't invite Clint!)

MAKES 8 OUNCES (DRAINED WEIGHT) OR ABOUT 15 SERVINGS OF 1 TABLESPOON EACH.

Per serving—Net carbohydrate:
0.6 grams; Protein: 0.2 grams; Fiber: 0.3 grams; Fat: 0 grams; Calories: 6

Total drained weight: 8 ounces or 227 grams

Weight per serving: ½ ounce or 14 grams

Preparation time: 10 minutes active, 25 minutes total plus chilling time.

Soft Drinks

It's easy to make your own sugar-free carbonated beverages without caffeine or aspartame. Express your creativity in your choice of flavors.

2 ounces (4 tablespoons) any flavor or combination of flavors of sugar-free syrup, such as DaVinci or Torani

8 ounces (1 cup) carbonated water

Pour over ice and stir.

VARIATION:

Italian Cream Sodas

Fill a glass with ice. Pour 8 ounces (1 cup) of carbonated water over the ice. Add 1 ounce (2 tablespoons) of heavy cream and 2 ounces (4 tablespoons) of any flavor of sugar-free syrup. Stir and enjoy.

Ice Cream Sodas

Put one scoop (½ cup or 65 grams) of **French Vanilla Ice Cream,** p. 308, in a tall glass. Add 2 ounces (4 tablespoons) any flavor or combination of flavors of sugar-free syrup, such as DaVinci's or Torani. Pour 8 ounces of carbonated water over the ice cream. Serve with a straw and a long spoon.

Ice Cream Floats

Put one scoop (½ cup or 65 grams) of **French Vanilla Ice Cream**, p. 308, in a tall glass. Pour 12 ounces of chilled, sugar-free cola or root beer over the ice cream. Serve with a straw and a long spoon.

MAKES 1 SERVING

Per serving—Net carbohydrate: 0 grams; Protein: 0 grams; Fiber: 0 grams; Fat: 0 grams; Calories: 0

Weight per serving 10 ounces or 284 grams, not counting ice

Preparation time: 3 minutes

MAKES 1 SERVING.

Per serving—Net carbohydrate: 0.8 grams; Protein: 0.6 grams; Fiber: 0 grams; Fat: 11.1 grams; Calories: 104

Weight per serving: 11 ounces or 312 grams, not counting ice

Preparation time: 3 minutes

MAKES 1 SERVING.

Per serving—Net carbohydrate: 2.3 grams; Protein: 3.6 grams; Fiber: 2.8 grams; Fat: 20.4 grams; Calories: 202

Total weight and weight per serving: 11¾ ounces or 40 grams

Preparation time: 3 minutes

MAKES 1 SERVING.

Per serving—Net carbohydrate: 2.3 grams; Protein: 3.6 grams; Fiber: 2.8 grams; Fat: 20.4 grams; Calories: 202

Total weight and weight per serving: 14⅝ ounces or 414 grams

Preparation time: 3 minutes

Baked Ham

If you like a sweet glaze, mix some prepared mustard with sugar-free apricot or orange jam and brush it over the ham during the last 20 minutes of baking time.

Sugar-free ham, such as Cure 81, 3 ounces per serving.

Prepare according to package directions; serve hot or at room temperature.

ONE SERVING OF ABOUT 3 OUNCES (84 GRAMS)

Net carbohydrate: 0 grams; Protein: 18.4 grams; Fiber: 0 grams; Fat: 3 grams; Calories: 89

Weight per serving: 3 ounces or 85 grams

Preparation time: see package directions.

Traditional foods for New Year's Day are not the festive, rich feasts of the recent holidays, but simple, rustic, everyday foods. The belief that eating such foods would ensure a plentiful supply of the same for the coming year has its roots in many folk customs. In Arkansas, where I grew up, eating pork and black-eyed peas guaranteed good fortune. My husband, from West Virginia, says his uncle Ben always had a bite of pork and sauerkraut on his fork ready to eat at the stroke of midnight on New Year's Eve.

Pigs symbolize luck, fertility, and abundance in many different cultures. Cabbage and greens signify paper money. Other lucky foods include beans of various kinds, which represent coins, and yellow-colored foods, like cornbread, which mean you will receive gold.

—*JBB*

HAM:

Cure 81 boneless hams from Hormel are sugar-free. Hormel also sells a fancy, spiral-sliced version, available year round, but easier to find around the Thanksgiving, Christmas, and Easter holidays. They are not completely sugar-free like the boneless hams. They come with an attached packet of brown-sugar glaze, which is included in the counts on the nutrition panel, but if you throw away the glaze, the ham will still have ½ gram of sugar and ½ gram of starch for a carbohydrate total of 1 net gram per serving (about 3 ounces). That's not too bad, and the bone-in hams do taste better.

Kurobuta hams from Snake River Farms are almost sugar-free. (The label lists sugar as an ingredient but gives the carb count as zero, which means it has less than 0.5 grams per serving.) Kurobuta uses purebred Berkshire pork, a heritage breed that is known for its marbling and excellent flavor. Kurobuta ham is dark, succulent, and rich, unlike most modern pork, which is pale, bland, and dry because it has been breed to be as lean as possible. Snake River Farms products are available in some areas on the West Coast and online from www. snakeriverfarms.com. See Sources.

Baked Ham

Bavarian Sauerkraut

Real, fermented sauerkraut is a traditional food that has many healthful properties. It can be used for a lot more than topping a hot dog!

1 (28 ounces as purchased) jar or package of fresh sauerkraut, drained
¼ cup water or white wine
1 apple, cored but not peeled, cut in half
1 onion, peeled and cut in half
¼ pound (3 to 4 slices) bacon

Buy fresh sauerkraut in a plastic bag or jar from the refrigerated case at the grocery or from a delicatessen. Put it in a colander and rinse it well under cold running water. Put it in a deep pot. Add water or white wine to the pot and bury the apple, cut side down, and the onion in the sauerkraut. Lay strips of bacon over the sauerkraut. Cover the pan and place over low heat. Cook for about an hour or until the apple and onion are very soft, checking occasionally and adding water if necessary. Remove the apple and onion before serving. (If you are careful not to move them, they can be scooped out with a spoon, even if they have disintegrated.)

MAKES ABOUT 3¾ CUPS OR 7½ SERVINGS OF ½ CUP.

Per serving—Net carbohydrate: 1.5 grams; Protein: 2.3 grams; Fiber: 3.1 grams; Fat: 8.8 grams; Calories: 104

Total weight: 1 pound 6⅓ ounces or 631 grams

Weight per serving: 3 ounces or 84 grams

Preparation time: 10 minutes active, 1 hour and 10 minutes total

(Count includes some of the sugar in the sauerkraut that will have been eaten during fermentation.)

Most sources list sauerkraut as having 1 gram of carbohydrate and 1 gram of fiber, giving it a net count of zero, probably because the numbers are rounded or the portions are small. At any rate, it is very low. Use it as a vegetable or side dish, or layer it with a variety of smoked meats, such as ham, smoked pork chops, or sausages to make the classic French one-pot meal called *Choucroute Garni*. If you use sugar-free meats, the carb count will be the same as for the recipe above.

Sauerkraut

Sauerkraut can also be served plain, for a quick and tasty side dish:

1 jar or package (28 ounces as purchased) of fresh sauerkraut, drained

Put sauerkraut in a colander and rinse it well under cold running water. Heat on stove-top or in microwave and serve as a side dish or serve cold and crisp as a salad or condiment.

MAKES ABOUT 3¾ CUPS OR 7½ SERVINGS OF ½ CUP.

Per serving—Net carbohydrate: 1.5 grams; Protein: 1 gram; Fiber: 3.1 grams; Fat: 0.1 grams; Calories: 20

Total weight: 1 pound 5⅓ ounces or 600 grams

Weight per serving: 2¾ ounces or 80 grams

Preparation time: 3 minutes active, 5 to 10 minutes total

SAUERKRAUT:
Fresh, crisp, sauerkraut can be found in glass jars or plastic pouches in the refrigerated cases at most grocery stores, usually near the fresh pickles. It is much better than canned. Some are labeled, "naturally fermented." (Buy smaller packages if you can find them, so you won't have leftovers that take up space in the refrigerator.)

Baked Ham, p. 214, Bavarian Sauerkraut, p. 216, Home Fries, p. 218, and Cheddar Biscuit, p. 220

Home Fries

RUTABAGA:

Some sources list the carbohydrate count for rutabaga as being higher than that for turnips; some list them as being about the same. I prefer rutabaga as a potato substitute because it is a bit milder and the texture is more like potatoes, but rutabagas and turnips can be used interchangeably in most recipes.

Buy the smallest, freshest rutabagas you can find. Fresh ones will be heavy for their size and they will feel firm to the touch. Avoid ones that have been waxed to give them a longer shelf life; they may feel hard but the older they are, the stronger they will taste.

This can be a lifesaver for a meat and potatoes *man (or woman).*

> 4 slices bacon (3¼ ounce or 93 grams)
> 2½ cups (15½ ounces) **Rutabaga *Faux* Potatoes,** p. 285
> ½ cup (2½ ounces) peeled and chopped onion
> Salt and pepper to taste

Cook the bacon in a skillet until crisp. Chop and reserve. Pour off the fat from the pan. Measure 2 tablespoons of bacon fat and return to pan or use oil. Sauté the cooked rutabaga, stirring occasionally, until browned. Add onion to the skillet with rutabaga and sauté until the onion is soft. Add the reserved bacon and the salt and pepper and cook until heated through.

MAKES 5 SERVINGS OF ½ CUP.

Per serving—Net carbohydrate: 7.8 grams; Protein: 3.7 grams; Fiber: 2 grams; Fat: 2.9 grams; Calories: 77

Total weight: 14 ounces or 398 grams

Weight per serving: 2¾ ounces or 78 grams

Preparation time: 5 minutes active; 20 total

"I appreciate the potato only as protection against famine, except for that, I know of nothing more eminently tasteless."

– *Jean Anthelme Brillat-Savarin,*
The Physiology of Taste, *1825*

Home Fries, p. 218

Cheddar Biscuits

JENNIFER'S HELPFUL HINTS:

If you don't have a pastry brush, an unused, clean, soft paint brush (small or medium size) works very well. If these biscuits are made ahead of time, reheat by placing biscuits directly on oven rack at 350° F and heat 10 minutes or more until very crisp, if desired.

The biscuits may be frozen. Microwave 40 seconds and place directly on oven rack in 350° F (180° C) oven for 10 minutes or until crisp.

I would have said it couldn't be done, but low-carb diva, Jennifer Eloff, has done it—low-carb cheese biscuits that rival those served at Red Lobster seafood restaurants! She says, "I love slicing the freshly baked biscuits in half and filling with grated cheese." My personal fantasy involves one of these luscious, crusty biscuits, piping hot, with a big pat of cold butter slowly sinking into its soft insides. Ummmmmm.

3½ cups (14.36 ounces or 407 grams) of **Biskmix**, p. 288
¼ teaspoon baking powder
2/3 cup (2.5 ounces or 70.9 grams) grated Cheddar cheese
2/3 cup water
3 tablespoon whipping cream

In large bowl, combine Biskmix and baking powder. Stir in Cheddar cheese. Make a well in center and pour in water and whipping cream. Using a wooden spoon, stir until soft dough forms. Beat with wooden spoon 30 seconds or so. Spoon onto greased cookie sheet by ¼ cupfuls. Do not flatten (they will naturally spread out) – just scoop out and drop them. Bake 10 minutes in 450° F (230° C) oven or until turning brown.

MAKES 12 BISCUITS.

Per serving—Net carbohydrate: 2.2 grams; Protein: 10.4 grams; Fiber: 1.9 grams; Fat: 20.6 grams; Calories: 235

Total weight: 1 pound 3¾ ounces or 561 grams.

Weight per serving: 1⅝ ounces or 47 grams

Preparation time: 10 minutes active, 20 minutes total

Garlic Butter

¼ cup (2 ounces or 57 grams) salted butter, melted
½ teaspoon garlic powder

In small bowl, combine melted butter and garlic powder. Brush over tops of baked, hot biscuits and serve immediately.

Recipe from Splendid Low-Carbing for Life, *Vol. 2, by best selling cookbook author, Jennifer Eloff (www.low-carb.us). Used by permission.*

Baked Custards

*This unpretentious, old-fashioned, comfort food is the basis for Crème Brule and **Crème Caramel**, p. 75, served in fine eating establishments around the world.*

2 large eggs
1 egg yolk
Sugar substitute equal to 1/3 cup sugar (see Sidebar).
1 1/3 cups heavy cream
2/3 cup water
1 teaspoon vanilla extract
Dash of ground nutmeg for each custard

Preheat oven to 350° F. You will need four 6-ounce custard cups or ramekins, a roasting pan that has been lined with a folded kitchen towel, and a kettle of boiling water.

In a medium-sized bowl, preferably one with a spout, whisk eggs and egg yolk. Add sweetener, cream, water, and vanilla and whisk until smooth. Pour into custard cups. Sprinkle with nutmeg. Arrange custard cups in pan so they do not touch. Carefully pour boiling water into pan until it reaches half way up sides of custard cups. Bake for 40 to 45 minutes or until custards are set and a knife inserted near the center comes out clean. Use potholders to remove ramekins from water bath to prevent overcooking. Serve warm or chilled.

MAKES 4 SERVINGS OF ½ CUP EACH.

Per serving—Net carbohydrate: 2.7 grams; Protein: 5.5 grams; Fiber: 0 grams; Fat: 33.1 grams; Calories: 328

Total weight: 1 pound 3 ounces or 540 grams

Weight per serving: 4¾ ounces or 136 grams

Preparation time: 10 minutes active, 55 minutes total

NOTE:
The carb count assumes a zero-carb sweetener. If using Splenda, add 1 gram of carbohydrate per serving (2 teaspoons or 1 packet) for the bulking agent. Crushed Splenda tabs will add almost no carbs.

When using Splenda in "plain vanilla" desserts, adding a small amount of another sweetener gives a more natural sweet taste. Replace the amount of Splenda equivalent to 2 teaspoons of sugar with Diabetisweet or Sweet One (both contain acesulfame potassium), stevia, or other high-intensity sweetener.

Steamed Artichokes with Garlic Lemon Butter

1 large fresh artichoke (about 1 to 1¼ pounds as purchased)
A cut lemon or some lemon juice and water
2 cloves garlic from a head of **Roasted Garlic**, p. 115
¼ cup of butter, melted
¼ teaspoon coarse salt
Freshly ground black pepper to taste

Prepare a cut lemon or a bowl of water with lemon juice added. After cutting the artichoke, rub it with lemon or dip in lemon-water mixture to prevent darkening.

Rinse artichoke and trim end of stem, leaving stem intact. Remove and discard small lower leaves. Cut off top one-third of artichoke. Use kitchen shears to trim tips of remaining leaves to remove thorns. Pare away all the green outer fibers from the stem until just the white core is left. Cut artichoke in half (it is easier if you start the cut from the stem end).

Put an inch or two of water in a steamer or large pot with a rack and bring to a simmer. Place artichoke halves, cut side down, on rack and cover pot with a lid. Steam for 25 minutes or until tender and leaves pull out easily. Remove, drain, and let cool.

Remove the small purple leaves above the choke (the furry white fibers in the center above the heart), being careful of the thorns on the tips. Using a paring knife or a spoon, scrape out the choke. A serrated grapefruit spoon works well for this.

Squeeze roasted garlic cloves out of skins and mash into melted butter with a fork. Add salt and pepper. Baste artichoke halves with garlic butter, spooning down between leaves. Sprinkle with coarse salt and serve with remaining garlic butter on side.

To eat, pull off leaves, dip base in butter, and scrape off the fleshy lower part of each leaf between teeth. (Provide a receptacle for discarded leaves, or you will have more on your plate after eating the artichoke than when you started.) Then cut up the heart and stem and dip in garlic butter.

MAKES 2 SERVINGS OF ½ ARTICHOKE EACH.

Per serving—Net carbohydrate: 3 grams; Protein: 2.2 grams; Fiber: 5.2 grams; Fat: 23.2 grams; Calories: 240

Total weight: 20 ounces or 570 grams

Weight per serving: 10½ ounces or 285 grams

Preparation time: 15 minutes active; 40 minutes total

Note: Some of the garlic butter included in the fat and calorie counts will be left over.

A sumptuous, sensual, sugar-free menu shows true love, the kind expressed by Robert Browning when he wrote, "Grow old along with me, the best has yet to be…." For love that lasts for a lifetime, keep the romance, but reduce the carbs.

—JBB

ARTICHOKES:
A cut artichoke will oxidize when exposed to air. Rub cut surfaces with a lemon slice or dip into a bowl of water with lemon juice added as you work to prevent it from turning dark. (The vitamin C in the lemon is an anti-oxidant.) Use stainless steel or other non-reactive knives and cooking utensils for artichokes, or they will blacken.

The stem of the artichoke is an extension of the heart. Pare away the tough outer fibers and it will be tender and delicious.

Artichokes affect the taste buds and change the taste of whatever food or drink follows immediately after eating one. They contain a chemical called *cynarin*, which for many people enhances sweet tastes. For this reason, they are considered incompatable with wine, however a very dry, acidic wine might actually be improved by the pairing.

Duck Breasts with Raspberry Glaze

Duck breast is red meat, like steak, and it tastes best when served medium-rare. Here's what the editor of Gourmet *magazine has to say:* "The USDA recommends cooking duck breasts to an internal temperature of 170º F to insure that any harmful bacteria are killed, but since we prefer the meat medium-rare, we cook it to only 135º F. To our taste, that yields the perfect degree of doneness."– Ruth Reichl, editor, *The Gourmet Cookbook*, 2004. (To follow the guidelines of the USDA, after pan searing, place the duck breasts in a preheated 350º oven for 6 to 10 minutes or until they reach an internal temperature of 170º F.)

2 (8-ounce) boneless duck breast halves
Salt and pepper to taste
Marinade, below
Glaze, below
6 fresh raspberries for garnish

MARINADE:
¾ teaspoon ground coriander
¾ teaspoon ground cumin
½ teaspoon ground cloves
½ teaspoon ground allspice
3 tablespoons minced shallots (¾ ounce)
3 tablespoons high-heat oil or fat

GLAZE:
¼ cup (1⅛ ounces) chopped shallots
2 tablespoons white wine
1 tablespoon chopped fresh rosemary leaves, stripped from stems
½ cup **Raspberry Vinegar**, p. 300
Sugar substitute equal to 2 teaspoons sugar
1 tablespoon butter
Salt and pepper to taste

DUCK:
Boneless, skin-on, duck breasts are available at many supermarkets, usually frozen, and from Maple Leaf Farms (see Sources).

Save the rendered fat from cooking the duck breasts and you can recoup much of their cost—the last time I checked, duck fat was selling for about half the price of the duck breasts. (Don't want the duck fat? Call me; I'll come get it.)

Duck fat contains 50% monounsaturated fat, 33% saturated, and 13% polyunsaturated. It is heat stable and makes a superlative fat for frying.

Peking duck, also called Long Island duck, is the most popular breed in the United States, representing ninety-five percent of the duck sold in restaurants and grocery stores. Peking Duck (with a capital "D"), is a traditional Chinese duck preparation.

Scoring is essential when cooking duck breasts as it helps render the fat and crisp the skin.

With a small, sharp knife, score skin on duck breasts in a ½-inch diamond pattern, cutting through the skin but not into the meat. (Some brands are conveniently pre-scored.) Sprinkle both sides of duck breasts with salt and pepper and set aside while making marinade.

TO MAKE MARINADE:

Mix coriander, cumin, cloves, and allspice together in a dry skillet. Stir over medium heat for about 2 minutes or until spices are lightly toasted and fragrant. Add shallots and oil and cook for an additional minute. Pour over duck breasts, turning to coat both sides. Place in refrigerator, covered, for several hours or overnight, turning occasionally.

Remove duck from marinade, drain, and blot dry. Preheat a heavy skillet on medium/low (325° F). Place duck breasts in skillet, skin-side-down, and cook for about 10 to 12 minutes or until skin is well browned, pouring off the rendered fat as it accumulates. Turn breasts over and cook for 2 or 3 minutes or until browned. Check with an instant-read thermometer for an internal temperature of 135° F. Transfer to cutting board and let rest, uncovered, for a few minutes. Slice and place in a fan pattern on warmed plates. Drizzle with glaze and garnish with 3 raspberries per plate and serve.

Recipe adapted from Chef Liu Jaing's award winning recipe for "Duck Breast with Balsamic Glaze," featured on the Maple Leaf website at http://www.mapleleaffarms.com/1.

FOR GLAZE:

While duck cooks, sauté shallots on medium-high for 3 or 4 minutes until softened. Add white wine and cook until almost completely evaporated. Add rosemary and raspberry vinegar. Simmer until liquid is reduced by half, about 5 to 8 minutes. Press through a sieve, scraping strained pulp from bottom of sieve back into pan. After slicing duck, add any meat juices from cutting board to the glaze and cook for an additional minute. Add butter and swirl in. Season with salt and pepper to taste. Makes 1½ cups glaze (strained). Note: There will be extra glaze; only ¼ cup is used per serving. Remaining glaze would be delicious on ham, lamb, pork, or chicken for another meal.

MAKES 2 SERVINGS.

Per serving—Net carbohydrate: 4.3 grams; Protein: 8 grams; Fiber: 1.7 grams; Fat: 28 grams (most stays in the pan); Calories: 321

Total weight: 14 ounces or 396 grams

Weight per serving: 7 ounces or 198 grams

Preparation time: 20 minutes, active; 35 minutes total plus marinating time

"The way to a Man's Heart if through his stomach."
    —Mrs. Sara Payson Parton (Fannie Flag)

"Anyone who thinks the way to a man's heart is through his stomach flunked geography."
    — Robert Byrne

Jicama, a root vegetable native to Mexico, has a smooth brown skin and crunchy, juicy, white flesh. It is low in carbohydrates and almost tasteless, so it can be flavored to imitate any crisp fruit or vegetable. (Here it is marinated in fruit-flavored vinegar and sweetener. Pear vinegar makes it taste like Asian pears; use cider vinegar and it will taste like apples.)

Jicama does not turn brown on exposure to air; it has a sweet, mild taste and crunchy texture, making it ideal to use on a crudity platter or as a carrier for dips or spreads. It can be used in Chinese dishes in place of water chestnuts.

MAKES 2 SERVINGS OF ABOUT 2½ CUPS EACH

Per serving—Net carbohydrate: 3.2 grams; Protein: 4.8 grams; Fiber: 3.5 grams; Fat: 30.3 grams; Calories: 312

Total weight: 9³⁄₈ ounces or 266 grams

Weight per serving: 4¾ ounces or 133 grams

Preparation time: 10 minutes active, 15 minutes total

Spinach Salad with Goat Cheese, "Pear," and Fennel

Low-carb salads don't have to be boring!

2 ounces (about ½ cup) jicama root (some are very large; use excess for another purpose)
2 tablespoons pear vinegar or apple cider vinegar
Sugar substitute equal to ½ teaspoon sugar
2 ounces (about ½ cup, sliced) fennel bulb
4 cups (about 3 ounces) baby spinach or other mild salad greens, rinsed and well dried
4 tablespoons extra virgin olive oil
2 tablespoons (1 ounce) fresh, soft-style goat cheese or kefir cheese
Coarse salt to taste
Freshly ground black pepper to taste

Peel a 2-ounce piece of jicama, cut into thin slices and then into narrow strips, about ⅛ inch thick by ½ inch wide. Marinate jicama slices in vinegar and sweetener for 5 to 10 minutes. Drain, reserving 1 tablespoon of the vinegar for dressing salads.

Cut off and discard stalks and fronds of fennel. Peel away any bruised or tough outer layers from bulb. Cut bulb vertically into quarters. Cut one quarter (about 2 ounces) into thin slivers, similar to jicama in size. (Reserve remaining fennel for another use.)

Divide salad greens between 2 plates. Scatter jicama and fennel slices over top. Drizzle salads with olive oil and reserved vinegar. Place 6 dots of goat cheese (about ½ teaspoon each for a total of 1 tablespoon per salad) around rim of each plate. Sprinkle salads with coarse salt and a few grinds of pepper. Serve immediately.

STRAWBERRIES:

Large strawberries make the most beautiful presentation, but small ones taste better. They are more flavorful and less likely to have a hard core or a hollow center, and there will be more chocolate in proportion to berry. Look for berries that are red all the way through without white "shoulders." If you have room for a few strawberry plants, you can harvest ripe, long-stemmed berries in season without the premium price tag.

Strawberries are high in vitamins, fiber, and antioxidants but very low in sugar. One medium-sized berry has about one gram of digestible carbohydrate.

CHOCOLATE:

Chocolate is silky, sensuous, and seductive. It contains a natural antidepressant similar to Prozac and more antioxidants than red wine, green tea, or any other fruit or vegetable. It is low in carbohydrates and half of that is fiber, which doesn't count. The good news is that this is one addiction that can be indulged without fear of getting arrested, intoxicated, or fat (provided it's sugar-free, of course).

The cacao tree is indigenous to Central America, where it was cultivated for at least a thousand years before the arrival of Columbus. Its botanical name is "theobroma," which means, "drink of the gods." The Aztecs believed cacao seeds were brought down from Paradise as a gift to man. They made a drink by mixing ground cacao nibs with water, vanilla, and spices but did not sweeten it. Chocolate was used as an aphrodisiac, as food, and as money. Europeans, who were the first to sweeten it, valued it for use in medicinal remedies. Premium, dark chocolate provides maximum health benefits. Inferior brands may substitute soy or cottonseed oil for the cocoa butter in the real thing.

Chocolate Dipped Strawberries

Gourmet chocolate-dipped treats are the perfect gift for that special someone in your life. Easy to make and not just good, but good for you!

> To make a beautiful gift, purchase a presentation box and fluted paper cups from a craft shop. Arrange the berries in the box and tie it all up with a pretty ribbon. Your friends will be amazed when you tell them you made them yourself. They will be even more amazed when you tell them that this extravagant confection could actually qualify as health food!

High-intensity liquid sweetener, such as sucralose or stevia, equal to ½ cup sugar
1 teaspoon no-trans-fat shortening, such as Spectrum
A few grains of salt
4 ounces unsweetened chocolate, either in disk form or chopped
12 to 16 fresh strawberries (½- to 1-ounce each for a total of about 10 ounces), with caps or stems attached

Note: Double the chocolate coating recipe for large berries.

Line a heavy sheet pan with waxed paper or foil and put in the refrigerator to chill. Wash and dry berries and put in the refrigerator. They should be very cold and very dry when you are ready to dip them.

Heat ½ inch of water to boiling in the bottom pan of a double boiler. Turn down the heat so it is hot but not bubbling. (A bowl that fits tightly over a pan can be used as a double boiler.) Be very careful not to get any water into the chocolate or it may separate or seize.

Place sweetener and salt in top pan of the double boiler and set over, but not touching, the water. Add shortening and stir until it is melted. Continue to stir for 1 minute more to let the liquid in the sweetener evaporate. Stir in chocolate and continue to stir until smooth. Stir the chocolate continuously with a flexible spatula as it melts.

Important: Chocolate melts at body temperature; which is why it has that wonderful, melt-in-your-mouth quality, but it separates or scorches if it gets much hotter than that. A small amount of melted chocolate that sits on the bottom of the hot pan for too long can ruin the whole batch. So be patient; don't be tempted to turn up the heat, and stir, stir, stir, thoroughly and constantly.

As soon as chocolate is melted, remove both pans from the heat. Leave the chocolate over the hot water while dipping.

Hold berry by the stem or cap or spear with a fork in the top where a stem would be if it had one. Dip the bottom ½ to ⅔ of each berry into the chocolate. Swirl the berry around then hold it upside down briefly so the chocolate will flow down for even coverage. Set on the cold pan. Repeat with remaining berries.

Place pan with berries in the fridge to chill for at least 15 minutes before serving. Store, loosely covered, for a few days. Do not cover tightly or moisture will condense and drip onto berries. (DO cover other things in the fridge so the berries don't pick up any off flavors.)

NOTES:
About half the chocolate dip will be left over because it will become too shallow for dipping. Pour it out as for **Chocolate Chips** (p. 43) or stir in some nuts or coconut and drop by tablespoonfuls on pan to make **Nut Clusters**.

MAKES 12 TO 16 STRAWBERRIES.

Per serving—Net carbohydrate: 1.7 grams; Protein: 0.7 grams; Fiber: 1.1 grams; Fat: 2.7 grams; Calories: 31

Total weight: 12 ounces or 341 grams

Weight per serving: 1 ounce or 28.4 grams

Preparation time: 25 minutes active and total, excluding time to chill berries

Chocolate Dipped Strawberries

Chocolate Dipped Strawberries

"The language of romance is written in chocolate."

—*Author Unknown*

Café Mocha

8 ounces strong, freshly brewed coffee
8 ounces **Hot Cocoa**, p. 231.
Whipped Cream, p. 312, for garnish
Dash of cinnamon or nutmeg

Combine the coffee and cocoa in an Irish coffee mug (a tall glass with a handle). Top with **Whipped Cream**, if desired, and a sprinkle of cinnamon or nutmeg.

MAKES 2 SERVINGS OF 1 CUP EACH.

Per serving—Net carbohydrate: 1.6 grams; Protein: 2.3 grams; Fiber: 1 gram; Fat: 15 grams; Calories: 142.5

Total weight: 16 ounces or 454 grams

Weight per serving: 8 ounces or 227 grams

Preparation time: 5 minutes

Café Mocha

ST. PATRICK'S DAY

Corned Beef
and Cabbage

6.9 net carbs

Bannock Bread
with Tomatillo Jam
and Butter

Bread: 3.7 net carbs;
jam: 1.2 net carbs

Rhubarb
Ginger Fool

2.2 net carbs

Menu total: 14 net carbs

TIP:
Divide the cabbage evenly,
leaving part of the core on each
wedge so it won't fall apart.

Corned Beef and Cabbage

I don't usually think about corned beef and cabbage until I see the seasonal specials in the stores in mid-March. It makes an easy, tasty, one-pot meal; I don't know why I don't make it more often. Try my walnut trick to keep the cooking odors from permeating the house and to make the rutabagas taste more like potatoes. (Technically, the following recipe is more like a New England Boiled Dinner, *which includes potatoes in addition to beef and cabbage.)*

1 (four-pound) corned beef brisket, spice packet included (weight may include liquid, but the meat should weight about 3 pounds and 10 ounces, raw)

1 (1½-pound) head of green cabbage, cut into 8 wedges

3 or 4 small rutabagas (1 pound as purchased), peeled and cut into roughly 1-inch chunks (about 14.5 ounces or 3 cups after it was peeled and cut up)

2 whole walnuts in the shell

Put the corned beef and the contents of the spice packet into a large pot and cover with cold water. Bring to a boil and then lower heat and simmer for 2½ to 3 hours or until almost tender. Add rutabagas and whole walnuts and simmer for 30 minutes more. Add the cabbage and continue to simmer for an additional 30 minutes or until the meat and vegetables are fork tender. Discard the walnuts. Slice the corned beef across the grain and surround with the vegetables. Serve with prepared mustard.

TO PREPARE IN SLOW COOKER:
Place rutabaga and walnuts in bottom of pot. Put brisket and spices from packet on top. Add 1½ cups water or enough to cover meat. Place lid on slow cooker. Cook on high for the first hour, and then continue to cook on high for 5 to 6 hours or reduce temperature to low and cook for 10 to 12 hours. Add cabbage wedges for last 3 hours.

VARIATION:

Reuben Sandwich

For a tasty Reuben Sandwich, toast one side of a slice of low-carb bread under broiler. Sprinkle with caraway seeds. Toast second slice on both sides. Put several slices of corned beef on the double-toasted bread slice and cover with drained sauerkraut. Lay slices of Swiss cheese over sauerkraut. Broil until cheese is melted. Put second bread slice on top, soft side up (this keeps it from abrading the roof of your mouth). Serve with dill pickles and mustard.

REUBENS CAN ALSO BE MADE WITH
LOW-CARB TORTILLAS:

Warm tortillas in a skillet or in the microwave and sprinkle with caraway seeds. Layer fillings directly in a greased pan and broil until cheese is melted. Use a spatula to place filling on tortilla, fold over, and serve with dill pickle and mustard.

Good Grief—Not Beef!

This custom the Yanks have invented,
Is an error they've never repented,
But bacon's the stuff
That all Irishmen scoff,
With fried cabbage it is supplemented.

– Frances Shilliday

CORNED BEEF:

Corned beef was cured with dry spices in Anglo-Saxon times to preserve it. *Corned* refers to the large grains of coarse salt used in the rub. The Oxford English Dictionary gives the meaning of the word *corn* as a "small, hard particle, a grain, as of sand or salt." Corned beef is now brined or pickled in liquid.

We think of corned beef and cabbage as a traditional Irish dish, but it is actually Irish/American. According to Bridgett Haggerty, of the Irish Cultures and Customs website, cows were used for milk in Ireland and were too valuable to eat. Pork was cheaper, so a side of bacon was cooked with cabbage for Easter. The Irish in New York substituted corned beef for bacon, borrowing from their Jewish neighbors, and it has come to be associated with St. Patrick's Day. She says that Irish pubs now serve corned beef and cabbage on St. Patrick's Day, but it is to please the tourists. Another bit of trivia—did you know that the national color of Ireland is blue?

Bannock Bread

See Sources for artificial honey made with xylitol. Maltitol sweetened honey substitutes are also available.

Bannock bread was a staple food in early Scotland where barley was easier to grow than wheat. Barley has very little gluten, necessary for raised bread, so it was originally a flatbread, cooked on a griddle. Wheat flour was added to the recipe later. I use whey protein, gluten flour, and baking powder to lighten my Bannock.

1 cup (3 ounces or 90 grams) Sustagrain barley flour or use oat flour and add 2.2 net carbs per serving

¼ cup (21 grams) sugar-free, vanilla whey protein powder (with 1 net carb per ¼ cup)

2 tablespoons (17 grams) vital wheat gluten flour

1¼ teaspoon baking powder

¾ teaspoon salt

1 egg

2 tablespoons artificial honey (with xylitol) or yacon syrup or sugar substitute equal to 2 tablespoons sugar

1 tablespoon olive oil, peanut oil, or melted coconut oil or butter

¼ cup cream

2 tablespoons water, more if needed

1 tablespoon Sustagrain barley flakes, rolled oats, or additional barley flour for dusting loaf

In a medium bowl, whisk barley flour, whey protein powder, gluten flour, baking powder, and salt together until blended and lumps are broken up. Set aside. Whisk egg until blended and whisk in sweetener, oil, cream, and water. Add wet ingredients to flour mixture while stirring with a wooden spoon until they form a smooth, stiff dough, adding more water a little at a time if too dry. Add a little more barley flour if necessary, but remember to add the carbs it contains (10 net grams per cup). Knead dough until smooth. Shape into a flat disk about 1 inch thick and 6 inches in diameter. Sprinkle loaf with Sustigrain barley flakes or rolled oats or dust with additional barley flour. Let rest in bowl covered with a damp towel in a warm place for 10 minutes. (Set a rack over a pan of hot water and set bowl with dough on rack.)

Preheat oven to 350° F.

Place loaf on a greased baking sheet and bake for 30 to 35 minutes or until well browned. Slice into wedges and serve warm with butter or follow directions below for **Barley Rusks**.

MAKES 1 LOAF OR 8 SERVINGS.

Per serving—Net carbohydrate: 3.7 grams (excluding 2 grams of sugar alcohol in xylitol honey); Protein: 5 grams; Fiber: 5.7 grams; Fat: 5.9 grams; Calories: 119

Total weight: 12½ ounces or 355 grams

Weight per serving: 1⅝ ounces or 45 grams

Preparation time: 10 minutes active; 55 minutes total

Note: Some of us tolerate grains better than others, but no one *needs* them. Any nutrients they contain can be obtained from better sources, ones that don't have the negative effects associated with cereal grains such as rice, corn, wheat, and wheat's gluten-containing relatives, oats, barley, and rye, which contain anti-nutrients, phytates, lectins, and gluten. Also, be aware that grain consumption can set off carb cravings for some people. If you find it hard to stop at one serving, it is best to avoid all breads and sweets.

"Declaring wheat a malicious food is like declaring that Ronald Reagan was a Communist…but I will make the case that the world's most popular grain is also the world's most destructive ingredient."
—*William Davis, M.D.,* Wheat Belly, *2011, Rodale.*

Bannock Bread, p. 234

VARIATION:

Bread made of barley does not keep well, but the dry rusks can be stored almost indefinitely. Twice-baked Bannock Bread rusks can be used as toast, crackers, and, with a little more sweetener, biscotti. They make an excellent base for bruschetta.

Shape **Bannock Bread** dough into a 4- x 7-inch rectangular loaf and bake as in recipe. Cut baked loaf in half and then cut at right angles into slices. Make slices thin or thick depending on how they will be used. Thin slices will be like Melba toast; thicker ones more like biscotti.

Return slices to oven set at 350º F and bake for 10 minutes. Turn slices over and bake for another 10 minutes. Remove from oven for rusks that are still a little soft in the middle. For dry rusks, turn oven off and leave slices in for 15 to 30 minutes more or until hard and dry.

MAKES 40 THIN RUSKS OR 20 THICKER ONES.

Net Carbohydrates: 0.09 grams for thin ones, 0.19 grams for thicker ones; Protein: 5 grams for thin, 10 grams for thick

Total weight: 10⁷/₈ ounces or 310 grams

Weight per serving for thicker rusk: ½ ounce or 13 grams

Weight per serving for thin rusk: ¼ ounce or 7 grams

Preparation time: 5 minutes active; 25 to 35 minutes total, not including time to make initial loaf

---

Barley rusks, dipped in water, are the traditional accompaniment for afternoon tea, called *Mezes*, in Greece. They are also part of a traditional **Greek Salad**, p. 134. Dip them in water, shake off the excess, break them up, and toss with the salad.

Tomatillo Jam

Our health organizations tell us that fruits and vegetables are the basis of a healthful diet. They always refer to "fruits and vegetables" as if they are one category and equally beneficial, but they can be as different as candy is from kale.

Technically, any part of a plant that contains seeds or is involved in reproduction is a fruit, while leaves, stems, and roots are vegetables. But in common usage, we classify plant foods based on sweetness. If it is sweet, we call it a fruit; if it is not, we call it a vegetable. If we want to cut down on sugar, we must limit or avoid some fruits. However, you'll have no trouble getting your recommended servings of fruit per day if you remember that avocados, zucchini, green beans, and olives are fruits. Pumpkin, cucumbers and tomatoes are fruits. And there is no end to the things you can do with these "vegetable" fruits.

1 pound of tomatillos, about 3½ cups, chopped
Sugar substitute equal to ½ cup sugar, preferably a sweet fiber
2 tablespoons of lemon juice
1 teaspoon of grated lemon zest (the thin, yellow part of the lemon rind)
Pinch of salt
1 (3-inch) cinnamon stick

Remove husks from tomatillos and wash off sticky residue. Chop into small pieces, reserving juice and seeds. Mix the fruit, the reserved juice and seeds, and the sweetener. Let stand for 24 hours to draw out the juices.

Place fruit and juice in a heavy saucepan. Grate zest into the pan and add the lemon juice. Bring mixture to a boil over high heat. Reduce heat to low and cook, uncovered, for about 40 minutes. Remove cinnamon. To thicken, purée about half of the mixture in a food processor or press through a sieve and return to the pan.

Use as jam, like cranberry or apple sauce, as a topping for yogurt or ice cream, or spread it in a low-carb tart crust. See variation below for **Pocket Pies**. Refrigerate or freeze. Jam can also be processed in a water bath; see the *USDA Complete Guide to Home Canning*, here: www.uga.edu.

RECIPE MAKES 1 CUP OF JAM OR 16 SERVINGS OF 1 TABLESPOON EACH.

Per serving—Net carbohydrate: 1.2 grams; Protein: 0.3 grams; Fiber: 0.5 grams; 0.3 Fat: 0.3 grams; Calories: 9

Total weight: 9⅔ ounces or 272 grams

Weight per serving: ½ ounce or 17 grams

Preparation Time: 20 minutes active; 1 hour total plus 24 hours to macerate fruit

Pocket Pies

Joseph's brand pitas are very thin and make a crisp, pastry-like crust. They have only 2 net grams of carbs in each half pita for a total of 6.8 net carbs per pie with filling.

Cut a low-carb pita pocket in half. Melt a tablespoon of butter in a skillet over medium heat. Add one pita half and fry until brown and crisp. Turn over. Carefully open the pita with a fork or spatula and spread ¼ cup of **Tomatillo Jam** inside. Continue to fry until second side is brown. Sprinkle with cinnamon and more granular sweetener and serve hot with a scoop of low-carb **Ice Cream**, p. 308. Wipe out the pan and repeat with other half.

NOTE:
When they are still crunchy and tart, green tomatoes make a perfect substitute for apples in jams, chutneys, sauces, and pies. Tomatillos, familiar to most of us as the main ingredient in salsa verde, are the little green fruits encased in a papery lantern commonly used in Mexican cuisine. While green tomatoes are only available in late summer, and then only if you have access to a local garden, tomatillos are easy to find fresh and canned year round.

Tomatillo Jam

Rhubarb Ginger Fool

A traditional fool *is made of puréed gooseberries and whipped cream. Gooseberries are large, tart, berries that are quite low in carbs. They are very popular in Europe, but difficult to find elsewhere. Rhubarb makes a perfect substitute.*

1 pound rhubarb (3½ cups cut up)
2 cups water
2 tablespoons (2 packets or ½ ounce) plain gelatin
2 tablespoons fresh grated ginger
Sugar substitute equal to 1 cup sugar
A few grains of salt
1 teaspoon sugar-free vanilla extract
3 ounces (1 small package) cream cheese
1 cup (8 ounces) heavy cream
Extra **Whipped Cream,** p. 312, and 6 small, sliced strawberries for garnish, optional

Place a mixing bowl and a whisk or the beaters to an electric mixer in the refrigerator to chill.

Cut away any green leaves and trim ends of rhubarb stalks. Peel to remove strings if desired. Slice into ¼-inch lengths. Put water in a medium saucepan and stir in the gelatin. Let stand for 5 minutes to soften gelatin. Place pan over medium heat and add sweetener, rhubarb, and ginger. Bring to a boil. Reduce heat to low and simmer for 10 minutes or until rhubarb is tender.

Place softened cream cheese in a small bowl and mix with a wooden spoon or spatula until creamy. Dip out ¼ cup of the liquid from the rhubarb mixture and mix into cream cheese until smooth (to prevent lumps). Stir cream cheese mixture into pan with hot rhubarb. Stir in vanilla. Let cool to room temperature.

In a large, chilled bowl, beat heavy cream to stiff peak stage. Fold in cooled rhubarb-gelatin mixture. Fill individual dishes, stemmed glasses, or a large serving bowl. Refrigerate for several hours. Serve with Whipped Cream and garnish with a sliced strawberry, if desired.

TIP:
A packet of gelatin weighs ¼ ounce or 7 grams and measures 1 tablespoonful. Gelatin also comes in sheet form—one packet is equal to 4 sheets of leaf gelatin.

MAKES 5½ CUPS OR ABOUT 11 SERVINGS OF ½ CUP.

Per serving—Net carbohydrate: 2.2 grams; Protein: 2.4 grams; Fiber: 0.7 grams; Fat: 10.6 grams; Calories: 117

Total weight: 36 ounces or 1021 grams

Weight per serving: 3¼ ounces or 93 grams

Preparation time: 15 minutes active, 35 minutes total, not including chilling time

Stuffed Eggs

Always welcome at picnics and barbecues, but also a perfect low-carb snack or appetizer.

6 **Hard Cooked Eggs,** p. 278, shelled and chilled
¾ teaspoon dry mustard
3 tablespoons heavy cream (more or less as needed)
2 teaspoons (¼ ounce) shallot, finely minced
1 tablespoon lemon juice
¼ teaspoon salt
⅛ teaspoon pepper
1 tablespoon fresh, snipped chives or parsley
⅛ to ¼ teaspoon smoked paprika

Slice eggs in half lengthwise. Reserve whites and crush yolks lightly with a fork. Add cream until yolks are moistened. Add shallot, lemon juice, salt, and pepper, and blend. Fill the egg-white shells with the mixture and garnish with fresh chives or parsley and a sprinkle of smoked paprika. Refrigerate until ready to serve.

MAKES 12 HALVES.

Per serving of ½ egg—Net carbohydrate: 0.4 grams; Protein: 3.3 grams; Fiber: 0.1 grams; Fat: 3.9 grams; Calories: 50

Total weight: 13⅜ ounces or 379 grams

Weight per serving: 1¼ ounces or 32 grams

Preparation time: 10 minutes active and total

EGGS TO GO:
Fill eggs and stick two halves together so they don't get smashed in transit in the lunch box or picnic basket.

EASTER DINNER

Stuffed Eggs
2 halves, 0.8 net carbs

Spring Radishes with Sweet Butter
1 net carb for 3

Roast Leg of Lamb
0 net carbs

Mint Jelly (p. 303)
1 tablespoon, 0.1 net carbs

Cheddar Biscuits with Butter (p. 220)
2.2 net carbs for 1 biscuit

French Style Peas
4.6 net carbs

Ambrosia Panna Cotta
6.6 net carbs

Menu total: 15.3 net carbs

Spring Radishes with Sweet Butter

SPRING RADISHES:
French breakfast radishes are the traditional choice for this simple appetizer. They are elongated, small radishes with a mild flavor. Small, round, *Easter egg* radishes, in a colorful array of pink, red, lavender, and white, are even prettier. They should be very fresh with tops still attached. Spring radishes don't keep as long as winter radishes, so use them within a few days of purchase.

Spring Radishes with Sweet Butter

The French have a custom of serving small, mild spring radishes with dishes of sweet butter and sea salt as an hors d'oeuvre. A clutch of pink, red, lavender, and white Easter Egg radishes is as charming as a bouquet of rosebuds, but the more traditional French Breakfast radishes are equally delectable.

1 bunch small spring radishes, Easter egg variety if available (12 to 15 radishes, about 1¼ ounces each, trimmed)
¼ cup unsalted butter, softened to room temperature
½ teaspoon coarse sea salt, or to taste

Rinse radishes in cool water. Remove larger leaves and any ragged ones, but leave a few to serve as handles. Trim root end if tough, but leave on if tender and attractive. (Larger radishes can be split in half.)

Cream salt into butter and place in shallow dishes for dipping radishes. Serve as an appetizer or snack.

Note: The cool, creamy butter cuts the bite of the radishes. If your doctor has advised you to cut down on salt, use salted butter or a salt substitute and omit the sea salt or use less. See p. xlix for more information about salt intake and high blood pressure.

MAKES 5 SERVINGS OF 3 RADISHES EACH.

Per serving—Net carbohydrate: 1 gram; Protein: 0.4 grams; Fiber: 0.8 grams; Fat: 9.5 grams; Calories: 90

Total weight: about 3 ounces or 85 grams, radishes only, not counting green tops

Weight per serving: ¾ ounce or 21 grams, radishes only, not counting green tops

Preparation time: 10 minutes active and total

Note: Some of the butter will be left over.

Roast Leg of Lamb

Food chemistry professor, J. Scott Smith, and his colleagues at Kansas State University discovered that adding certain spices to fried, broiled, or grilled foods could inhibit the formation of heterocyclic amines (HCAs), compounds that may be carcinogenic. Rosemary had the strongest protective effect of the spices tested, reducing the potentially harmful substances by up to 79 percent.[86]

Ask the butcher to remove both the aitch bone and the leg bone for easier carving. My local Costco sells Australian leg of lamb already boned, trimmed, and tied and at a very attractive price.

1 oven-ready, boned leg of lamb, about 5 pounds
2 garlic cloves (¼ ounce total), more to taste
2 or 3 sprigs of fresh rosemary or ½ teaspoon of finely-crushed, dried rosemary
1 small lemon
2 tablespoons olive oil
Salt and pepper to taste

Grease a large roasting pan and rack. One hour before cooking, remove lamb from refrigerator.

Peel and mince the garlic. If using fresh rosemary, strip the leaves from the stems and chop. Remove the thin yellow rind from the lemon with a zester. Crush the garlic into the olive oil and mix in the fresh or dried rosemary and lemon zest.

Cut the lemon in half and rub over the meat, including the inside pocket from which the bones were removed, squeezing to release juice. Sprinkle with salt and pepper and spread the garlic and oil mixture over the meat, inside and out. Reshape roast, tie if desired, and place on rack in roasting pan. Let roast sit for the remainder of the hour.

Preheat oven to 350° F.

Place lamb on lower rack in oven and roast for about 20 minutes per pound for medium-rare, or until an instant-read meat thermometer registers 125° to 130° F. Remove lamb to a platter and tent with foil or cover with a large, inverted bowl. Let rest in a warm place for 10 to 15 minutes before carving.

---

86   Footnote: From a news release from the Food Safety Consortium, May 18, 2010.

TO MAKE PAN GRAVY (AU JUS):

While meat rests, pour juices from roasting pan into a narrow container or a gravy separator and let sit until fat rises to the top. Meanwhile, place pan over burners on stovetop. Scrape any browned bits from the rack into the pan. Add ¼ cup of cold water to pan, turn heat to medium, and bring to a simmer, scraping up any caramelized juices and browned drippings from the pan.

Pour off fat from container or separator or use a bulb baster to recover meat juices and add to roasting pan. Add 1 cup of chicken stock and bring to a boil. Reduce heat and simmer until slightly thickened. After carving roast, add any juices from the platter and the cutting board to the gravy and heat to simmering. Taste and adjust seasonings. Strain into a sauceboat. Drizzle lamb slices with *au jus*.* Serve with **Mint Jelly**, p. 303, if desired.

*Makes about 1 cup of pan gravy depending on amount of pan juices. It will have zero grams of carbohydrate if made with pan juices and **Stock,** p. 279.

A 5-POUND, BONELESS LAMB ROAST MAKES 9 SERVINGS

Per serving—Net carbohydrate: 0 grams; Protein: 44.6 grams; Fiber: 0 grams; Fat: 34.8 grams; Calories: 504

Total weight: 3 pounds 9 ounces or 1.6 kilograms

Weight per serving: 6⅓ ounces or 180 grams

Preparation time: 20 minutes active; 1 hour 50 minutes total including standing time before and after cooking.

French Style Peas

Peas, lettuce, and onions are a classic French combination. (Julia Child insisted that her version should be a separate course, served with chilled white wine, and eaten with a spoon.) My recipe is far from traditional, but it has become a family favorite. The sugar snap peas contribute fresh pea flavor but with added crunch and less sugar.

2 tablespoons butter
2½ cups fresh sugar snap peas (about 8 ounces)
1½ cups thinly sliced, white onion (about 5 ounces)
3 cups thinly sliced iceberg lettuce (6 ounces or about one third of a
    6-inch head)
½ teaspoon of salt
Dash of pepper

Wash the peas. Break off ends and remove any strings. Cut pea pods into ½–inch lengths. Melt butter in a skillet over low heat. Add peas and onions to the pan and raise the heat to medium-high. Sauté for about 3 minutes, stirring frequently. Add lettuce, salt, and pepper and continue to cook and stir for about 2 minutes more or until tender but still crisp. Serve at once.

MAKES 6 SERVINGS OF ½ CUP.

Per serving—Net carbohydrate: 4.6 grams; Protein: 1.4 grams; Fiber: 1.6 grams; Fat: 4 grams; Calories: 65

Total weight: 1 pound 1½ ounces or 497 grams

Weight per serving: 3 ounces or 82 grams

Preparation time: 15 minutes active; 20 minutes total

"Let nothing which can be treated by diet be treated by other means."

— *Maimonides*

Ambrosia Panna Cotta

Enjoy the heavenly taste of Ambrosia, usually verboten *to low carbers, in this delectable orange and coconut dessert.*

FOR PANNA COTTA:

  1 package plain gelatin (¼ ounce or 7 grams)

  3 tablespoons water

  1 cup heavy cream

  Sugar substitute equal to ¾ cup sugar

  A few grains of salt

  1 (14-ounce) can regular, not *lite*, unsweetened coconut milk

  1 teaspoon vanilla extract

  ½ teaspoon coconut extract

Soften the gelatin in the 3 tablespoons of water for 5 minutes. Place cream, sweetener, and salt in a saucepan and bring to a simmer over medium heat. Add the softened gelatin and stir until dissolved. Remove pan from heat and stir in coconut milk and extracts. Pour into six serving dishes or molds and chill until set.

FOR ORANGE AND COCONUT TOPPING:

  1 medium naval orange (4.3 ounces, peeled and segmented)

  2 teaspoons Grand Marnier optional (adds 0.36 net carbs per serving)

  1 cup (2¼ ounces) unsweetened, large flake coconut, toasted

Remove zest (thin orange-colored part of peel) in thin strips from orange. Set aside some for garnish and place remainder in a small bowl. Working over the bowl to collect any juice, peel orange and separate segments, removing the white fibers and core. Cut segments into small pieces. Add Grand Marnier, if using. Stir, and place in refrigerator to chill.

When ready to serve, top each dessert with a sixth of the oranges and a sixth of the toasted coconut. Garnish with orange zest.

TO TOAST COCONUT:

Spread coconut on a baking sheet and bake in an oven set to 325° F for about 10 minutes or until lightly browned, stirring occasionally. Alternately, stir coconut in a dry skillet over medium heat for a few minutes until browned.

Panna Cotta is Italian for "cooked cream." The traditional recipe calls for a cup of cream and a cup of milk. By substituting coconut milk for the milk, we subtract a few grams of carbohydrates and add lots of flavor.

COCONUT MILK:

Brands of coconut milk vary in carbohydrate content. I have found some with 4 carbs per cup and some with up to 8. Check the label and choose one on the lower end of the range.

"Lite" coconut milk has been thinned with water. If you prefer a thinner product, it is more economical to buy the real thing and add your own water.

MAKES 6 SERVINGS OF ½ CUP.

Per serving—Net carbohydrate: 6.6 grams; Protein: 4 grams; Fiber: 3.2 grams; Fat: 34.9 grams; Calories: 369

Total weight: 31 ounces or 878 grams

Weight per serving: 5 ounces or 146 grams

Preparation time: 20 minutes active, 25 minutes total plus chilling time

Roast Turkey

Is it really worth the effort to have a turkey that looks like a Norman Rockwell illustration? Or could you be happy with one that cooks quickly and doesn't need a lot of attention but is dependably juicy, tender, flavorful, and crispy-skinned? It might not win a beauty contest, but it will never be dry or chewy either.

1 (11- to 12-pound) frozen turkey, completely thawed in refrigerator
Butter
2 teaspoons salt (omit salt if turkey is kosher or self-basting, such as a frozen Butterball)
1 teaspoon black pepper
1 medium onion, peeled and cut in half
2 carrots
2 stalks celery with tops
1 apple, cut in half
3 sprigs fresh thyme or 3 teaspoons dried
5 tablespoons butter, melted
1 cup water

Remove thawed turkey from refrigerator and let stand at room temperature for 1 hour. Preheat oven to 400° F. Place oven rack in lower third of oven, removing other racks. Grease a large, oval roasting pan with a lid. Place a V-shaped rack inside the pan and grease the rack also. Puncture a piece of parchment paper at 1- to 2-inch intervals with a meat fork or knife tip to make drainage holes and use it to line the rack. (You could use foil, but I prefer paper in contact with food.)

Remove giblets, neck, and liver from body and/or neck cavities of turkey. Set giblets and neck aside for making stock. (See recipe below for directions.) Refrigerate liver until needed if using for gravy.

Rinse turkey and pat dry inside and out. Remove deposits of fat from body cavities and discard. Using your fingers, starting from the neck opening, loosen the skin all the way down to the thighs, being careful not to tear it. Rub turkey, with butter, inside and out, and under the loosened skin. Mix together 2 teaspoons salt, if using, and 1 teaspoon black pepper; sprinkle inside and out, including the neck cavity and under the skin. *Note: do not use salt on kosher or pre-basted turkeys, as they already contain enough salt.*

Put onion, carrots, celery, half the apple, and thyme in body cavity. Tie drumsticks together loosely, if desired. (This is for appearance only and will make the thighs take longer to cook.) Place remaining half-apple in neck cavity, rounded-side-up. Trussing is optional. (See Sidebar on p. 119. Untrussed birds will cook more evenly.) Fold wings up and place wing tips under turkey.

Brush top and sides of turkey with butter and place breast-side-down on rack in roasting pan. Brush back of turkey with melted butter. Cover pan and place in oven. Roast for 1 hour. Baste with pan juices and add a cup of water to pan. Continue to roast, covered, for about 1 hour longer or until an instant-read thermometer inserted into each thigh (not touching bone) registers 170° F. (Ovens vary, so start checking doneness after 30 minutes.) Turn turkey over so it is breast-side-up, baste with remaining butter, and roast, uncovered, for about 15 minutes more or until skin is nicely browned. (If your oven has a convection feature, this is a good time to use it.)

Lift turkey so juices from cavity drain into pan. Transfer turkey to a platter, tent loosely with foil, and let stand for 30 minutes. The temperature of the thigh meat should continue to rise until it reaches 175° to 180° F. Discard the apple used in the body cavity. Discard vegetables from body cavity or save for making stock (see Sidebar). Leave apple in neck cavity until ready to carve, so turkey will look plump and attractive for presentation, and then discard it. Place turkey on cutting board, carve, and serve.

"A turkey roast is the Squire's boast;
A turkey boiled is a turkey spoiled;
A turkey braised, may the Lord be praised."

— *Anonymous English rhyme*

TIPS:
Allow at least ¾ pound raw weight per person, but 1 pound will ensure plenty of leftovers.

Enameled, oval roasting pans with lids can be purchased inexpensively from hardware stores or supermarkets, especially around the holidays. These are the old-fashioned, speckled ones called "graniteware." The fancy cookware stores sell stainless steel versions if you care to invest in one. To use a regular roasting pan without a lid, cover turkey with a piece of greased parchment paper and then with foil. Uncover for last part of cooking time as in recipe above.

MAKES ABOUT 15 SERVINGS OF 6 OUNCES EACH.

Per serving—Net carbohydrate: 0 grams; Protein: 54.6 grams; Fiber: 0 grams; Fat: 21.2 grams; Calories 424

Total weight: a 12 pound turkey yields about 6.4 pounds of cooked meat

Preparation time: 25 minutes active, 2½ to 3 hours total, not including 1 hour standing time before cooking.

TURKEYS:

Fresh or frozen?

Processed turkeys labeled as *fresh* are kept at temperatures low enough to allow the formation of ice crystals. Slight temperature fluctuations cause the ice crystals to melt and refreeze multiple times, resulting in water loss from damaged cells and yielding tough, dry meat. So unless your turkey came straight from the farm, frozen may be better than *fresh*.

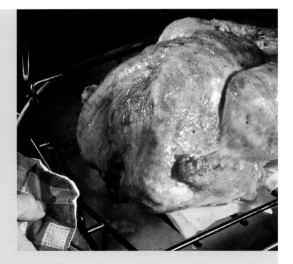

Organic? Free Range?

An "organic" label on a product guarantees that it has no additives, so organic turkeys cannot be injected with a salt and sugar solution. They must be raised on pesticide-free feed, but it can still be corn and soy rather than a natural diet of plants and insects. This affects the taste as well as the nutrition profile. If you buy a "free range" turkey, there is at least a chance that it may have eaten an occasional bug or sprig of grass.

All Natural? Kosher?

Modern turkeys are bred to have more white meat and to grow faster on less feed. The commercially grown Broad-Breasted White is ready for market in three and a half months compared to seven or eight for heritage varieties. This has advantages for the producers, but it makes for lean birds. Turkeys need time to develop the layer of fat that makes them tender and tasty. The turkey growers compensate by using brining solutions containing salt, sugar, oil, and phosphate. The labels say they are "pre-basted." So an *all natural* turkey may not be moist.

Kosher turkeys are washed multiple times with a salt solution, which has the effect of brining, making them juicy and tender without additional soaking. However, you need to allow extra time when preparing a kosher turkey to remove pinfeathers. Religious rules prohibit the use of boiling water for processing the birds. Several machines are used to remove the feathers, each with a different plucking motion, but they leave many pinfeathers behind which must be removed with tweezers or fingers.

To brine or not to brine?

Self-basting turkeys (such as frozen Butterballs) do not need to be brined. They have been injected with a solution of salt, sugar, and chemicals to keep them moist. Brining is also unnecessary for Kosher turkeys or for any turkey roasted upside down in a covered pan.

Hen or Tom?

Tom turkeys are bigger, but hens have proportionally more meat. The bargain turkeys used to lure shoppers at Thanksgiving are usually Toms. I prefer an 11 to 14 pound hen—big enough to feed the family, but small enough to lift and maneuver by myself.

"Those picture-perfect birds gracing the holiday table of that food catalogue are most often an illusion. As a food stylist, I know that often those birds in the photos are raw and simply painted with a toxic combination of shoe polish, vegetable oil, and soy sauce."
– *Virginia Willis,* Tender Turkey Talk, *November 13, 2008, www.aldenteblog.com/ about-al-dente.html*

Brown Sauce

Potato flour and butter give this sauce its rich flavor and deep color.

2 tablespoons of butter

2 chopped shallot segments (about 1 ounce)

2¼ teaspoons potato flour

1 cup turkey or beef stock, homemade or zero-carb canned stock

¼ teaspoon salt

1/8 teaspoon pepper

Melt the butter or bacon fat in a saucepan, add the shallot and cook on low heat until translucent. Stir in the potato flour. Gradually stir in the broth. Bring to a boil, reduce heat to low, and simmer, stirring for 2 minutes. Taste and correct the seasonings. Strain to remove the shallot. Keep hot over very low heat or in the top of a double boiler until ready to serve.

MAKES 1 CUP OR 8 SERVINGS OF 2 TABLESPOONS EACH.

Per serving—Net carbohydrate: 0.8 grams; Protein: 0.3 grams; Fiber: 0.1 grams; Fat: 3.2 grams; Calories: 33

Total weight: 8¼ ounces or 233 grams

Weight per serving: 1 ounce or 29 grams

Preparation time: 10 minutes active and total

Potato flour turns out to be the best of the traditional thickeners for sauces. It is higher in carbohydrate than wheat flour, but you need only 1/3 the amount. It is also higher than cornstarch, but you need only half the amount, so there is still an advantage. Use 1½ teaspoons of potato flour to thicken 1 cup of liquid for a light sauce. Use more for a thicker sauce.

To thicken gravy without adding carbs, stir in xanthan gum, a small amount at a time, to desired consistency.

Turkey Dressing with Mushrooms and Hominy

It's *stuffing* if it's baked in the bird; *dressing* if it's baked in a separate pan. The turkey will be more juicy and tender if it is cooked without the stuffing inside.

You can make regular dressing with low-carb bread, but if old-fashioned cornbread dressing is more to your liking, here's another option. Traditional seasonings plus a little hominy suggest the taste of Southern-style cornbread dressing.

3 tablespoons light olive oil, bacon fat, butter, or a combination
1 pound ground, fresh turkey (preferably not all white meat)
6½ ounces leek (1 large or 2 small as purchased) or onion
    (1½ cups chopped)
6½ ounces fresh celery (1½ cups diced), cut into ¼-inch dice
8 ounces fresh mushrooms (3 cups chopped into ½-inch dice)
½ cup dry white wine
1 cup (⅓ of a 29 ounce can) Mexican style hominy, chopped as in recipe
    for **Hominy *Faux* Rice,** p. 284
2 tablespoons stone-ground cornmeal, optional
½ cup (2½ ounces) chopped walnuts
½ teaspoon poultry seasoning
1 teaspoon dried thyme
1 teaspoon dried sage
1 teaspoon salt or to taste
1 teaspoon pepper or to taste
2 eggs, lightly beaten

Grease an 8-inch square dish. Preheat oven to 350° F. Trim root end of leeks, cut off green tops, and quarter lengthwise. Cut into ½-inch slices. Rinse in a basin of water, let dirt settle to bottom, and dip leek pieces out. Set aside.

Heat oil or fat in a large saucepan on medium-high heat and cook the ground turkey 5 to 7 minutes or until it is no longer pink. Remove from pan and reserve. Sauté the leeks and celery in the same pan, adding a little more oil if necessary, over medium heat until translucent and starting to brown, about 10 minutes. Add mushrooms and continue to cook and stir for another 5 to 10 minutes. Turn the heat to medium-high and add the wine. Cook for a minute or two and then turn heat to low and simmer for 10 minutes or until most of the liquid is cooked off. Stir in reserved ground turkey and let cool for 5 minutes. Mix in chopped hominy, cornmeal (if using), walnuts, thyme, and sage. Add salt and pepper to taste. Beat eggs with a fork and stir into mixture until evenly moistened.

Place dressing in baking dish and bake at 350º F for 30 minutes or until brown on top. Cut into 9 servings.

MAKES 9 SERVINGS OF ABOUT ¾ CUP EACH.

Per serving—Net carbohydrate: 3.7 grams; Protein: 13.2 grams; Fiber: 2.6 grams; Fat: 15.1 grams; Calories: 225

Total weight: 2 pounds 6½ ounces or 1 kilogram

Weight per serving: 4⅓ ounces or 122 grams

Preparation time: 30 minutes active; 1 hour total

Roast Turkey p. 248, Brown Sauce, p. 251, Turkey Dressing with Mushrooms and Hominy, Cauliflower with Herbed Cheese, p. 254, and Cranberry Sauce, p. 255

Cauliflower with Herbed Cheese

The delicious sauce is really just purchased garlic- and herb-flavored cheese spooned over the cauliflower while it is hot.

1 medium head of cauliflower, about 2 pounds, as purchased (1 pound 14 ounces, trimmed)
5.2 ounces (1 package) of Boursin garlic and herb cheese or other soft herbed cheese
½ teaspoon salt
Water for the pot

Take the cheese out of the refrigerator to warm up for 45 minutes.

Remove the green leaves from the cauliflower and cut off the stalk, leaving the head in one piece. Cut a deep "X" in the stem so it will cook evenly, but do not cut into the small stems of the florets.

Bring 2 to 3 quarts of water to a boil in a large pot. Place the cauliflower, stem end down, into the boiling water. Reduce heat to a simmer, and cook for 10 minutes. Turn head over and cook for about 10 minutes more or until tender but not mushy. Remove from water and drain well. Place in a serving dish and spread softened cheese over the top of the hot cauliflower. Cut into 8 wedges with a long knife to serve.

TO PREPARE IN A MICROWAVE:
Place trimmed cauliflower head in a microwave-safe dish. Add 3 tablespoons of water and a little salt. Cover and cook on high for 4 to 5 minutes. Turn head over and cook for an additional 3 to 4 minutes or until tender. Drain, place in serving dish, and top with cheese and slice as in above recipe.

MAKES 8 SERVINGS OF ABOUT ½ CUP.

Per serving—Net carbohydrate: 1.7 grams; Protein: 3.1 grams; Fiber: 1.1 grams; Fat: 1.7 grams; Calories: 37

Total weight: 2 pounds and 2½ ounces or 982 grams

Weight per serving: 4¼ ounces or 122 grams

Preparation time: 10 minutes active, 30 minutes total (10 active, 20 total in microwave)

Cranberry Sauce

Beautiful, tart-sweet cranberry sauce adds zing to any meal. It's not just for holidays!

3 cups fresh or frozen cranberries (one 12-ounce bag)
Sugar substitute equal to 1 cup sugar
1 cup water
A few grains of salt

Wash and pick over cranberries; remove any stems and any berries with soft spots. Mix the sweetener and water in a saucepan and bring to a boil. Add the cranberries. Return to boiling, reduce heat, and simmer for 10 minutes, stirring occasionally, until the cranberries burst. Cool to room temperature and then cover and refrigerate.

MAKES 2 1/8 CUPS TOTAL OR 9 SERVINGS OF 1/4 CUP EACH.

Per serving—Net carbohydrate: 2.6 grams; Protein: 0.1 grams; Fiber: 1.5 grams; Fat: 0 grams; Calories: 15

Total weight: 17 3/8 ounces or 494 grams

Weight per serving: 2 ounces or 55 grams

Preparation time: 5 minutes active; 15 minutes total

TIP:
Packages of fresh cranberries can be put directly in the freezer without blanching, and frozen cranberries can be used in any recipe in place of fresh, although they may take a little longer to cook.

Fennel Citrus Salad

You can make this salad a day ahead.

1 medium head of fennel, about a pound as purchased (bulb should
weigh about 11 ounces after trimming)
1 small shallot segment, about 1 ounce
2 ounces of orange segments, about ¼ of a medium orange, chopped
3 tablespoons of extra virgin olive oil
1 tablespoon of lemon juice
Sugar substitute equal to 2 teaspoons of sugar, or to taste
½ teaspoon finely grated orange zest
½ teaspoon finely grated lemon zest
Salt to taste
Freshly ground black pepper to taste.

**MAKES ABOUT
4 CUPS OF SALAD
OR 8 SERVINGS OF
½ CUP.**

Per serving—Net carbohydrate:
2.3 grams; Protein: 0.5 grams;
Fiber: 1.1 grams; Fat: 5.1 grams;
Calories: 59

Total weight: 16 ounces or
453 grams

Weight per serving: 2 ounces or
57 grams

Preparation time: 15 minutes active
and total

Trim the bottom of the fennel bulb and cut off the stalks
and fronds. Finely chop about ¼ cup of the fronds and
reserve. Trim away any damaged or discolored parts of the
fennel bulb. Cut in half and cut out the core. Slice core
into matchsticks and slice bulb crosswise into very thin
slices or shave on a mandoline.

Peel shallot and cut in half lengthwise and then cut crosswise into thin slices. Put fennel, shallot, and orange pieces
in a large bowl. Whisk together olive oil, lemon juice,
sweetener, orange and lemon zest, salt, and pepper. Pour
over salad and toss. Sprinkle chopped fennel fronds over
top and serve, or refrigerate for up to a day.

Fennel Citrus Salad

Pumpkin Pie

Partially cooking the filling before putting it in the shell is the secret to this rich, creamy pumpkin pie.

9-inch **Almond Pie Crust**, p. 168
2 large eggs
1½ cups half-and-half (or use ¾ cup cream plus ¾ cup Calorie Count-
    down, LC Foods low carb milk, or "**Milk**" recipe, p. 14)
1 teaspoon vanilla extract
15 ounces (1 can) canned pumpkin or about 2 cups pumpkin purée
Sugar substitute equal to ½ cup plus 3 tablespoons sugar
2 tablespoons Brown Sugar Replacement, such as Diabetisweet
¼ teaspoon salt
1 teaspoon ground cinnamon
¾ teaspoon ground ginger
1/8 teaspoon ground cloves

Preheat oven to 400º F. Place a baking sheet on lowest oven rack.

Whisk eggs, half and half, and vanilla together in a medium bowl and set aside. Combine pumpkin purée, sugar sub-stitute, salt, and spices in a large, heavy saucepan. Set over medium heat, stirring occasionally, until it starts to simmer, which will take about 5 minutes. (Mixture will splutter and spit, so use a deep pan or a splatter shield.) Continue to stir and simmer for 10 minutes until thickened.

Remove pan from heat and whisk in egg mixture until smooth. Press out any lumps or strain if necessary. Pour fill-ing into warm pre-baked pie shell. Use pie crust shields or foil to protect edges from over-browning. Set pie on pre-heated baking sheet in 400º F oven. Bake for 10 minutes. Reduce heat to 300º F and continue to bake until edges of filling are set but it is still wobbly in the center, about 20 to 35 minutes longer. An instant-read thermometer inserted near the center should register 175º. Set pie on a rack and let cool for 2 to 3 hours until room temperature. Refrigerate pie when cool. Garnish with **Whipped Cream**, p. 312.

"For pottage and puddings and custard and pies,

Our pumpkins and parsnips are common supplies.

We have pumpkin at morning and pumpkin at noon;

If it were not for pumpkin we should be undoon."

—*Anonymous early American rhyme*

MAKES 8 SERVINGS.

Per serving (for filling and crust):
Net carbohydrate: 6.8 grams;
Protein: 7.3 grams; Fiber 3.8 grams;
Fat 18.3 grams; Calories: 225

Total weight: 1 pound 102/3 ounces or 752 grams

Weight per serving: 31/3 ounces or 94 grams

Preparation time: 25 minutes active; 55 minutes total

Pumpkin Soup

This thick, fragrant soup makes a wonderfully warming lunch on a blustery day or the perfect start to a festive holiday feast.

2 tablespoons butter
½ cup of chopped onion (2½ ounces)
½ cup chopped celery (1¾ ounces)
1½ teaspoons yellow curry powder
½ teaspoon ground cinnamon
½ teaspoon ground ginger
1/8 teaspoon ground cloves
1/8 teaspoon ground nutmeg
¼ teaspoon salt
1/8 teaspoon black pepper
2 cups or 1 (14½ -ounce) can pumpkin purée (not pumpkin pie filling)
Sugar substitute equal to 2 teaspoons of sugar (use more or less, depending on the sweetness of the pumpkin)
2 cups chicken stock, homemade, or one (14½ -ounce) can
1 cup water
2/3 cup heavy cream

Melt butter over low heat in a large saucepan. Add onions and celery and cook for 10 minutes, stirring occasionally, until softened. Add spices and seasonings and continue to cook and stir for 2 minutes more until fragrant. Stir in pumpkin, sweetener, stock, and water. Bring to a boil. Reduce heat to low and simmer, covered, for 15 minutes. Strain soup or use a slotted spoon to dip our onion and celery pieces. Add cream and heat through. Garnish with chopped fresh parsley and toasted pumpkin seeds, if desired.

MAKES 5 SERVINGS OF SLIGHTLY LESS THAN 1 CUP EACH AS A STARTER.

Per serving—Net carbohydrate: 5.5 grams; Protein: 2.1 grams; Fiber: 2.7 grams; Fat: 14.2 grams; Calories: 162

Total weight: 2 pounds 12 ounces or 1.25 kilograms

Weight per serving: 7⅓ ounces or 207 grams

Preparation time: 15 minutes active; 40 minutes total

CHRISTMAS DINNER

Pumpkin Soup with Parmesan Almond Crisps (p. 304)

Soup, 5.5 net carbs;
2 crisps, 0.4 net carbs

Standing Beef Rib Roast With Brown Sauce

0.8 net carbs

Faux Duchess Potatoes (p. 282)

2.2 net carbs

Cranberry Jelly Mold

1.4 net carbs

Steamed Broccoli with Browned Butter Sauce

Broccoli, 1.4 net carbs,
Butter sauce, 0.4 net carbs

Christmas Pudding, Cranberry Syrup, and Custard Sauce

Pudding and syrup: 5.7 net carbs;
Custard Sauce: 0.8 net carbs

Menu total 19.4 net carbs

Standing Beef Rib Roast

TIP AND NOTES:
The best ribs for a standing rib roast come from the small end of the rib cage, toward the tenderloin rather than the shoulder.

———

The end cuts will be less rare than the center; save those to offer to guests who prefer it that way.

———

My favorite meat thermometer has a probe that stays in the meat as it cooks and a cord that connects it to a counter-top monitor. The cord can be closed in the oven door. It will sound an alarm when a preset temperature is reached, eliminating multiple door openings so the oven doesn't cool down.

"Searing seals in the juices, right? Wrong. The reason for searing is flavor."

—Shirley O. Corriher

Sous vide (cooking under vacuum) is a technique used in many restaurants, especially for expensive cuts of beef. For sous vide, the food is sealed in a plastic bag, the air is pumped out, and it is submerged in water held at precisely the target temperature that the finished product should reach. Deli roast beef is also cooked this way so it stays red and rare, but is safe to eat. Long, slow cooking eliminates shrinkage, retains moisture, and produces prime rib that is uniformly rare throughout, rather than well done on the outside and rare in the middle like conventional cooking methods. This recipe is as close as the home cook can come to achieving the same results without an expensive piece of equipment.

> One 3-rib beef roast (about 7 pounds)
> 2 tablespoons high-heat cooking oil or melted fat
> Salt and pepper to taste

Ask the butcher for a roast from the loin end of the rib, dry-aged if the budget allows. Have him sever the ribs from the roast and tie in place. Take the roast out of the refrigerator and let stand for two hours until it is near room temperature. Position oven rack in lower third of oven and remove other racks. Preheat oven to 200º F. (Roasting at 200° F will produce meat that is uniformly medium-rare rather than well-done toward the outside with just a small, rare center.)

Place a large, heavy roasting pan (not non-stick) or large iron skillet on stovetop and heat on medium-high. Untie the strings from the roast and remove the bones. Rub the roast and the bones with oil. Sear the roast (but not the bones) on all sides except the one where the ribs were attached, for a total of about 8 minutes, or until nicely browned and some of the fat is rendered. Remove roast to cutting board and let cool for ten minutes.

Tie ribs back on in original position with four pieces of kitchen twine. Rub roast with salt and freshly-ground black pepper. Place back in pan, fat-side-up, so ribs form a natural rack. Transfer pan to preheated oven and roast for 30 minutes per pound or until an instant-read thermometer inserted into the center of the roast (not touching fat or bone) reaches 125º F for very rare or 130º F for medium rare.

Remove roast from pan and place on cutting board; tent with foil or cover with a large mixing bowl and let rest for 20 to 30 minutes. (Meat that is slow roasted will only rise in temperature by 1 or 2 degrees while standing, so cook it to the desired degree of doneness.)

Remove strings and bones and slice meat into ¾- to 1-inch-thick slices and serve.

MAKES ABOUT 7 SERVINGS.

Per serving—Net carbohydrate: 0 grams; Protein: 61.9 grams; Fiber: 0 grams; Fat: 81.2 grams; Calories: 998

Total weight: 6 pounds 7¾ ounces or 2.9 kilograms

Weight per serving, including bones: 14¾ ounces or 420 grams

Preparation time: 20 minutes active, 3½ to 4 hours total, excluding standing time.

TIPS:

If the roast is done early, turn the heat down very low (150º to 170º F) and leave it in the oven until ready to serve.

Grease the pan before cooking roast beef or turkey so it will release the pan juices and the browned glaze.

"…And he brought back the toys! And the food for the feast! And he… HE HIMSELF…! The Grinch carved the roast beast!"

– *Dr. Suess*, How the Grinch Stole Christmas

Well known low-carb experts, Drs. Michael and Mary Dan Eades, have developed the first *sous vide* machine for home use. It is the *Sous Vide Supreme*, and it can be purchased from their website. (www.protein-power.com) or in retail stores.

_____

If beef is not in the budget or if you just want to simplify things at this busy season, have ham for your holiday dinner. Boneless Cure 81 hams from Hormel are the only widely available hams that are sugar-free. Hormel also sells a fancy, spiral-sliced version. You are more likely to find it around the holidays. It comes with an attached packet of brown-sugar glaze, which is included in the counts on the nutrition panel, but if you throw away the glaze, the ham has only 1 net gram of carbohydrate per serving. If you like a sweet glaze, mix some prepared mustard with sugar-free apricot or orange jam and brush it over the ham during the last 20 minutes of baking time.

Cranberry Jelly Mold

One gorgeous jelly mold or several small ones will add sparkle to your holiday table.

1 (12 ounce) package frozen or fresh cranberries
1 (1 ounce) slice fresh orange with peel (about 1/8 of a medium orange)
½ cup water
Sugar substitute equal to 1 cup sugar
A few grains of salt
1 teaspoon orange extract
2 teaspoons Grand Marnier (optional)
2 packets (4 teaspoons or ½ ounce) plain powdered gelatin
½ cup cold water
1 cup boiling water
1 cup cold water or part ice cubes
½ cup (2 ounce) chopped walnuts
Fresh cranberries, walnut halves, and orange zest for garnish, optional

Rinse and pick over cranberries. Reserve a few for garnish, if desired. Cut orange slice into several pieces. Coarsely chop cranberries and orange slice in the bowl of a food processor. Put in a medium saucepan with ½ cup water. Heat to a simmer and cook, stirring occasionally, for about 5 minutes. Add sweetener, salt, and flavorings and remove from heat.

Meanwhile, soak gelatin in ½ cup cold water for 2 or 3 minutes to soften. Heat 1 cup of water to boiling. Add boiling water to softened gelatin and stir until completely melted. Stir in 1 cup cold water. (For faster setting, fill a 1-cup measure with ice cubes and then add water to make 1 cup.) Combine gelatin mixture with cooked cranberries and stir in walnuts. (If using part ice, stir until ice is melted.)

Rinse a 4-cup mold with water to make removal easier and fill with jelly. Chill for about 4 hours or until set. Unmold onto a wet serving plate so it can be repositioned, if necessary, and decorate with fresh cranberries, walnut halves, and kumquats or curls of orange zest, if desired.

TIPS:

To unmold:
Loosen the edges from the mold with a thin knife. Wet the serving plate so the jelly will slide if it needs to be centered. Place the serving plate over the mold, hold together tightly, and turn upside down. If mold doesn't release, place a towel dipped in hot water over it for a few seconds or until you can shake it loose.

The easy way:
Just pour the jelly into a pretty glass bowl and serve with a spoon. Set the bowl on a plate, garnish with cranberries, nuts, orange zest, and greenery and you will still have a gorgeous centerpiece for your table.

MAKES 4 CUPS OR 16 SERVINGS OF ¼ CUP EACH.

Per serving—Net carbohydrate: 1.4 grams; Protein: 1.4 grams; Fiber: 0.9 grams; Fat: 0.2 grams; Calories: 34

Total weight: 1 pound and 15 ounces or 876 grams

Weight per serving: 2 ounces or 55 grams

Preparation time: 15 minutes active; 20 total, plus 4 hours to set

Steamed Broccoli

Don't over-cook it. That's really all you need to know.

1 bunch of broccoli tops (about 1 pound as purchased)
¼ cup water
Salt to taste

Rinse broccoli and cut a deep "x" in the large stem end. Cut stem crosswise into 1-inch lengths, so that pieces are similar in size. Separate tops into florets, cutting larger ones into halves or quarters so they are about the same size. Put stems in microwave-safe dish and add water. Cover and cook on high for 2 minutes. Add florets to dish and microwave, covered, for an additional 5 to 7 minutes or until tender-crisp, stirring once or twice so everything cooks evenly. It should be bright green and tender but never mushy. Salt lightly or provide salt at the table.

TIP:
To avoid burns when using the microwave to steam foods, use a vented cover or protect your hands when removing the cover.

MAKES 4 CUPS OR 8 SERVINGS OF ½ CUP.

Per serving—Net carbohydrate: 1.4 grams; Protein: 1 gram; Fiber: 0.9 grams; Fat: 0.1 grams; Calories: 12

Total weight: 2 pounds 12 ounces or 1.2 kilograms

Weight per serving: 5½ ounces or 156 grams

Preparation time: 6 minutes active; 13 minutes total

Browned Butter Sauce

This simple sauce makes any dish sublime. Pour it over tender-crisp broccoli, Brussels sprouts, or asparagus, or toss it with Dreamfields *spaghetti.*

4 tablespoons (¼ cup) salted butter
1 tablespoon fresh lemon juice
1 teaspoon chopped fresh sage leaves, optional
Black pepper to taste

Cook butter in small saucepan over medium-low heat until it is golden brown and has a nutty fragrance, about 3 or 4 minutes. Watch it carefully so it doesn't burn. Remove pan from heat and add lemon juice. (It is very hot and it will foam, so be careful.) Stir in sage, if using, and pepper. Allow 1 to 2 tablespoons per serving.

MAKES 5 TABLESPOONS OR 2½ SERVINGS

Per serving—Net carbohydrate: 0.4 grams; Protein: 0.2 grams; Fiber: 0 grams; Fat: 11.7 grams; Calories: 164

Total weight: 2⅛ ounces or 61 grams

Weight per serving: ⅞ ounce or 24 grams

Preparation time: 6 minutes active and total

Christmas Puddings with Cranberry Syrup and Custard Sauce

A spectacular finale for a festive holiday meal.

1 recipe of **Candied Fruit and Syrup**, p. 266
¼ cup (½ ounce) sugar-free **Dried Cranberries**, p. 12, or purchased, sugar-free cranberries
1 cup nuts (4 ounces), roughly chopped
2 tablespoons (½ ounce) dried currants, optional (adds 1.4 net carbs)
¼ cup plus 2 teaspoons sugar-free vanilla whey protein powder, divided
2 eggs, at room temperature
High intensity sugar substitute equal to ½ cup sugar
1 teaspoon black strap molasses or yacon syrup
2 tablespoons butter, melted and cooled
2 tablespoons cream
1 teaspoon vanilla extract
¼ teaspoon almond extract
½ cup (2 ounces or 57 grams) almond flour
¾ teaspoon baking powder
½ teaspoon baking soda
2 tablespoons (½ ounce or 15 grams) white whole-wheat flour
A pinch of cream of tartar (omit if beating egg whites in a copper bowl)

TOPPING:
1 recipe (1½ cups) of **Custard Sauce**, p. 91.

Preheat the oven to 325º F. Butter 10 cups of a 12 cup muffin pan and a piece of foil to cover the top.

Place the drained **Candied Fruit** mixture, **Dried Cranberries,** and currants, if using, in a bowl and sprinkle with ¼ cup of the whey protein powder. Toss to coat, separating pieces by hand. Stir in nuts.

Separate the eggs, putting the whites in one mixing bowl and the yolks in another. Add sugar substitute and remaining 2 teaspoons whey powder to the bowl with the egg yolks. Beat until thick. Beat in the molasses, melted butter, cream, and extracts. In a third bowl, whisk the almond flour, baking powder, baking soda, and whole-wheat flour together and then stir into the batter.

In a clean bowl, with clean beaters, beat the egg whites until foamy; add the cream of tartar (if using), and beat to the stiff-peak stage. Gently fold one-fourth of the egg whites into the batter to lighten, and then fold in the rest of the whites. Pour the batter over the fruit and nut mixture and stir until evenly coated. Spoon the batter into 10 cups of the prepared pan. Cover the pan with buttered foil and bake for 15 minutes until risen. Remove the foil and bake for an additional 10 minutes, or until the puddings are firm in the middle and brown on the edges. Place the pan on a rack to cool for 10 minutes.

Remove the puddings from the pan. Invert onto serving dishes and drizzle with a spoonful of the syrup from the **Candied Fruit**. Serve warm, topped with **Custard Sauce** and garnished with reserved candied cranberries.

> **MAKES 10 PUDDINGS OF ABOUT ½ CUP EACH.**
>
> Per serving—Net carbohydrate for pudding and cranberry syrup: 5.7 grams (6.5 net grams with 2½ tablespoons of **Custard Sauce**); Protein: 9 grams; Fiber: 13 grams; Fat: 15.5 grams; Calories: 211
>
> Total weight: 1 pound ¼ ounce or 466 grams (excluding **Custard Sauce**)
>
> Weight per serving: 1¾ ounces or 47 grams
>
> Preparation time: 1 hour active; 1½ hours total

NOTE:
If you substitute **Splendid Low Carb Bake Mix**, p. 287, for the white whole-wheat flour, you can reduce the carb count per pudding from 5.7 to 4.9 net grams.

Rich, delectable holiday food doesn't have to be off limits. You can enjoy all your seasonal favorites, such as breads, cookies, delicious stand-ins for potatoes and yams, and even desserts. This sumptuous menu shows just how satisfying, festive, and traditional low-carb food can be.

— JBB

Candied Fruit and Syrup for Christmas Puddings

Polydextrose has the texture and mouth feel of table sugar and adds missing bulk in recipes made with high-intensity sweeteners. It also browns and caramelizes like regular sugar, but it behaves like soluble fiber when ingested. It is widely used in commercial products to allow a reduction in the amount of sugar or fat needed and to add beneficial fiber. One ounce has a total of 27 grams of carbohydrate and 25 grams of fiber for a net carb count of 2 grams. See Ingredients and Sources for more information. Recipes was tested with Stay-lite III polydextrose from Honeyville Grain.

NOTE:

Nutrition information for Candied Fruit and Syrup is included with the Christmas Pudding recipe, p. 265.

1 cup (3½ ounces or 100 grams) whole, frozen or fresh cranberries
2 tablespoons (½ ounce) fresh ginger root
2 tablespoons grated orange zest (amount from 1 medium orange)
¾ cup water
½ cup (3½ ounces or 99 grams) polydextrose
High intensity sugar substitute (such as sucralose or stevia) equal to
1 cup sugar

TO MAKE CANDIED FRUIT:

Cut cranberries in half. Peel ginger root and cut into very thin slices and then into small dice. Remove zest (thin, orange-colored part of peel) from orange in thin strips with a zesting tool or remove with a vegetable peeler and cut crosswise into thin strips.

Place halved cranberries, ginger, and orange zest in a shallow pan just large enough to hold them in one layer and add water. Stir in polydextrose and sweetener. Heat to boiling. Reduce heat to simmer and cook on low heat, stirring, occasionally at first, and more often as the syrup thickens, until most of the water is evaporated and the fruit is very sticky and glossy, about 30 to 40 minutes. Lift fruit out with a slotted spoon and place in a strainer set over the pan so any liquid drains back into the pan. Set pan with drained juice and gooey residue, the utensil used for stirring, and strainer aside to make syrup for finished puddings. Reserve a few cranberry pieces for garnish.

TO MAKE SYRUP:

Put ½ cup water into the pan used for making Candied Fruit. Stir with original utensil and swish the strainer in the liquid to dissolve and recover any sticky residue. Cook over low heat until reduced to a thick syrup.

Christmas Pudding, p. 164, with Cranberry Syrup, p. 266, and Custard Sauce, p. 91

> "…It's like kissing the sea on the lips."
> —*Léon-Paul Fargue, French poet, on eating oysters.*

Oyster Bisque

I've been clipping articles from The Seattle Times *by Greg Atkinson, one of my favorite food writers, for years. I found this recipe in my stash and he generously granted me permission to use it.*

"It defies logic that a simple soup with just a handful of ingredients could be as complex as this one is. But the mysterious mineral-toned flavor and the creamy-meaty texture make for a compelling first course. On some winter evenings, this soup is supper in itself." – Greg Atkinson

3 dozen small, live oysters
2 cups water
4 tablespoons butter
4 shallots (3½ ounces as purchased), peeled and sliced (2¼ ounces)
½ teaspoon ground pepper
About 1/8 teaspoon freshly grated nutmeg, or to taste
½ cup sherry or Madeira
2½ cups heavy cream
½ cup heavy cream for garnish
¼ cup freshly chopped parsley leaves

Scrub the oysters and bring 2 cups of water to a full rolling boil in a 1-gallon Dutch oven or enameled kettle over high heat. Put the oysters in the kettle, cover the pan, reduce the heat to medium and let them steam until they open, about 8 minutes. Lift the oysters out of the kettle and save the water.

Remove the steamed oysters from their shells and put them in a blender. Strain the liquid in which they were steamed into the blender and blend the oysters and their liquid to make a fairly smooth puree.

Put the butter in a heavy soup pot or Dutch oven over medium-high heat and add the shallots. Sauté until the shallots are soft and transparent (about 3 to 4 minutes). Add the pepper, nutmeg, and sherry and cook until the sherry has evaporated and the shallots have begun to sizzle in the pan once again (about 4 minutes more). Add 2½ cups of the cream and bring this mixture to a full rolling boil; stir to prevent the cream from boiling over. Stir the oyster puree into the boiling cream mixture and reduce the heat to a simmer. The soup may be served at once, or chilled and reheated just before serving.

Whip the remaining ½ cup of cream. Garnish hot soup with dollops of whipped cream and chopped parsley and serve.

Recipe by Greg Atkinson, used by permission.

MAKES 8 SERVINGS OF ABOUT ²/₃ CUPS.

Per serving—Net carbohydrate: 7.3 grams; Protein: 8.2 grams; Fiber: 0.3 grams; Fat: 41.2 grams; Calories: 437

Total weight: 2 pounds 9¾ ounces or 1.2 kilograms

Weight per serving: 5¼ ounces or 148 grams

Preparation time: 25 minutes active; 30 minutes total

NOTE:
If live oysters are not readily available, you may substitute raw oysters from a jar. A 10-ounce jar of extra-small, raw oysters should contain about a dozen. They come packed in their own juice and are not treated with chemicals or preservatives.

"The whipped-cream garnish looks best if a hot, wet spoon is used to scoop the cream into a neat oval to plant on top of each bowl."
— *Greg Atkinson, cookbook author, Seattle Culinary Academy teacher, and* Seattle Times *food writer.*

With a feast like this, your actions will match your words when you raise a glass and toast, "To your health!"

— JBB

Cheese Platter

RESVERATROL:
Resveratrol is an anti-fungal compound produced by grapes grown in cool, wet conditions. A study published in the August 2009 *FASEB Journal* suggests how resveratrol may work to treat and prevent inflammatory diseases. Researchers found that resveratrol prevented the body from creating sphingosine kinase and phospholipase D, two molecules known to trigger inflammation.[87]

"Beulah, peel me a grape."

— *Mae West,*
I'm No Angel,
1933

Choose several varieties of cheese with contrasting tastes and textures, from soft to firm and from mild to sharp. Arrange on a large platter and garnish with any of the following: **Dried Cranberries,** p. 12, **Stuffed Grapes**, below, fresh kumquats, nuts, olives, and cornichons. Serve with a selection of the following: **Barley Rusks,** p. 237, thin slices of toasted **Whole Grain Bread,** p. 290, **Almond Crisps**, p. 304, and/or **Easy Biskmix Crackers** p. 289.

Stuffed Grapes

In most fruits, the part that is good for you is the dark skin, not the pale, sweet pulp. Big, juicy, black grapes, bursting with healthful nutrients are, unfortunately, also bursting with sugar. Here's a delicious way to get the benefits and reduce the sugar hit.

12 (3 ounces or 86 grams) black grapes
1½ ounces soft cheese, such as goat cheese or Boursin
24 pecan halves, optional

Slice grapes in half. Using a small melon ball scoop or a grapefruit spoon, scoop out the center of each grape half, leaving a thin wall of pulp next to the skin. Dip up about ½ teaspoonful of goat or herb cheese and fill grapes, mounding slightly. Top with a pecan half, if desired, or put together in pairs. Serve as hors d'oeuvres or arrange around the rim of a **Cheese Platter**.

MAKES 24 HALVES OR 6 SERVINGS OF 4 HALF-GRAPES EACH.

Per serving of 4 grape halves—Net carbohydrate: 1.8 grams; Protein: 1.4 grams; Fiber: 0.1 grams; Fat: 1.5 grams; Calories: 26

Total weight: 3²/₃ ounces or 104 grams

Weight per serving: ²/₃ ounce or 17 grams

Preparation time: 10 minutes active and total

Note: Three ounces of grapes with centers scooped out weighed 2 ounces, so ¹/₃ less than their original weight

---

87   Priya D. A. Issuree, Peter N. Pushparaj, Shazib Pervaiz, and Alirio J. Melendez, "Resveratrol attenuates C5a-induced inflammatory responses *in vitro* and *in vivo* by inhibiting phospholipase D and sphingosine kinase activities," *FASEB J.* 2009 23: 2412-2424; published online as doi:10.1096/fj.09-130542..

Cheese Platter

"...Low carb means never having to say you're hungry."

—*Joan Hedman, joan'sdiet.blogspot.com*

Candied Fennel Tart

TIPS:

See p. 147 for instructions for using star fruit instead of fennel.

The **Mascarpone Cream**, topped with **Candied Fennel** or other fruit, can solo as a quick dessert on its own.

I smacked my forehead and said, "Why didn't I think of that?" when Gourmet *magazine featured an upside-down cake topped with fennel.*[88] *Fennel is a vegetable, similar to celery, that imparts a delicate anise flavor and aroma to desserts and candies. It's graceful, tulip shape makes it a perfect alternative for fruit for this tart.*

Baked 9-inch **Almond Pie Crust**, p. 168
Mascarpone Cream, p. 313
Candied Fennel in Syrup, opposite

Spoon **Mascarpone Cream** over pastry. Arrange the candied fennel slices on top of the mascarpone cream, placing them around the outside of the tart with the base of the *tulip* facing out. (Trim to fit by removing outer "petals" if necessary.) Cut smaller pieces to fit and place decoratively in the center. Drizzle some of the reserved anise-flavored syrup over the top of the fennel. Cut into wedges and serve. (Assemble close to serving time so crust will not soften.)

MAKES 8 SERVINGS.

Per serving for mascarpone cream filling and fennel topping only--Net carbohydrate: 3.5 grams; Protein: 2 grams; Fiber: 6.1 grams; Fat: 18.6 grams; Calories: 181

Per serving for filling, fennel, and crust—Net carbohydrate: 5.5 grams; Protein: 5.8 grams; Fiber: 8.2 grams; Fat: 30.3 grams; Calories: 310

Total weight for cream and fennel with syrup: 17 1/8 ounces or 485 grams

Weight per serving for filling and fennel topping only: 2.85 ounces or 80 grams

Total weight for tart: 23 ounces or 650 grams

Weight per serving for tart: 3 ounces or 81 grams

Preparation time: 30 minutes active; 50 minutes total

---

88 *Gourmet Magazine*, April, 2009.

Candied Fennel in Syrup

*Candied Fennel in syrup is also wonderful spooned over soft cheese with **Almond Crisps,** p. 304.*

1 fennel bulb, about 1 pound as purchased with tops (bulb alone weighs about 8½ ounces) *Note: I prefer to buy two and use only inside slices.*
½ cup water
¼ cup polydextrose
High intensity sugar substitute equal to ½ cup sugar
½ teaspoon fennel seed or 2 whole stars of anise
1 stick cinnamon
A few grains of salt (optional)

Rinse fennel, cut off stalks, and slice bulb horizontally into ¼-inch slices. Remove any green, fern-like leaves from center of slices. Rinse again if any dirt has been trapped between layers. Drain and place in a large skillet with water, sweetener, and spices. Bring to a boil, reduce heat to low, and cover pan. Simmer for 10 minutes. Turn slices over carefully so they don't fall apart and simmer for another 10 minutes, stirring and basting occasionally. When fennel is tender, uncover pan, turn heat to medium-high, and cook for about 10 minutes, turning once, until water is evaporated and fennel is starting to brown and caramelize. Dip fennel slices out with a slotted spatula when ready to use. Add a little water to thin the syrup, if necessary, and drizzle over fennel.

Serve warm or cold as a condiment or dessert, over ice cream or yogurt, or use to make the **Candied Fennel Tart,** p. 272.

VARIATION:
Add a slice of fresh ginger and/or 2 teaspoons of grated lemon zest to the fennel as it cooks.

MAKES 8 SERVINGS AS TART TOPPING; 6 SERVINGS OF 1½ SLICES AS FRUIT TOPPING.

Per each of 8 servings—Net carbohydrate: 1.7 grams; Protein: 0.4 grams; Fiber: 6.1 grams; Fat: 1.3 grams; Calories: 16

Total weight of fennel with some of the syrup: 3¾ ounces or 3.7 ounces or 106 grams

Weight per serving: 3 ounces or 80 grams

Preparation time: 10 minutes active, 40 minutes total

Candied Fennel Tart

PART 4

Basic Recipes

Carnitas
(Basic Recipe used for Tacos and Carnitas Soup)

4-POUND PICNIC ROAST MAKES 6 CUPS SHREDDED PORK OR 6 SERVINGS OF 1 CUP.

5-pound roast makes 7.5 cups or 7½ servings

Per serving—Net carbohydrate: 0 grams; Protein: 50.5 grams; Fiber: 0 grams; Fat: 61 grams; Calories: 765

Weight for 4 pound, cooked roast, meat only: 1 pound 14½ ounces or 866 grams

Weight for 5 pound cooked roast, meat only: 2 pounds 6⅛ ounces or 1,082 kilograms

Weight per serving: 5 ounces or 142 grams

Preparation time: 15 minutes active; 3½ hours total

4- to 5-pound bone-in pork roast, with a layer of fat
Water to cover meat
2 teaspoons of salt
½ teaspoon dried oregano
½ teaspoon dried cumin
2 cups roughly chopped onion (2 onions or 11 ounces)
Additional salt to taste
Black pepper to taste

Put the roast in a deep pot and cover with water. Add other ingredients. Cover pot and bring to a boil. Reduce heat and simmer on low for 2½ hours.

Preheat oven to 350º F. Grease a roasting pan.

Remove meat from the cooking liquid and place in roasting pan. Bake for 45 minutes to an hour or until very brown and tender. Take the meat off the bone, roughly chop it, and then tear it into shreds. Serve as pulled pork or use as filling for **Tacos** (p. 74). Skim and reserve the broth to use with the leftover meat to make **Carnitas Soup** (p. 60).

Poached Chicken

Moist, tender chicken to use hot or cold for main dishes, salads, enchiladas, tacos, and soups.

1 pound boneless, skinless chicken breast halves
1 teaspoon salt
3 cups chicken stock or water or just enough to cover chicken

Cut each breast half crosswise through thickest part into two pieces. Sprinkle both sides of the chicken breasts with some of the salt. Let stand at room temperature for 15 minutes.

Heat water and remaining salt to a boil in a medium saucepan. Add chicken and reduce heat to simmer. Cook, uncovered, for 6 minutes. Remove pan from heat. Cover and let stand for 20 minutes or until chicken is just cooked, but still very moist and tender. Cut into the thickest part of one of the pieces to check. If it is still pink, leave it in the hot liquid for another 5 minutes and recheck.

Store in the refrigerator, covered with the poaching liquid, until needed.

MAKES 2¾ CUPS OF CUBED CHICKEN OR 4 SERVINGS OF ABOUT ²/₃ CUP.

Per serving—Net carbohydrate: 0 grams; Protein: 33 grams; Fiber: 0 grams; Fat: 3.4 grams; Calories: 171

Total weight: 14¾ ounces or 419 grams

Weight per ²/₃ cup: 3¾ ounces or 105 grams

Preparation time: 5 minutes active; 45 minutes total

Hard Cooked Eggs

Cooking eggs upright in an egg rack will help keep the yolks centered, a useful thing, both for esthetics and for having a uniform container of egg white to hold a filling. Another way to center the yolks: put a rubber band around the carton of raw eggs and store it on its side in the refrigerator.

Put eggs in warm water to bring them up to room temperature. Place them in a heavy pan and cover with water to a depth of 1½ inches over the top of the eggs. Place a lid on the pan so that it is partially covered and bring the water to a full boil. Immediately turn the heat to low and cover the pan. Continue to cook for 30 seconds, then remove the pan from the heat and let stand, covered, for 15 minutes. Drain eggs and plunge into cold water until cool.

Roll eggs on the counter until the shells are cracked all over. Peel the eggs, starting at the large end where the air pocket allows you to get under the membrane without damaging the whites. Store the eggs in the refrigerator for a quick breakfast or snack or to use for **Stuffed Eggs** (p. 241) or tuna or egg salad.

TIPS:

Eggs cooked in the shell are less likely to crack if you prick the large end before cooking. You may find a special tool for this, or you can use a thumbtack (the kind with a plastic head so there's something to hold onto, not the flat metal ones).

For perfectly cooked eggs, use an electric egg cooker. Most accommodate 6 to 7 eggs and can be set for soft or hard cooked. Some also include an egg poacher. The eggs turn out beautifully with shells that slip right off.

I like to slightly under-cook my eggs so the yolks are creamy rather than dry. If you have an electric egg cooker, set it at the lower end of the hard-cooked range.

EGGS:

Brown or white? They all have the same nutrition values, but brown eggs have thicker shells, which makes them slightly harder to crack. Also, brown eggs are more likely to have blood spots, as the dark shells make defects more difficult to detect when the eggs are sorted (the spots are harmless, but you can remove them with a spoon if you prefer).

Chickens lay eggs the same color as their ears. (Yes, they have ears.) Push back the feathers on the side of a hen's head and you can predict the color of her eggs: brown, white, green, or blue.

SERVING SIZE: 1 LARGE EGG

Per serving—Net carbohydrate: 0.6 grams; Protein: 6.3 grams; Fiber: 0 grams; Fat: 5.3 grams; Calories: 78

Weight of 1 shelled egg: 1¾ ounces or 51 grams

Preparation time: 3 minutes active; 18½ minutes total

Stock

Hands down, my favorite way to make stock is in a slow-cooker (see Sidebar). I usually have a stash in the freezer from a previous chicken or turkey to use for gravy. If I don't have any on hand, here is my second favorite way.

Giblets (except liver) and neck from turkey or about a pound of chicken wings or backs
½ a medium onion, cut into chunks
1 tablespoon butter
3 cups water
1 carrot, cut into pieces
1 stalk celery, cut into pieces
2 sprigs fresh thyme or 1 teaspoon dried
2 sprigs fresh sage or 1 teaspoon dried
Salt and pepper to taste
1 tablespoon vinegar or lemon juice

Brown giblets, neck, onion, carrot, and celery in butter in a large, heavy saucepan on medium-high heat, turning and stirring occasionally, for about 15 minutes or until well browned. Add remaining ingredients, bring to a boil, reduce heat, and simmer for about 1½ hours. Remove giblets and reserve. Strain stock into a narrow, heatproof container and discard solids. Let sit until fat rises to top and skim off. If stock is not going to be used right away, cool it quickly by setting stock pot in a sink of cold water, then refrigerate. A layer of fat will harden on top of the chilled stock that can be lifted off with a slotted spoon. Use stock for making gravy and dressing to serve with chicken or turkey or divide into containers and freeze for making soups and sauces.

MAKES ABOUT 3 CUPS.

Per cup (nutrition data from Shelton's Chicken Broth, Regular)—Net carbohydrate: 0 grams; Protein: 2 grams; Fiber: 0 grams; Fat: 2.5 grams; Calories: 35

Preparation time: 25 minutes active; 2 hours total.

VARIATION:

Brown beef marrow bones rather than giblets and poultry parts to make **Beef Stock**.

STOCK THAT MAKES ITSELF:

After a long day in the kitchen preparing a beautiful holiday meal, the last thing I want to deal with is leftovers. The kitchen is a mess, the sink is full of dirty dishes, the family has gone off to watch the game, and yet the turkey must be dealt with before it spoils. Here's the solution: put away the sliced meat and toss the carcass and the vegetables from the body cavities into the slow cooker. Break it up a bit if necessary so the lid will fit. Cover the whole thing with water. Add a tablespoon of vinegar or lemon juice to the pot to extract calcium from the bones for an added nutritional bonus. Put on the lid and set the cooker on low.

Have dessert, visit, relax, and wake up the next morning to the delicious aroma of dark, rich, flavorful turkey stock. Place the slow-cooker insert in a sink full of cold water to cool it quickly then strain it into containers and store in the freezer.

Purchased broth and stock usually contain water, MSG, sugar, salt, and very little else. It can't compare to what you make yourself. "Real" stock, unlike the kind from a can or a cube, will gel when chilled because of the high protein content.

Cauliflower *Faux* Potatoes
(Basic Recipe used for *Faux* Mashed Potatoes, *Faux* Duchess Potatoes, and Cottage Pie)

TIPS:

To make recipe in a microwave:
Prepare cauliflower as in recipe above. Place in microwave-safe dish, add 3 tablespoons of water and a little salt. Cover and cook on high for about 6 minutes. Stir and microwave for 4 to 6 minutes more or until fork tender. Drain, let cool for a few minutes, and continue as in following recipes.

To make without a food processor:
Use a food mill or a potato masher or ricer to purée cauliflower and mix by hand or with an electric mixer.

MAKES 4 CUPS OR 8 SERVINGS OF ½ CUP.

Per serving—Net carbohydrate: 2.2 grams; Protein: 3.2 grams; Fiber: 1.1 grams; Fat: 6.4 grams; Calories: 80

Total weight: 1 pound 14⅓ ounces or 861 grams

Weight per serving: 3¾ ounces or 108 grams

Preparation time: 10 minutes active; 40 minutes total

See specific recipes for complete information.

1 head cauliflower (about 1 pound 15 ounces as purchased, or
   1 pound 8 ounces, trimmed)
4 garlic cloves, peeled (½ ounce)
3 ounces cream cheese (one small package), softened
1 tablespoon butter, softened
¾ teaspoon salt
¼ teaspoon black pepper
2 large eggs

Wash and trim cauliflower. Quarter the head and cut vertically into ½-inch slices. Place cauliflower and garlic on steaming rack in large saucepan. Add water to pan (not touching rack) and bring to a boil. Reduce heat and steam until fork tender, about 25 to 35 minutes.

Let cool for a few minutes. Place in work bowl of food processor and process for 1 minute. Scrape down bowl and process for about 1 minute more, or until smooth. Add cream cheese, butter, salt, and pepper and process until blended. Let mixture cool for a few minutes (so it won't cook the eggs) and add the eggs. Process until blended.

Continue with recipe for **Faux** Mashed Potatoes (p. 281), **Faux** Duchess Potatoes (p. 282), or **Cottage Pie** (p. 88). (Recipe above requires additional cooking as in one of the following recipes.)

"Training is everything. The peach was once a bitter almond; cauliflower is nothing but cabbage with a college education."

— *Mark Twain*, Pudd'nhead Wilson

Cauliflower *Faux* Mashed Potatoes

Follow recipe for **Cauliflower *Faux* Potatoes**. Return cauliflower mixture to pan after blending in the eggs and cook and stir over low heat for 6 to 10 minutes until thickened and mixture has the consistency of mashed potatoes. Taste and correct seasoning if needed. Serve hot with butter or gravy.

"….As food for cattle, sheep or hogs, this is the worst of all the green and root crops; but of this I have said enough before; and therefore, I now dismiss the Potato with the hope, that I shall never again have to write the word, or see the thing."

— *William Cobbett (1763-1835),*
British writer and reformer

Yes, cauliflower really can taste as good as potatoes!

MAKES 4 CUPS OR 8 SERVINGS OF ½ CUP.

Per serving—Net carbohydrate: 2.2 grams; Protein: 3.2 grams; Fiber: 1.1 grams; Fat: 6.4 grams; Calories: 80

Total weight: 1 pound 14⅓ ounces or 861 grams

Weight per serving: 3¾ ounces or 108 grams

Preparation time: 10 minutes active (plus time to prepare **Cauliflower *Faux* Potatoes**, p. 280.

Cauliflower Faux Mashed Potatoes

Faux Duchess Potatoes

A simple dish that makes an elegant presentation.

1 recipe *Faux* **Mashed Potatoes**, p. 281
A pinch of nutmeg
½ teaspoon of baking powder
8 teaspoons of butter, melted, or use cooking spray

Preheat oven to 400º F. Grease a baking sheet.

Add nutmeg and baking powder to *Faux* Mashed Potato recipe. Thicken the mixture as in recipe and fill a pastry bag fitted with a ½-inch star tip. Pipe 8 mounds onto baking sheet, refilling bag as necessary, or drop individual ½-cup servings onto baking sheet and swirl top with a spoon. Drizzle each mound with 1 teaspoon melted butter or coat with cooking spray. Place baking sheet in oven and bake for 18 to 20 minutes or until lightly brown on top. Use convection heat if your oven has that option, or put under broiler briefly, if necessary. Serve hot as a side dish with more butter.

MAKES 4 CUPS OR 8 SERVINGS OF ½ CUP.

Per serving—Net carbohydrate: 2.2 grams; Protein: 3.2 grams; Fiber: 1.1 grams; Fat: 6.4 grams; Calories: 80

Total weight: 1 pound 14⅓ ounces or 861 grams

Weight per serving: 3¾ ounces or 108 grams

Preparation time: 10 minutes active; 30 minutes total (plus time to make *Faux* **Mashed Potatoes**, p. 281)

Faux Duchess Potatoes

Cauliflower *Faux* Rice
(Basic Recipe)

½ head cauliflower or about 1 pound as purchased (trimmed weight 14 ounces)
Salt to taste

Rinse cauliflower and trim away any discolorations. Discard the stem end with green leaves attached. Cut core and florets into ½ inch thick slices. Put through shredder blade on food processor or pulse with metal blade in place until cauliflower resembles rice. (If using metal blade, remove top and stir once while chopping.) To chop without a food processor, use a chef's knife to make rice-sized granules.

Put cauliflower into a microwave-safe dish and cover tightly. Do not add water. Microwave for 4 to 6 minutes. It can also be steamed on the stovetop. It should be cooked but still firm and fluffy. Add salt and use like rice.

MAKES ABOUT 2 ¼ CUPS OR 4 ½ SERVINGS OF ½ CUP EACH.

Per serving—Net carbohydrate: 1.1 grams; Protein: 0.8 grams; Fiber: 1 gram; Fat: 0.1 grams; Calories: 10

Total weight: 13 ounces or 369 grams

Weight per serving: 2⅞ ounces or 83 grams

Preparation time: 10 minutes active, 15 minutes total

"A diet that consists predominantly of rice leads to the use of opium, just as a diet that consists predominantly of potatoes leads to the use of liquor."

– Friedrich Nietzsche (1844-1900)

Hominy *Faux* Rice

Mexican-style hominy can be used whole in soups in place of dumplings or noodles and in chili instead of beans, and it can be served with butter as a side dish. When chopped in a food processor, it can be used like rice, bulgur, or grits.

Hominy brands vary a great deal in carbohydrate content, so check the nutrition information on the label to be sure it says "Mexican Style." Juanita's and Teasdale brands list 10 grams of carbohydrates, of which 6 are fiber, leaving just 4 grams of digestible carbs in each ½ cup serving. (Most corn products, and even other brands of hominy, have from 13 to 25 grams in the same half-cup amount.) You will find it with the Mexican foods at most grocery stores.

Per serving—Net carbohydrate: 4 grams; Protein: 2 grams; Fiber: 6 grams; Fat: 0.5 grams; Calories: 60

Total drained weight: 15 ounces or 429 grams (whole can weighs 1 pound and 13 ounces or 864 grams with liquid)

Weight per serving: 5 ounces or 142 grams

Preparation time: 5 minutes active and total

1 (29-ounce) can Juanita's or Teasdale's Mexican style hominy (weight includes liquid)

Drain hominy and pulse it in the bowl of a food processor fitted with the metal blade or chop by hand into grains the size of rice kernels. Use as you would cooked rice in recipes or serve as a side dish.

Rutabaga *Faux* Potatoes
(Basic Recipe)

Try this when you are missing those hash browns and home fries. They may not pass for russets, but they are very much like Yukon gold potatoes. Unless you tell them, your guests may be convinced that they are eating potatoes.

  3 small rutabagas (about 1¼ pounds total)
  2 walnuts in the shell
  1 slice of lemon with peel, optional
  Salt and pepper to taste
  Sweetener, if needed

Peel the rutabaga and dice into ½- to 1-inch cubes. Simmer for 10 minutes in a generous amount of water to which you have added salt and pepper and the 2 whole walnuts. Change the water if desired, add the lemon, if using, and continue to cook for 10 to 15 minutes more or until fork tender. Drain well. Discard walnuts and lemon. Return the rutabaga to the pan on low heat and stir a minute or two longer to dry. Taste the rutabaga and if it is bitter, sprinkle with a small amount of Splenda or other sugar substitute. Use like potatoes in soups or chowders or to make *Faux* potato salad or **Home Fries** (see p. 218).

> **MAKES 5 SERVINGS OF ½ CUP EACH.**
>
> Per serving—Net carbohydrate: 6.5 grams; Protein: 1.4 grams; Fiber: 2.9 grams; Fat: 0.2 grams; Calories: 41
>
> Total weight: 15½ ounces or 440 grams
>
> Weight per serving: 3 ounces or 88 grams
>
> Preparation time: 15 minutes active; 35 minutes total

Adding walnuts in the shell to the cooking liquid will neutralize the odor of cooking cabbage; I have discovered that it also helps counteract the turnip or cabbage flavor of similar vegetables, like cauliflower and rutabaga. Lemon also helps to neutralize strong flavors. Changing the water once while boiling makes them even milder.

If the recipe you will be using calls for cream, rinse the rutabaga well after draining to remove any trace of the lemon so the cream won't curdle.

"There is nothing so tragic on earth as the sight of a fat man eating a potato."
— *Vance Thompson,* Eat and Grow Thin, *1914*

Spaghetti Squash

This very mild, stringy squash is a good choice for those who are gluten intolerant and those who need to avoid grains. It can be used in almost any pasta recipe. It has so little taste of its own that it can serve as the base for all your favorite sauces and toppings. It has a crisp texture, and although it's a stretch to say it resembles al dente *spaghetti, you may find you like it as well as the real thing. It can also be chopped and used in place of rice with curry dishes.*

1 spaghetti squash (about 2½ pounds)

Pierce squash several times (so it won't explode) and microwave for about 2 to 5 minutes or just until the skin is soft enough to cut. Don't overcook it at this point; it is easier to remove the center fibers while the squash is still firm and raw. After it is cooked, the rest of the squash turns to fibers as well, and they tend to pull out along with the seedy ones.

Split the squash lengthwise. Remove the seeds and stringy fibers from the center. A grapefruit spoon with a serrated edge works well for this. One at a time, place the halves, cut-side-down, in a dish with ½-inch of water. Cover and cook on high in the microwave until tender. This may take 4 or 5 minutes per half, but there are many variables, so check it several times for doneness. When it is ready, you should be able to squeeze the sides in and see the strands start to separate at the edges. (There is no *al dente* stage; it's crisp, or it's mush.) Alternately, you can bake the squash in a 375º F oven for 30 to 45 minutes.

Let the squash cool enough to handle—you can speed it up by running cold water over it. Tease out the strands, one layer at a time, from the shell using a combing motion with a fork. If you have a very cooperative squash, you may be able to loosen the strands around the edges with a fork, and then pull them out with your fingers. To use as a side dish, sprinkle squash with salt and pepper and top with butter, use like spaghetti or noodles, or chop to use like rice.

NOTES:

Medium-sized squash (2 to 3 pounds) are easier to handle than the very large ones. If they are much smaller than 2 pounds, the strands may be too thin.

Spaghetti squash will continue to weep each time it's heated. Drain it well and serve it with a slotted spoon or blot up the excess liquid with a paper towel.

MAKES 6 CUPS FOR 6 SERVINGS OF 1 CUP OR 12 SERVINGS OF ½ CUP.

Per serving—Net carbohydrate: 7.8 grams; Protein: 1 gram; Fiber: 2.2 grams; Fat: 0.4 grams; Calories: 42

Total weight: 1 pound 10 ounces 738 grams

Weight per serving: 2¼ ounces or 123 grams

Preparation time: 15 minutes active, 35 minutes total, not counting cooling time

Splendid Low-Carb Bake Mix

This is one of many of Jennifer Eloff's bake mix combinations. It is used in **Favorite Chocolate Chip Cookies**, *p. 41,* **Cheddar Cheese Muffins**, *p. 46, and* **Biskmix**, *p. 288, (her low-carb version of Bisquik), which she generously allowed me to use in this book. Jennifer says this tasty bake mix reduces carbohydrates in a recipe by about 75%!*

She has dozens more recipes using this bake mix and others in her books available at **www.low-carb.us** *and on her blog at* **www.low-carb-news.blogspot.com**. *She has authored 7 books that use Splenda, 5 of which are low-carb. Four of Jennifer's books made the Canadian best sellers list!*

1²/3 rounded cups (7.4 ounces or 210 grams) ground almonds

²/3 cup (2.1 ounces or 60 grams) natural whey protein powder or vanilla whey protein powder

²/3 cup (3.5 ounces or 98 grams) vital wheat gluten, such as Bob's Red Mill 75% Protein Vital Wheat Gluten

In a large bowl, combine ground almonds, vanilla whey protein, and vital wheat gluten. Use a large wooden spoon to stir and mix well or place in sealed container and shake to combine. Store in an airtight container at room temperature for short-term storage or in freezer for longer term storage.

TO USE THIS BAKE MIX:

For every cup of flour in your recipe, replace with 1 cup **Plus** 2 to 4 tablespoons of Low-Carb Bake Mix. Always add liquid cautiously to your own recipes. Sometimes as much as ½ cup less wet ingredients will be required (this includes ingredients such as butter, olive oil, applesauce, pumpkin, water, yogurt, sour cream, cream, etc.). Typically, ¼ cup of wet ingredients will need to be omitted from your regular recipe. If the batter is too moist, add more bake mix.

NOTE:

Vital wheat gluten: 75 to 80% will work well in most recipes. Bob's Red Mill vital wheat gluten (75%) is very good quality.

TIP:

Ground hazelnuts or pecans may be used instead of almonds. This bake mix is useful for pie crusts, muffins, loaves, many cakes, cookies and squares, some cooking applications, and it guarantees lower carbs as well. The nutritional analysis of the bake mix is calculated using the individual weights of the ingredients rather than the cup measures for extra accuracy.

───────

Be sure to use a sugar-free version of vanilla whey protein. For savory recipes, it is possible to replace vanilla whey protein, which is sweetened, with natural whey protein powder.

MAKES 3 CUPS OR 9 SERVINGS OF ¹/3 CUP.

Per serving—Net carbohydrate: 3.3 grams; Protein: 17.8 grams; Fiber: 3 grams; Fat: 12.4 grams; Calories: 202

Total weight: 13 ounces or 368 grams

Weight per ¹/3 cup serving: 1½ ounces of 41 grams

Preparation time: 5 minutes active and total

Jennifer's Biskmix

This recipe is from Splendid Low-Carbing for Life, Vol. 2, *by best selling cookbook author, Jennifer Eloff (www.low-carb.us). It can be used similarly to Bisquick in many favorite recipes; however, it will not work with yeast applications. (Bisquick, a Betty Crocker product, is the trademark of General Mills.)*

2¼ cups (10 ounces or 280 grams) *Splendid Low-Carb Bake Mix*, p. 287.
4½ teaspoons baking powder
½ teaspoon salt (omit if using salted butter)
½ cup (4 ounces or 113 grams) unsalted, ice cold butter

In food processor bowl with sharp S-blade, combine Low-Carb Bake Mix, baking powder, and salt. Add butter, cut into smaller pieces; process only until mixture is crumbly (you don't want a dough ball.) If the food processor is too powerful, rub the butter in by hand. Leftovers can be stored at room temperature in an airtight container for about a week and transferred to the refrigerator or freezer for longer storage. Biskmix that is weeks old might need a boost with a little extra baking powder. Baked goods are best fresh. Chilled or day-old baking is often better reheated either in the oven or microwave.

EASY INSTRUCTIONS FOR SUBSTITUTING BISKMIX IN RECIPES REQUIRING BISQUICK:

Replace each cup of Bisquick with 1 cup **plus an extra ¼ cup** Biskmix and typically use 2 tablespoons less fluid than indicated in the recipe per cup of Bisquik that will be replaced.

For example, if your particular recipe requires 2 cups of Bisquick and 1 cup of fluid, you'd need to use 2½ cups Biskmix and ¾ cup fluid. Simple math!

Sometimes, for convenience, it is possible to approximate the amount of Biskmix required. For example, instead of using 1 cup plus 14 tablespoons, use a full 2 cups and adjust the fluid requirements accordingly. Experienced bakers will know what a cookie batter looks like versus a cake, loaf, or muffin batter, etc. Use plain whey protein in **Splendid Low-Carb Bake Mix** for savory applications and the vanilla whey protein for desserts, if desired.

Recipe used by permission.

JENNIFER'S HELPFUL HINT:

Leftover Splendid Low-Carb Bake Mix is also great as filler in hamburgers and meatloaf and for "breading" vegetables and meats.

MAKES 3½ CUPS OF BISKMIX OR 14 SERVINGS OF ¼ CUP EACH.

Per serving—Net carbohydrate: 1.8 grams; Protein: 8.3 grams; Fiber: 1.5 grams; Fat: 12.5 grams; Calories: 154

Total weight: 14⅓ ounces or 407 grams

Weight per ¼ cup: 1 ounce or 29 grams

Preparation time: 10 minutes active and total

Easy Biskmix Crackers

Great for using up leftover Biskmix. Overcooked the crackers? Crumble and use as "Cheese Bits" on casseroles or instead of bacon bits. Spread the crackers with sugarless preserves.

½ cup (2 ounces or 57 grams) grated Cheddar cheese
1/3 cup (1½ ounce or 43 grams) Biskmix
2 teaspoons water

In a small bowl, combine Cheddar cheese, Biskmix and water. Place on greased dinner plate and using plastic wrap, press out dough to fill inside of plate. Microwave on high power 2 to 4 minutes until crisp.

Recipe used by permission from *Splendid Low-Carbing for Life, Vol. 2*, by best-selling cookbook author Jennifer Eloff (www.low-carb.us).

TO ACCURATELY MEASURE BISKMIX:
Spoon into measuring cup, then level top with a flat knife. Do not scoop it or pack it down.

MAKES 2 SERVINGS.

Per serving—Net carbohydrate: 1.5 grams; Protein: 12 grams; Fiber: 0.9 grams; Fat: 16.9 grams; Calories: 206

Total weight of crackers: 3¾ ounces or 107 grams

Weight per serving: 2 ounces or 53.5 grams

Preparation time: 8 minutes active; 10 minutes total

Whole Grain Bread
1 Loaf, Bread Machine Recipe

JENNIFER'S HELPFUL HINT:
The loaves are easier to slice
with a sharp bread knife when
completely cool. For crustier
buns, toast lightly on both sides
in nonstick pan. The buns are
somewhat chewy.

This exceptional low-carb bread is from More Splendid
Low-Carbing *by Jennifer Eloff. The recipe makes one large
loaf. The variation that follows makes 2 smaller loaves, 12 to
14 hamburger buns, 9 hotdog buns, or 24 rolls. Jennifer says
this wonderful-tasting bread almost pops the top off a bread
machine with a vertical pan.*

FOR 1 LARGE LOAF BAKED IN LARGE BREAD MACHINE:

1 cup water

3 tablespoons olive oil

1 large egg

1 cup (5½ ounces or 155 grams) 70-80% vital wheat gluten

2/3 cup (3¾ ounces or 108 grams) whole wheat pastry flour

½ cup (1 1/3 ounces or 37 grams) wheat bran

¼ cup (1 1/3 ounces or 38 grams) additional whole wheat pastry flour,
or

    ¼ cup (1 1/8 ounces or 32 grams) ground flax seeds

4 teaspoons rapid/quick rise yeast

1 tablespoon Splenda Granular or sugar substitute equal to
    1 tablespoon sugar

1 tablespoon granulated sugar (to feed the yeast)

1 teaspoon salt

1 teaspoon vanilla extract

1 teaspoon baking powder

½ teaspoon molasses, optional

MAKES 18 SLICES

Per serving without flax—
Net carbohydrate: 4.9 grams;
Protein: 7.4 grams; Fiber: 1.6
grams; Fat: 2.8 grams; Calories: 74

Per serving with flax—
Net carbohydrate: 4.2 grams;
Protein: 7.5 grams; Fiber: 1.9
grams; Fat: 5.4 grams; Calories: 83

Total weight: 21 ounces or
594 grams

Weight per slice: 1¼ ounce or
33 grams

Preparation time: 15 minutes
active; total varies with bread
machine

In small bowl, heat water in microwave 1 minute. In pan of
bread machine, place water, olive oil, egg, vital wheat gluten,
2/3 cup whole wheat pastry flour, wheat bran, an additional
¼ cup whole wheat pastry flour or ground flax seeds, rapid
rise yeast, Splenda, sugar, salt, vanilla extract, baking powder,
and molasses, if using. Program bread machine to *Bread
Rapid* setting and color to *Medium*. Remove 30 minutes
before baking time is over or when brown in color.

Recipe used with permission from *More Splendid Low-Carbing* by best-
selling cookbook author, *Jennifer Eloff (www.low-carb.us).*

Two-Loaf, Oven-Baked Recipe

For two smaller loaves, mixed and kneaded in either a bread machine or a mixer with a dough hook, and baked in a regular oven:

Use 1 cup water (one may need up to 3 tablespoon more, but not always), 2 eggs, 1¼ cups vital wheat gluten and 2 teaspoons baking powder. Follow recipe above with these changes. Program bread machine to *Pizza Cycle* (see hint in sidebar) or knead in a Kitchenaid mixer until dough is moist and elastic, about 16 minutes. Do not knead too long or the dough will be ruined (using a bread machine takes the guess work out of things). Divide dough in two equal portions (only one rise in total with Kitchenaid mixer). Place each portion in greased 8 x 4 x 2½ in (948 mL) loaf pan (line pan with waxed paper and grease to make removal of loaves easier). Place pans on bottom shelf in preheated 225° F oven, which is turned off. Allow to rise 40 minutes. Set oven to 350° F, leaving loaves inside. (In some newer ovens, the broiler comes on when the oven is preheating. If you cannot turn off this feature, just let your bread rise in a warm place, but do not put it in the oven until it is preheated to the proper temperature.) Bake 30 minutes and remove loaves. Place on wire rack to cool. The bread or buns may be frozen, if desired.

JENNIFER'S HELPFUL HINT: Some people prefer the texture of the bread when they remove the dough before the rise in the pizza cycle.

Per serving without flax— Net carbohydrate for each of 44 slices: 2.2 grams; Protein: 3.8 grams; Fiber: 0.7 grams; Fat: 1.3 grams; Calories: 38

Per serving with flax— Net carbohydrate for each of 44 slices: 1.9 grams; Protein: 3.8 grams; Fiber: 0.8 grams; Fat: 1.5 grams; Calories: 39

Total weight: 1½ pounds or 594 grams

Weight per slice: ½ ounce or 13.5 grams

FOR HAMBURGER BUNS, HOT DOG BUNS, OR DINNER ROLLS:

Shape dough into 14 hamburger buns, 9 hot dog buns, or 24 dinner rolls. Place on greased pizza pan. Spray buns with nonstick cooking spray. Proceed as above and bake 20 minutes.

> Per serving without flax—Net carbohydrate for each of 14 hamburger buns: 6.9 grams; Protein: 11.9 grams; Fiber: 2.2 grams; Fat: 4.1 grams; Calories: 119
>
> Per serving with flax—Net carbohydrate for each of 14 hamburger buns: 6 grams; Protein: 11.9 grams; Fiber: 2.5 grams; Fat: 4.7 grams; Calories: 123
>
> Total weight: 1½ pounds or 663 grams
>
> Weight per bun: 1¾ ounces or 47 grams
>
> Per serving without flax —Net carbohydrate for each of 9 hotdog buns: 10.8 grams; Protein: 18.6 grams: Fiber: 3.4 grams: Fat: 6.4 grams; Calories: 186
>
> Per serving with flax—Net carbohydrate for each of 9 hotdog buns: 9.3 grams; Protein: 18.6 grams; Fiber: 3.9 grams; Fat: 7.3 grams; Calories: 191
>
> Total weight: 1½ pounds or 663 grams
>
> Weight per bun: 2½ ounces or 74 grams
>
> Per serving without flax—Net carbohydrate for each of 24 dinner rolls: 4; Protein: 7 grams; Fiber: 1.3 grams; Fat: 2.4 grams; Calories:70
>
> Per serving with flax—Net carbohydrate for each of 24 dinner rolls: 3.5 grams; Protein: 7 grams;
> Fiber: 1.5 grams; Fat: 2.8 grams; Calories: 72
>
> Total weight: 1½ pounds or 663 grams
>
> Weight per roll: 1 ounce or 28 grams

JENNIFER'S HELPFUL HINT: Whole wheat pastry flour, also known as graham flour, is available from The King Arthur Flour Company or in some health food or grocery stores. Arrowhead Mills makes a whole grain, organic pastry flour (this is the one Jennifer uses).

VARIATIONS:

Bread Crumbs:

Toast **Whole Grain Bread** and tear into pieces. Place in blender with seasonings; blend.

Croutons:

Cut **Whole Grain Bread** into cubes and toss in olive oil with desired seasonings (salt, garlic, Parmesan cheese, etc.). Bake on cookie sheet in 325° F oven until crisp (toss occasionally).

Barbecue Sauce

Make a double batch of sauce to keep on hand for meatballs, pulled pork, spare ribs, meatloaf, and other dishes. Just a few tablespoonfuls can really perk up a pot roast.

½ onion, finely chopped (about 3 ounces)

2 tablespoons olive oil

2 garlic cloves (¼ ounce), peeled and chopped

2 (8-ounce) cans tomato sauce

1 teaspoon Worcestershire sauce

2 teaspoons liquid smoke, hickory or mesquite flavored

1 teaspoon hot sauce, such as Tabasco

½ teaspoon gravy flavoring (like Kitchen Bouquet or Gravy Master)

Sugar substitute to equal ¼ cup sugar

½ cup cider vinegar

½ teaspoon salt

¼ teaspoon pepper

Sauté onion in the olive oil. Add the chopped garlic and sauté a little longer. Mix in other ingredients and simmer, uncovered, on low heat for 30 minutes. Purée in a food processor in batches if you prefer a smooth sauce. Refrigerate until needed.

MAKES ABOUT 3 CUPS OR 24 SERVINGS OF 2 TABLESPOONS.

Per serving—Net carbohydrate: 1.2 grams; Protein: 0.3 grams; Fiber: 0.3 grams;

Fat: 1.2 grams; Calories: 18

Total weight: 13 ounces or 369 grams

Weight per serving: 1¼ ounces or 30 grams

Preparation time: 10 minutes active, 40 minutes total

Ketchup

½ cup (2 ounces) onion, chopped

1 (15-ounce can) tomato sauce

Sugar substitute equal to ¼ cup sugar

1 teaspoon each of the following whole spices: allspice, cloves, celery seed, and peppercorns

½-inch piece of stick cinnamon

1/8 teaspoon dry mustard

1 garlic clove (1/8 ounce), minced

½ a Turkish bay leaf

Salt and black or cayenne pepper to taste

¼ cup cider vinegar

Bring all ingredients except vinegar, salt, and pepper to a boil in a medium saucepan. Simmer, stirring occasionally, until reduced by half, about 20 to 25 minutes. Add the vinegar. Simmer 10 minutes more. Strain out spices and onion. Add salt and pepper to taste if needed. Put into a container, cover and store in refrigerator or divide into smaller containers and freeze.

MAKES 1 CUP OR 16 SERVINGS OF 1 TABLESPOON EACH.

Per serving—Net carbohydrate: 1.5 grams; Protein: 0.4 grams; Fiber: 0.5 grams; Fat: 0.1 grams; Calories: 10

Total weight: 8 ounces or 256 grams

Weight per serving: ½ ounce or 16 grams

Preparation time: 25 minutes active; 1 hour total

Marinara Sauce

1 tablespoon olive oil

½ cup (2 ounces) onion, chopped

2 garlic cloves, peeled and minced

2 (8-ounce) cans tomato sauce

16 ounces Pomi Chopped Tomatoes or 1 (14½-ounce) can
    chopped tomatoes

4 tablespoons fresh parsley, minced, or 2 tablespoons dried

2 teaspoons fresh basil, minced, or 1 teaspoon dried

½ teaspoon salt

¼ teaspoon pepper

Heat olive oil in a medium saucepan. Cook onion until softened. Add garlic and cook for a minute or two longer. Add the tomato sauce and tomatoes, including the liquid from the can, the parsley, basil, salt, and pepper. Simmer, uncovered, stirring occasionally, for about 45 minutes or until thickened.

**MAKES 2¾ CUPS
OR 11 SERVINGS
OF ¼ CUP.**

Per serving made with Pomi Strained Tomatoes—Net carbohydrate: 1.8 grams; Protein: 0.9 grams; Fiber: 2.3 grams; Fat: 1.3 grams; Calories: 32

Total weight: 1 pound 9¼ ounces or 717 grams

Weight per serving: 2⅓ ounces or 66 grams

Preparation time: 8 minutes active, 58 minutes total

Meat Sauce

If you are on a system that doesn't allow tomato products, try replacing canned tomatoes with puréed, **Roasted Red Peppers**, *p. 78. The carbohydrate counts will be about the same.*

1 pound lean ground beef
½ cup (2 ounces) onion, chopped
2 (¼ ounce) garlic cloves, minced
2 (8-ounce) cans tomato sauce
1 (14½-ounce) can tomatoes, crushed (preferred) or diced
4 tablespoons fresh parsley, minced, or 2 tablespoons dried
2 teaspoons fresh basil, minced, or 1 teaspoon dried
1 teaspoon salt
½ teaspoon pepper

Cook the ground beef in a lightly greased skillet until it is no longer pink. Add the onion and cook until the onion is softened and the meat starts to brown. Add the garlic and cook for a minute or two longer; drain. Add the tomato sauce and tomatoes, including the liquid, the parsley, basil, salt, and pepper. Simmer, uncovered, stirring occasionally, for about 35 to 40 minutes or until thickened.

MAKES 4 CUPS OR 8 SERVINGS OF ½ CUP.

Per serving—Net carbohydrate: 2.5 grams; Protein: 12.5 grams; Fiber: 3.1 grams; Fat: 5.7 grams; Calories: 129

Total weight: 2 pounds 3 ounces or 995 grams

Weight per serving: 4½ ounces or 124 grams

Preparation time: 15 minutes active, 60 minutes total

NOTES:
Some ready-made spaghetti and marinara sauces are naturally low-carb. Look for ones that are imported from Italy; they are unlikely to have added sugar. I have found some that are as low as 2 net grams of carbohydrates in ½ cup. Avoid any that list sugar in the ingredients. See Sources.

Most brands of canned tomatoes, tomato sauce, and paste contain added sugar. The Italian Pomi brand, in a red and white carton rather than a can, is the lowest I've found. It is available in stores and online. (None are really sugar-free, because tomatoes naturally contain a small amount of sugar.)

Crème Fraîche

Crème Fraîche can be whipped like cream, and it can be boiled without curdling, so it works well in sauces and in cream soups. It also makes a great topping for fruit and desserts. It is available from the cooler in most groceries, or you can make this less expensive version at home.

Combine 1 cup of heavy cream with 2 tablespoons of buttermilk (with live cultures) in a glass container. Cover and let stand at room temperature (about 70° F) for 8 to 24 hours, or until very thick. Stir well, cover, and refrigerate for up to ten days.

MAKES 1 1/8 CUPS OR 9 SERVINGS OF 2 TABLESPOONS EACH.

Per serving—Net carbohydrate: 0.9 grams; Protein: 0.7 grams; Fiber: 0 grams; Fat: 9.9 grams; Calories: 93

Total weight: 9 ounces or 270 grams

Weight per serving: 1 ounce or 30 grams

Preparation time: 5 minutes active; 8 to 24 hours total

TIP:
For a quick substitute for **Crème Fraîche**, mix equal parts sour cream and heavy cream.

"Dr. Atkins taught us that eating fat doesn't necessarily make us fat, and in fact it makes us thin. He was absolutely right and should have been taken more seriously by the nutrition establishment."

— *Dr. Arthur Agaston,*
author of The South Beach Diet *series*

Mayonnaise

About.com has directions for pasteurizing egg yolks at: http://culinaryarts.about.com/od/eggsdairy/ht/pasteurize_eggs.htm.

Dr. Michael Eades gives most of the credit to his wife for the success of their latest project: they have developed and brought to market a sous vide *machine for the home kitchen! You can read about this latest innovation on their blog at: www.proteinpower.com.*

Below is a recipe for blender mayonnaise that appeared on Dr. Mary Dan's blog. Is there anything this woman can't do?

A BIT OF ADVICE:
"Making mayonnaise may seem daunting, but it's really simplicity itself. I'll share my blender version, but a word of caution. Don't use your good quality, extra-virgin, olive oil for making mayonnaise. It will become bitter in the blender. I haven't a clue why, but it happens quite regularly, so don't waste your money on the good oil."– *Dr. Mary Dan Eades*

> 1 raw egg yolk (pasteurized in the shell, if available)
> 2 teaspoons champagne vinegar or white wine vinegar
> ¼ teaspoon salt
> ½ lemon, juice only (about 1 tablespoon)
> ¼ teaspoon dry mustard
> Dash cayenne pepper
> 1 packet Splenda (optional, but gives it a slight sweetness like Miracle Whip)
> ¾ to 1 cup light olive oil, such as Bertoli

Crack egg and put yolk only into the blender

Add the vinegar and salt and blend on low speed.

With the motor running, add all the remaining ingredients, except the oil.

With the motor still running, add the oil in a slow, steady stream until it makes mayonnaise of the consistency you desire. Be careful not to add the oil too fast or add too much oil or you may break the emulsion and the mayonnaise will separate and clump. Don't despair if your mayonnaise breaks, and don't throw out the result. While, once broken, it will not likely ever thicken into a spread-able form, you can save it in a jar in the refrigerator and whisk herbs and garlic and a bit more salt into it to make a nice mayonnaise-based dressing, which demands a looser emulsion anyway.

Store in the refrigerator in a clean jar or a container with a tight-fitting lid for up to a week.

Recipe used by permission.

MAKE 1 CUP OR 16 SERVINGS OF 1 TABLESPOON.

Per serving—Net carbohydrate: 0.1 grams; Protein: 0.2 grams; Fiber: 0 grams; Fat: 10.5 grams; Calories: 94

Total weight: 6 ounces or 170 grams

Weight per serving: ⅓ ounce or 11 grams

Preparation time: 10 minutes active and total

"Mayonnaise…is a delicious and healthy low-carb food, if made with good oil. Therein lies the problem for most commercial mayonnaise: they're usually made with nasty soybean oil or canola oil, basically a trans-fat slurry…. And if you've read our books, you know that one of the most important aspects of good nutrition is the quality (not the quantity) of the fat you put into your mouth."

— *Dr. Mary Dan Eades*

Raspberry Vinegar

*Purchased raspberry vinegar contains sugar. This sugar-free version is a snap to make and tastes better too. Use it in my **Duck Breasts with Raspberry Glaze** recipe or to make vinaigrette for dressing salads.*

1 cup (4½ ounces) fresh or sugar-free frozen raspberries
1½ cups white wine vinegar

Rinse a 16-ounce glass jar and lid with boiling water. Rinse raspberries and place in jar. Heat vinegar to boiling in a small non-reactive saucepan (stainless steel, enamel, or ceramic). Pour vinegar over berries. Place lid on jar but let stand until cool before tightening lid. Leave at room temperature in a dark place for a few days to infuse. Strain and refrigerate.

MAKES 1½ CUPS (STRAINED) OR 12 SERVINGS OF 2 TABLESPOONS AS SALAD DRESSING.

Per serving—Net carbohydrate: 0 grams; Protein: 0 grams; Fiber: 0 grams; Fat: 0 grams; Calories: 5

Total weight: 12 ounces 341 grams

Weight per serving: 2 ounces or 57 grams

Preparation time: 5 minutes; 10 minutes total plus several days infusion time

---

Red Wine Vinaigrette

¼ cup red wine vinegar
Sugar substitute equal to 1 teaspoon sugar
2 garlic cloves, minced
½ teaspoon salt
¼ teaspoon fresh black pepper
¾ cup olive oil

Combine vinegar, sweetener, garlic, salt, and pepper in a small bowl. Whisk in the olive oil until thickened and emulsified. Can be stored in refrigerator for up to 2 weeks.

MAKES 1 CUP OF DRESSING OR 16 SERVINGS OF 1 TABLESPOON.

Per serving—Net carbohydrate: 0.1 grams; Protein: 0 grams; Fiber: 0 grams; Fat: 10.1 grams; Calories: 91

Total weight: 8 fluid ounces or 227 grams

Weight per serving: ½ ounce or 14 grams

Preparation time: 5 minutes active and total

Roasted Garlic and "Balsamic" Vinaigrette

You may use my recipe for roasting a whole head of garlic on p. 115 and use the extra for another purpose or cook just two cloves in the microwave (see Sidebar).

2 garlic cloves (¼ ounce) from a head of **Roasted Garlic,** p. 115
3 tablespoons (1½ ounces) red wine vinegar
Sugar substitute equal to ¼ teaspoon sugar
½ teaspoon Dijon mustard
5 tablespoons (2½ ounces) extra virgin olive oil
Salt and freshly ground pepper to taste

Squeeze the pulp from two cloves of roasted garlic into a bowl and mash with a fork. Add vinegar, sweetener, and mustard and whisk together until smooth. Pour olive oil in a thin stream into the mixture while continuing to whisk. Add salt and ground pepper to taste.

MAKES ABOUT ½ CUP OR 4 SERVINGS OF 2 TABLESPOONS EACH.

Per serving—Net carbohydrate: 0.5 grams; Protein: 0.1 grams; Fiber: 0.1 grams; Fat: 16.9 grams; Calories: 154

Total weight: 3½ ounces or 98 grams

Weight per serving: 7/8 ounce or 25 grams

Preparation time: 5 minutes active and total

TIP:
To roast just 2 garlic cloves in microwave:
Remove cloves from head of garlic but do not peel. Cut off tips to expose pulp. Microwave on high for 45 to 60 seconds or until very soft, turning once or twice.

Cherry Jelly

Agar agar is made from a red seaweed called gracilaria. It makes a clear, firm jelly and is popular as a vegan replacement for gelatin. It is rich in iodine and trace minerals; it has no carbohydrate and adds no taste to the finished dish.

Acidic ingredients, like lemon juice, will require more agar agar to set, and the enzymes in some raw fruits, like pineapple, kiwi, and papaya, will interfere with its ability to set.

There are many no-sugar-added jams and jellies in the stores, but I haven't seen any that were sugar-free and fruit-free. Perhaps the manufacturers are not allowed to call it jelly or jam if it doesn't contain fruit or fruit juice. I don't have that constraint.

½ cup water
½ cup cherry-flavored, sugar-free syrup, such as DaVinci or Torani
1 teaspoon agar agar flakes or 1/3 teaspoon agar agar powder
A few grains of salt
Sugar substitute equal to 2 tablespoons sugar
1 teaspoon almond extract

Put water and syrup in a small saucepan. Stir in agar agar and let sit for 15 minutes. Bring to a boil and simmer for 10 minutes, stirring, or until agar agar is completely dissolved. Stir in extract. Let cool until set, about 45 minutes to an hour. Keep refrigerated.

MAKES ½ CUP OF JELLY OR 8 SERVINGS OF 1 TABLESPOON EACH

Per serving—Net carbohydrate: 0.1 grams; Protein: 0 grams; Fiber: 0 grams; Fat: 0 grams; Calories: 0.4

Total weight: 4 ounces or 114 grams

Weight per serving: ½ ounce or 14 grams

Preparation time: 5 minutes active; 30 minutes total plus setting time.

TIPS:

Test the jelly by placing a little on a saucer; it will set in about half a minute. Add more agar agar for a firmer gel, more liquid for a softer one. The jelly will become firm at room temperature or in the refrigerator in about 45 minutes to an hour. Once set it will not melt until it reaches 136º F.

Almond extract and amaretto liqueur intensify cherry flavors because, out of context, it is impossible to tell the difference between the flavor of almonds and cherries.

Grape Jelly

Substitute grape-flavored sugar-free syrup for cherry in **Cherry Jelly** recipe. Substitute 1 tablespoon red wine for almond extract.

Mint Jelly

Especially good with lamb.

  1 cup water
  1 teaspoon agar agar flakes or $1/3$ teaspoon agar agar powder
  Sugar substitute equal to ½ cup sugar
  A few grains of salt
  ½ cup finely chopped, fresh mint leaves, divided
  1 teaspoon mint extract

Put water, agar agar, sweetener, salt, and ¼ cup of the mint leaves in a small saucepan. Let sit for 15 minutes. Bring to a boil and simmer for 10 minutes, stirring, or until agar agar is completely dissolved. Strain out the mint and add the remaining fresh mint to the hot jelly. Stir in extract. Let cool until set, about 45 minutes to an hour. Keep refrigerated or process in a water bath to make jelly that can be stored on the shelf. (See the USDA Complete Guide to Home Canning: www.uga.edu/nchfp/publications/publications_usda.html.)

> **MAKES** 5/8 **CUP OR 14 SERVINGS OF 1 TABLESPOON.**
>
> Per serving—Net carbohydrate: 0.1 grams; Protein: 0 grams; Fiber: 0 grams; Fat: 0 grams; Calories: 0.4
>
> Total weight: 7¼ ounces or 198 grams
>
> Weight per serving: ½ ounce or 14 grams
>
> Preparation time: 10 minutes active; 15 minute total

MORE VARIATIONS:
Combine any flavor or flavors of sugar-free syrup with a compatible extract or liquor for more jelly variations. See Sources for other brands of syrups.

You can also make **Mint Jelly** with mint-flavored sugar-free syrup in the same way as **Cherry** or **Grape Jelly** by substituting mint extract for almond. DaVinci and Torani both make a Crème de Menthe flavored sugar-free syrup. See Sources.

Almond Crisps

Here's what we've been looking for—simple crackers or cookies that taste good, are super-easy, and super-low in carbs. These are substantial enough to use with dips or spreads and the variations are limited only by your imagination.

MAKES 48 CRISPS.

Net carbohydrate per crisp:
0.2 grams; Protein: 0.6 grams;
Fiber: 0.3 grams; Fat: 1.2 grams;
Calories: 14

Total weight: 3¼ ounces or
92 grams

Weight per crisp: 0.06 ounces or
2 grams

Preparation time: 10 minutes active,
20 minutes total (depending on
number of pans used)

1 egg white from a large egg
1 cup (4 ounces) almond flour or almond meal
Sugar substitute equal to 2 teaspoons sugar (recipe was tested with
    1 drop of EZ-Sweetz liquid sucralose)
A pinch of salt

Preheat oven to 325° F. Place a piece of parchment paper on a baking sheet. You will also need something for pressing the crisps, like a flat meat pounder or a measuring cup with a flat bottom, and some plastic wrap.

Whisk egg white until blended. Add remaining ingredients and mix well. Form dough into 48 small balls. They should be about ½-inch across. Place balls about 3 inches apart (to make room for tool used to press crisps) on parchment-lined pans. Cover with a sheet of plastic wrap and flatten balls into thin circles, roughly 2 inches across, with a flat implement. Carefully remove plastic. Place in preheated oven and bake for about 10 to 12 minutes or until golden brown and crisp. Repeat with remaining balls. Store in an airtight container.

Almond Parmesan Crisps

Gourmet crackers to serve with soups or dips and spreads.

Make basic **Almond Crisps**, p. 304. Add 3 tablespoons (⅜ ounce) of finely grated Parmesan cheese and a dash of freshly-ground black pepper to mixture. Sprinkle crisps with coarse salt before baking.

MAKES 48 CRACKERS.

Per serving—Net carbohydrate: 0.2 grams; Protein: 0.7 grams; Fiber: 0.3 grams; Fat: 1.3 grams; Calories: 16

Total weight: 4 ounces or 120 grams

Weight per cracker: 0.08 ounces or 2.5 grams

Preparation time: 10 minutes active, 20 minutes total

TIP:

You will be tempted to eat these like chips. Make a few at a time and refrigerate the remaining dough to help with portion control.

Almond Crisp Cookies

1 egg white from large egg
1 cup (4 ounces) almond flour or meal
Sugar substitute equal to 8 teaspoons sugar
A pinch of salt
1 teaspoon vanilla, lemon, or other extract

Make according to directions for **Almond Crisps**, p. 305.

MAKES 48 COOKIES.

Per serving—Net carbohydrate: 0.2 grams; Protein: 0.6 grams; Fiber: 0.3 grams; Fat: 1.2 grams; Calories: 14

Total weight: 4 ounces or 114 grams

Weight per cookie: 0.08 ounces or 2.5 grams

Preparation time: 10 minutes active, 20 minutes total

OTHER VARIATIONS:

For sweet or savory crisps:
Use other nut flours, such as hazelnut or pecan in place of the almond flour.

Substitute poppy or chia seeds, or ground sesame, pumpkin, sunflower, or flax seeds for some of the almond flour or sprinkle on crisps before baking.

For savory crisps:
Add a pinch of one or more of the following to the dough: garlic powder, onion powder, red pepper flakes, ground black pepper, curry powder, dry mustard, paprika, or choice of other spices and herbs.

Top with coarse salt and freshly-ground black pepper, smoked paprika or dried herbs, chopped nuts, or seeds before baking.

Cassia   Ceylon

CINNAMON:

Dr. Anderson, of the USDA Human Nutrition Research Center in Beltsville, Maryland, and his colleagues were looking into the effects of chromium on insulin action. While testing various foods, they found something that had a much greater influence on blood sugar, cholesterol, and triglycerides: it was apple pie. It turned out to be the cinnamon in the pie that produced what Anderson called the "most significant nutritional discovery he'd seen in 25 years."[1]

Since the insulin-like properties of cinnamon were discovered, it has become a popular treatment for insulin resistance and diabetes, but there is a potential danger in taking too much or the wrong kind. Cinnamon contains coumarin, an anti-coagulant and possibly carcinogenic substance that can cause liver inflammation.

There are two kinds of cinnamon, but product labels do not usually specify the type. Ceylon, or true cinnamon (Cinnamomum zwylanicum), is a pale tan color; it is milder, sweeter, and more expensive than cassia. Cassia, or common cinnamon (Cinnamomum cassia), is redder, stronger in flavor, and cheaper in price. Ceylon cinnamon sticks are tight rolls of thin, shaggy layers; cassia sticks are hollow scrolls of thick bark. Cassia contains 0.5 percent coumarin, while Ceylon contains only 0.0004 percent. Most of the cinnamon sold in the US is cassia. The beneficial compounds in cinnamon are soluble in water, coumarin is not, so a water extract of cinnamon will not contain any of the hazardous substance. Dr. Anderson recommends that anyone who wants to take more than ¼ to 1 teaspoonful a day should use a water extract rather than powdered cinnamon.

Note: Those of us who eat a low carb diet may not see additional benefits from cinnamon supplementation, since we have already reduced our need for insulin.

Two final bits of advice from Dr. Anderson: "First, eating great quantities of cinnamon straight from the can is not a good idea. Table cinnamon is not water soluble, meaning it can build up in the body with unknown consequences. Second, the powdered cinnamon has another limitation. Dr. Anderson's personal 60-point decline in total cholesterol occurred only after he switched from sprinkling cinnamon on his breakfast cereal to taking it in a capsule. Saliva contains a chemical harmful to cinnamon."[2]

---

1   Valerie Reitman, A dash of cinnamon may help, *The Los Angeles Times*, January 26, 2004.

2   From a press release from the Federation of American Societies for Experimental Biology.

Ginger Crisp Cookies

These are reminiscent of Anna's Swedish Thins.

Basic **Almond Crisp Cookie** dough, p. 305
1 teaspoon ground ginger (or more to taste)
½ teaspoon ground cinnamon
1/8 teaspoon ground cloves
¼ teaspoon freshly grated lemon zest

Make according to directions for **Almond Crisps**, p. 305.

MAKES 48 COOKIES.

Per serving—Net carbohydrate: 0.2 grams; Protein: 0.6 grams; Fiber: 0.3 grams;
Fat: 1.2 grams; Calories: 14

Total weight: 4 ounces or 112 grams

Weight per cookie: 0.08 ounces or 0.25 grams

Preparation time: 10 minutes active, 20 minutes total

Cinnamon Crisp Cookies

Basic **Almond Crisp Cookie** dough, p. 305
½ teaspoon ground cinnamon
¼ teaspoon vanilla extract

TOPPING:

1 teaspoon granular sugar substitute, such as Splenda or a stevia blend
¼ teaspoon ground cinnamon

Make by directions for **Almond Crisps**, p. 304. Mix cinnamon and sweetener together and sprinkle over cookies before baking.

MAKES 48 COOKIES.

Per cookie—Net carbohydrate: 0.2 grams; Protein: 0.6 grams; Fiber: 0.3 grams;   Fat: 1.2 grams; Calories: 14

Total weight: 4 ounces or 114 grams

Weight per cookie: 0.08 ounces or 0.25 grams

Preparation time: 12 minutes active, 22 minutes total

MORE VARIATIONS:
For sweet crisps:
Add one or more of the following: cocoa powder, grated coconut, a dash of cinnamon, ginger, or cloves. Add a bit of fresh lemon or orange zest, and/or other spices or flavorings.

Put two cookies together with **Ganache**, p. 132, or **Butter Cream Frosting**, p. 126, for filled cookies.

Break several cookies into a bowl in lieu of a cone and top with ice cream.

French Vanilla Ice Cream

Ice cream is the perfect low-carb dessert.

FOR THE CUSTARD:
- ¼ cup (1¾ ounces or 50 grams) polydextrose
- ¼ cup (3½ ounces or 48 grams) granular erythritol
- 1 teaspoon no-sugar fruit pectin, such as Ball's
- ¼ teaspoon salt
- High intensity sugar substitute equal to ¼ cup sugar (such as liquid sucralose, stevia, or Splenda)
- 6 egg yolks from large eggs (reserve whites)
- ¾ cup half and half
- 2 teaspoons sugar-free vanilla extract

TO FINISH:
- 6 egg whites (see Sidebar about egg safety)
- A pinch of cream of tartar (do not use cream of tartar if beating whites in a copper bowl)
- 3 cups heavy cream

Prepare a large bowl of ice water for cooling the pan after cooking the custard.

Whisk the polydextrose, erythritol, pectin, salt, and any dry sweetener, if using, together in a medium bowl. Break up lumps and mix dry ingredients thoroughly. In a medium bowl, beat the egg yolks with a whisk until smooth. Whisk in any liquid sweetener and the half and half. Sprinkle dry mixture over egg-yolk mixture and whisk until well blended.

Heat one-half inch of water in the bottom of a double boiler to a simmer. Put the custard mixture in the top pan and place over, but not touching, the hot water. Cook, stirring constantly with a heat-resistant spatula, until slightly thickened and an instant-read thermometer reads 175° to 180° F. This may take about 8 to 12 minutes. Scrape the sides of the pan often with the spatula and scrape off the custard that sticks to the spatula itself with a knife or a second spatula while cooking, to prevent any lumps from forming. (If you do get

---

I often see recipes for low-carb ice cream made with Splenda, but the ones I've tried always turn to cement after a few hours in the freezer. Maybe there is something I don't know, or maybe it is meant to be eaten immediately after it is made while it is still like soft-serve, but even commercial ice creams made with sugar contain emulsifiers and ingredients that depress their freezing point to keep them scoopable. (Premium ice creams made with real cream are naturally harder than cheap ones, which contain a lot of air.)

The high-intensity sweetener can be of your choice. When using sucralose or Splenda, a small amount of acesulfame potassium (acesulfame K) will give a more natural sweet taste than sucralose alone. (Sweet One, Sunette, and Diabetisweet contain acesulfame K.) Stevia can be used instead. Stevia blends, which contain stevia and fructooligosaccharide or inulin can be used in place of both the poly-d and the high-intensity sweetener if desired, but keep the erythritol.

lumps, remove the custard from the heat and whisk vigor-
ously until smooth.) Remove pan from the heat and stir in
vanilla. Strain the custard into a bowl and place the bowl in
the ice bath to cool it quickly. Continue to stir until cold.
Cover and chill the custard thoroughly (8 hours or overnight) in the refrigerator.

Whip the egg whites until foamy and add cream of tartar (if
not using a copper bowl). Continue to whip until stiff but
not dry. In a second bowl, with the same beaters, whip the 3
cups of cream until thick but not stiff, being careful not to
over beat (or it will make butter). Stir the custard mixture,
pressing out any lumps that may have formed and gently
fold the cream and egg whites into the custard.

Churn according to the directions for your ice cream maker.
(It takes about 25 minutes with my Kitchen Aid Mixer attachment.) Scrape ice cream into a shallow container and
cover with a piece of parchment paper laid directly on top of
the ice cream. Cover container tightly with a lid or foil and
place in freezer for 2 to 3 hours to ripen before serving. If
frozen for longer, let soften in refrigerator until scoop-able.

SERVING:

All homemade ice cream that has been stored in the freezer
for more than a few hours needs to soften in the refrigerator
before serving. The length of time depends on how solidly
it is frozen and the thickness of the layer of ice cream in the
container. One recipe of **French Vanilla Ice Cream**, frozen in
a 2-inch layer, may soften in as little as 10 minutes. If the layer
is thicker, it may take up to 30 minutes or more. Set a timer
and check it every 10 minutes until you learn how long it
takes. Freezing the ice cream in several smaller containers will
make it faster to bring one portion up to serving temperature
and will prolong the storage life of the rest of the batch, which
will not then be subjected to repeated softening and refreezing.

MAKES ABOUT 2 QUARTS OR 16 SERVINGS OF ½ CUP.

Per serving—Net carbohydrate: 2.3 grams (count excludes 3 grams of sugar alcohol);
Protein: 3.6 grams; Fiber: 2.8 grams; Fat: 20.4 grams; Calories: 202

Total weight: 42 ounces or 1.2 kilograms

Weight per serving: 2⅝ ounces or 74 grams

Preparation time: 1 hour active; 11 hours total, including chilling and freezing time.

NOTES:

This recipe will work for tub-
style, manual or electric ice
cream makers, the kind that
use salt and ice. The instructions for the Kitchen Aid ice
cream attachment say the
bowl holds 2 quarts, but this
amount overflows the bowl,
so for the Kitchen Aid and the
small counter-top models, like
Cuisinart (which hold 1 quart),
cut the recipe in half.

———————

I used egg yolks as an emulsifier and erythritol to lower the
freezing temperature in this
recipe to make it creamy and
scoopable. A small amount of
pectin also helps keep it soft.

A ROSE BY ANY OTHER NAME?
Rose water was first distilled from fragrant damask roses grown in Persia and Bulgaria. Turkish delight candy gets its distinctive taste from rose water, which is called *gulub jal* in India and *goolub* in Iran. Do you think it still smells as sweet?

VARIATIONS:

Rose-Flavored Ice Cream

One of the most memorable desserts I ever had was a tiny scoop of rose-flavored ice cream nestled in the heart of a perfect, pale pink rose. It was presented simply, with no cookie or cake to steal the limelight. There were hundreds of guests at the event, and yet every petal was perfect and the ice cream was seemingly suspended in that fleeting, meltingly-spoonable-but-still-firm stage. To pull off such an ambitious feat was a staggering achievement for the restaurant staff. I don't remember exactly where or when it happened, but I'll never forget the night we ate roses.

Add ¾ teaspoon rose water and reduce vanilla extract to 1 teaspoon in recipe for **French Vanilla Ice Cream**, above. Add a tiny bit of red food coloring or red fruit juice if you want a pink tint.

Coconut Ice Cream

Make custard for **French Vanilla Ice Cream** as in recipe above, but reduce vanilla extract to 1 teaspoon and add 1 teaspoon coconut extract. Stir one cup (8½ ounces) of coconut milk into finished custard and chill for 8 hours or overnight as directed. When ready to finish ice cream, use 2 cups of heavy cream rather than 3 cups. (You are just replacing some of cream with an equal amount of coconut milk.) Proceed according to instructions.

MAKES ABOUT 16 SERVINGS OF ½ CUP ICE CREAM.

Per serving—Net carbohydrate: 2.3 grams; Protein: 3.5 grams; Fiber: 2.8 grams; Fat: 16.3 grams; Calories: 172

Total weight: 42 ounces or 75 grams

Weight per serving: 2⅝ ounces or 74 grams

Preparation time: 1 hour active; 11 hours total, including chilling and freezing time.

Vanilla Extract

"Plain vanilla" is a very misleading description of the world's most popular flavor. Kids often think "vanilla" means unflavored, but just try making a pudding or custard without this aromatic, mellow ingredient, and you will discover how important it is. And imagine what it would have been like to live in a plain gray world before the discovery of the Americas—with no vanilla (or chocolate!).

However, most vanilla extracts contain corn syrup, even when the label says "pure vanilla extract." I've found several brands that contain no sugar (see Sources). You can also make your own vanilla quite easily. Here's how I do it:

Split a vanilla bean lengthwise, being careful to retain all the tiny seeds, and place it in a small glass bottle (fold or cut bean to fit). Cover with brandy, rum, or vodka, making sure the vanilla bean is completely submerged, and cap the bottle. Give the bottle a shake occasionally. It will be usable in about 4 weeks. Replenish the liquor in the bottle as it is used. When the vanilla bean loses its scent, replace it with a fresh one. The strength of the extract will vary with time, so taste it and use more or less if necessary.

Orchids make up the largest group of flowering plants in the world, but only one, the vanilla plant, produces an edible fruit.

Whipped Cream

Thanks to the new interest in fresh, local foods, I can now buy cream from a local dairy at the grocery store. It comes in glass bottles with a hefty deposit, and it is not ultra-pasteurized. It comes from cows eating a natural diet of grass, and it tastes wonderful.

1 cup heavy cream (8 ounces)
Sugar substitute equivalent to 1 tablespoon sugar or more to taste
1 teaspoon sugar-free vanilla extract, optional

Chill the bowl and beaters of an electric mixer. The cream should be 45º F or cooler, or it may turn to butter when it is beaten. Beat cream, sweetener, and vanilla, if using, on high speed until it starts to thicken, and then switch to low, watching carefully. Whip just until it forms soft peaks that droop over when the beaters are raised. Serve at once or refrigerate, covered, for an hour or two.

MAKES 2 CUPS OR 16 SERVINGS OF 2 TABLESPOONS.

Per serving—Net carbohydrate: 0.16 grams; Protein: 0.3 grams; Fiber: 0 grams; Fat: 2.2 grams; Calories: 52

Total weight: 8 ounces or 227 grams

Weight per serving: ¼ ounce or 7 grams

Preparation time: 5 minutes active and total

For cream that holds up longer, soften 1 teaspoon (not a whole packet) of gelatin in 2 tablespoons of water for a few minutes, then heat just until melted. Cool until it is barely warm before beating it into the whipped cream. (The gelatin needs to be slightly warm or the cold cream will cause it to solidify before it is blended.)

You can buy dispensers for whipped cream that can be filled with fresh cream and sweetened to taste. They use a nitrous oxide (N20) cartridge to aerate the cream.

Mascarpone Cream

½ cup (4 ounces or ½ carton) mascarpone cheese
3 tablespoons artificial honey or sugar substitute equal to
    3 tablespoons sugar
1 cup heavy cream

Place a medium bowl and beaters in the freezer for 5 minutes.

In a second bowl, beat the mascarpone and sweetener until fluffy. In the chilled bowl, whip the cream to soft peaks. Fold in the mascarpone and sweetener. Refrigerate until ready to serve.

MASCARPONE CHEESE SUBSTITUTE:
Heat 2 cups heavy cream to 180º F in a stainless steel saucepan. Stir in $1/8$ teaspoon of tartaric acid (available from pharmacists or drugstores). Pour into a clean bowl and refrigerate overnight.

MAKES 8 SERVINGS AS PIE FILLING.

Per serving—Net carbohydrate: 1.8 grams; (count excludes 3 grams of sugar alcohol); Protein: 1.6 grams; Fiber: 0 grams; Fat: 17.3 grams; Calories: 165

Total weight: 17⅛ ounces or 485 grams

Weight per serving: 2⅛ ounces or 61 grams

Preparation time: 10 minutes active and total

Recipe for Mascarpone Cream and Mascapone Cheese Substitute adapted from Shirley O. Corriher's book, Cookwise.

Mascarpone is a rich, Italian-style cream cheese. It can be found in the cheese case in larger supermarkets or specialty stores. In my experience, Trader Joe's usually has the best prices on this as well as other premium cheeses. You may use the Mascarpone Cheese Substitute on this page or regular cream cheese.

PART 5

Snacks, Food for Travel, and "Freebies"

Recipes for entries in boldface are included in this book.

Snacks:

Parmesan Fricos

Easy Biskmix Crackers

Cheese

Protein Shake

Berry Protein Shake

Chocolate Avocado Smoothie

Beef jerky (see Sources for zero-carb jerky)

"Milk"

Chocolate "Milk"

Hot Cocoa

Celery filled with peanut butter or cream cheese

Stuffed Celery or Stuffed Vegetables

Italian Sodas

Jicama Slices with Lime Wedges and Chili Powder

Fresh vegetables with **Blue Cheese Dressing**

Spring Radishes with Sweet Butter

Herb Roasted Olives

Pork rinds (chicharones)

Cheese Puffs and **Cheese Puff sandwiches**

Nuts: almonds, macadamias, pistachios, pecan, or walnuts (Peanuts and cashews are higher in carbs than true nuts.)

Pumpkin seeds

Eggplant and Sun-dried Tomato Mini Pizzas

Mystic Pizza

Fluffy Omelet

Hard Cooked Eggs

Stuffed Eggs

Ready to eat salmon or tuna cups

Tinned sardines

Pâtés and canned pâté spreads

Bacon

Ham with cheese slices, rolled or lettuce wrapped

Smoked salmon and cream cheese roll ups with capers

Coco-choco-chia Bars

Peanut Butter Cookies

Protein Bars

Riccota cheese or plain yogurt with sugar-free flavoring syrup

Fruit Gelatin, p. 54, or prepared, sugar-free gelatin cups. (Don't make it from a boxed powder, which has carbs.)

Almond Crisp Crackers or Cookies

Bran crackers and peanut butter

Chocolate Granola

Snack mix made with nuts, sugar-free chocolate chips, dried cranberries, and flaked coconut

Food for Travel:

It's not difficult to find menu items in restaurants that fit the low-carb lifestyle, but eating while you are in transit or stranded in an unfamiliar place can be a challenge. The vending machines in most hotels and rest stops dispense nothing but junk, and the food choices when you are flying are often even worse. Take along a few foods that don't require refrigeration so you won't be tempted to order out for pizza or to eat the airplane pretzels.

Nuts and seeds

Sugar-free Hot Cocoa mix in individual packages

Meal replacement shake mix in individual packets

Individual, wax-coated cheeses, such as Laughing Cow

Sugar-free chocolate and candy bars

Beef jerky (see sources for zero-carb jerky)

Pre-cooked bacon (Unopened packages can be taken on trips. Refrigeration is not necessary for many brands until the package is opened.)

Small cans of tuna, salmon, sardines, pate, or vienna sausages with tiny jars of mustard, gerkins, or capers (Cost Plus World Market stores sell lots of condiments in small jars.)

Low-carb meal-replacement bars or **Protein Bars**

Pork rinds

Almond Crisp Crackers or **Cookies**

Peanut Butter, Chocolate Chip, or other low-carb cookies

Bran crackers and individual packets of peanut butter

Chocolate Granola

Snack mix of nuts, seeds, sugar-free **Chocolate Chips**, **Dried Cranberries**, and flaked coconut

Sugar-free puddings and Jell-o cups, purchased (Choose a brand that doesn't require refrigeration (not the ones sold from the refrigerator case)

Individual cartons or small cans of coconut or almond milk

"Chips" made of fried, cut up low-carb tortillas

Crackers made of cut up and toasted sheets of Joseph's flatbread.

"Freebies:"

Here are some ideas for foods that are so low in carbs that they almost don't count. (There really are no "freebies"; even a food without carbohydrates can stimulate insulin release if the volume is great enough. The sheer bulk of something like lettuce can stretch the gut enough to cause an insulin response in anticipation of carbs, even if none are actually present. Remember, too, that protein can be converted into a small amount of sugar, so that must also be taken into consideration.)

Bacon

Beef jerky (see Sources for zero-carb jerky)

Ready to eat salmon or tuna cups

Tinned sardines

Pâtés and canned pâté spreads

Sugar free Jell-o, purchased, not made from powder or **Fruit Gelatin**

Pork rinds

Oven Fried Chicken

Roast beef

Sashimi

Steak tartar

Sugar-free cold cuts

Italian Cream Sodas

Flavored coffee drinks

Sugar-free Soft Drinks

Hot broth, plain or with kelp or shirataki noodles, shrimp, chicken, beef, pork, or fish, and herbs or spices as desired.

Bran crackers

Fish or shrimp wrapped in toasted nori

ADVICE FROM THE EXPERTS:

"I have observed anecdotally, and Dr. Mike Eades (from *Protein Power*) saw this regularly in his clinic, that the three things that look okay on a low-carb diet but may actually be trouble are cheese, nuts, and peanut butter."

– Dr. Richard D. Feinman,
SUNY Downstate in Brooklyn, New York;
Co-Editor-In-Chief of Nutrition & Metabolism.

Recommended Reading:
Books, Blogs, and Websites

Books:

Atkins, Robert C. 2002 (revised edition). *Dr. Atkins' New Diet Revolution*. NY: HarperCollins.

Atkins, Robert C. with Vernon, Mary C., and Eberstein, Jacqueline A. 2004. *Atkins Diabetes Revolution: The Groundbreaking Approach to Preventing and Controlling Type 2 Diabetes*. NY: HarperCollins.

Berkowitz, Keith and Berkowitz, Valerie. 2009. *The Stubborn Fat Fix: Eat Right to Lose Weight and Cure Metabolic Burnout without Hunger or Exercise*. NY: Rodale Inc.

Bernstein, Richard K. 2007. *Dr. Bernstein's Diabetes Solution: The Complete Guide to Achieving Normal Blood Sugars*. NY: Little, Brown and Company.

Bowden, Jonny. 2010. *Living Low Carb: Controlled-Carbohydrate Eating for Long-Term Weight Loss*. NY: Sterling Publishing.

Bowden, Jonny. 2010. *The Most Effective Ways to Live Longer*. Beverly, MA: Fair Winds Press.

Briffa, John. 2007. *The True You Diet: The revolutionary diet programme that identifies your unique body chemistry and reveals the foods that are right for YOU*. London, UK: Hay House.

Carlson, James. 2008. *Genocide: How Your Doctor's Dietary Ignorance Will Kill You!!!!*. Charleston, SC: BookSurge Publishing.

Cordain, Loren. 2002. *The Paleo Diet: Lose Weight and Get Healthy by Eating the Food You Were Designed to Eat*. Hoboken, NJ: John Wiley & Sons.

Davis, William, MD, 2011. *Wheat Belly*. NY: Rodale Books.

Donaldson, Blake F. 1962. *Strong Medicine*. Garden City, NY: Doubleday.

Eades, Michael R and Eades, Mary Dan. 2009. *The 6-Week Cure for the Middle-Aged Middle: The Simple Plan to Flatten Your Belly Fast!* NY: Crown Publishing.

Eades, Michael R and Eades, Mary Dan. 2001. *The Protein Power Lifeplan*. Grand Central Publishing.

Enig, Mary and Fallon, Sally. 2006. *Eat Fat, Lose Fat: The Healthy Alternative to Trans Fats*. NY: Plume.

Fallon, Sally with Enig, Mary G. 1999 (revised edition). *Nourishing Traditions: The Cookbook that Challenges Politically Correct Nutrition and the Diet Dictocrats*. Washington, DC: New Trends Publishing, Inc.

Gedgaudas, Nora. 2009. *Primal Body-Primal Mind: Empower Your Total Health The Way Evolution Intended (...And Didn't)*. Portland, OR: Primal Body-Primal Mind Publishing.

Groves, Barry. 2007. *Natural Health & Weight Loss*. London, UK: Hammersmith Press Ltd.

Groves, Barry. 2008. *Trick And Treat – how 'healthy eating' is making us ill*. London, UK: Hammersmith Press Ltd.

Hahn, Fred, Eades, Mary Dan and Eades, Michael R. 2002. *The Slow Burn Fitness Revolution: The Slow Motion Exercise That Will Change Your Body in 30 Minutes a Week*. NY: Broadway.

Hahn, Frederick. 2008. *Strong Kids, Healthy Kids: The Revolutionary Program for Increasing Your Child's Fitness in 30 Minutes a Week*. NY: AMACOM.

Kauffmann, Joel M. 2006. *Medical Myths: Why Medical Treatment Causes 200,000 Deaths in the USA Each Year, and How to Protect Yourself*. West Conshohocken, PA: Infinity Publishing.

Keith, Lierre. 2009. *The Vegetarian Myth: Food, Justice, and Sustainability*. Oakland, CA: PM Press.

Kendrick, Malcolm. 2008. *The Great Cholesterol Con: The Truth About What Really Causes Heart Disease and How to Avoid It*. London, UK: John Blake.

McCleary, Larry. 2007. *The Brain Trust Program: A Scientifically Based Three-Part Plan to Improve Memory, Elevate Mood, Enhance Attention, Alleviate Migraine and Menopausal Symptoms, and Boost Mental Energy*. NY: Perigee Books.

McCleary, Larry, 2010. *Feed Your Brain Lose Your Belly*. Teocalli, LLC.

McCully, Kilmer S. and McCully, Martha. 2000. *The Heart Revolution: the Extraordinary Discovery That Finally Laid the Cholesterol Myth to Rest*. NY: Harper Paperbacks.

Moore, Jimmy. 2005. *Livin' La Vida Low-carb: My Journey from Flabby Fat to Sensationally Skinny in One Year*. Bangor, ME: Booklocker.com.

Moore, Jimmy. 2009. *21 Life Lessons From Livin' La Vida Low-Carb: How the Healthy Low-Carb Lifestyle Changed Everything I Thought I Knew*. Book Surge Publishing. D. S.

Phinney, Stephen D., and Volek, Jeff S. 2011. *The Art and Science of Low Carbohydrate Living: An Expert Guide to Making the Life-Saving Benefits of Carbohydrate Restriction Sustainable and Enjoyable.* Beyond Obesity LLC.

Price, Weston A. 1939. *Nutrition and Physical Degeneration.* NY: McGraw-Hill.

Ravnskov, Uffe. 2009. *Fat and Cholesterol are Good for You.* Yale, OK: GB Publishing.

Rosedale, Ron. 2005. *The Rosedale Diet; Turn off Your Hunger Switch!* Harper Paperbacks.

Ruhl, Jenny. 2008. *Blood Sugar 101: What They Don't Tell You About Diabetes*, Technion Books.

Sisson, Mark. 2009. *The Primal Blueprint: Reprogram Your Genes for Effortless Weight Loss, Vibrant Health, and Boundless Energy.* Malibu, CA: Primal Nutrition, Inc.

Su, Robert K., MD, 2009. *Carbohydrates Can Kill.* Portsmouth, VA: JEV Publishing.

Taubes, Gary. 2008. *Good Calories, Bad Calories: Fats, Carbs, and the Controversial Science of Diet and Health.* NY: Anchor.

Taubes, Gary, 2010. *Why We Get Fat and What to Do About It.* NY: Knopf.

Volek, Jeff and Campbell, Adam. 2008. *Men's Health TNT Diet: The Explosive New Plan to Blast Fat, Build Muscle, and Get Healthy in 12 Weeks.* NY: Rodale Inc.

Westman, Eric C., Phinney, Stephen D., Volek, Jeff S. 2010. *New Atkins for a New You: The Ultimate Diet for Shedding Weight and Feeling Great.* NY: Fireside.

Low-Carb Cookbooks:

Bernstein, Richard K., M.D. 2005. *The Diabetes Diet.* Little, Brown, and Company.

Carpender, Dana. 2002. *500 Low-Carb Recipes from Snacks to Dessert That the Whole Family Will Love.* Fair Winds Press (MA)

Carpender, Dana. 2005. *200 Low-Carb Slow Cooker Recipes: Healthy Dinners That Are Ready When You Are!*

Baker, Judy Barnes. 2007. *Carb Wars; Sugar is the New Fat.* Duck in a Boat.

Eades, Mary Dan, M.D., and Eades, Michael R., M.D. 2005. *The Low Carb CookwoRX Cookbook.* Wiley.

Eades, Mary Dan, M.D. and Solom, Ursula. 2005. *The Low-Carb Comfort Food Cookbook.* Wiley.

Eloff, Jennifer. 2003 and 2004. *Splendid Low-Carbing for Life, Volume 1 and 2.* Eureka

Publishing.

Eloff, Jennifer. 2004. *Splendid Low-Carb Desserts*. Eureka Publishing.
McLagan, Jennifer. 2008. *Fat; An Appreciation of a Misunderstood Ingredient, With Recipes.* Ten Speed Press.

McCullough, Fran. 2003. *Good Fat: Low-Carb: with 100 Recipes*. New York: Scribner.

Stella, George and Stella, Christian. *Eating Stella Style: 2006. Low-Carb Recipes for Healthy Living*. Simon & Schuster

Stella, George. 2009. *George Stella's Good Carb Family Cookbook*. Dynamic Housewares Inc.

Blogs and Websites:

About.com, Laura Dolson, www.lowcarbdiets.about.com

Dr. Berstein's Diabetes Solution, www.diabetes-book.com

Blood Sugar 101, Jenny Ruhl, www.phlaunt.com/diabetes/

Dr. John Briffa, www.drbriffa.com/

Dr. Jonny Bowden, www.jonnybowden.com/blogger.html

Adam Campbell, www.thefitnessinsider.menshealth.com

The Brain Trust Program, Dr. Larry McCleary, www.drmccleary.com

Carbohydrates Can Kill, Dr. Robert K. Su, www.carbohydratescankill.com

The Cholesterol Myths, Uffe Ravnskov, M.D., Ph.D., www.ravnskov.nu/cholesterol.htm

Controlled Carbohydrate Nutrition, Jacqueline Eberstein, www.controlcarb.com

Diabetes Health, www.diabeteshealth.com

Diet Doctor, Dr. Andreas Eenfeldt, www.dietdoctor.com

Jennifer Eloff, www.low-carb-news.blogspot.com

Fat Head, the Movie, Tom Naughton, www.fathead-movie.com

Dr. Richard Feinman, www.rdfeinman.wordpress.com

Female Fitness and Nutrition, Cassandra Forscythe, www.cassandraforsythe.blogspot.com

Lauren Benning, www.healthyindulgences.blogspot.com
Hold The Toast, Dana Carpender, www.holdthetoast.com

Innovative Metabolic Solutions, Dr. Mary C. Vernon, Dr. Eric Westman, and Gary Taubes
www.myimsonline.com

In Search of the Perfect Human Diet, CJ Hunt, www.perfecthumandiet.us

Junkfood Science, Sandy Szwarc, www.junkfoodscience.blogspot.com

Livin' La Vida Low-Carb, Jimmy Moore, www.livinlavidalowcarb.com/blog

Living With Diabetes, David Mendosa, www.mendosa.com

Low Carb Daily, www.lowcarbdaily.com

Mark's Daily Apple, Mark Sisson, www.marksdailyapple.com

Nutrition Data about any food, www.nutritiondata.com

The Nutrition and Metabolism Society, www.www.nmsociety.org

Protein Power, Drs. Michael and Mary Dan Eades, www.proteinpower.com

Second Opinions , Dr. Barry Groves, www.second-opinions.co.uk/index.htm

Slow Burn, Fred Hahn, www.slowburnfitness.com

Gary Taubes, www.www.garytaubes.com/blog

USDA National Nutrient Database, www.nal.usda.gov/fnic/foodcomp/search

Weston A. Price Foundation for Wise Traditions, www.westonaprice.org

Lists for Customizing Menus

Substitutes for breads, crackers, pasta, rice, and potatoes, with net carb counts:

Breads

Bannock Bread - 3.9 g per slice

Cheddar Biscuits - 2.2 g each

Cheddar Cheese Muffins - 3 g each

Cheese Puffs - 0.3 g per 1 whole slice or 4 quarter-slices

Lettuce leaves - 0.4 g per large leaf

Low-carb tortillas - (see Sources) 3.0 g each for 6- to 7-inch; 7 g for large

Low-carb Breads, Pizza Crusts, Bagels, Etc. (See Sources)

Oopsie Buns - 0.9 g each

Whole Grain Bread - 1-Loaf Recipe Without Flax: Slice 4.9 G

Whole Grain Bread - 1 Loaf Recipe With Flax: Slice 4.2 G

Whole Grain Bread - 2-loaf recipe without flax: slice 2.2 g;
     Roll 4 G, Hamburger Bun 6.9 G; Or Hot Dog Bun: 10.8 G

Whole Grain Bread - 2-Loaf Recipe With Flax: Slice 1.9 G; Roll: 3.5 G; Hamburger Bun:
     6 G; Or Hot Dog Bun: 9.3 G

Crackers

Almond Crisps And Variations - 0.2 g each

Barley Rusks - 1 g each (thin) or 2 g each (thick)

Cheese Puffs - 0.3 g per slice

Easy Biskmix Crackers - 0.8 g for a half batch

Fricos - 0.3 net g

Joseph's Flatbread (see Sources), cut up and toasted, ½ g for each of
     16 crackers per sheet

Low-Carb Crackers (see Sources)

Low-carb Tortillas, cut into strips or squares, (see Sources) 3 g for each 6- to 7-inch tortilla

Pasta

Atkins Penne (see Sources) 19 net g per serving

Dreamfields Pasta - (see Sources) 5 digestible g per 2 ounces dry

Kelp Noodles - 0 g per serving

Shirataki Noodles - 0 g per serving

Spaghetti Squash - 7.8 g per half cup, cooked

Rice

Cauliflower Faux Rice - 1.1 g per half cup

Chana Dal - 21.1 g per half cup (high in carbs, but very low glycemic)

Hominy Faux Rice - (Mexican-style only) 4.0 g per half cup

Potato

Celery Root Gratin - 6.6 g per half cup

Celery Root Purée - 8.2 g per half cup

Faux Duchess Potatoes (Cauliflower) - 2.2 g per half cup

Faux Mashed Potatoes (Cauliflower) - 2.2 g per half cup

Faux Potatoes (Cauliflower)- 2.2 g per half cup

Faux Potatoes (Rutabaga) - 6.5 g per half cup

French Fries (Fried Green Beans) - 3.3 per half cup

Ginger Pumpkin Purée - 7.1 g per half cup

Home Fries (Rutabaga) - 7.8 g per half cup

Jicama Shoestring Fries - 4.9 g per half cup

Sources

This is not meant to be an exhaustive list; it is just the things I've come across or heard about from others. Brands and availability will vary widely from one region to another.

Some sources that have multiple entries are marked with an asterisk, and their contact information is listed in the Directory of Sources at the end. If there is only one item from a particular source, contact information for that source is listed with the entry.

Always check the labels when you buy commercial products. Ingredients and nutrition data are constantly in flux, and something that was once OK may not be the next time you purchase it.

Try new products that claim to be low in carbs cautiously to see how you react. If they are sold on sites that solicit customer reviews, check the reports from others before ordering.

BREADS, CAKES, COOKIES, CRACKERS, AND TORTILLAS

Controlled Carb Gourmet (www.controlledcarbgourmet.com) sells rolls, breads, and bagels with zero to 5 net carbs. They also sell low-carb cakes, muffins, and *Big Classic Brownies* with 1 net carb and 16 grams of sugar alcohol per 2-ounce serving, (not a whole brownie.)

Carb Kruncher's (www.low-carbbakery.com) sliced bread has 2.25 net carbs per slice; their bagels and rolls have 5.7 net carbs each. They also make pita bread. All have similar ingredients, which include almond, soy, bran, whole wheat, oat, soy, and sesame flours.

Damascus Bakeries (www.damascusbakery.com) makes a 6 net carb *Flax Roll-Up* and a 10 net carb *Whole Wheat Pita*. There is a store locator on the website.

FlatOut Flatbread (www.flatoutbread.com) makes *Healthy Grain Multigrain with Flax Flatbread* with 8 net carbs. One large *Light FlatOut* flatbread has 6 net carbs. Available in supermarkets nationwide. There is a store finder on the website.

Foods Alive (www.foodsalive.com) makes four kinds of low-carb organic flax crackers. Their other crackers contain maple syrup, molasses, or agave syrup and are not recommended. Available at *Whole Foods** and various Low-Carb Internet Stores.*

Franz Family Bakery (www.usbakery.com) in Oregon sells *Smart Nutrition Net 4*, reduced-carb, high-fiber bread, available in stores nation-wide.

GG Scandinavian Bran Crispbreads are fiber crackers with zero net carbs each. They are available in retail and internet Stores.

Healthwise Bakery (www.healthwisebakery.com) makes breads and bagels with zero net carbs, a multigrain bread with 2 net per slice, and other baked goods. Available from www.lindasdietdelites.com and other online and health stores.

Joseph's Middle East Bakery's Low-Carb Lavash and *Reduced-Carb/Flax, Oat Bran & Whole Wheat Pita Bread*, both of which are available from *Netrition.** Their *Lavash Roll-Ups* have 8 net carbs in each large sheet. (To make crackers, cut a sheet of lavash into pieces, toast on both sides, brush with olive oil, and sprinkle with coarse salt. For cookies, top with cinnamon and granular sweetener. They can also be used as a quick pie crust, topped with sugar-free pudding, jam, or lemon curd.)

Julian's Bakery (www.julianbakery.com) makes several low-carb breads, including *Smart Carb #1,* with only 1 net carb per slice, and *Manna from Heaven* with 2. The company advises diabetics to take readings before and after eating their bread. (One of my recipe testers reported that he had a high blood glucose response to this, so do check to see how you react.) Order from their website or purchase from stores in California and some other states.

La Banderita (www.olemexicanfoods.com) has a *Low Carb Soft Taco* with 5 net carbs.

La Nouba makes sugar-free *Belgian Waffles* with 7 net carbs and *Belgian Coffee Wafers* with 3.4 net per serving of 3. See the listing under CANDY AND SWEETS.

La Tortilla Factory (www.latortillafactory.com) makes low-carb tortillas in two sizes. The original Whole-wheat Tortillas (6- to 7-inch) have 3 net carbs each; the large ones have 5. They make others that are not low-carb, so check the label. They are widely distributed (see store locator on website) or you can order them online from many Internet Stores.*

Low Carb Connoisseur* has a *7 Grain Low Carb Bread* with 2 net carbs and a *7 Grain Cinnamon Raisin Low Carb Bread* with 3 net carbs.

LC Foods for Low Carb Living* sells a wide variety of low-carb products including breads, crackers, cereals, ready-to-bake breads, and mixes. They also sell flours, sweeteners, and baking ingredients for home-baked products with recipes included.

Pepperidge Farm (www.pepperidgefarm.com) makes *Very Thin Soft 100% Whole Wheat Bread* with 6 net carbs per slice. Their *Light Style Extra Fiber* and *Light Style Soft Wheat Bread* have less than 7 net carbs per slice. *Pepperidge Farm* products are widely available.

Rault Foods, Inc. produces *Smackaroos* (www.smackaroos.com), low-carb crackers with 1 net carb, in six flavors: plain, garlic, onion, rye, sesame, and cinnamon. Available from some low-carb internet stores.*

A number of baked cheese crackers are available from low-carb internet stores, including *Kitchen Table Bakers'* (kitchentablebakers.com) *Gourmet Cheese Crisps*, which come in 8 flavors, including Aged Parmesan, Garlic, and Italian Herb. A serving of three has less than 1 net carb. *Grace Island Baked Cheese Crisps*, come in four varieties: Asiago, Parmesan and Italian Herb, Romano and Black Pepper, and Baby Swiss. A packet of 14 small crackers has 1 net carb.

Mama Lupe's (www.tortillaking.com) *Low Carb Tortillas* with 3 net carbs can be purchased in stores and online from *Low Carb Connoiseur** and *Netrition.**

Mission Foods (www.missionmenus.com) sells a line of *Carb Balance Tortillas* consisting of 6-inch *Whole Wheat and Flour Tortillas* (6 net carbs); 8-inch flour tortillas (7 net), and 10-inch whole wheat (10 net).

Hill & Valley Inc. (www.hillandvalley.net) sells over 200 varieties of trans fat-free, sugar-free, and no-sugar-added baked goods, but only a few are low-carb. They are made with regular flour, sugar alcohols, and Splenda. Their products are sold in some supermarket bakeries (refer to their store locator) or order online.

Maine Cottage Foods makes *Low Carb Chocolate Chunk Brownies* (2.4 net carbs), *Nut Cupcakes* (1.2 and 1.8 net carb), and *Ricotta Kisses* (under 1 net carb). See also under CANDY.

Safe at the Plate! (www.carb-one.com) sells *Carb-one* muffins with 1 net carb and breads with 3 per serving. Their products are formulated for those with diabetes and celiac disease. All are sugar-free, grain-free, dairy-free, trans-fat-free, and gluten-free. (Dr. Richard Bernstein recommends the chocolate muffins as a meal replacement, especially for those with type 1 diabetes; he believes they actually have more than one gram of carbs, but are digested very slowly and can be covered with a small dose of insulin.) The company provides only standard shipping, so online ordering is feasible only for those who live in the Northeast.

Toufayan Bakeries' Low-Carb Pita Bread can be purchased from *Netrition.com*.

Wellness Bakeries (www.wellnessbakeries.com) sells a gluten-free mix for *Chocolate Bliss Cake* and *Chocolate Ganache Frosting*. Ingredients in the mix include almond flour and whey protein isolate; it is sweetened with erythritol and stevia for 3 net carbs per slice.

BEANS

Chana dal, also called Bengal dram beans, are sweet, nutty, split baby garbanzo beans. They have a much lower glycemic index than regular garbanzos. You can find them in Indian groceries, Asian stores, and some supermarkets, though care must be taken since yellow split-peas with a much higher glycemic load may be wrongly labeled as chana dal. Dependable sources for chana dal are available from David Mendosa's site at: www.mendosa.com/chanadal.

Eden sells black soy beans, garbanzo beans, and black beans. They are cooked in cans that are not lined with bisphenol-A, a plastic that is thought to contain an endocrine disrupting chemical.

BEVERAGES

BOTTLED AND CANNED DRINKS AND DRINK MIXES

Adirondack fruit-flavored spring water, *Clear'n'Natural* and *Waist Watcher* diet soft drinks are made using a blend of sucralose and acesulfame K. They are only available in fifteen eastern states. The website (www.adirondackbeverages.com) has a store locator.

Diet Rite Cola (www.dietrite.com), introduced in 1958, was the first diet soft drink. In 2000, it became the first soft drink made with Splenda, although they have since added acesulfame K. It contains no caffeine and no sodium. Available nationwide.

Carbsmart* sells Splenda-sweetened *CS Lemonade* with 1 net carb per serving. There are many other sugar-free powders available, but most of them contain aspartame.

Hansen's Natural (www.hansens.com) *Fruit-Flavored Diet Soft Drinks* have zero calories, no caffeine, and no preservatives. They are sweetened with Splenda and acesulfame K. Hansen's products are widely available.

Jones Soda Company (www.jonessoda.com) has three *Zilch Zero Calorie*, Splenda-sweetened, caffeine-free, carbonated beverages: black cherry, pomegranate, and vanilla. Their website includes a store locator.

Kool-Aid, the original version, is still sugar-free, readily available, and inexpensive. You can choose any sweetener you like and make it with plain or carbonated water.

The National Beverage Company makes *La Croix* (www.lacroixwater.com) *Sparkling Spring Waters* and several lightly flavored, calorie- and carb-free sodas (orange, lemon, lime, grapefruit, berry, and cran-raspberry). These beverages are available at supermarkets, Target, and large warehouse stores.

WHITE TEA

The antioxidant, healthful properties of green tea are due to its polyphenols, which are even higher in mild, sweet white tea, which is minimally processed and naturally low in caffeine.

Celestial Seasonings (www.celestialseasonings.com) sells decaffeinated white teabags called *China White Pearl*, widely available.

The Republic of Tea (www.republicoftea.com) sells 9 different flavors of white tea, but only the *Kiwi Pear* flavor is decaffeinated. *Cost Plus World Market** and *Starbuck's* carry *The Republic of Tea* brand but may not stock all the varieties.

See MILK, CREAM, AND SUBSTITUTES for sugar-free milk, coconut milk, and almond milk.

CANDY, SWEETS, AND MEAL-REPLACEMENT AND PROTEIN BARS

Asher's, Atkins, Russell Stover, Whitman's, Ross, and Judy's Candy Co. are just some of the low-carb candy brands available. Most of them are sweetened with maltitol and carry warnings about excess consumption. Any that combine other sweeteners with maltitol will have fewer unpleasant side effects, but candy sweetened with soluble fibers like oligofructose, inulin, and polydextrose, are a better choice. One caveat: be sure to check the serving size—the carb count in large print may sound low for a whole candy bar, but it may really be the amount in a small portion. The low-carb internet stores* carry most of the brands listed here.

Atkins makes *Advantage* and *Daybreak* meal replacement bars and *Endulge* candy bars in many flavors. All are widely available in stores and online.

Asher's (www.ashers.com) makes cordial cherries with liquid centers with less than 1 net carb in 3 pieces. They are made with maltitol, sorbitol, and sucralose. They also make sugar-free chocolate bars, fudge, jellies, and caramels, but most contain maltitol. They are available in many grocery stores or online.

D-lectable's (www.d-lectable.com or www.citynutandcandyonline.com) *Healthy Option Candies* and *Chocolates* are sweetened with either maltitol or an all-natural sweetener made from inulin and polydextrose. Their *Sugar-free Dark Chocolate Melting & Shaving Bar* is made with inulin and polydextrose. Their products are available online and in some *Trader Joe's*.*

Jelly Belly (www.jellybelly.com) makes sugar-free jelly beans with maltitol and Splenda.

Judy's Candy Company (www.judyscandy.com) makes sugar-free caramels (with maltitol, but real cream).

La Nouba (www.lanouba.be) is based in Belgium. Their *Sugar-Free Marshmallows* have zero net carbs (sweetened with isomalt and maltitol, so exercise some caution). They also make sugar-free *Chocolate Covered Marshmallows* and no-sugar-added *Fruit Spreads* (1.6 net carb per tablespoon), *Dark Chocolate Bars* (1.1 net carbs), and *Belgian Chocolate Bars* (3.5 net carbs). Their no-sugar-added *Belgian Waffles* have 7 net carbs and thin ones called *Belgian Coffee Waffles* have 3.4 net carbs in three waffles. (The thin ones are my favorites. I like put one in the toaster oven to crisp and enjoy it with a cup of coffee.) They can be ordered by the case from the website. *Netrition*,* *Carbsmart*,* and *Low Carb You**sell *La Nouba* products.

Low Carb Specialties Inc. (www.lowcarbspecialties.com) sells Choco*perfection* bars in dark, milk chocolate, raspberry, and almond flavors. These delectable bars are sweetened with oligofructose, a beneficial prebiotic fiber, and stevia. Each bar has 2 digestible grams of carbohydrate and 14 grams of fiber. They also sell chocolate chips and Sweet*perfection*, a granular sweetener. All can be ordered from the website or the stores in the Sources Directory. Health food stores also sell them.

Marich sells chocolate covered nuts, dried cherries, espresso beans, caramels, and bridge mix through *Carbsmart*.*

Maine Cottage Foods (www.mainecottagefoods.com) makes sugar-free, maltitol-free chocolate, and low-carb, gluten-free baked goods sweetened with erythritol and inulin. *Their Sugar Free Chocolate Bars* (1 to 2 net carbs) and *Chocolate Bark* (1 to 2.4 net carbs) are available from *Carbsmart*.* All their products, including their *Low Carb Chocolate Chunks* (less than 1 net carb) and their baked *Low Carb Chocolate Chunk Brownies* (2.4 net carbs), *Nut Cupcakes* (1.8 net carb), and a doughnut-like pastry called *Baci di Ricotta* (1 net carb), are available on their website.

Quest Bars are not just thinly disguised candy, like other nutrition bars, according to the makers. They have 20 grams of protein, no sugar alcohols or soy, and only 4 or 5 net grams of digestible carbs, all of which come from nuts. They are sweetened with lo han guo and sucralose. Available online at: www.questproteinbar.com or by calling: 1-888-212-0601.

Walden Farms (www.waldenfarms.com) makes marshmallow cream with no calories, no carbs, and no fat. Widely available in stores and online.

York (www.hersheyssugarfree.com), now owned by *Hershey's*, sells *Sugar-Free Peppermint Patties* that are indistinguishable from the originals, but they are heavy on the maltitol. They are widely available; see Sources Directory.

See CHOCOLATE for additional choices.

CHEESE

Mascarpone cheese (Italian cream cheese) from *BelGioioso* (www.belgioioso.com) is not hard to find, but the price varies a great deal. *Trader Joe's** usually has a good value for mascarpone and many other kinds of cheese. The big box stores like *Costco* also have good prices on premium cheese, but you must buy it in larger quantities. This and other brands of mascarpone are available from *Amazon,** but the shipping may be prohibitive.

Parmigiano-Reggiano is made from raw milk from grass-fed cows. The name can only be used for cheese imported from certain regions in Northern Italy, but similar cheeses called simply *Parmesan* are widely available. It is expensive, but *Trader Joe's* and *Costco* sell it for less.

CHOCOLATE

COCOA POWDER

Droste (www.droste.nl) *Dutch Cocoa*, and *Saco* (www.sacofoods.com) *Premium Dutched Cocoa* have 1 net gram of carbohydrate per tablespoon. Widely available.

Ghirardelli's (www.ghirardelli.com) natural cocoa powder is available at many grocery stores. It has 1 net gram per tablespoon.

SEMI-SWEET CHOCOLATE CHIPS, BAKING CHOCOLATE, AND CHOCOLATE COATING

Callebaut (www.callebaut.com) makes *No Added Sugar Dark Chocolate, Milk Chocolate*, and *White Chocolate Blocks* sweetened with maltitol, and *Unsweetened Chocolate Liquor Blocks* and *Chunks*. These can be purchased at *Chocosphere** or www.*Worldwidechocolate.com*.

Dixie Diner's 1 net carb, semi-sweet, *Carb Counters Chocolate Chunkies*, sweetened with sucralose are available from *Netrition.**

Ghirardelli's (ghirardelli.com) *100% Cacao Unsweetened Chocolate Baking Bar* (1.7 net carbs per section) is available in stores.

Guittard unsweetened *Baking Chocolate* (2 net carbs per ½ oz) and unsweetened chocolate in convenient 1-inch disks, called *Bittersweet Chocolate Onyx Wafers* (5 net carbs per ½ oz), can be ordered from *The King Arthur Flour Company.* * *Chocosphere** also has the wafers but calls them *Guittard's Classic 'Oban' Cocoa Liquor Wafers.*

*The King Arthur Flour Company** sells *Sugar-Free Semisweet Chocolate Chips* sweetened with maltitol. They have about 1 net carb per ½ oz.

Low Carb Specialties Inc. (www.lowcarbspecialties.com) sells chocolate chips made with oligofructose and stevia.

Nevada Manna sugar-free, mini-sized chocolate chips with no sugar alcohols are available from *Carbsmar*t (www.carbsmart.com). They are sweetened with acesulfame K and sucralose and contain 1 net gram of carbohydrate and 7 grams of fiber (polydextrose) in two tablespoons.

Maine Cottage Foods (www.mainecottagefoods.com) makes erythritol-sweetened *Low-Carb Chocolate Chunks.*

Merckens' Milk and Dark Chocolate Dietetic Coating can be ordered from *Kitchen Krafts* (www.kitchenkrafts.com). It contains maltitol.

Nestlé's Toll House pre-melted, unsweetened *Choco Bake* chocolate (2 net carbs) is widely available in stores.

Scharffen Berger makes an *Unsweetened 99% Cocoa Mini-Chef Bar* and *Unsweetened Couverture Block* with 99% cocoa content. These can be purchased at *Chocosphere** or www.*Worldwidechocolate.com.*

Valrhona has a number of different varieties of 100% cocoa, *Unsweetened Pure Cocoa Paste Blocs,* and *Xocoline Sugar-Free Milk* and *Dark Chocolate* sweetened with maltitol. Available from *Chocosphere** or www.*Worldwidechocolate.com.*

See CANDY for chocolate bars and chocolate candy.

COCONUT
Unsweetened coconut is usually available with the baking products or in the bulk bins at grocery stores. *Bob's Red Mill** sells it in stores and online. *The King Arthur Flour * Company* also sells it online.

Coconut flour is not as easy to find as grated or flaked coconut, but it is becoming more common with the increased demand for gluten-free baking ingredients. Most of the Low-Carb Internet Stores* have it. You may also find it in health food stores and some groceries.

See FATS AND OILS for sources for coconut butter or oil.

See MILK, CREAM, AND SUBSTITUTES for sources for coconut milk as a beverage and canned coconut milk.

CONDIMENTS, PICKLES, AND SAUCES

KETCHUP AND BARBECUE SAUCE

Heinz Reduced Sugar Ketchup has 1 gram of carbs per serving. It is sweetened with sucralose. Available in some stores and from low-carb sites listed in Sources Directory below.

Jok'n Al makes low carb ketchup and barbecue sauce, available from the sites in Sources Directory.

Nature's Hollow makes a sugar-free barbecue sauce sweetened with xylitol with 2 net carbs per tablespoon. It can be ordered from *Netrition.**

MAYONNAISE

Most commercial mayonnaise is made with vegetable oil (usually soy) and is loaded with omega-6 oils, trans fats, sugar, and MSG. Some brands are made with part olive oil, but most still have sugar, so also check the carb count.

Duke's brand is sugar-free, but it is made with soy oil. It is commonly available in the Southeast or it can be ordered from www.southernconnoisseur.com.

Hellman's Real Mayonnaise is also sugar free, but, again, the first ingredient is soy oil.

Spectrum makes an organic mayonnaise with olive oil, but the first ingredient is still soy.

Walden Farms* makes a zero-carb, zero-fat mayonnaise.

PICKLES AND PICKLED PEPPERS

Mount Olive makes a full line of sugar-free sweet pickles sweetened with sucralose, including a sweet pickle relish. Information is here: www.mtolivepickles.com. They also make no-sugar-added sweet gherkins. Mt Olive has a store locator on their website. You can order online from www.low-carb.com.*

Sport peppers: You can order the Original, bite-sized, hot peppers used for Chicago-style hot dogs from *Vienna Beef (www.viennabeef.com).* They warn, "Caution: contents may make you the life of the party." *Hollywood Sauce* (www.hollywoodsauce.com) carries a similar product, *Il Primo Hot Dog Sport Peppers.*

Vlasic makes sugar-free relish and sugar-free bread and butter pickles that can be chopped to use as relish. *Vlasic* products are available at retail grocers.

SALSA

Salsa Verde is available from grocery stores or online from *www.mexgrocer.com* or *Amazon.** The label for *Embasa* brand lists a net carb count of zero.

CRANBERRIES

Fresh and frozen cranberries are easy to find in the fall. Fresh ones can be frozen in the original package, just as they come from the store, so stock up with enough to last through the year. Dried cranberries usually contain a lot of sugar. Unsweetened, they are too tart to be palatable, and many that say "sugar-free" have been sweetened with fruit juice or a high-carb form of sugar other than sucrose. (Check the carb count on the label to see if they contain sugar.)

Shoreline Fruit (www.shorelinefruitcompany.com) sells unsweetened dried cranberries online. They sound expensive by the pound, but they are very lightweight.

LC Foods for Low Carb Living* sells dried cranberries and other dried fruits without sugar or sugar alcohols.

EGGS AND EGG PRODUCTS

I hesitate to recommend substitutes for fresh eggs. Eggs are a good source of natural protein and healthful fats, but some people may prefer an alternative for recipes that are not cooked. They are also useful when you need just a little and don't want to sacrifice a whole egg or when you need a lot of whites and don't want to waste the yolks.

Liquid egg whites are available in cartons in the refrigerated case at grocery stores. Check the label; some brands have been heated too much to whip properly.

Davidson's Pasteurized Eggs in the shell, (www.safeeggs.com) are available in many supermarkets nationwide. See website for store locator.

Deb El Just Whites, powdered egg whites can be found in most supermarkets.

Crystal Farms (www.betterneggs.com) pasteurized, liquid *Better'n Eggs* and *All Whites* are widely available. The *All Whites* can't be used for whipping but will work for other purposes and are available in most supermarkets. *Better'n Eggs* is a pasteurized, whole-egg replacement made from egg whites. It does not contain real yolks, which are needed as emulsifiers in many recipes, such as ice creams and sauces.

Nulaid Foods Inc. (www.nulaid.com) *ReddiEgg Real Egg Product* is a liquid, whole-egg replacement made from egg whites. It is sold mainly on the East Coast.

Powdered whole eggs, egg whites, and yolks, can be ordered from *The King Arthur Flour Company**, the *Eggstore* (www.eggstore.com*), Barry Farm Foods* (www.barryfarm.com), and others. Unlike the liquid egg white products, reconstituted, powdered egg whites can be whipped.

EXTRACTS AND FLAVORINGS

Better Than Bouillon Premium (www.superiortouch.com) cooking bases can be used in small amounts to flavor soups, sauces, and stock. They have 1 net carb per teaspoon. Do not add extra salt when using without tasting first. They can be found in supermarkets and at *Costco*.

Rose flower water is available at Egyptian and Lebanese ethnic grocery stores, some Asian stores, and in the ethnic section of larger supermarkets. *Al Wadi* brand can be ordered by mail or online from *The King Arthur Flour Company*.*

SUGAR-FREE VANILLA EXTRACT, VANILLA BEANS, AND POWDER

I've listed some brands of vanilla extract without corn syrup or sugar below. Most of these companies also sell whole vanilla beans.

Spice Islands vanilla is available at grocery stores and from www.spiceadvice.com._

Simply Organic vanilla is available at www.frontiercoop.com. They also sell Almond, Orange, Lemon, and Peppermint flavors. Their products are sold in health food stores and co-ops.

Cook's Choice vanilla extract is carried in some stores and can be ordered from www.cooks-vanilla.com.

Trader Joe's Tahitian Blend vanilla extract is sugar-free. (*Trader Joe's* sells several kinds of vanilla, so be sure to get the one that lists only "bourbon, Tahitian vanilla beans, alcohol, and water" as ingredients.)

Singing Dog, all natural, fair trade, organic, and sugar-free vanilla is available in natural food stores nationwide and online from www.singingdogvanilla.com and low-carb.com.* They also sell vanilla beans and vanilla powder. (*What's a singing dog? Singing Dog vanilla is made from vanilla beans grown in Papua New Guinea, home of a wild dog that does not bark but "sings" like a whale. You can hear the song on their website.*)

Kirkland Signature Rodelle vanilla beans are available from Costco. Five, big, plump, moist vanilla beans in 2 glass vials come attached to a pretty card with a picture of an orchid on it. You get 10 vanilla beans at an excellent price.

NOW Organic Vanilla Extract is available from *Netrition*.*

FATS AND OILS

BUTTER

Organic dairy is the best place to put your money if you can't afford to buy everything organic. Most dairy cows are fed cottonseed; unrefined cottonseed contains a natural pesticide and the plants are treated with chemicals that are not approved for use on food crops. Organic butter from pastured cows, which contains a lot of the beneficial fatty acid called CLA, is even better. Primo, pastured butter, both the ones imported from Ireland and the domestic brands, often comes wrapped in green foil.

Trader Joe's * and *Costco* * carry organic butter at good prices.

LARD

Fiedler Family Farms (www.fiedlerfamilyfarms.com) will ship non-hydrogenated, regular and leaf lard.

Prairie Pride (www.prairiepridepork.com) sells non-hydrogenated leaf lard. (Lard is just melted and strained pork fat; cut up some fat and put it in a slow oven and you can make your own. But if you want leaf lard, you will have to ask the butcher to order the special fat needed to make it.)

RICE BRAN OIL

This oil has a fatty acid profile similar to olive oil (47% monounsaturated), but it holds up better to heat. It is usually available at Asian markets or with the Asian foods at larger groceries. It has a smoke point of 490º F. The *California Rice Oil Company* (www.californiariceoil.com) has information on this oil and lists distributors in the U.S.

COCONUT OIL OR COCONUT BUTTER

It's liquid oil above 76º F, and solid butter below. It can be used as an alternative to shortening. It has the advantage that even extra-virgin oil can be used for frying or baking. Most stores carry it with the oils and salad dressings, or it can be ordered from many online retailers. Compare prices for the best buy. (Avoid any coconut oils that are partially hydrogenated.)

SHORTENING

Spectrum (www.spectrumorganics.com) sells organic, vegetable shortening with no trans fats made of expeller-pressed palm oil. There is a store locator on their website. (This is the one I use when I need shortening, which isn't often.)

Earth Balance (www.earthbalance.net) shortening is an expeller-pressed natural oil blend (palm fruit, soybean, canola seed, and olive oils). It can be found at health food stores and with the organic foods at the grocery store.

CEREALS, GRAINS, FLOURS, THICKENERS, AND FLOUR SUBSTITUTES

CEREAL

Dixie Carb Counters' Sweet Commute Carb Controlled Granola (4 net carbs) is available at the low-carb internet Stores in the Directory of Sources or from the manufacturer.

Flax Z Snax makes *No Sugar Added Granola* with 1 net carb per ½ cup serving and *Hot Cereal* with 1 to 2 net carbs.

LC Foods for Low Carb Living* sells a wide variety of cereal mixes.

FLOURS, BLENDS, AND FLOUR SUBSTITUTES

LOW-CARB BAKING MIX

Bob's Red Mill* sells a low-carb baking mix. They also sell a complete range of other flours, including nut flours, gluten, oat, and barley flour.

New Atkins* All Purpose Baking Mix can be purchased from the *Atkins* website or from some of the online stores listed in the Sources Directory.

LC Foods for Low Carb Living* makes 5 specialty flours for low-carb baking and cooking. The choices include: *#1* for multigrain breads, rolls, and crackers, *#2* for white bread, hamburger and hot dog rolls, *#3* for pizza, calzones, stomboli, and bagels, *#4* for flaky pastries and biscuits, and *#5* for cakes, muffins, brownies, and cookies. All produce baked goods with only 1 to 2 digestible grams of carbohydrate per serving.

Gluten flour (vital wheat gluten) is widely available at regular and health food stores and direct from *Bob's Red Mill,** *Honeyville Grain,** and the *King Arthur Flour Company.**

Oat flour is widely available at regular food stores and direct from *Bob's Red Mill** and the *King Arthur Flour Company.**

Sustagrain Barley has 2 to 3 times the fiber and about half the starch compared to other common cereal grains. It is available from *The King Arthur Flour Company** in two forms: as *Barley Flour*, which can be used like oat flour, and *Barley Flakes*, which can be used like rolled oats, with the addition of extra liquid in the recipes.

Tova Industries' Carbalose (www.carbalose.com) is a low-carb flour substitute that can be used like all-purpose flour with a few changes. *Carbalose* Flour can be purchased from *Netrition.** *Carbquik* is a low-carb baking and biscuit mix (similar to *Bisquik*) made with *Carbalose* flour. It contains 90% fewer net carbs than *Bisquik* and has no trans fats or soy. The *Carbquik* box and website have recipes and the website has a store finder. It can be ordered online from many low-carb internet stores.*

White whole-wheat flour is available in stores and online from the *King Arthur Flour Company** and *Bob's Red Mill.** Milled from the hard white wheat berry, it is only slightly lower in carbs than all-purpose flour, but it has same nutrients as whole wheat with a taste similar to white flour. More information is available from the American White Wheat Producers Association (www.farmerdirectfoods.com).

See also WHEY PROTEIN POWDER, often used to replace some of the flour in low-carb recipes.

GARLIC AND HERBS

Dorot Garlic and Herbs (www.dorot.co.il) produces frozen chopped basil, coriander, dill, parsley, and crushed garlic and ginger in trays of 20 cubes each. They are sold in the U.S. at *Trader Joe's** stores.

MEXICAN STYLE HOMINY

Be sure the label says "Mexican Style," as other kinds of hominy are much higher in carbs.

Juanita's (www.juanitasfoods.com) canned Mexican-style hominy has only 4 net carbs per serving. It can be found on the aisle with the Mexican foods in grocery stores.

Teasdale is a similar brand, also carried in many groceries.

ICE CREAM AND FROZEN TREATS

Breyers (www.breyers.com) makes *Carb Smart Ice Cream* and novelties. Many stores carry *Carb Smart* products. The ice cream flavors are sweetened with Splenda and sorbitol and most have 4 net carbs in ½ cup; the *Fudge Bars* have 3.

*LC Foods for Low Carb Living** makes an ice cream mix.

Well's Blue Bunny (www.bluebunny.com) *Sweet Freedom Bars* have 2 to 5 net carbs and are available nationwide. The carb content of their "no-sugar-added" products is much higher.

JAMS, MARMALADE, AND PRESERVES

Jok'n'Al's jams and preserves have only 2 grams of carbs per serving. Their products are available online from many of the stores in the Source Directory.

*Walden Farms** products have no calories, no carbs, and no fat. They are made of water with gums and thickeners and flavored to taste like jams, sauces, mayonnaise, even marshmallow cream. Sucralose is the sweetener in all their products. Their *No Carbs Fruit Spreads* are made with concentrated fruit extracts and natural flavors. (My friend Mary-Clare Holst says the *Strawberry Spread* containing dehydrated strawberries is very good. "It's thick but a few seconds in the microwave fixes this.") *Walden Farms* products can be purchased at the low-carb internet stores and at many grocery stores.

Smucker's (www.smuckers.com) makes 7 favors of sugar-free jam, marmalade, and preserves with 5 net grams of carbohydrate per tablespoon. They also make breakfast syrup sweetened with aspartame with 1 net in ¼ cup and hot fudge topping sweetened with sorbitol and sucralose with 5 net carbs in 2 tablespoons. (Most of their products include polydextrose as the third ingredient, but list no fiber. They may be counting the poly-D as sugar, which might alter the "true" count.) All the major grocery chains carry *Smucker's* products. They are made with NutraSweet or with Splenda and NutraSweet.

See the *La Nouba* listing under CANDY for their fruit spreads.

MEATS AND POULTRY

Regular groceries are starting to carry more products from local farms, and many specialty shops have sprung up as a result of the renewed interest in local, pastured, and free-range meat, poultry, eggs, and dairy products. You may soon have one in your area; I'm thrilled to say I do! Bill the Butcher has opened several shops near me that sell grass-fed, dry-aged beef and house-made bacon and sausages.

Eat Wild (www.eatwild.com) is a website where grass farmers can advertise their products. Over 700 suppliers offer pastured beef, pork, chicken, lamb, goat, bison, venison, and rabbit. The site also lists sources for dairy products from grazing cows and eggs from pastured chickens. Check their Directory of Pasture-Based Farms for sources near you. Some farms will sell meat in bulk for your freezer, or you may find a farmer's market or butcher where you can buy individual cuts.

BEEF

*Carb Smart** has a beef and turkey *Sugar-Free Gourmet Jerky* with 1 net carb and no added sweetener.

Laura's Lean Beef (www.laurasleanbeef.com) is raised without the use of antibiotics, hormones, or animal by-products. They raise Limousin and Charolais cattle, breeds that produce lean beef. They're based in Kentucky, but market nationally. The website has a store locator.

Lasater Grasslands Beef (www.lgbeef.com) is in Colorado. Their cattle spend their entire lives grazing in open pastures, i.e., they're never fed grain, and they're free of growth hormones, antibiotics, and pesticides.

Maverick Ranch Natural Meats (www.maverickranch.com) sells organic beef, pork, lamb, chicken, and cage-free eggs. They do not use hormones, pesticides, or antibiotics. *Maverick Ranch* products are carried in over 2,000 stores nationwide.

Wild Ride Zero Carb Beef Jerky is sold on *Amazon.** It comes in four flavors, all with zero carbs.

BUFFALO

Buffalo meat is becoming more available in stores. *Beefalo*, a cross between beef and buffalo is another option. Choose meat from animals that are entirely grass fed, not grain finished, if possible.

CHILI

Homestyle Fresh (www.homestylefresh.com), in Portland Oregon, sells ready-to-eat chili in microwavable containers that do not require refrigeration. Their beef and bean chili has 4 net carbs per serving of 1 cup, their chicken chili has 5 net. Available at Smart Eats,* Netrition,* or from the website.

PORK

Hormel Cure 81 (www.hormel.com) hams list zero carbs per serving and do not have added water or sugar. Their spiral-sliced hams have a little sugar and come with an optional glaze, but the ham itself has ½ gram of sugar and ½ gram of starch for a net of 1 gram in 3 ounces.

Kurobuta hams from *Snake River Farms* are almost sugar-free. (The label lists sugar as an ingredient but gives the carb count as zero, which means it has less than 0.5 grams per serving.) *Kurobuta* uses Berkshire pork, a heritage breed that is known for its marbling and excellent flavor. Their ham is dark, succulent, and rich, unlike most modern pork, which is pale, bland, and dry because it has been bred to be as lean as possible. *Snake River Farms* products are available on the West Coast or online from www.snakeriverfarms.com.

Maple Leaf (www.mapleleaf.com) all-natural, smoked ham is not preserved, and the label states that it is minimally processed. It has zero grams of carbohydrate (the label lists turbinado sugar, so there is a little).

Niman Ranch (www.nimanranch.com) pork can be ordered online and the website has a list of retailers and restaurants that sell their meat.

Wellshire Farms' (www.wellshirefarms.com) thick-sliced, uncured, dry-rubbed bacon is minimally processed. It is made from all-natural pork raised without antibiotics. They also sell franks, burgers, hams, deli meats, cheese, sausage, and turkey. The Website has a store locator.

PORK RINDS

Check out www.porkrind.com for lots of information about fried or roasted pig skin and a wonderful photo of a pork-rind pig sculpture.) Known as chicharrón *in Spain and Latin America, they can be dipped in salsa, crumbled for coating or casserole topping, or just enjoyed plain like potato chips.*

Old Dutch is marketing pork rinds as *Bac'n Puffs* in supermarkets, and many other brands and flavors can be found on Taquitos.net (www.taquitos.net). *Golden Flake* makes pork skins in several flavors (some have sugar). They are popular in the Southern states and can be ordered by the case of 16 bags from the website at www.store.goldenflake.com. Pork rinds are available with the chips in most grocery stores.

POULTRY

Maple Leaf Farms' all-natural, USDA grade A ducks are raised without antibiotics. Independent animal welfare experts audit their farms, and their products bear an Animal Well-being Assured seal. The Website has a store locator, or you can order online at www.mapleleaffarms.com.

MILK, CREAM, AND SUBSTITUTES

MILK

Hood (www.hphood.com) *Calorie Countdown* makes a milk substitute that uses Splenda and acesulfame K to replace the natural sugar (lactose). It comes in 2%, fat-free, and 2% chocolate. The 2% tastes like real milk and has the same amount of calcium. It can be used like milk in recipes. Many stores carry only the fat-free one, but you can add a little cream to make it taste better. The 2% and fat-free versions have 3 net carbs per cup; the chocolate has 4. *Hood* products are widely available in stores.

*LC Foods for Low Carb Living** sells powdered mixes for low-carb milk and chocolate milk. Add water and cream to make whole milk products without lactose (milk sugar). They also sell a mix for making sour cream, available from www.LCFoodscorp.com.

A low carb alternative to milk is *Blue Diamond* (www.bluediamond.com) *Almond Breeze Almond Milk.* The original and vanilla flavors have only 1 net carb per cup, the chocolate has 2. *Blue Diamond's* website has a store locator.

COCONUT MILK

Use canned coconut milk for cooking rather than the thinner kind sold as a beverage from the dairy case. Canned coconut milk is available in most grocery stores and health food stores. It is often displayed with the Asian foods. Check the label for the carb count and choose one in the lower range. Also check the serving size, as that varies with brand. Avoid the ones labeled "lite," as they are just thinned with water, so not a good buy. Coconut cream is the thick layer that rises to the top, which should be stirred back in when using coconut milk.

So Delicious Coconut Milk beverage can be found in cartons like regular milk in the dairy case. Only the unsweetened version is low in carbs, as the "original" and the other flavors have sugar added. It is tasty, but you may want to add a little sweetener. Other brands of unsweetened coconut milk beverages in single-serving cartons, such as *Aroy-D*, imported from Thailand, are displayed on the aisles with the Asian foods. Note: this is not the same as canned coconut milk called for in recipes, which is thicker than those sold as beverages.

CREAM AND SOUR CREAM

Regular pasteurized cream tastes better than ultrapasteurized and less processing preserves nutrients, but it doesn't keep as long. Avoid cream with added sugar or thickeners.

Cream from a local dairy would be your best choice if that is an option. I love the *Golden Glen Creamery* (in Bow, Washington) near me that sells cream in glass bottles with a hefty deposit, so good cream and good for the environment as well.

Daisy brand sour cream lists "cultured cream" as its only ingredient. It has 1 net carb in 2 tablespoons, but like other fermented dairy products, the microbes in the live culture will have eaten some of the sugar and reduced the count. (Don't buy the "lite" version, which contains skim milk and has 2 net carbs per serving.) *Daisy* products are widely available.

*LC Foods for Low Carb Living** sells a powdered mix for making sour cream.

Organic Valley's (www.organicvalley.com) half-pint container of pasteurized heavy whipping cream has "grade A organic cream" as the only ingredient. Their ultrapasteurized cream contains additional ingredients (carrageenan and gums).

*Trader Joe's** sells fresh cream and usually has good prices.

NUTS AND SEEDS

Choose raw nuts over roasted when possible to get the maximum benefit from the healthful oils they contain. They can be roasted in the oven or a dry pan on the stove when necessary. Search online to find the best prices for nuts, nut flour, and nut meal.

NUTS AND NUT FOUR

Nut flour, also called nut meal, provides a low-carb substitute for wheat flour for baking. Almonds and other nuts can be ground in a food processor if you include some dry ingredients to absorb the oil (otherwise you may get nut butter rather than flour). A coarser grind can be used in muffins and a more finely ground mixture in cakes.

Authentic Foods almond meal in a 12-ounce bag can be ordered from www.glutenfreemall.com.

*Bob's Red Mill** sells almond meal/flour made from blanched almonds.

*Honeyville Grain, Inc.** sells natural and blanched almond flours in 5-pound bags. They also sell sesame seeds, granular erythritol, polydextrose, vital wheat gluten flour, almond flour, and other products at good prices. They will ship your entire order for one low price.

*The King Arthur Flour Company** offers almond and hazelnut flour and pecan meal.

Trader Joe's* is a good source for nuts and almond meal at good prices.

Nuts4U (www.nuts4u.com) sells all kinds of nuts as well as nut flours.

Netrition* carries *NOW Almond Flour*, in a 10-ounce bag.

Most low carb internet stores* carry almond and coconut flour.

NUT BUTTERS

Regular peanut butter is full of sugar and unhealthy oils. Look for products labeled "natural" that contain only nuts or nuts and salt. Health food stores and co-ops often sell nut butters in jars and in bulk. Some stores have grinders so you can make fresh nut butter from whole nuts.

Butters made from tree nuts have similar low-carb content, for example, Netrition* *carries* MaraNatha Natural Macadamia *and* Natural Raw Almond Butters *with 1 and 2 net carbs respectively. Nut butters are available at* Trader Joe's*, *health food stores, and grocery stores. But do check the ingredients and counts on the labels.*

Adam's Natural Peanut Butter is available nationwide.

Trader Joe's* sells *Crunchy* and *Creamy Peanut Butter* made from unblanched peanuts with 3 net carbs in 2 tablespoons.

Smucker's Natural Peanut Butter is available nationwide.

Walden Farms' Whipped Peanut Spread includes natural, fresh roasted peanut flavoring, natural peanut extract, and peanut flour. (My friend, Mary-Clare Holst, says, "It is some-what sweet and lacks the stick-to-your-mouth texture of ground peanuts, but for zero carbs and zero calories, it's not bad.")

La Nouba sells a *Chocolate Hazelnut Spread*, which is a sugar-free version of Nutella. See listing under CANDY.

SEEDS

Chia seed is available at *LC Foods,** health food stores, supplement and vitamin stores, and from the internet stores listed in the Directory of Sources. It is not as perishable as flax. *Vita Cost* (www.vitacost.com), *Sharp Web Labs* (www.SharpWebLabs.com), and many other venders sell *Chia Life* online.

Flax is now commonly available as whole flax seed, flax meal, and flax oil. The polyun-saturated omega-3 oil in flax is extremely fragile and goes rancid quickly. Buy only whole flax seed, especially if you have it shipped, and grind it just before using to be sure it is not rancid. The ground meal can be stored frozen, but only for a few weeks.

Bob's Red Mill* whole, flax seed is available from grocery stores, health food stores, and *Amazon.**

PASTA AND SUBSTITUTES

Atkins* offers a penne pasta with 19 grams of digestible carbohydrate per ½ cup dry, or about half that of regular pasta. It can be ordered from *Atkins* or from low-carb internet stores.*

Dreamfields (www.dreamfieldsfoods.com) pasta is made with real semolina flour and is indistinguishable from regular pasta. It has 5 digestible grams of carbohydrate in a generous 2-ounce serving, compared to more than 40 for regular pasta. It comes as spaghetti, linguini, macaroni, lasagna, rotini, angel hair, and two sizes of penne. You can find it in many groceries or order it from the low-carb internet stores.* There is a store finder on their website. Please note that people respond differently to *Dreamfields*, and the company encourages careful monitoring of blood glucose, especially for those with diabetes.

Shirataki noodles are made from konjac root and consist mainly of gelatinous fiber. They have no carbs, fat, or protein. Tofu shiratki has a small amount of tofu added, which gives it the texture of soft egg noodles and adds a small amount of carbohydrate. Both are available in the refrigerated cases with the Asian foods in many groceries or they can be ordered from the low-carb sites in the Sources Directory.

Kelp noodles are made of kelp and sodium alginate, a salt derived from brown seaweed. They can be found with the Korean foods in some groceries or in stores that specialize in Asian foods. They can be ordered from the *Sea Tangle Noodle Company* in San Diego at www.kelpnoodles.com.

SWEETENERS AND SYRUPS

ACESULFAME K

Sweet One (www.sweetone.com), also called Sunette, contains acesulfame K with a little sugar as a bulking agent. One packet is equal to two teaspoons of sugar. It is available at many groceries, or you can order it from the website. Acesulfame K is one of the sweeteners in DiabetiSweet, widely available with diabetic products in drugstores.

LO HAN GUO

Lo han guo is a natural sugar alternative made from a Chinese melon called monk fruit. It is 300 times as sweet as sugar and has zero calories. Different brands use different bulking agents, so the nutrition counts and strengths vary. *TriMedica's Slim Sweet* is a blend of lo han guo and fructose (levulose). It has a tendency to absorb moisture and become lumpy when humid. *NuNaturals* sells an extract made with glycerin, alcohol, and water. *Jarrow Formulas' Lo Han Sweet* also contains xylitol and inulin-FOS. *LC Foods* sells a sweetener that contains lo han guo, stevia, and sucralose, bulked with inulin.

SUCRALOSE

Splenda is the leading sugar substitute in the U.S. It contains the sweetener sucralose and one of three natural sugars, maltodextrine, dextrose, or lactose, as a bulking agent. It comes in a granular form which measures like sugar, in packets, and as tablets in a dispenser. It provides a sweet taste, but doesn't brown, caramelize, or add volume like sugar. The sugar used as a bulking agent in granular Splenda adds 24 grams of carbohydrate and 96 calories per cup. Each Splenda packet, which replaces two teaspoons of sugar, contains 0.9 grams of carbohydrate and 2 calories. Splenda Mini Tabs have only 0.04 grams of carbs and 0.2 calories per tab, which is equal to 1 teaspoon of sugar in sweetness. Splenda and similar generic brands are widely available.

LIQUID SUCRALOSE

Unlike sweeteners such as Splenda Granular and Nutrasweet, which use sugar as a bulking agent, liquid sucralose is truly calorie- and carbohydrate-free.

American Health Foods and Ingredients (www.ahfni.com) sells liquid sucralose at an excellent price in a 4-ounce glass bottle with a dropper and a 16-ounce refill size. Three drops equal 2 teaspoons of sugar. AHF also sells pure powdered sucralose and powdered neotame, a sweetener made by NutraSweet that is between 7,000 and 13,000 times sweeter than sugar.

EZ-Sweetz liquid sucralose (www.ez-sweetz.com) can be ordered from the website in 0.25- and 0.5-ounce dispensers (1 drop equals 2 teaspoons of sugar) and a 2-ounce bottle (1 drop equals 1 teaspoon of sugar). Order it from the website or the stores in the Directory of Sources. *Nutragenics Fiberfit Sucralose-sweetened Dietary Fiber* is liquid sucralose plus guar gum and Irish moss. It is much less concentrated than the ones listed above, but even so, 1 teaspoon has 8 teaspoons of sweetening power. It is available from the stores listed in the Directory of Sources.

Sweetzfree (www.sweetzfree.com) is a sucralose solution without sugar as a bulking agent. One drop has the sweetening power of 1½ teaspoons of sugar; a 4-ounce container equals 96 cups of sugar. Order from the website.

SUGAR ALCOHOLS

DIABETISWEET

DiabetiSweet is made by *HCP Health Care Products* (www.diabeticproducts.com). *Original* and *Brown Sugar DiabetiSweet* contain isomalt (a sugar alcohol) and acesulfame K. These products are available with the diabetic supplies in drug stores and online from HCP.

ERYTHRITOL

Erythritol is a natural sugar alcohol with a high digestive tolerance. It is 70% as sweet as sugar. It can be ordered from the stores listed in the Directory of Sources and from *Now Foods* (www.nowfoods.com). *Netrition** sells *Now* erythritol crytals and *Sensato* erythritol powder.

XYLITOL

Xylitol is a natural sugar alcohol. It can be substituted measure for measure for sugar, and it does not deteriorate when heated, so it can be used for baking. It can cause digestive problems when eaten in excess, usually described as more than 25 grams per day. It has an odd cooling taste when used as the only sweetener in a recipe. It is sold by *Epic, XyloSweet, Jarrow,* and *Now Foods*. It comes in packets, bags, and shakers.

SUGAR-FREE SYRUPS AND HONEY

DaVinci (www.davincigourmet.com) zero-carb syrups (sweetened with sucralose) come in 45 flavors. Many grocery stores, big discount stores, and low-carb internet stores* stock some flavors, but all can be ordered from the company. *Cash and Carry* stores in the Northwest have a large selection of sugar-free flavors at discount prices. *DaVinci* also sells sugar-free caramel and chocolate sauce in ½ gallon jugs.

Maple Grove Farms (www.maplegrove.com) *Vermont Sugar Free Syrup* is sweetened with Splenda, acesulfame K, and sorbitol and has 2 net carbs per serving. See Directory of Sources.

Torani makes sugar-free syrups that contain acesulfame K and Splenda. They are widely available in stores and at *Cost Plus World Markets.**

*Walden Farms** Calorie-Free Syrups (chocolate, strawberry, blueberry, and pancake) are thicker than the DaVinci Gourmet or Torani syrups; they are good on low-carb ice cream or other desserts. They are widely available or they can be ordered online.

HONEY SUBSTITUTES

Honey substitutes made with xylitol or maltitol are available retail and from the online stores listed in the Directory of Sources.

Global Sweet Smart Sweet Xylitol Honey has 2 net carbs per serving.

Nature's Hollow Tastes Like Honey is sweetened with xylitol. It lists zero net carbs.

SWEET FIBERS AND BLENDS

Several blends of erythritol combined with a stevia extract called rebaudiana (Reb A) were introduced in 2009. These are now available on supermarket shelves with the sugars and sweeteners as well as from internet sites.

Just Like Sugar (www.JustLikeSugarInc.com) sells natural sugar substitutes made from iulin, calcium, vitamin C, and orange peel extract that have no calories or carbs. The granular form comes in packets or in a shaker. It is also available powdered (for baking), and as brown sugar by the pound. The powdered one is measured by weight for baking, the granular by volume. Use the granular when a clear finished product is desirable. *Just Like Sugar* can be ordered from the website. There is a store locator on the site.

LC Foods for Low Carb Living* sells *LC Sweet,* a blend of stevia, lo han guo, sucralose, and inulin in several forms, including, brown sugar, white sugar, powdered sugar, liquid white and brown sugar, and one that will caramelize.

NOW Foods (www.nowfoods.com) produces a polysaccharide sweetener made from inulin (derived from chicory root and other natural sources). Available from *Netrition.**

Nuva contains a Reb A, erythritol, an inulin.

Polydextrose is not very sweet, but it has many of the qualities of sugar that are missing in high-intensity sweeteners. It contains 2 net grams of carbohydrate and 25 grams of soluble fiber per ounce. I used *Sta-lite III* polydextrose from *Honeyville Grain** to test some of my recipes. It comes in five-pound bags. *Netrition** also sells polydextrose; their *Life Source Foods PolyD Fiber* is similar to the one from *Honeyville Grain*, but they also have one sweetened with sucralose, called *PolyD Fiber Plus*. Both products are sold in one-pound bags.

PureVia contains erythritol, isomaltulose, and Reb A. It is available in stores and can be ordered from *Vitacost.com*, *Drugstore.com*, *Amazon*,* and *Netrition.**

SomerSweet in packets and *SomerSweet Baking Blend* can be ordered from www.suzanne-somers.com. It contains chicory root fiber, erythritol, fructose, and orange peel extract. The baking blend measures like sugar; the packets are equal to 1 teaspoon of sugar.

Sweetleaf Sweetener in packets contains stevia extract with inulin as a bulking agent. It also comes as a powder; ¼ teaspoon is equal to 1 teaspoon of sugar. It is available in packets from *Carbsmart** and as packets or powder from *vitacost.com*. (It may be called Sweetleaf Stevia Plus on the Vitacost website.) You may also find it in health food stores and grocery stores.

Sweetperfection, from *Low Carb Specialties, Inc.* is made of oligofructose sweetened with stevia extract. It can be used like sugar in recipes. One cup has 5 net carbs and 122 grams of fiber. It can be ordered from www.lowcarbspecialties.com or bought in health food stores.

Trader Joe's * sells inulin as a fiber supplement.

Truvia contains erythritol, Reb A, and natural flavors. It is available in stores and from *Netrition,** *Vitacost.com*, and *Carbsmart.**

Yacon syrup is available at health food stores, at *Whole Foods Markets,* and it can be ordered from *Amazon** and other internet sites. The *Live Super Food* website (www.livesuperfoods.com) sells it as a syrup, a powder, and as raw, dried chips. Most brands give the nutrition information for yacon as if it were all sugar with no fiber, but I did find two who said it has about 1 net gram of carbohydrate per teaspoon. Since it is 4 times as sweet as honey or sugar, it could have a significant advantage.

THICKENERS AND STABILIZERS

Agar agar is a type of seaweed used for thickening and as a gelling agent. It is more common than gelatin in Chinese cooking. Look for it online or with the Chinese foods at grocery stores or in an Asian grocery store.

LC Foods for Low Carb Living* makes a variety of low-carb thickeners for sauces, gravies, and potato substitutes.

Quick & Thick Low Carb Food Thickener and Texturizer is available from *Carbsmart.** It is made of acacia, guar, carob, and xanthan gums and can be used like cornstarch. It has a net carb count of zero. (One teaspoon thickens like 1 teaspoon of cornstarch, but one tablespoon thickens like 2 tablespoons of cornstarch.)

Xanthan gum and guar gum are available from *Bob's Red Mill Natural Foods*.* Many groceries display them with flour or organic foods. *The King Arthur Flour Company** and *LC Foods** also sell xanthan gum and both guar and xanthan gum can be ordered from the low-carb stores listed in the Directory of Sources.

TOMATO PRODUCTS

TOMATOES

Pomi Strained Tomatoes, imported from Italy, contain nothing but tomatoes and have 2 net carbs in ½ cup. The label says, "strained tomatoes," but it can be used like tomato sauce. *Pomi Chopped Tomatoes* have 1 net carb in ½ cup, compared to 5 or more for other brands. *Pomi* also sells *Marinara Sauce*, but it contains sugar.

PASTA SAUCE

Most of the sugar-free pasta sauces I have found are imported from Italy. Cost Plus World Market* stores usually carry several Italian brands, and many are available at regular groceries.

Alessi Marinara Pasta Sauce (www.vigo-alessi.com) is made with olive oil and has only 2 net carbs in ½ cup. It is imported from Sicily and is available in many grocery stores.

Bella Vita says "low carb" on the label. It has 4 net carbs per ½ cup, but it contains soy oil and partially hydrogenated soy oil, so not the best choice. It can be ordered from Netrition.*

Don Pomodoro (www.beltesoro.com) *Marinara Sauce* is made in Italy from all-natural, organic ingredients. It contains 3 net grams of carbohydrate in ½ cup. *Don Pomodoro* makes other tomato-based sauces and a *Garlic Oil & Chili Pepper Sauce*. Available in stores or online.

WHEY PROTEIN POWDER

Biochem Sports (www.biochem-fitness.com) makes whey protein with 1 net carb per serving.

*Bob's Red Mill** sells plain, unsweetened, whey protein powder that works well for baking when you don't want the sweetener.

MRM All Natural whey protein powder comes in Dutch chocolate or vanilla. It is stevia sweetened. Each scoop (a little over ¼ cup) has 1.5 grams of carbohydrate and 18 grams of protein. *MRM* can be found in health food stores or ordered online from *Bodybuilding. com*. It comes in canisters or in individual packets, good for travel.

*Trader Joe's** sells *Designer Whey* protein powder. The French vanilla flavor has less than 2 net carbs per serving. It is made by *Next Proteins*, www.designerwhey.com.

YOGURT AND KEFIR

Be sure the label says "contains live cultures." If it does, the actual carb count will probably be less than what is shown on the nutrition panel.

Kefir can be found with the yogurt in the dairy case at most groceries and at health food stores. Goat milk kefir is often available as well as cow's milk. Unfortunately, many stores only carry low-fat or non-fat kefir.

Brands of Greek yogurt include: *Fage*, *Oikos*, and *Chobani*. *Greek Gods* is also good, but it contains pectin for thickening, so it is not totally authentic. They are widely available.

DIRECTORY OF SOURCES AND INTERNET STORES

Amazon
www.amazon.com

Atkins
www.atkins.com

Bob's Red Mill Natural Foods
www.bobsredmill.com

Carbsmart
www.carbsmart.com

Chocosphere
1-877-992-4626
www.chocosphere.com

Controlled Carb Gourmet
www.controlledcarbgourmet.com

Cost Plus World Market
1-877-967-5362
www.worldmarket.com
The website has a store locator.

Dixie Diner
1-800- 233-3668
www.dixiediner.com

Honeyville Grain Inc.
1-888-810-3212, ext. 121
www.honeyvillegrain.com

King Arthur Flour Company,
The Baker's Catalogue
1-800-827-6836
www.kingarthurflour.com

LC Foods for Low Carb Living
www.LCFoodscorp.com

Low Carb Connoisseur
www.low-carb.com

Low Carb You
www.locarbu.com

Netrition
www.netrition.com

Smart Eats
www.smarteatsusa.com

Spices etc.
1-800-827-6373
www.spicesetc.com

Trader Joe's
www.traderjoes.com
Stores throughout the country;
store locator on the website.

Viva Low Carb Superstore
www.vivlowcarb.com

Walden Farms
www.waldenfarms.com

Index